W9-AUC-248

SAINT OF THE DAY

Saint of the Day

UPDATED & EXPANDED

EDITED BY LEONARD FOLEY, O.F.M.
REVISED BY PAT McCLOSKEY, O.F.M.

Franciscan
MEDIA
Cincinnati, Ohio

RESCRIPT

In accord with the *Code of Canon Law*, I hereby grant my permission to publish *Saint of the Day: Updated and Expanded*.
Most Rev. Joseph R. Binzer
Auxiliary Bishop and Vicar General
Archdiocese of Cincinnati
Cincinnati, Ohio
July 30, 2013

The *Permission to Publish* is a declaration that a book or pamphlet is considered to be free of doctrinal or moral error. It is not implied that those who have granted the *Permission to Publish* agree with the contents, opinions or statements expressed.

Scripture citations are taken from *The New American Bible with Revised New Testament*, copyright ©1986 by the Confraternity of Christian Doctrine, and are used by permission. All rights reserved. Some excerpts from the documents of Vatican II are taken from Austin P. Flannery, ed. *Documents of Vatican II*.

Original photo of stained glass for cover, St. James Basilica, Jamestown, ND,
©The Crosiers/Gene Plaisted o.s.c.
Cover and interior design by Mark Sullivan.

LIBRARY OF CONGRESS CATALOGING-IN-PUBLICATION DATA
Saint of the day : updated and expanded / edited by Leonard Foley ; revised by Pat McCloskey. —
Seventh edition
pages cm
Summary: "Biographies and lessons from the lives of the saints, linked to their feast days. Each of the more than two hundred entries includes a short biography of the saint, a comment linking the example of this life relevant to our own and an appropriate quotation from Scripture, the words of the saint or another spiritual writer for reflection"— Provided by publisher.
Includes bibliographical references and index.
ISBN 978-1-61636-653-7 (pbk.)
1. Christian saints—Calendar. 2. Christian saints—Biography. I. Foley, Leonard, 1913- II. McCloskey, Patrick.
BX4655.3.S25 2013
270.092'2—dc23
[B]
2013011917

ISBN 978-1-61636-653-7

Copyright ©2013, Franciscan Media. All rights reserved.

Published by Franciscan Media
28 W. Liberty St.
Cincinnati, OH 45202
www.FranciscanMedia.org

Printed in the United States
Printed on acid-free paper.
15 16 17 5 4 3

• • •

CONTENTS

● ● ●

INTRODUCTION

A loving God offers us friendship, and the result of that gracious act is our holiness.

God alone is holy: to be God is to be holy. Not to be God is not to be holy. It is not right or natural for us to live the life of God. But God creates God's own life in us and makes it right for God to love us. When God finds divine life and love in us, it becomes natural for us to live supernatural or divine lives.

This was God's eternal plan: "[God] chose us in [Christ], before the foundation of the world, to be holy and without blemish before him" (Ephesians 1:4). "I am the vine, you are the branches. Whoever remains in me and I in him will bear much fruit, because without me you can do nothing" (John 15:5).

With faith, all this is obvious. Without faith, it contradicts obvious human experience. A prime heresy of all ages has been the one that says holiness is what we create by our own efforts.

It seems so evident that it is *my* strength of character that refuses to take revenge; *my* hard-won decision to remain faithful that sustains my marriage; *my* endurance that brings me to Mass every Sunday; *my* devotion that prompts me to fast twice a week and give tithes on all I possess. Why shouldn't I thank God that I'm not like the rest of the world—at least many people?

Faith is the answer.

Faith is not a naïve abandonment of reason to certain mysterious truths, or a feverish scrambling to put together a respectable life of good works. Faith is the gift whereby we are able to receive a gift. We are able to open ourselves to God's friendship, communion, oneness. Our freedom becomes total freedom when we let Christ enfold it in his own.

It is true that we must work at being holy—keeping the commandments, being on the alert for others' needs, disciplining ourselves. But even this effort is God's gift. The more we realize that, the more we will use the gift.

xv

We have absolutely nothing to give God—except himself. One Eucharistic Prayer for weekdays says, "our thanksgiving is itself your gift."

The supreme example of human holiness is that which Jesus received—as *truly human*—from his Father. His heart was totally open to the gift of his Father's love, and by his death and resurrection he is the living source whereby the Holy Spirit flows into us and through us.

The saints and blesseds whose lives are described in this book are special signs of God's activity. Their surrender to God's love was so generous an approach to the total surrender of Jesus that the Church recognizes them as heroes and heroines worthy to be held up for our inspiration. They remind us that the Church is holy, can never stop being holy, and is called to show the holiness of God by living the life of Christ.

Our holiness is the same as theirs—God's holiness. Their lives were indeed conditioned by the culture and history of their own day; their expression of holiness is partly different from what it would be in the twenty-first century. But the essence is the same: They received God's gift with joy. They call to us to do likewise: "Do you not know that you are the temple of God, and that the Spirit of God dwells in you? If anyone destroys God's temple, God will destroy that person; for the temple of God, which you are, is holy" (1 Corinthians 3:16–17).

A Unique Holiness

On January 16, 1903, Angelo Roncalli (later Blessed John XXIII, October 11) wrote in his journal: "From the saints I must take the substance, not the accidents of their virtues. I am not St. Aloysius, nor must I seek holiness in his particular way, but according to the requirements of my own nature, my own character, and the different conditions of my life. I must not be the dry, bloodless reproduction of a model, however perfect. God desires us to follow the examples of the saints by absorbing the vital sap of their virtues and turning it into our own life-blood, adapting it to our own individual capacities and particular circumstances. If St. Aloysius had been as I am, he would have become holy in a different way."

This comes from a man who turned twenty-one two months earlier and was studying in Rome for ordination as a priest in the Diocese of Bergamo. He was writing about St. Aloysius Gonzaga (June 21), a Jesuit who died at the age of twenty-three and is buried in Rome's Sant'Ignazio Church, not far from where Roncalli was living.

There are obvious similarities among the saints. Augustine of Hippo (August 28) and Thomas Aquinas (January 28) were great theologians; Elizabeth of Hungary (November 17) and Jeanne Jugan (August 30) showed extraordinary compassion to everyone, especially the poor. Thomas More (June 22) and Teresa Benedicta of the Cross (August 9) were martyred for their faith.

Blessed John XXIII, however, was certainly correct: Someone becomes a saint not by being "the dry, bloodless reproduction of a model, however perfect." An individual becomes a saint by cooperating generously with God's grace, according to that person's "individual capacities and particular circumstances."

God apparently loves diversity! The stories of saints reaffirm that holiness is not restricted by age, sex, nationality, geography, or time in which a person lives. Saints represent almost every occupation and family background. Holy women and men use their diverse, God-given talents by witnessing in their unique way to God's compassionate love; there are no clones among the saints.

Saints and Blesseds

The process starts on the diocesan level, where witnesses testify to the heroic virtue of the person. When that work is officially received by the Congregation for the Causes of the Saints, the person is then known as "Servant of God." After further investigation, including the study of that person's writings, a decree of heroic virtue may be issued, recognizing that person as "Venerable." Designation of the person as a martyr killed "in hatred of the faith" or the acceptance of a miraculous healing clears the way for the person's beatification. Acceptance of a second miracle leads to canonization.

The difference between canonized saints and those officially recognized as blessed is not whether they are in heaven or merely close to it. The key difference is where their liturgical feast may be publicly celebrated. A saint's feast can be celebrated anywhere in the world; a blessed's feast can be celebrated in the country where he or she lived and in other places where the bishops' conference requests this and receives approval from the Holy See. If the beatified person belonged to a religious congregation, then other members of that congregation can celebrate that feast anywhere in the world. Thus, officially speaking, the feast of Blessed Teresa of Kolkata (September 5) can be celebrated liturgically only in Albania (where she was born), in India (where she lived most of her life), and in the three religious congregations she founded.

For centuries, local bishops officially recognized saints. Because this was so important a declaration, the Catholic Church eventually reserved the canonization process—likewise the designation of someone as "blessed"—to the bishop of Rome

One of Pope Benedict XVI's first decisions was that normally beatifications would be celebrated in the diocese where that person lived and that the prefect of the Congregation for the Causes of the Saints would preside. Otherwise, a cardinal or the local bishop presides. Beatification is still a pontifical act, following the same procedures as before. Pope Benedict XVI decided that he would preside at canonizations. This new procedure was confirmed in a communiqué from the congregation on September 29, 2005. Even so, Pope Benedict XVI beatified John Henry Newman (October 9) in 2010 and Pope John Paul II (October 22) the following year.

Legends and Facts

There are two kinds of biography for saints. First, there is practical hagiography (from *hagios*—"holy"—and *graphein*—"to write"). From the earliest times, lists of martyrs were drawn up so that their anniversaries could be remembered. Narratives of martyrdom were also written by their contemporaries. Finally, later writers wrote accounts to edify or to satisfy curiosity. Collections were made, finally developing into what were called *legendaries*.

Scientific hagiography began in the seventeenth century. A Jesuit, Rosweyde, first conceived the project of a collection of the lives of the saints. The project was actually carried out by J. Bollandus and others (hence the name "Bollandists"). As much as the state of historical science then permitted, the material of the lives of the saints was subjected to severe critical analysis. Later, with the development of archaeology, philology, and paleography, greater advances were made in determining the factual content of saints' biographies.

In this book we clearly label legend as such. We have included the legendary material because it is part of the tradition (small *t*) of the Church. Ages previous to ours were not blessed (or afflicted) with our passion for historical accuracy. Whether this saint actually walked on the water or not, whether the sacred Host flew from the hands of the priest to the saint's heart or not was of no real concern. God had worked infinitely greater miracles of grace in the lives of these heroes and heroines of Christ. If what we call legend is not factually true, it is often true to the character and spirit of the saint involved. Legends always convey a truth deeper than what a video camera can capture.

We have kept and identified some of these legends, therefore, as the quaint and human poetry of countless ordinary Christians whose imaginations knew no bounds when divine friendship with God's holy ones was involved.

Other Celebrations

This revised edition of *Saint of the Day* includes other commemorations on the Roman calendar. This volume includes the solemnities of Jesus, which claim no Sunday, or holy day as their own, the feasts of the premier saint, Mary, and celebrations that commemorate the dedication of important churches and honor the angels. Last, but by no means least, we have included the days which honor the whole galaxy of unnamed stars among God's people: All Saints and All Souls. Saints and blesseds of special interest in the United States, Canada, and Mexico are also here.

The highest class of liturgical celebration is the *solemnity*. There are three that honor specific saints: Joseph, Peter and Paul, John the Baptist; two are solemnities of the Lord; and two honor Mary.

The next class consists of *feasts*. Saints whose commemorations are ranked as feasts are those of the apostles, Paul, Mark, Luke, Stephen, Lawrence, and the Holy Innocents. Other feasts include the Visitation, the Transfiguration, the Triumph of the Cross, Mary's birthday, and the Dedication of St. John Lateran.

Memorials are divided into two classes. About one-third of the saints' days are *obligatory* memorials, that is, they must be celebrated unless superseded by a higher ranking celebration (for example, a day of Lent). The other celebrations of saints' days are *optional*.

Renewed Interest

Since 1975, when the first edition of this book was published, there has been a renewed interest in the saints, especially through books, videos, and Web sites devoted to the saints. Blessed John Paul II beatified and canonized more women, men, and children than all his predecessors in the previous one thousand years. This seventh edition of *Saint of the Day* updates many previous entries and includes new ones for Blesseds John Henry Newman, Pope John Paul II, and Sts. Paul of the Cross, Mary of the Cross MacKillop, Hildegard of Bingen, Joan of Arc, John of Avila, and the Solemnity of Jesus's birth. There is also an Appendix of additional saint-related print, audio, and DVD resources.

In his highly acclaimed book, *Making Saints: How the Catholic Church Determines Who Becomes a Saint, Who Doesn't and Why*, Kenneth Woodward says of Pope John Paul II, "As a poet and playwright, he understands the primordial power of stories; his many beatifications and canonizations are dramatic validation of this book's central argument: *that saints exist in and through their stories*." Woodward goes on to write:

> A saint is always someone through whom we catch a glimpse of what God is like—and of what we are called to be. Only God "makes" saints, of course. The Church merely identifies from time to time a few of these for emulation. The Church then tells the story. But the author is the Source of the grace by which saints live. And there we have it: a saint is someone whose story God tells.

The story of every saint is the story of God's grace and human cooperation, of God's faithful love and the person's often circuitous route to appreciating that love, of God's constancy and human weakness. Saints differ greatly in the details of their lives, in the circumstances in which God's grace takes root in their lives, but saints are identical in this: allowing God's grace to bear fruit in their lives, in faith, hope, and love, in works of compassion, in the witness of a life lived generously in praise of God.

In her book *Friends of God and Prophets: A Feminist Theological Reading of the Communion of Saints*, Elizabeth Johnson describes two ways that Christians have related to saints: as companions on our faith journey or as patrons to whom we related as clients. Although the companion model was stronger in the first three hundred years of Christianity, the patron-client model (based on Roman society) prevailed for the next twelve centuries. The companion paradigm has made a comeback since the sixteenth century. Johnson writes: "The profound connection that *Lumen Gentium* [the Dogmatic Constitution on the Church] forges between the people of God, called to be holy, and those faithful friends of God already in glory articulate the biblical and early martyrs' pattern in a new idiom. Far from being isolated patrons, saints in heaven are enfolded into the whole people of God as companions in Christ who are the beginning of the great harvest."

The patron-client paradigm could leave the impression that saints are simply allies in persuading God to do something. People commonly seek allies to further a change in one's family (for an intervention about someone's addictive, self-destructive behavior), in the academic world (to introduce a program or discontinue a program), or in business (to market a new product or discontinue an existing one).

The companion paradigm, however, suggests that saints resemble our best teacher, coaches, coworkers, family members, or friends, encouraging us to use our talents in constructive new ways. "You can do this" or "You'll be great," they sometimes say. In Preface I of Saints, the presider proclaims: "For you are praised in the company of your Saint and, in crowning their merits, you crown your own gifts. By their way of life you offer us an example, by communion with them you give us companionship, by their intercession, sure support, so that, encouraged by so great a cloud of witnesses, we may run as victors in the race before us and win with them the imperishable crown of glory, through Christ our Lord."

The Roman Missal's Preface II of Saints says: "For in the marvelous confession of your Saints, you make your Church fruitful with strength ever new and offer us sure signs of your love. And that your saving mysteries may be fulfilled, their great example lends us courage, their fervent prayers sustain us in all we do." In the Eucharistic Prayer for Reconciliation I, the presider prays: "Help us to work together for the coming of your Kingdom, until the hour when we stand before you, Saints among the Saints in the halls of heaven...." Similar expressions occur in the Mass prayers for the Solemnity of All Saints.

During a September 2011 pastoral visit to Germany, Pope Benedict XVI presided over an outdoor prayer service with young people. With candles lighting up the evening sky and after recalling Christ as the light of the world, the pope continued:

> To be sure, those who believe in Jesus do not lead lives of perpetual sunshine, as though they could be spared suffering and hardship, but there is always a bright glimmer there, lighting up the path that leads to fullness of life. The eyes of those who believe in Christ see light even amid the darkest night, and they already see the dawning of a new day. Light does not remain alone. All around, other lights are flaring up. In their gleam, space acquires contours, so that we can find our bearings. We do not live alone in this world. And it is for the important things of life that we have to rely on other people. Particularly in our faith, then, we do not stand alone; we are links in the great chain of believers. Nobody can believe unless he is supported by the faith of others, and conversely, through my faith, I help to strengthen others in their faith.

He was describing every saint, officially canonized or not.

In his general audience on January 16, 2013, the pope said that the desire to see and know God is innate in everyone, even nonbelievers.

Kenneth Woodward opened his book *Making Saints* by quoting from Leon Bloy, "There is but one sadness…and that is for us not to be saints *(La Femme Pauvre)*."

This current volume seeks to present the truly wonderful variety and the powerful unity of lives open to God's grace—wherever that may lead.

Authors

This book is the result of a cooperative effort of Franciscan friars of St. John the Baptist Province and the staff of Franciscan Media. Contributors include Franciscan friars John Bach, Murray Bodo, John Boehman, Leander Blumlein, Robert Buescher, Timothy Carmody, Bede Clancy, Steve Connair, George Darling, Berard Doerger, Roy Effler, Austin Ernstes, William Faber, William Farris, Aldric Heidlage, Alan Hirt, Jerome Kaelin, Christopher Kerr, Jerome Kircher, Cletus Kistner, Hilarion Kistner, Lawrence Landini, William Linesch, Nicholas Lohkamp, Patrick McCloskey, George Miller, Pio O'Connor, Norbert Oldegeering, Anthony Panozzo, Peter Poppleton, Joseph Ricchini, Peter Ricke, Gary Sabourin, Boniface Sack, Jeffrey Scheeler, Anthony Walter, and Michael Wohler.

Contributing members of the Franciscan Media staff have been: Lisa Biedenbach, Leonard Foley, Jeremy Harrington, Carol Luebering, Norman Perry, Mary Lynne Rapien, and Jack Wintz.

Leonard Foley edited the original book (1975), plus its second and third editions (1981 and 1990). Pat McCloskey prepared the fourth, fifth, sixth, and seventh editions, benefitting from the wise advice of Judy Ball, who for many years developed and updated the Saint of the Day website at www.FranciscanMedia.org. He continues that task.

JANUARY 1 + SOLEMNITY

Mary, Mother of God

Mary's divine motherhood broadens the Christmas spotlight. Mary has an important role to play in the Incarnation of the Second Person of the Blessed Trinity. She consents to God's invitation conveyed by the angel (Luke 1:26–38). Elizabeth proclaims: "Most blessed are you among women and blessed is the *fruit of your womb*. And how does this happen to me, that *the mother of my Lord* should come to me?" (Luke 1:42–43, emphasis added). Mary's role as mother of God places her in a unique position in God's redemptive plan.

Without naming Mary, Paul asserts that "God sent his Son, born of a woman, born under the law" (Galatians 4:4). Paul's further statement that "God sent the spirit of his Son into our hearts, crying out 'Abba, Father!'" helps us realize that Mary is mother to all the brothers and sisters of Jesus.

Some theologians also insist that Mary's motherhood of Jesus is an important element in God's creative plan. God's first thought in creating was Jesus. Jesus, the incarnate Word, is the one who could give God perfect love and worship on behalf of all creation. As Jesus was first in God's mind, Mary was second insofar as she was chosen from all eternity to be his mother.

The precise title "Mother of God" goes back at least to the third or fourth century. In the Greek form *Theotokos* (God-bearer), it became the touchstone of the Church's teaching about the Incarnation. The Council of Ephesus in 431 insisted that the holy Fathers were right in calling the holy virgin *Theotokos*. At the end of this particular session, crowds of people marched through the street shouting: "Praised be the *Theotokos*!" The tradition reaches to our own day. In its chapter on Mary's role in the Church, Vatican II's *Dogmatic Constitution on the Church* calls Mary "Mother of God" twelve times.

COMMENT: Other themes come together at today's celebration. It is the Octave of Christmas: Our remembrance of Mary's divine motherhood injects a further note of Christmas joy. It is a day of prayer for world peace: Mary is the mother of the Prince of Peace. It is the first day of a new year: Mary continues to bring new life to her children—who are also God's children.

QUOTE: "The Blessed Virgin was eternally predestined, in conjunction with the incarnation of the divine Word, to be the Mother of God. By decree of divine Providence, she served on earth as the loving mother of the divine Redeemer, an associate of unique nobility, and the Lord's humble handmaid. She conceived, brought forth, and nourished Christ" (Dogmatic Constitution on the Church, 61).

• • •

JANUARY 2 + MEMORIAL

Basil the Great and Gregory Nazianzen
BISHOPS AND DOCTORS

Basil the Great (329–379). Basil was on his way to becoming a famous teacher when he decided to begin a religious life of Gospel poverty. After studying various modes of religious life, he founded what was probably the first monastery in Asia Minor. He is to monks of the East what St. Benedict is to the West, and Basil's principles influence Eastern monasticism today.

He was ordained a priest, assisted the archbishop of Caesarea (now southeastern Turkey), and ultimately became archbishop himself, in spite of opposition from some of the bishops under him, probably because they foresaw coming reforms.

One of the most damaging heresies in the history of the Church, Arianism, which denied the divinity of Christ, was at its height. Emperor Valens persecuted orthodox believers and put great pressure on Basil to remain silent and admit the heretics to communion. Basil remained firm, and Valens backed down. But trouble remained. When the great St. Athanasius (May 2) died, the mantle of defender of the faith against Arianism fell upon Basil. He strove mightily to unite and rally his fellow Catholics who were crushed by tyranny and torn by internal dissension. He was misunderstood, misrepresented, accused of heresy and ambition. Even appeals to the pope brought no response. "For my sins I seem to be unsuccessful in everything."

He was tireless in pastoral care. He preached twice a day to huge crowds, built a hospital that was called a wonder of the world (as a youth he had organized famine relief and worked in a soup kitchen himself) and fought the prostitution business.

Basil was best known as an orator. Though not recognized greatly in his lifetime, his writings rightly place him among the great teachers of the Church. Seventy-two years after his death, the Council of Chalcedon described him as "the great Basil, minister of grace who has expounded the truth to the whole earth."

COMMENT: As the French say, "The more things change, the more they remain the same." Basil faced the same problems as modern Christians. Sainthood meant trying to preserve the spirit of Christ in such perplexing and painful problems as reform, organization, fighting for the poor, maintaining balance, and peace in misunderstanding.

QUOTE: St. Basil said: "The bread which you do not use is the bread of the hungry; the garment hanging in your wardrobe is the garment of him who is naked; the shoes that you do not wear are the shoes of the one who is barefoot; the money that you keep locked away is the money of the poor; the acts of charity that you do not perform are so many injustices that you commit."

Gregory Nazianzen (329–390). After his baptism at thirty, Gregory gladly accepted his friend Basil's invitation to join him in a newly founded monastery. The solitude was broken when Gregory's father, a bishop, needed help in his diocese and estate. It seems that Gregory was ordained a priest practically by force and only reluctantly accepted the responsibility. He skillfully avoided a schism that threatened when his own father made compromises with Arianism. At forty-one, Gregory was chosen as bishop of a diocese near Caesarea and at once came into conflict with Valens, the emperor, who supported the Arians. An unfortunate by-product of the battle was the cooling of the friendship of two saints. Basil, his archbishop, sent him to a miserable and unhealthy town on the border of unjustly created divisions in his diocese. Basil reproached Gregory for not going to his see.

When protection for Arianism ended with the death of Valens, Gregory was called to rebuild the faith in the great see of Constantinople, which had been under Arian teachers for three decades. Retiring and sensitive, he dreaded being drawn into the whirlpool of corruption and violence. He first stayed at a friend's home, which became the only orthodox Church in the city. In such surroundings, he began giving the great sermons on the Trinity for which he is famous. In time, Gregory did rebuild the faith in the city, but at the cost of great suffering, slander, insults, and even personal violence. An interloper even tried to take over his archdiocese.

His last days were spent in solitude and austerity. He wrote religious poetry, some of it autobiographical, of great depth and beauty. He was acclaimed simply as "the Theologian."

COMMENT: It may be small comfort, but turmoil in the Church today is a mild storm compared to the devastation caused by the Arian heresy, a trauma the Church has never forgotten. Christ did not promise the kind of peace we would love to have—no problems, no opposition, no pain. In one way or another, holiness is always the way of the cross.

QUOTE: "God accepts our desires," wrote Gregory, "as though they were a great value. He longs ardently for us to desire and love him. He accepts our petitions for benefits as though we were doing him a favor. His joy in giving is greater than ours in receiving. So let us not be apathetic in our asking, nor set too narrow bounds to our requests; nor ask for frivolous things unworthy of God's greatness."

● ● ●

JANUARY 3 + OPTIONAL
Most Holy Name of Jesus

In a world of fiercely guarded corporate names and logos, it should be easy to understand this feast. The letters IHS are an abbreviation of *Jesous*, the Greek name for Jesus.

Although St. Paul might claim credit for promoting devotion to the Holy Name because he wrote in Philippians that God the Father gave Christ Jesus "that name that is above every name" (see 2:9), this devotion became popular because of twelfth-century Cistercian monks and nuns but especially through the preaching of St. Bernardine of Siena, a fifteenth-century Franciscan (May 20).

Bernardine used devotion to the Holy Name of Jesus as a way of overcoming bitter and often bloody class struggles and family rivalries or vendettas in Italian city-states. The devotion grew, partly because of Franciscan and Dominican preachers. It spread even more widely after the Jesuits began promoting it in the sixteenth century.

In 1530, Pope Clement V approved an Office of the Holy Name for the Franciscans. In 1721, Pope Innocent XIII extended this feast to the entire Church.

COMMENT: Jesus died and rose for the sake of all people. No one can trademark or copyright Jesus's name. Jesus is the Son of God and son of Mary. Everything that exists was created in and through the Son of God (see Colossians 1:15–20). The name of Jesus is debased if any Christian uses it as justification for berating non-Christians. Jesus reminds us that because we are all related to him we are, therefore, all related to one another.

QUOTE: "Glorious name, gracious name, name of love and of power! Through you sins are forgiven, through you enemies are vanquished, through you the sick are freed from their illness, through you those suffering in trials are made strong and cheerful. You bring honor to those who believe, you teach those who preach, you give strength to the toiler, you sustain the weary" (St .Bernardine of Siena).

• • •

JANUARY 4 + MEMORIAL (U.S.A.)
Elizabeth Ann Seton
RELIGIOUS (1774–1821)

Mother Seton is one of the keystones of the American Catholic church. She founded the first American religious community for women, the Sisters of Charity. She opened the first American parish school and established the first American Catholic orphanage. All this she did in the span of forty-six years while raising her five children.

Elizabeth Ann Bayley Seton is a true daughter of the American Revolution, born August 28, 1774, just two years before the Declaration of Independence. By birth and marriage, she was linked to the first families of New York and enjoyed the fruits of high society. Reared a staunch Episcopalian by her mother and stepmother, she learned the value of prayer, Scripture, and a nightly examination of conscience. Her father, Dr. Richard Bayley, did not have much use for churches but was a great humanitarian, teaching his daughter to love and serve others.

The early deaths of her mother in 1777 and her baby sister in 1778 gave Elizabeth a feel for eternity and the temporariness of the pilgrim life on earth. Far from being brooding and sullen, she faced each new "holocaust," as she put it, with hopeful cheerfulness.

At nineteen, Elizabeth was the belle of New York and married a handsome, wealthy businessman, William Magee Seton. They had five children before his business failed, and he died of tuberculosis. At thirty, Elizabeth was widowed and penniless, with five small children to support.

While in Italy with her dying husband, Elizabeth witnessed Catholicity in action through family friends. Three basic points led her to become a Catholic: belief in the Real Presence, devotion to the Blessed Mother and conviction that the Catholic Church led back to the apostles and to Christ. Many of her family and friends rejected her when she became a Catholic in March 1805.

To support her children, she opened a school in Baltimore. From the beginning, her group followed the lines of a religious community, which was officially founded in 1809.

The thousand or more letters of Mother Seton reveal the development of her spiritual life from ordinary goodness to heroic sanctity. She suffered great trials of sickness, misunderstanding, the death of loved ones (her husband and two young daughters), and the heartache of a wayward son. She died January 4, 1821, and became the first American-born citizen to be beatified (1963) and then canonized (1975). She is buried in Emmitsburg, Maryland.

COMMENT: Elizabeth Seton had no extraordinary gifts. She was not a mystic or stigmatic. She did not prophesy or speak in tongues. She had two great devotions: abandonment to the will of God and an ardent love for the Blessed Sacrament. She wrote to a friend, Julia Scott, that she would prefer to exchange the world for a "cave or a desert." "But God has given me a great deal to do, and I have always and hope always to prefer his will to every wish of my own." Her brand of sanctity is open to everyone if we love God and do his will.

QUOTE: Elizabeth Seton told her sisters, "The first end I propose in our daily work is to do the will of God; secondly, to do it in the manner he wills it; and thirdly, to do it because it is his will."

· · ·

JANUARY 5 + MEMORIAL (U.S.A.)
John Neumann
BISHOP (1811–1860)

Perhaps because the United States got a later start in the history of the world, it has relatively few canonized saints, but their number is increasing.

John Neumann was born in what is now the Czech Republic. After studying in Prague, he came to New York at twenty-five and was ordained a priest. He did missionary work in New York until he was twenty-nine, when he joined the Redemptorists and became its first member to profess vows in the United States. He continued missionary work in Maryland, Virginia and Ohio, where he became popular with the Germans.

At forty-one, as bishop of Philadelphia, he organized the parochial school system into a diocesan one, increasing the number of pupils almost twentyfold within a short time.

Gifted with outstanding organizing ability, he drew into the city many teaching communities of sisters and the Christian Brothers. During his brief assignment as vice provincial for the Redemptorists, he placed them in the forefront of the parochial movement.

Well-known for his holiness and learning, spiritual writing and preaching, on October 13, 1963, John Neumann became the first American bishop to be beatified. Canonized in 1977, he is buried in St. Peter the Apostle Church in Philadelphia.

COMMENT: Neumann took seriously our Lord's words, "Go and teach all nations." From Christ he received his instructions and the power to carry them out. For Christ does not give a mission without supplying the means to accomplish it. The Father's gift in Christ to John Neumann was his exceptional organizing ability, which he used to spread the Good News.

Today the Church is in dire need of men and women to continue in our times the teaching of the Good News. The obstacles and inconveniences are real and costly. Yet when Christians approach Christ, he supplies the necessary talents to answer today's needs. The Spirit of Christ continues his work through the instrumentality of generous Christians.

QUOTE: "All people of whatever race, condition or age, in virtue of their dignity as human persons, have an inalienable right to education. This education should be suitable to the particular destiny of the individuals, adapted to their ability, sex and national cultural traditions, and should be conducive to amicable relations with other nations in order to promote true unity and peace in the world. True education aims to give people a formation which is directed towards their final end and the good of that society to which they belong and in which, as adults, they will have their share of duties to perform" (Declaration on Christian Education, 1).

* * *

JANUARY 6 + MEMORIAL (CANADA)
André Bessette
RELIGIOUS (1845–1937)

Brother André expressed a saint's faith by a lifelong devotion to St. Joseph.

Sickness and weakness dogged André from birth. He was the eighth of twelve children born to a French Canadian couple near Montreal. Adopted at twelve, when both parents had died, he became a farmhand. Various trades followed: shoemaker, baker, blacksmith—all failures. He was a factory worker in the United States during the boom times of the Civil War.

At twenty-five, he applied for entrance into the Congregation of the Holy Cross. After a year's novitiate, he was not admitted because of his weak health. But with an extension and the urging of Bishop Bourget (see Marie-Rose Durocher, October 6), he was finally received. He was given the humble job of doorkeeper at Notre Dame College in Montreal, with additional duties as sacristan, laundry worker, and messenger. "When I joined this community, the superiors showed me the door, and I remained forty years."

In his little room near the door, he spent much of the night on his knees. On his windowsill, facing Mount Royal, was a small statue of St. Joseph, to whom he had been devoted since childhood. When asked about it he said, "Some day, St. Joseph is going to be honored in a very special way on Mount Royal!"

When he heard someone was ill, he visited to bring cheer and to pray with the sick person. He would rub the sick person lightly with oil taken from a lamp burning in the college chapel. Word of healing powers began to spread.

When an epidemic broke out at a nearby college, André volunteered to nurse. Not one person died. The trickle of sick people to his door became a flood. His superiors were uneasy, diocesan authorities were suspicious, and doctors called him a quack. "I do not cure," he said again and again. "St. Joseph cures." In the end, he needed four secretaries to handle the eighty thousand letters he received each year.

For many years the Holy Cross authorities had tried to buy land on Mount Royal. Brother André and others climbed the steep hill and planted medals of St. Joseph. Suddenly, the owners yielded. André collected two hundred dollars to build a small chapel and began receiving visitors there—smiling through long hours of listening, applying St. Joseph's oil. Some were cured, some not. The pile of crutches, canes, and braces grew.

The chapel also grew. By 1931 there were gleaming walls, but money ran out. "Put a statue of St. Joseph in the middle. If he wants a roof over his head, he'll get it." The magnificent Oratory on Mount Royal took fifty years to build. The sickly boy who could not hold a job died at ninety.

He is buried at the Oratory and was canonized in 2010.

COMMENT: Rubbing ailing limbs with oil or a medal? Planting a medal to buy land? Isn't this superstition? Aren't we long past that?

Superstitious people rely only on the magic of a word or action. Brother André's oil and medals were authentic sacramentals of a simple, total faith in the Father who lets his saints help him bless his children.

QUOTE: "It is with the smallest brushes that the artist paints the most exquisitely beautiful pictures," said St. André Bessette.

• • •

JANUARY 7 + OPTIONAL
Raymond of Peñafort
PRIEST (1175–1275)

Since Raymond lived into his hundredth year, he had a chance to do many things. As a member of the Spanish nobility, he had the resources and the education to get a good start in life.

By the time he was twenty, he was teaching philosophy. In his early thirties he earned a doctorate in both canon and civil law. At forty-one he became a Dominican. Pope Gregory IX called him to Rome to work for him and to be his confessor. One of the things the pope asked him to do was to gather together all the decrees of popes and councils that had been made in eighty years since a similar collection by Gratian. Raymond compiled five books called the *Decretals*. They were looked upon as one of the best organized collections of Church law until the 1917 codification of canon law.

Earlier, Raymond had written a book of cases for confessors. It was called *Summa de Casibus Poenitentiae*. More than simply a list of sins and penances, it discussed pertinent doctrines and laws of the Church that pertained to the problem or case brought to the confessor.

At the age of sixty, Raymond was appointed archbishop of Tarragona, the capital of Aragon. He didn't like the honor at all and ended up getting sick and resigning in two years.

He didn't get to enjoy his peace long, however, because when he was sixty-three he was elected by his fellow Dominicans to be the head of the whole order, the successor of St. Dominic. Raymond worked hard, visited on foot all the Dominicans, reorganized their constitutions, and managed to put through a provision that a master general be allowed to resign. When the new constitutions were accepted, Raymond, then sixty-five, resigned.

He still had thirty-five years to oppose heresy and work for the conversion of the Moors in Spain. He convinced St. Thomas Aquinas to write his work *Against the Gentiles*.

In his hundredth year the Lord let Raymond retire.

COMMENT: Raymond was a lawyer, a canonist. Legalism can suck the life out of genuine religion if it becomes too great a preoccupation with the letter of the law to the neglect of the spirit and purpose of the law. The law can become an end in itself, so that the value the law was intended to promote is overlooked. But we must guard against going to the opposite extreme and seeing law as useless or something to be lightly regarded. Laws ideally state those things that are for the best interests of everyone and make sure the rights of all are safeguarded. From Raymond, we can learn a respect for law as a means of serving the common good.

QUOTE: "He who hates the law is without wisdom, / and is tossed about like a boat in a storm" (Sirach 33:2).

* * *

JANUARY 12 + MEMORIAL (CANADA)
Marguerite Bourgeoys
RELIGIOUS (1620–1700)

"God closes a door and then opens a window," people sometimes say when dealing with their own disappointment or someone else's. That was certainly true in Marguerite's case. Children from European as well as Native American backgrounds in seventeenth-century Canada benefited from her great zeal and unshakable trust in God's providence.

Born the sixth of twelve children in Troyes, France, Marguerite at the age of twenty believed that she was called to religious life. Her applications to the Carmelites and Poor Clares were unsuccessful. A priest friend suggested that perhaps God had other plans for her.

In 1654, the governor of the French settlement in Canada visited his sister, an Augustinian canoness in Troyes. Marguerite belonged to a sodality connected to that convent. The governor invited her to come to Canada and start a school in Ville-Marie (eventually the city of Montreal). When she arrived, the colony numbered two hundred people with a hospital and a Jesuit mission chapel.

Soon after starting a school, she realized her need for coworkers. Returning to Troyes, she recruited a friend, Catherine Crolo, and two other young women. In 1667 they added classes at their school for Indian children. A second trip to France three years later resulted in six more young women and a letter from King Louis XIV, authorizing the school. The Congregation of Notre Dame was established in 1676 but its members did not make formal religious profession until 1698 when their Rule and constitutions were approved.

Marguerite established a school for Indian girls in Montreal. At the age of sixty-nine, she walked from Montreal to Quebec in response to the bishop's request to establish a community of her sisters in that city. By the time she died, she was referred to as the "Mother of the Colony." Marguerite was canonized in 1982.

COMMENT: It's easy to become discouraged when plans that we think that God must endorse are frustrated. Marguerite was called not to be a cloistered nun but to be a foundress and an educator. God had not ignored her after all.

QUOTE: In his homily at her canonization, Pope John Paul II said, "In particular, [Marguerite] contributed to building up that new country

[Canada], realizing the determining role of women, and she diligently strove toward their formation in a deeply Christian spirit." He noted that she watched over her students with affection and confidence "in order to prepare them to become wives and worthy mothers, Christians, cultured, hardworking, radiant mothers."

• • •

JANUARY 13 + OPTIONAL
Hilary
BISHOP AND DOCTOR (315?–368)

This staunch defender of the divinity of Christ was a gentle and courteous man, devoted to writing some of the greatest theology on the Trinity and was like his Master in being labeled a "disturber of the peace." In a very troubled period in the Church, his holiness was lived out in both scholarship and controversy. He was bishop of Poitiers in France.

COMMENT: Christ said his coming would bring not peace but a sword (see Matthew 10:34). The Gospels offer no support for us if we fantasize about a sunlit holiness that knows no problems. Christ did *not* escape at the last moment, though he did live happily ever after—after a life of controversy, problems, pain and frustration. Hilary, like all saints, simply had more of the same.

STORY: This immovable defender of orthodoxy was very gentle in reconciling the bishops of France who, in fear or ignorance, had accepted the Arian creed, which denied Christ's divinity. And while he wrote a blistering indictment of the emperor for sponsoring heresy, he could also point out, calmly, that sometimes the difference between heretical and orthodox doctrines was in the words rather than the ideas. He counseled bishops of the West, therefore, to be reserved in their condemnation. And this, of course, won him new enemies.

• • •

JANUARY 17 + MEMORIAL
Anthony
ABBOT (251–356)

The life of Anthony will remind many people of St. Francis of Assisi. At twenty, Anthony was so moved by the Gospel message, "Go, sell what you have, and give to [the] poor" (Mark 10:21b) that he actually did just that with his large inheritance. He is different from Francis in that most of Anthony's life was spent in solitude. He saw the world completely covered with snares and gave the Church and the world the witness of solitary asceticism, great personal mortification, and prayer. But no saint is antisocial, and Anthony drew many people to himself for spiritual healing and guidance.

At fifty-four, he responded to many requests and founded a sort of monastery of scattered cells. Again like Francis, he had great fear of "stately buildings and well-laden tables."

At sixty, he hoped to be a martyr in the renewed Roman persecution of 311, fearlessly exposing himself to danger while giving moral and material support to those in prison. At eighty-eight, he was fighting the Arian heresy, that massive trauma from which it took the Church centuries to recover. "The mule kicking over the altar" denied the divinity of Christ.

Anthony is associated in art with a T-shaped cross, a pig, and a book. The pig and the cross are symbols of his valiant warfare with the devil—the cross his constant means of power over evil spirits, the pig a symbol of the devil himself. The book recalls his preference for the book of nature over the printed word.

Anthony died in solitude at age 105.

COMMENT: In an era that smiles at the notion of devils and angels, a person known for having power over evil spirits must at least make us pause. And in a day when people speak of life as a rat race, one who devotes a whole life to solitude and prayer points to an essential of the Christian life in all ages. Anthony's hermit life reminds us of the absoluteness of our break with sin and the totality of our commitment to Christ. Even in God's good world, there is another world whose false values constantly tempt us.

STORY: Lest we be misled by the awesomeness of Anthony's asceticism, we have a statement from his biographer (Athanasius, May 2) that emphasizes the meaning and result of all Christian life: "Strangers knew him from among his disciples by the joy on his face."

Even the great Emperor Constantine wrote to him, asking for his prayers. Anthony told his friends, "Don't be surprised that the emperor writes to me—he's just another man, as I am. But be astounded that God should have written to us, and that he has spoken to us by his Son."

* * *

JANUARY 20 + OPTIONAL

Fabian

POPE AND MARTYR (C. 250)

Fabian was a Roman layman who came into the city from his farm one day as clergy and people were preparing to elect a new pope. Eusebius, a Church historian, says a dove flew in and settled on the head of Fabian. This sign united the votes of clergy and laity, and he was chosen unanimously.

He led the Church for fourteen years and died a martyr's death during the persecution of Decius in A.D. 250. St. Cyprian wrote to his successor that Fabian was an "incomparable" man whose glory in death matched the holiness and purity of his life.

In the catacombs of St. Callistus, the stone that covered Fabian's grave may still be seen, broken into four pieces, bearing the Greek words, "Fabian, bishop, martyr."

COMMENT: We can go confidently into the future and accept the change that growth demands only if we have firm roots in the past, in a living tradition. A few pieces of stone in Rome are a reminder to us that we are bearers of more than twenty centuries of a living tradition of faith and courage in living the life of Christ and showing it to the world. We have brothers and sisters who have "gone before us with the sign of faith," as the First Eucharistic Prayer puts it, to light the way for us.

QUOTE: "The blood of the martyrs is the seed of the Church" (Tertullian).

•　•　•

JANUARY 20 + OPTIONAL

Sebastian

MARTYR (257?–288?)

Nothing is historically certain about St. Sebastian except that he was a Roman martyr, was venerated in Milan even in the time of St. Ambrose (December 7), and was buried on the Appian Way, probably near the present Basilica of St. Sebastian. Devotion to him spread rapidly, and he is mentioned in several martyrologies as early as A.D. 350.

The legend of St. Sebastian is important in art, and there is a vast iconography. Scholars now agree that a pious fable has Sebastian entering the Roman army because only there could he assist the martyrs without arousing suspicion. Finally he was found out, brought before Emperor Diocletian and delivered to Mauritanian archers to be shot to death. His body was pierced with arrows, and he was left for dead. But he was found still alive by those who came to bury him. He recovered, but refused to flee. One day he took up a position near where the emperor was to pass. He accosted the emperor, denouncing him for his cruelty to Christians. This time the sentence of death was carried out. Sebastian was beaten to death with clubs. He was buried on the Appian Way, close to the catacombs that bear his name.

COMMENT: The fact that many of the early saints made such a tremendous impression on the Church—awakening widespread devotion and great praise from the greatest writers of the Church—is proof of the heroism of their lives. As has been said, legends may not be literally true. Yet they may express the very substance of the faith and courage evident in the lives of these heroes and heroines of Christ.

STORY: Another legend describes Sebastian's effectiveness in bolstering the courage of those in prison. Two men under sentence of death seemed about to give in to their captors. Sebastian made such an impassioned exhortation to constancy that it not only confirmed the two in their original convictions but won over many other prisoners in the jail. Again, this particular story may not be historically accurate. But it is true that all saints witness to Jesus both by word and action.

* * *

JANUARY 21 + MEMORIAL

Agnes

VIRGIN AND MARTYR (D. 258?)

Almost nothing is known of this saint except that she was very young—twelve or thirteen—when she was martyred in the last half of the third century. Various modes of death have been suggested—beheading, burning, strangling.

Legend has it she was a beautiful girl whom many young men wanted to marry. Among those she refused, one reported her to the authorities for being a Christian. She was arrested and confined to a house of prostitution. The legend continues that a man who looked upon her lustfully lost his sight and had it restored by her prayer. She was condemned, executed, and buried near Rome in a catacomb that eventually was named after her. The daughter of Constantine built a basilica in her honor.

COMMENT: Like that of modern Maria Goretti (July 6), the martyrdom of a virginal young girl made a deep impression on a society enslaved to a materialistic outlook. Like Agatha, who died in similar circumstances, Agnes is a symbol that holiness does not depend on length of years, experience, or human effort. It is a gift God offers to all.

QUOTE: "This is a virgin's birthday; let us follow the example of her chastity. It is a martyr's birthday; let us offer sacrifices; it is the birthday of holy Agnes: let men be filled with wonder, little ones with hope, married women with awe, and the unmarried with emulation. It seems to me that this child, holy beyond her years and courageous beyond human nature, received the name of Agnes (Greek: pure) not as an earthly designation but as a revelation from God of what she was to be" (from St. Ambrose's discourse on virginity).

* * *

Vincent
DEACON AND MARTYR (D. 304)

When Jesus deliberately began his journey to death, Luke says that he "set his face" to go to Jerusalem. It is this quality of rocklike courage that distinguishes the martyrs.

Most of what we know about this saint comes from the poet Prudentius. His *Acts* have been rather freely colored by the imagination of their compiler. But St. Augustine, in one of his sermons on St. Vincent, speaks of having the *Acts* of his martyrdom before him. We are at least sure of his name, his being a deacon, and the place of his death and burial.

According to the story we have (and as with some of the other early martyrs the unusual devotion he inspired must have had a basis in a very heroic life), Vincent was ordained deacon by his friend St. Valerius of Zaragossa in Spain. The Roman emperors had published their edicts against the clergy in 303, and the following year against the laity. Vincent and his bishop were imprisoned in Valencia. Hunger and torture failed to break them. Like the youths in the fiery furnace (Daniel 3), they seemed to thrive on suffering.

Valerius was sent into exile, and Dacian, the Roman governor, now turned the full force of his fury on Vincent. Tortures that sound very modern were tried. But their main effect was the progressive disintegration of Dacian himself. He had the torturers beaten because they failed.

Finally he suggested a compromise: Would Vincent at least give up the sacred books to be burned according to the emperor's edict? He would not. Torture on the gridiron continued, the prisoner remaining courageous, the torturer losing control of himself. Vincent was thrown into a filthy prison cell—and converted the jailer. Dacian wept with rage but, strangely enough, ordered the prisoner to be given some rest.

Friends among the faithful came to visit him, but he was to have no earthly rest. When they finally settled him on a comfortable bed, he went to his eternal rest.

COMMENT: The martyrs are heroic examples of what God's power can do. It is humanly impossible, we realize, for someone to go through tortures such as Vincent had and remain faithful. But it is equally true that by human power alone, no one can remain faithful even without torture or suffering. God does not come to our rescue at isolated, special moments. God is supporting the super-cruisers as well as children's toy boats.

QUOTE: "Wherever it was that Christians were put to death, their executions did not bear the semblance of a triumph. Exteriorly they did not differ in the least from the executions of common criminals. But the moral grandeur of a martyr is essentially the same, whether he preserved his constancy in the arena before thousands of raving spectators or whether he perfected his martyrdom forsaken by all upon a pitiless flayer's field" (Ludwig Hertling and Engelbert Kirschbaum, *The Roman Catacombs and Their Martyrs*).

● ● ●

JANUARY 23 + MEMORIAL (U.S.A.)
Marianne Cope
RELIGIOUS (1838–1918)

Though leprosy scared off most people in nineteenth-century Hawaii, the disease sparked great generosity in the woman who came to be known as Mother Marianne of Molokai. Her courage helped tremendously to improve the lives of its victims in Hawaii, a territory annexed to the United States during her lifetime (1898).

Mother Marianne's generosity and courage were celebrated at her beatification in Rome on May 14, 2005. She was a woman who spoke "the language of truth and love" to the world, said Cardinal José Saraiva Martins, prefect of the Congregation for the Causes of Saints. Cardinal Martins, who presided at the beatification Mass in St. Peter's Basilica, called her life "a wonderful work of divine grace." Speaking of her special love for persons suffering from leprosy, he said, "She saw in them the suffering face of Jesus. Like the Good Samaritan, she became their mother."

On January 23, 1838, a daughter was born to Peter and Barbara Cope of Hessen-Darmstadt, Germany. The girl was named after her mother. Two years later, the Cope family emigrated to the United States and settled in Utica, New York. Young Barbara worked in a factory until August 1862, when she went to the Sisters of the Third Order of St. Francis in Syracuse, New York. After profession in November of the next year, she began teaching at Assumption parish school.

Marianne held the post of superior in several places and was twice the novice mistress of her congregation. A natural leader, three different times she was superior of St. Joseph Hospital in Syracuse, where she learned much that would be useful during her years in Hawaii.

Elected provincial in 1877, Mother Marianne was unanimously reelected in 1881. Two years later the Hawaiian government was searching for someone to run the Kakaako Receiving Station for people suspected of having leprosy. More than fifty religious communities in the United States and Canada were asked. When the request was put to the Syracuse sisters, thirty-five of them volunteered immediately. On October 22, Mother Marianne and six other sisters left for Hawaii, where they took charge of the receiving station outside Honolulu. On the island of Maui they also opened a hospital and a school for girls.

In 1888, Mother Marianne and two sisters went to Molokai to open a home for "unprotected women and girls" there. The Hawaiian government was quite hesitant to send women for this difficult assignment; they need not have worried about Mother Marianne! On Molokai she took charge of the home that Damien de Veuster (d. 1889, see May 10 entry) had established for men and boys. Mother Marianne changed life on Molokai by introducing cleanliness, pride, and fun to the colony. Bright scarves and pretty dresses for the women were part of her approach.

Awarded the Royal Order of Kapiolani by the Hawaiian government and celebrated in a poem by Robert Louis Stevenson, Mother Marianne continued to work faithfully. Her sisters have attracted vocations among the Hawaiian people and still work on Molokai.

Mother Marianne died on August 9, 1918, and was canonized in 2012.

COMMENT: The government authorities were reluctant to allow Mother Marianne to be a mother on Molokai. Thirty years of dedication proved their fears unfounded. God grants gifts regardless of human shortsightedness and allows those gifts to flower for the sake of the kingdom.

QUOTE: Soon after Mother Marianne died, Mrs. John F. Bowker wrote in the *Honolulu Advertiser*: "Seldom has the opportunity come to a woman to devote every hour of 30 years to the mothering of people isolated by law from the rest of the world. She risked her own life in all that time, faced everything with unflinching courage and smiled sweetly through it all."

•   •   •

JANUARY 24 + MEMORIAL

Francis de Sales

BISHOP AND DOCTOR (1567–1622)

Francis was destined by his father to be a lawyer so that the young man could eventually take his elder's place as a senator from the province of Savoy in France. For this reason Francis was sent to Padua to study law. After receiving his doctorate, he returned home and, in due time, told his parents he wished to enter the priesthood. His father strongly opposed Francis in this, and only after much patient persuasiveness on the part of the gentle Francis did his father finally consent. Francis was ordained and elected provost of the Diocese of Geneva, then a center for the Calvinists. Francis set out to convert them, especially in the district of Chablais. By preaching and distributing the little pamphlets he wrote to explain true Catholic doctrine, he had remarkable success.

At thirty-five he became bishop of Geneva. While administering his diocese he continued to preach, hear confessions, and catechize the children. His gentle character was a great asset in winning souls. He practiced his own axiom, "A spoonful of honey attracts more flies than a barrelful of vinegar."

Besides his two well-known books, *An Introduction to the Devout Life* and *A Treatise on the Love of God*, he wrote many pamphlets and carried on a vast correspondence. For his writings, he has been named patron of the Catholic press. His writings, filled with his characteristic gentle spirit, are addressed to laypeople. He wants to make them understand that they too are called to be saints. As he wrote in *An Introduction to the Devout Life*: "It is an error, or rather a heresy, to say devotion is incompatible with the life of a soldier, a tradesman, a prince, or a married woman…. It has happened that many have lost perfection in the desert who had preserved it in the world."

In spite of his busy and comparatively short life, he had time to collaborate with another saint, Jane Frances de Chantal (August 12), in the work of establishing the Sisters of the Visitation. These women were to practice the virtues exemplified in Mary's visit to Elizabeth: humility, piety, and mutual charity. They at first engaged to a limited degree in works of mercy for the poor and the sick. Today, while some communities conduct schools, others live a strictly contemplative life.

COMMENT: Francis de Sales took seriously the words of Christ, "Learn of me for I am meek and humble of heart." As he said himself, it took him twenty years to conquer his quick temper, but no one ever suspected he had such a problem, so overflowing with good nature and kindness was his usual manner of acting. His perennial meekness and sunny disposition won for him the title of "Gentleman Saint."

QUOTE: Francis de Sales tells us: "The person who possesses Christian meekness is affectionate and tender towards everyone: he is disposed to forgive and excuse the frailties of others; the goodness of his heart appears in a sweet affability that influences his words and actions, presents every object to his view in the most charitable and pleasing light."

. . .

Conversion of Paul

APOSTLE

Paul's entire life can be explained in terms of one experience—his meeting with Jesus on the road to Damascus. In an instant, he saw that all the zeal of his dynamic personality was being wasted, like the strength of a boxer swinging wildly. Perhaps he had never seen Jesus, who was only a few years older. But he had acquired a zealot's hatred of all Jesus stood for, as he began to harass the Church, "entering house after house and dragging out men and women, he handed them over for imprisonment" (Acts 8:3b). Now he himself was "entered," possessed, all his energy harnessed to one goal—being a slave of Christ in the ministry of reconciliation, an instrument to help others experience the one Savior.

One sentence determined his theology: "I am Jesus, whom you are persecuting" (Acts 9:5b). Jesus was mysteriously identified with people—the loving group of people Saul had been running down like criminals. Jesus, he saw, was the mysterious fulfillment of all he had been blindly pursuing.

From then on, his only work was to "present everyone perfect in Christ. For this I labor and struggle, in accord with the exercise of his power working within me" (Colossians 1:28b–29). "For our gospel did not come to you in word alone, but also in power and in the Holy Spirit and [with] much conviction" (1 Thessalonians 1:5a).

Paul's life became a tireless proclaiming and living out of the message of the cross: Christians die baptismally to sin and are buried with Christ; they are dead to all that is sinful and unredeemed in the world. They are made into a new creation, already sharing Christ's victory and someday to rise from the dead like him. Through this Risen Christ, the Father pours out the Spirit on them, making them completely new.

So Paul's great message to the world was: You are saved entirely by God, not by anything you can do. Saving faith is the gift of total, free, personal, and loving commitment to Christ, a commitment that then bears fruit in more works than the Law could ever contemplate. According to tradition, he was beheaded in Rome around A.D. 64.

COMMENT: Paul is undoubtedly hard to understand. His style often reflects the rabbinical style of argument of his day, and often his thought skips on mountaintops while we plod below. But perhaps our problems are accentuated by the fact that so many beautiful jewels have become part of the everyday coin in our Christian language.

QUOTE: "Love is patient, love is kind. It is not jealous, [love] is not pompous, it is not inflated, it is not rude, it does not seek its own interests, it is not quick-tempered, it does not brood over injury, it does not rejoice over wrongdoing but rejoices with the truth. It bears all things, believes all things, hopes all things, endures all things" (1 Corinthians 13:4–7).

• • •

JANUARY 26 + MEMORIAL
Timothy and Titus
BISHOPS

Timothy (d. 97?). What we know from the New Testament of Timothy's life makes it sound like that of a modern harried bishop. He had the honor of being a fellow apostle with Paul, both sharing the privilege of preaching the Gospel and suffering for it.

Timothy had a Greek father and a Jewish mother named Eunice. Being the product of a "mixed" marriage, he was considered illegitimate by the Jews. It was his grandmother, Lois, who first became Christian. Timothy was a convert of Paul around the year 47 and later joined him in his apostolic work. He was with Paul at the founding of the church in Corinth. During the fifteen years he worked with Paul, he became one of his most faithful and trusted friends. He was sent on difficult missions by Paul—often in the face of great disturbance in local churches that Paul had founded.

Timothy was with Paul in Rome during the latter's house arrest. At some period Timothy himself was in prison (Hebrews 13:23). Paul installed him as his representative at the church of Ephesus.

Timothy was comparatively young for the work he was doing. ("Let no one have contempt for your youth," Paul writes in 1 Timothy 4:12a.) Several references seem to indicate that he was timid. And one of Paul's most frequently quoted lines was addressed to him: "Stop drinking only water, but have a little wine for the sake of your stomach and your frequent illnesses" (1 Timothy 5:23).

COMMENT: Nostalgia for the good old days in the Church—especially the early Church—should not blind us to the fact that the servants have never been greater than the Master. Their holiness was lived out in day-to-day perplexities, sufferings, and apparent failure. The world is not saved by what we do, but by what God does through the life he creates for us.

QUOTE: Paul writes, "I remind you to stir into flame the gift of God that you have through the imposition of my hands. For God did not give us a spirit of cowardice but rather of power and love and self-control. So do not be ashamed of your testimony to our Lord, nor of me, a prisoner for his sake; but bear your share of hardship for the gospel with the strength that comes from God" (2 Timothy 1:6–8).

Titus, bishop (d. 94?). Titus has the distinction of being a close friend and disciple of Paul as well as a fellow missionary. He was Greek, apparently from Antioch. Even though Titus was a Gentile, Paul would not let him be forced to undergo circumcision at Jerusalem. Titus is seen as a peacemaker, administrator, and great friend. Paul's Second Letter to the Corinthians affords an insight into the depth of his friendship with Titus, and the great fellowship they had in preaching the Gospel: "When I went to Troas…I had no relief in my spirit because I did not find my brother Titus. So I took leave of them and went on to Macedonia…. For even when we came into Macedonia, our flesh had no rest, but we were afflicted in every way—external conflicts, internal fears. But God, who encourages the downcast, encouraged us by the arrival of Titus" (2 Corinthians 2:12a, 13; 7:5–6).

When Paul was having trouble with the community at Corinth, Titus was the bearer of Paul's severe letter and was successful in smoothing things out.

Paul writes he was strengthened not only by the arrival of Titus but also "by the encouragement with which he was encouraged in regard to you, as he told us of your yearning, your lament, your zeal for me, so that I rejoiced even more…. And his heart goes out to you all the more, as he remembers the obedience of all of you, when you received him with fear and trembling" (2 Corinthians 7:7a, 15).

The Letter to Titus addresses him as the administrator of the Christian community on the island of Crete, charged with organizing it, correcting abuses, and appointing presbyter-bishops.

COMMENT: In Titus we get another glimpse of life in the early Church: great zeal in the apostolate, great communion in Christ, great friendship. Yet always there is the problem of human nature and the unglamorous details of daily life: the need for charity and patience in "quarrels with others, fears within myself," as Paul says. Through it all, the love of Christ sustained them. At the end of the Letter to Titus, Paul says that when the temporary substitute comes, "hurry to me."

QUOTE: "But when the kindness and generous love / of God our Savior appeared, / not because of any righteous deeds we had done / but because of his mercy, / he saved us through the bath of rebirth / and renewal by the holy Spirit, / whom he richly poured out on us / through Jesus Christ our savior, / so that we might be justified by his grace / and become heirs in hope of eternal life. / This saying is trustworthy" (Titus 3:4–8).

* * *

JANUARY 27 + OPTIONAL
Angela Merici
VIRGIN (1470?–1540)

Angela has the double distinction of founding the first teaching congregation of women in the Church and what is now called a "secular institute" of religious women.

As a young woman she became a member of the Third Order of St. Francis (now known as the Secular Franciscan Order) and lived a life of great austerity, wishing, like St. Francis, to own nothing, not even a bed. Early in life she was appalled at the ignorance among poorer children, whose parents could not or would not teach them the elements of religion. Angela's charming manner and good looks complemented her natural qualities of leadership. Others joined her in giving regular instruction to the little girls of their neighborhood.

She was invited to live with a family in Brescia (where, she had been told in a vision, she would one day found a religious community). Her work continued and became well known. She became the center of a group of people with similar ideals.

She eagerly took the opportunity for a trip to the Holy Land. When they had gotten as far as Crete, she was struck with blindness. Her friends wanted to return home, but she insisted on going through with the pilgrimage, and visited the sacred shrines with as much devotion and enthusiasm as if she had her sight. On the way back, while praying before a crucifix, her sight was restored at the same place where it had been lost.

At fifty-seven, she organized a group of twelve girls to help her in catechetical work. Four years later the group had increased to twenty-eight. She formed them into the Company of St. Ursula (patron of medieval universities and venerated as a leader of women) for the purpose of re-Christianizing family life through solid Christian education of future wives and mothers. The members continued to live at home, had no special habit, and took no formal vows, though the early Rule prescribed the practice of virginity, poverty, and obedience. The idea of a teaching congregation of women was new and took time to develop. The community thus existed as a secular institute until some years after Angela's death.

COMMENT: As with so many saints, history is mostly concerned with their activities. But we must always presume deep Christian faith and love in one whose courage lasts a lifetime and who can take bold new steps when human need demands.

QUOTE: In a time when change is problematic to many, it may be helpful to recall a statement this great leader made to her sisters: "If according to times and needs you should be obliged to make fresh rules and change certain things, do it with prudence and good advice."

● ● ●

JANUARY 28 + MEMORIAL

Thomas Aquinas

PRIEST AND DOCTOR (1225–1274)

By universal consent, Thomas Aquinas is the preeminent spokesman of the Catholic tradition of reason and of divine revelation. He is one of the great teachers of the medieval Catholic Church, honored with the titles Doctor of the Church and Angelic Doctor.

At five he was given to the Benedictine monastery at Monte Cassino in his parents' hopes that he would choose that way of life and eventually become abbot. In 1239, he was sent to Naples to complete his studies. It was here that he was first attracted to Aristotle's philosophy.

By 1243, Thomas abandoned his family's plans for him and joined the Dominicans, much to his mother's dismay. On her order, Thomas was captured by his brother and kept at home for over a year.

Once free, he went to Paris and then to Cologne, where he finished his studies with Albert the Great (November 15). He held two professorships at Paris, lived at the court of Pope Urban IV, directed the Dominican schools at Rome and Viterbo, combated adversaries of the mendicants, as well as the Averroists, and argued with some Franciscans about the teachings of Aristotle.

His greatest contribution to the Catholic Church is his writings. The unity, harmony, and continuity of faith and reason, of revealed and natural human knowledge, pervade his writings. One might expect Thomas, as a man of the Gospel, to be an ardent defender of revealed truth. But he was broad enough, deep enough, to see the whole natural order as coming from God the Creator and to see reason as a divine gift to be highly cherished.

The *Summa Theologiae*, his last and, unfortunately, uncompleted work, deals with the whole of Catholic theology. He stopped work on it after celebrating Mass on December 6, 1273. When asked why he stopped writing, he replied, "I cannot go on.... All that I have written seems to me like so much straw compared to what I have seen and what has been revealed to me." He died March 7, 1274.

COMMENT: We can look to Thomas Aquinas as a towering example of Catholicism in the sense of broadness, universality, and inclusiveness. We should be determined anew to exercise the divine gift of reason in us, our power to know, learn, and understand. At the same time we should thank God for the gift of his revelation, especially in Jesus Christ.

QUOTE: "Hence we must say that for the knowledge of any truth whatsoever man needs divine help, that the intellect may be moved by God to its act. But he does not need a new light added to his natural light, in order to know the truth in all things, but only in some that surpasses his natural knowledge" (*Summa Theologiae*, I-II, 109, 1).

• • •

JANUARY 31 + MEMORIAL
John Bosco
PRIEST (1815–1888)

John Bosco's theory of education could well be used in today's schools. It was a preventive system, rejecting corporal punishment and placing students in surroundings removed from the likelihood of committing sin. He advocated frequent reception of the sacraments of reconciliation and Holy Communion. He combined catechetical training and fatherly guidance, seeking to unite the spiritual life with one's work, study, and play.

Encouraged during his youth to become a priest so he could work with young boys, John was ordained in 1841. His service to young people started when he met a poor orphan and instructed him in preparation for receiving Holy Communion. He then gathered young apprentices and taught them catechism.

After serving as chaplain in a hospice for working girls, John opened the Oratory of St. Francis de Sales for boys. Several wealthy and powerful patrons contributed money, enabling him to provide two workshops for the boys, shoemaking and tailoring.

By 1856, the institution had grown to 150 boys and had added a printing press for publication of religious and catechetical pamphlets. His interest in vocational education and publishing justify him as patron of young apprentices and Catholic publishers.

John's preaching fame spread and by 1850 he had trained his own helpers because of difficulties in retaining young priests. In 1854 he and his followers informally banded together, inspired by Francis de Sales.

With Pope Pius IX's encouragement, John founded the Salesians in 1859. Their activity concentrated on education and mission work. Later, he organized a group of Salesian Sisters to assist girls.

COMMENT: John Bosco educated the whole person—body and soul united. He believed that Christ's love and our faith in that love should pervade everything we do—work, study, and play. For John Bosco, being a Christian was a full-time effort, not a once-a-week, Mass-on-Sunday experience. It is searching and finding God and Jesus in everything we do, letting God's love lead us. Yet, because John realized the importance of job training and the self-worth and pride that come with talent and ability, he trained his students in the trade crafts, too.

QUOTE: "Every education teaches a philosophy; if not by dogma then by suggestion, by implication, by atmosphere. Every part of that education has a connection with every other part. If it does not all combine to convey some general view of life, it is not education at all" (G.K. Chesterton, *The Common Man*).

• • •

Presentation of the Lord

At the end of the fourth century, a woman named Etheria made a pilgrimage to Jerusalem. Her journal, discovered in 1887, gives an unprecedented glimpse of liturgical life there. Among the celebrations she describes is the Epiphany (January 6), the observance of Christ's birth, and the gala procession in honor of his Presentation in the Temple forty days later—February 15. (Under the Mosaic Law, a woman was ritually unclean for forty days after childbirth, when she was to present herself to the priests and offer sacrifice—her purification. Contact with anyone who had brushed against mystery—birth or death—excluded a person from Jewish worship.) This feast emphasizes Jesus's first appearance in the Temple more than Mary's purification.

The observance spread throughout the Western Church in the fifth and sixth centuries. Because the Church in the West celebrated Jesus's birth on December 25, the Presentation was moved to February 2, forty days after Christmas.

At the beginning of the eighth century, Pope Sergius inaugurated a candlelight procession; at the end of the same century the blessing and distribution of candles which continues to this day became part of the celebration, giving the feast its popular name: Candlemas.

COMMENT: In Luke's account, Jesus was welcomed in the Temple by two elderly people, Simeon and the widow Anna. They embody Israel in their patient expectation; they acknowledge the infant Jesus as the long-awaited Messiah. Early references to the Roman feast dub it the feast of St. Simeon, the old man who burst into a song of joy that the Church still sings at day's end.

QUOTE: "Christ himself says, 'I am the light of the world. ' And we are the light, we ourselves, if we receive it from him…. But how do we receive it, how do we make it shine?… [T]he candle tells us: by burning, and being consumed in the burning. A spark of fire, a ray of love, an inevitable

31

immolation are celebrated over that pure, straight candle, as, pouring forth its gift of light, it exhausts itself in silent sacrifice" (Paul VI).

• • •

Blaise

BISHOP AND MARTYR (D. 316)

We know more about the devotion to St. Blaise by Christians around the world than we know about the saint himself. His feast is observed as a holy day in the Eastern Church. The Council of Oxford, in 1222, prohibited servile labor in England on Blaise's feast day. The Germans and Slavs hold him in special honor, and for decades many United States Catholics have sought the annual St. Blaise blessing for their throats.

We know that Bishop Blaise was martyred in his episcopal city of Sebastea, Armenia, in 316. The legendary *Acts of Saint Blaise* was written four hundred years later. According to them, Blaise was a good bishop, working hard to encourage the spiritual and physical health of his people. Although the Edict of Toleration (311), granting freedom of worship in the Roman Empire, was already five years old, persecution still raged in Armenia. Blaise was apparently forced to flee to the backcountry. There he lived as a hermit in solitude and prayer, making friends with the wild animals. One day a group of hunters seeking wild animals for the amphitheater stumbled upon Blaise's cave. They were first surprised and then frightened: The bishop was kneeling in prayer surrounded by patiently waiting wolves, lions, and bears.

As the hunters hauled Blaise off to prison, the legend has it, a mother came with her young son who had a fish bone lodged in his throat. At Blaise's command, the child was able to cough up the bone.

Agricolaus, governor of Cappadocia, tried to persuade Blaise to sacrifice to pagan idols. The first time Blaise refused, he was beaten. The next time he was suspended from a tree and his flesh torn with iron combs or rakes. (English wool combers, who used similar iron combs, took Blaise as their patron. They could easily appreciate the agony the saint underwent.) Finally, he was beheaded.

COMMENT: Four centuries give ample opportunity for fiction to creep in with fact. Who can be sure how accurate Blaise's biographer was? But biographical details are not essential. Blaise is seen as one more example of the power of those who have given themselves entirely to Jesus. As Jesus told his apostles at the Last Supper, "If you remain in me and my words remain in you, ask for whatever you want and it will be done for you" (John 15:7). With faith we can follow the lead of the Church in asking for Blaise's protection.

QUOTE: "Through the intercession of St. Blaise, bishop and martyr, may God deliver you from ailments of the throat and from every other evil. In the name of the Father, and of the Son and of the Holy Spirit" (Blessing of St. Blaise).

• • •

FEBRUARY 3 + OPTIONAL
Ansgar
BISHOP (801–865)

The "apostle of the north" (Scandinavia) had enough frustrations to become a saint—and he did. He became a Benedictine at Corbie, France, where he had been educated. Three years later, when the king of Denmark became a convert, Ansgar went to that country for three years of missionary work, without noticeable success. Sweden asked for Christian missionaries, and he went there, suffering capture by pirates and other hardships on the way. Less than two years later, he was recalled to become abbot of New Corbie (Corvey) and bishop of Hamburg. The pope made him legate for the Scandinavian missions. Funds for the northern apostolate stopped with Emperor Louis's death. After thirteen years' work in Hamburg, Ansgar saw it burned to the ground by invading Northmen. Sweden and Denmark returned to paganism.

He directed new apostolic activities in the north, traveling to Denmark and being instrumental in the conversion of another king. By the strange device of casting lots, the king of Sweden allowed the Christian missionaries to return.

Ansgar's biographers remark that he was an extraordinary preacher and a humble and ascetical priest. He was devoted to the poor and the sick, imitating the Lord in washing their feet and waiting on them at table. He died peacefully at Bremen, Germany, without achieving his wish to be a martyr.

Sweden became pagan again after Ansgar's death and remained so until the coming of missionaries two centuries later.

COMMENT: History records what people do, rather than what they are. Yet the courage and perseverance of men and women like Ansgar can only come from a solid base of union with the original courageous and persevering Missionary. Ansgar's life is another reminder that God writes straight with crooked lines. Christ takes care of the effects of the apostolate in his own way; he is first concerned about the purity of the apostles themselves.

STORY: One of his followers was bragging about all the miracles the saint had wrought. Ansgar rebuked him by saying "If I were worthy of such a favor from my God, I would ask that he grant me this one miracle: that by his grace he would make of me a good man."

. . .

FEBRUARY 5 + MEMORIAL

Agatha
VIRGIN AND MARTYR (D. 251?)

As in the case of Agnes, another virgin-martyr of the early Church, almost nothing is historically certain about this saint except that she was martyred in Sicily during the persecution of Emperor Decius in 251.

Legend has it that Agatha, like Agnes, was arrested as a Christian, tortured and sent to a house of prostitution to be mistreated. She was preserved from being violated and was later put to death.

She is claimed as the patron of both Palermo and Catania. The year after her death, the stilling of an eruption of Mt. Etna was attributed to her intercession. As a result, people continued to ask her prayers for protection against fire.

COMMENT: Those of a scientific mind wince at the thought of a volcano's might being contained by God because of the prayers of a Sicilian girl. Still less welcome, probably, is the notion of that saint being the patron of such varied professions as those of foundry workers, nurses, miners, and alpine guides. Yet, in our desire for historical precision, have we lost an essential human quality of wonder and poetry and even our belief that we come to God by helping each other, both in action and prayer?

QUOTE: When Agatha was arrested, the legend says, she prayed: "Jesus Christ, Lord of all things! You see my heart, you know my desires. Possess all that I am—you alone. I am your sheep; make me worthy to overcome the devil." And in prison: "Lord, my creator, you have protected me since I was in the cradle. You have taken me from the love of the world and given me patience to suffer. Now receive my spirit."

●　●　●

FEBRUARY 6 + MEMORIAL
Paul Miki and Companions
MARTYRS (D. 1597)

Nagasaki, Japan, is familiar to Americans as the city on which the second atomic bomb was dropped, immediately killing about forty thousand people. Three and a half centuries before, twenty-six martyrs of Japan were crucified on a hill, now known as the Holy Mountain, overlooking Nagasaki. Among them were priests, brothers, laymen, Franciscans, Jesuits, and members of the Secular Franciscan Order; there were catechists, doctors, simple artisans, servants, old men, and innocent children—all united in a common faith and love for Jesus and his Church.

Brother Paul Miki, a Jesuit and a native of Japan, has become the best known among the martyrs of Japan. While hanging upon a cross, Paul Miki preached to the people gathered for the execution:

> The sentence of judgment says these men came to Japan from the Philippines, but I did not come from any other country. I am a true Japanese. The only reason for my being killed is that I have taught

the doctrine of Christ. I certainly did teach the doctrine of Christ. I thank God it is for this reason I die. I believe that I am telling only the truth before I die. I know you believe me and I want to say to you all once again: Ask Christ to help you to become happy. I obey Christ. After Christ's example I forgive my persecutors. I do not hate them. I ask God to have pity on all, and I hope my blood will fall on my fellow men as a fruitful rain.

When missionaries returned to Japan in the 1860s, at first they found no trace of Christianity. But after establishing themselves they found that thousands of Christians lived around Nagasaki and that they had secretly preserved the faith. Beatified in 1627, the martyrs of Japan were finally canonized in 1862.

COMMENT: Today a new era has come for the church in Japan. Although the number of Catholics is not large, the church is respected and has total religious freedom. The spread of Christianity in the Far East is slow and difficult. Faith such as that of the twenty-six martyrs is needed today as much as in 1597.

QUOTE: "Since Jesus, the Son of God, showed his love by laying down his life for us, no one has greater love than they who lay down their lives for him and for their sisters and brothers (see 1 John 3:16; John 15:13). Some Christians have been called from the beginning, and will always be called, to give this greatest testimony of love to everyone, especially to persecutors. Martyrdom makes disciples like their master, who willingly accepted death for the salvation of the world, and through it they are made like him by the shedding of blood. Therefore, the Church considers it the highest gift and as the supreme test of love. And while it is given to few, all, however, must be prepared to confess Christ before humanity and to follow him along the way of the cross amid the persecutions which the Church never lacks" (Dogmatic Constitution on the Church, 42).

• • •

Josephine Bakhita
VIRGIN (1869–1947)

For many years, Josephine Bakhita was a slave, but her spirit was always free and eventually that spirit prevailed.

Born in Olgossa in the Darfur region of southern Sudan, Josephine was kidnapped at the age of seven, sold into slavery, and given the name Bakhita, which means *fortunate*. She was resold several times, finally in 1883 to Callisto Legnani, Italian consul in Khartoum, Sudan.

Two years later he took Josephine to Italy and gave her to his friend Augusto Michieli. Soon Bakhita became babysitter to Mimmina Michieli, whom she accompanied to Venice's Institute of the Catechumens, run by the Canossian Sisters. While Mimmina was being instructed, Josephine felt drawn to the Catholic Church. She was baptized and confirmed in 1890, taking the name Josephine.

When the Michielis returned from Africa and wanted to take Mimmina and Josephine back with them, the future saint refused to go. During the ensuing court case, the Canossian sisters and the patriarch of Venice intervened on Josephine's behalf. The judge concluded that since slavery was illegal in Italy, she had actually been free since 1885.

Josephine entered the Institute of St. Magdalene of Canossa in 1893 and made her profession three years later. In 1902, she was transferred to the city of Schio (northeast of Verona), where she assisted her religious community through cooking, sewing, embroidery, and welcoming visitors at the door. She soon became well loved by the children attending the sisters' school and the local citizens. She once said, "Be good, love the Lord, pray for those who do not know Him. What a great grace it is to know God!"

The first steps toward her beatification began in 1959. She was beatified in 1992 and canonized eight years later.

COMMENT: Josephine's body was mutilated by those who enslaved her, but they could not touch her inner spirit. Her baptism set her on an eventual path toward asserting her civic freedom and then service to God's people as a Canossian sister.

She who worked under many "masters" was finally happy to address God as "Master" and carry out everything that she believed to be God's will for her.

QUOTE: During his homily at her canonization Mass in St. Peter's Square, Pope John Paul II said that in St. Josephine Bakhita, "we find a shining advocate of genuine emancipation. The history of her life inspires not passive acceptance but the firm resolve to work effectively to free girls and women from oppression and violence, and to return them to their dignity in the full exercise of their rights."

* * *

FEBRUARY 8 + OPTIONAL

Jerome Emiliani

PRIEST (1481–1537)

A careless and irreligious soldier for the city-state of Venice, Jerome was captured in a skirmish at an outpost town and chained in a dungeon. In prison Jerome had a lot of time to think, and he gradually learned how to pray. When he escaped, he returned to Venice where he took charge of the education of his nephews—and began his own studies for the priesthood.

In the years after his ordination, events again called Jerome to a decision and a new lifestyle. Plague and famine swept northern Italy. Jerome began caring for the sick and feeding the hungry at his own expense. While serving the sick and the poor, he soon resolved to devote himself and his property solely to others, particularly to abandoned children. He founded three orphanages, a shelter for penitent prostitutes, and a hospital.

Around 1532, Jerome and two other priests established a congregation, the Clerks Regular of Somasca, dedicated to the care of orphans and the education of youth. Jerome died in 1537 from a disease he caught while tending the sick. He was canonized in 1767. In 1928 Pius XI named him the patron of orphans and abandoned children.

COMMENT: Very often in our lives it seems to take some kind of imprisonment to free us from the shackles of our self-centeredness. When we're caught in some situation we don't want to be in, we finally come to know the liberating power of Another. Only then can we become another for the imprisoned and the orphaned all around us.

QUOTE: "'The father of orphans and the defender of widows is God in his holy dwelling. God gives a home to the forsaken; he leads forth prisoners to prosperity; only rebels remain in the parched land' (Psalm 68).... We should not forget the growing number of persons who are often abandoned by their families and by the community: the old, orphans, the sick and all kinds of people who are rejected.... We must be prepared to take on new functions and new duties in every sector of human activity and especially in the sector of world society, if justice is really to be put into practice. Our action is to be directed above all at those men and nations which, because of various forms of oppression and because of the present character of our society, are silent, indeed voiceless, victims of injustice" (*Justice in the World,* 1971 World Synod of Bishops).

● ● ●

FEBRUARY 10 + MEMORIAL
Scholastica
VIRGIN (480–542?)

Twins often share the same interests and ideas with an equal intensity. Therefore, it is no surprise that Scholastica and her twin brother, Benedict (July 11), established religious communities within a few miles from each other.

Born in 480 of wealthy parents, Scholastica and Benedict were brought up together until he left central Italy for Rome to continue his studies.

Little is known of Scholastica's early life. She founded a religious community for women near Monte Cassino at Plombariola, five miles from where her brother governed a monastery.

The twins visited each other once a year in a farmhouse because Scholastica was not permitted inside the monastery. They spent these times discussing spiritual matters.

According to the *Dialogues of Saint Gregory the Great*, the brother and sister spent their last day together in prayer and conversation. Scholastica sensed her death was close at hand, and she begged Benedict to stay with her until the next day.

He refused her request because he did not want to spend a night outside the monastery, thus breaking his own Rule. Scholastica asked God to let her brother remain, and a severe thunderstorm broke out, preventing Benedict and his monks from returning to the abbey.

Benedict cried out, "God forgive you, Sister. What have you done?" Scholastica replied, "I asked a favor of you and you refused. I asked it of God and he granted it."

Brother and sister parted the next morning after their long discussion. Three days later, Benedict was praying in his monastery and saw the soul of his sister rising heavenward in the form of a white dove. Benedict then announced the death of his sister to the monks and later buried her in the tomb he had prepared for himself.

COMMENT: Scholastica and Benedict gave themselves totally to God and gave top priority to deepening their friendship with him through prayer. They sacrificed some of the opportunities they would have had to be together as brother and sister in order better to fulfill their vocation to the religious life. In coming closer to Christ, however, they found they were also closer to each other. In joining a religious community, they did not forget or forsake their family but rather found more brothers and sisters.

QUOTE: "All religious are under an obligation, in accordance with the particular vocation of each, to work zealously and diligently for the building up and growth of the whole mystical body of Christ and for the good of the particular churches. It is their duty to foster these objectives primarily by means of prayer, works of penance, and by the example of their own lives" (Decree on the Pastoral Office of Bishops, 33).

• • •

Our Lady of Lourdes

On December 8, 1854, Pope Pius IX proclaimed the dogma of the Immaculate Conception in the apostolic constitution *Ineffabilis Deus*. A little more than three years later, on February 11, 1858, a young lady appeared to Bernadette Soubirous. This began a series of visions. During an apparition on March 24, the lady identified herself with the words: "I am the Immaculate Conception."

Bernadette was a sickly child of poor parents. Their practice of the Catholic faith was scarcely more than lukewarm. Bernadette could pray the Our Father, the Hail Mary, and the Creed. She also knew the prayer of the Miraculous Medal: "O Mary, conceived without sin."

During interrogations Bernadette gave an account of what she saw. It was "something white in the shape of a girl." She used the word *aquero,* a dialectic term meaning "this thing." It was "a pretty young girl with a rosary over her arm." Her white robe was encircled by a blue girdle. She wore a white veil. There was a yellow rose on each foot. A rosary was in her hand. Bernadette was also impressed by the fact that the lady did not use the informal form of address (*tu*), but the polite form (*vous*). The humble virgin appeared to a humble girl and treated her with dignity.

Through that humble girl, Mary revitalized and continues to revitalize the faith of millions of people. People began to flock to Lourdes from other parts of France and from all over the world. In 1862 Church authorities confirmed the authenticity of the apparitions and authorized the cult of Our Lady of Lourdes for the diocese. The feast of Our Lady of Lourdes was first celebrated worldwide in 1907.

COMMENT: Lourdes has become a place of pilgrimage and healing, but even more of faith. Church authorities have recognized over sixty miraculous cures, although there have probably been many more. To people of faith this is not surprising. It is a continuation of Jesus's healing miracles—now performed at the intercession of his mother.

SAINT OF THE DAY

Some would say that the greater miracles are hidden. Many who visit Lourdes return home with renewed faith and a readiness to serve God in their needy brothers and sisters. There still may be people who doubt the apparitions of Lourdes. Perhaps the best that can be said to them are the words that introduce the film *The Song of Bernadette*: "For those who believe in God, no explanation is necessary. For those who do not believe, no explanation is possible."

QUOTE: "Lo! Mary is exempt from stain of sin, Proclaims the Pontiff high; And earth applauding celebrates with joy Her triumph, far and high. Unto a lowly timid maid she shows Her form in beauty fair, And the Immaculate Conception truth Her sacred lips declare" (Unattributed hymn from the *Roman Breviary*).

*   *   *

FEBRUARY 14 + MEMORIAL

Cyril and Methodius
MONK (D. 869) AND BISHOP (D. 884)

Because their father was an officer in a part of Greece inhabited by many Slavs, these two Greek brothers ultimately became missionaries, teachers, and patrons of the Slavic peoples.

After a brilliant course of studies, Cyril (called Constantine until he became a monk shortly before his death) refused the governorship of a district such as his brother had accepted among the Slavic-speaking population. Cyril withdrew to a monastery where his brother Methodius had become a monk after some years in a governmental post.

A decisive change in their lives occurred when the Duke of Moravia (the present-day Czech Republic) asked the Eastern Emperor Michael for political independence from German rule and ecclesiastical autonomy (having their own clergy and liturgy). Cyril and Methodius undertook the missionary task.

Cyril's first work was to invent an alphabet, still used in some Eastern liturgies. His followers probably formed the Cyrillic alphabet (used, for example, in modern Russian) from Greek capital letters. Together they translated the Gospels, the psalter, Paul's letters, and the liturgical books into Slavonic, and composed a Slavonic liturgy, highly irregular then.

That and their free use of the vernacular in preaching led to opposition from the German clergy. The bishop refused to consecrate Slavic bishops and priests, and Cyril was forced to appeal to Rome. On the visit to Rome, he and Methodius had the joy of seeing their new liturgy approved by Pope Adrian II. Cyril, long an invalid, died in Rome fifty days after taking the monastic habit.

Methodius continued mission work for sixteen more years. He was papal legate for all the Slavic peoples, consecrated a bishop, and then given an ancient see (now in the Czech Republic). When much of their former territory was removed from their jurisdiction, the Bavarian bishops retaliated with a violent storm of accusation against Methodius. As a result, Emperor Louis the German exiled Methodius for three years. Pope John VIII secured his release.

Because the Frankish clergy, still smarting, continued their accusations, Methodius had to go to Rome to defend himself against charges of heresy and uphold his use of the Slavonic liturgy. He was again vindicated.

Legend has it that in a feverish period of activity, Methodius translated the whole Bible into Slavonic in eight months. He died on Tuesday of Holy Week, surrounded by his disciples, in his cathedral church.

Opposition continued after his death, and the work of the brothers in Moravia was brought to an end and their disciples scattered. But the expulsions had the beneficial effect of spreading the spiritual, liturgical and cultural work of the brothers to Bulgaria, Bohemia, and southern Poland. Patrons of Moravia, and specially venerated by Catholic Czechs, Slovaks, Croatians, Orthodox Serbians, and Bulgarians, Cyril and Methodius are eminently fitted to guard the long-desired unity of East and West. In 1980, Pope John Paul II named them additional copatrons of Europe (with Benedict).

COMMENT: Holiness means reacting to human life with God's love: human life as it is, crisscrossed with the political and the cultural, the beautiful and

43

the ugly, the selfish and the saintly. For Cyril and Methodius, much of their daily cross had to do with the language of the liturgy. They are not saints because they got the liturgy into Slavonic, but because they did so with the courage and humility of Christ.

QUOTE: "Even in the liturgy, the Church has no wish to impose a rigid uniformity in matters which do not involve the faith or the good of the whole community. Rather she respects and fosters the spiritual adornments and gifts of the various races and peoples.... Provided that the substantial unity of the Roman rite is maintained, the revision of liturgical books should allow for legitimate variations and adaptations to different groups, religions, and peoples, especially in mission lands" (Constitution on the Sacred Liturgy, 37, 38).

* * *

FEBRUARY 17 + OPTIONAL

Seven Founders of the Order of Servites

(THIRTEENTH CENTURY)

Can you imagine seven prominent men of Boston or Denver banding together, leaving their homes and professions, and going into solitude for a life directly given to God? That is what happened in the cultured and prosperous city of Florence in the middle of the thirteenth century. The city was torn with political strife as well as the heresy of the Cathari, who believed that physical reality was inherently evil. Morals were low and religion seemed meaningless.

In 1240 seven noblemen of Florence mutually decided to withdraw from the city to a solitary place for prayer and direct service of God. Their initial difficulty was providing for their dependents, since two were still married and two were widowers.

Their aim was to lead a life of penance and prayer, but they soon found themselves disturbed by constant visitors from Florence. They next withdrew to the deserted slopes of Monte Senario.

In 1244, under the direction of St. Peter of Verona, O.P., this small group adopted a religious habit similar to the Dominican habit, choosing to live under the Rule of St. Augustine and adopting the name of the Servants of Mary. The new order took a form more like that of the mendicant friars than that of the older monastic orders.

Members of the community came to the United States from Austria in 1852 and settled in New York and later in Philadelphia. The two American provinces developed from the foundation made by Fr. Austin Morini in 1870 in Wisconsin.

Community members combined monastic life and active ministry. In the monastery, they led a life of prayer, work, and silence while in the active apostolate they engaged in parochial work, teaching, preaching, and other ministerial activities.

COMMENT: The time in which the seven Servite founders lived is very easily comparable to the situation in which we find ourselves today. It is "the best of times and the worst of times," as Dickens once wrote. Some, perhaps many, feel called to a countercultural life, even in religion. All of us are faced in a new and urgent way with the challenge to make our lives decisively centered in Christ.

QUOTE: "Let all religious therefore spread throughout the whole world the good news of Christ by the integrity of their faith, their love for God and neighbor, their devotion to the Cross and their hope of future glory.... Thus, too, with the prayerful aid of that most loving Virgin Mary, God's Mother, 'Whose life is a rule of life for all,' religious communities will experience a daily growth in number, and will yield a richer harvest of fruits that bring salvation" (Decree on the Renewal of Religious Life, 25).

• • •

FEBRUARY 20 + OPTIONAL
Blesseds Jacinta and Francisco Marto
LAYPEOPLE (1910–1920 AND 1908–1919)

Between May 13 and October 13, 1917, three children, Portuguese shepherds from Aljustrel, received apparitions of Our Lady at Cova da Iria, near Fatima, a city 110 miles north of Lisbon. At that time, Europe was involved in an extremely bloody war. Portugal itself was in political turmoil, having overthrown its monarchy in 1910. The government disbanded religious organizations soon after.

At the first appearance, Mary asked the children to return to that spot on the thirteenth of each month for the next six months. She also asked them to learn to read and write and to pray the rosary "to obtain peace for the world and the end of the war." They were to pray for sinners and for the conversion of Russia, which had recently overthrown Czar Nicholas II and was soon to fall under communism. Up to ninety thousand people gathered for Mary's final apparition on October 13, 1917.

Less than two years later, Francisco died of influenza in his family home. He was buried in the parish cemetery and then reburied in the Fatima basilica in 1952. Jacinta died of influenza in Lisbon, offering her suffering for the conversion of sinners, peace in the world, and the Holy Father. She was reburied in the Fatima basilica in 1951. Their cousin, Lucia dos Santos, became a Carmelite nun and was still living when Jacinta and Francisco were beatified in 2000. Lucia died five years later. The shrine of Our Lady of Fatima is visited by up to twenty million people a year.

COMMENT: The Church is always very cautious about endorsing alleged apparitions, but it has seen benefits from people changing their lives because of the message of Our Lady of Fatima. Prayer for sinners, devotion to the Immaculate Heart of Mary, and praying the rosary—all these reinforce the Good News Jesus came to preach.

QUOTE: In his homily at their beatification, Pope John Paul II recalled that shortly before Francisco died, Jacinta said to him, "Give my greetings to Our Lord and to Our Lady and tell them that I am enduring everything they want for the conversion of sinners."

. . .

FEBRUARY 21 + OPTIONAL
Peter Damian
BISHOP AND DOCTOR (1007–1072)

Maybe because he was orphaned and had been treated shabbily by one of his brothers, Peter Damian was very good to the poor. It was the ordinary thing for him to have a poor person or two with him at table, and he liked to minister personally to their needs.

Peter escaped poverty and the neglect of his own brother when his other brother, who was archpriest of Ravenna, took him under his wing. His brother sent him to good schools, and Peter became a professor.

Already in those days Peter was very strict with himself. He wore a hair shirt under his clothes, fasted rigorously, and spent many hours in prayer. Soon, he decided to leave his teaching and give himself completely to prayer with the Benedictines of the reform of St. Romuald (June 19) at Fonte Avellana. They lived two monks to a hermitage. Peter was so eager to pray and slept so little that he soon suffered from severe insomnia. He found he had to use some prudence in taking care of himself. When he was not praying, he studied the Bible.

The abbot commanded that when he died Peter should succeed him. Abbot Peter founded five other hermitages. He encouraged his brothers in a life of prayer and solitude and wanted nothing more for himself. The Holy See periodically called on him, however, to be a peacemaker or problem solver between two abbeys in dispute or a cleric or government official in some disagreement with Rome.

Finally, Pope Stephen IX made Peter the cardinal-bishop of Ostia. He worked hard to wipe out simony (the buying of Church offices) and encouraged his priests to observe celibacy and urged even the diocesan clergy to live together and maintain scheduled prayer and religious observance. He wished to restore primitive discipline among religious and priests, warning against needless travel, violations of poverty, and too-comfortable living. He even wrote to the bishop of Besançon, complaining that the canons there sat down when they were singing the psalms in the Divine Office.

He wrote many letters. Some 170 are extant. We also have fifty-three of his sermons and seven lives, or biographies, that he wrote. He preferred examples and stories rather than theory in his writings. The liturgical offices he wrote are evidence of his talent as a stylist in Latin.

He asked often to be allowed to retire as cardinal-bishop of Ostia, and finally Alexander II consented. Peter was happy to become once again just a monk, but he was still called to serve as a papal legate. When returning from such an assignment in Ravenna, he was overcome by a fever. With the monks gathered around him saying the Divine Office, he died on February 22, 1072.

In 1828 he was declared a Doctor of the Church.

COMMENT: Peter was a reformer and if he were alive today would no doubt encourage the renewal started by Vatican II. He would also applaud the greater emphasis on prayer that is shown by the growing number of priests, religious and laypersons who gather regularly for prayer, as well as the special houses of prayer recently established by many religious communities.

QUOTE: "Let us faithfully transmit to posterity the example of virtue which we have received from our forefathers" (St. Peter Damian).

• • •

Chair of Peter
APOSTLE

This feast commemorates Christ's choosing Peter to sit in his place as the servant-authority of the whole Church (see June 29).

After the lost weekend of pain, doubt, and self-torment, Peter hears the Good News. Angels at the tomb say to Magdalene, "The Lord has risen! Go, tell his disciples and Peter." John relates that when he and Peter ran to the tomb, the younger outraced the older, then waited for him. Peter entered, saw the wrappings on the ground, the headpiece rolled up in a place by itself. John saw and believed. But he adds a reminder: "They did not yet understand the scripture that he had to rise from the dead" (John 20:9). They went home. There the slowly exploding, impossible idea became reality. Jesus appeared to them as they waited fearfully behind locked doors. "Peace be with you," he said (John 20:21b), and they rejoiced.

The Pentecost event completed Peter's experience of the risen Christ. "They were all filled with the holy Spirit" (Acts 2:4a) and began to express themselves in foreign tongues and make bold proclamation, as the Spirit prompted them.

Only then can Peter fulfill the task Jesus had given him: "Once you have turned back, you must strengthen your brothers" (Luke 22:32). He at once becomes the spokesman for the twelve about their experience of the Holy Spirit—before the civil authorities who wished to quash their preaching, before the council of Jerusalem, for the community in the problem of Ananias and Sapphira. He is the first to preach the Good News to the Gentiles. The healing power of Jesus in him is well attested: the raising of Tabitha from the dead, the cure of the crippled beggar. People carry the sick into the streets so that when Peter passes his shadow might fall on them.

Even a saint experiences difficulty in Christian living. When Peter stopped eating with Gentile converts because he did not want to wound the sensibilities of Jewish Christians, Paul says, "I opposed him to his face because he clearly was wrong.... [T]hey were not on the right road in line with the truth of the gospel" (Galatians 2:11b, 14a).

At the end of John's Gospel, Jesus says to Peter, "Amen, amen, I say to you, when you were younger, you used to dress yourself and go where you wanted; but when you grow old, you will stretch out your hands, and someone else will dress you and lead you where you do not want to go" (John 21:18). What Jesus said indicated the sort of death by which Peter was to glorify God. On Vatican Hill, in Rome, during the reign of Nero, Peter did glorify his Lord with a martyr's death, probably in the company of many Christians.

Second-century Christians built a small memorial over his burial spot. In the fourth century, the Emperor Constantine built a basilica, which was replaced in the sixteenth century.

QUOTE: Peter described our Christian calling in the opening of his First Letter, "Blessed be the God and Father of our Lord Jesus Christ, who in his great mercy gave us a new birth to a living hope through the resurrection of Jesus Christ from the dead" (1 Peter 1:3a).

STORY: This saintly man's life is perhaps best summed up at his meeting with Jesus after the resurrection in the presence of the men Peter was to lead. In imitation of Peter's triple denial, Jesus asked him three times, "Simon, son of John, do you love me?" (John 21:16b). Peter answered, "Yes, Lord, you know that I love you.... Lord, you know everything; you know that I love you" (John 21:16–17b).

• • •

Polycarp

BISHOP AND MARTYR (D. 156)

Polycarp, bishop of Smyrna (modern Izmir, Turkey), disciple of St. John the Apostle, and friend of St. Ignatius of Antioch, was a revered Christian leader during the first half of the second century.

St. Ignatius, on his way to Rome to be martyred, visited Polycarp at Smyrna and later at Troas wrote him a personal letter. The Asia Minor churches recognized Polycarp's leadership by choosing him as a representative to discuss with Pope Anicetus the date of the Easter celebration in Rome—a major controversy in the early Church.

Only one of the many letters written by Polycarp has been preserved, the one he wrote to the church of Philippi in Macedonia.

At eighty-six, Polycarp was led into the crowded Smyrna stadium to be burned alive. The flames did not harm him, and he was finally killed by a dagger. The centurion ordered the saint's body burned. The *Acts of Martyrdom* is the earliest preserved, fully reliable account of a Christian martyr's death. He died in 156.

COMMENT: Polycarp was recognized as a Christian leader by all Asia Minor Christians—a strong fortress of faith and loyalty to Jesus Christ. His own strength emerged from his trust in God, even when events contradicted this trust. Living among pagans and under a government opposed to the new religion, he led and fed his flock. Like the Good Shepherd, he laid down his life for his sheep and kept them from more persecution in Smyrna. He summarized his trust in God just before he died: "Father...I bless Thee, for having made me worthy of the day and the hour" (*Acts of Martyrdom*, Chapter 14).

QUOTE: "Stand fast, therefore, in this conduct and follow the example of the Lord, 'firm and unchangeable in faith, lovers of the brotherhood, loving each other, united in truth,' helping each other with the mildness of the Lord, despising no man" (Polycarp, *Letter to the Philippians*).

• • •

MARCH 3 + MEMORIAL (U.S.A.)

Katharine Drexel

VIRGIN (1858–1955)

If your father is an international banker and you ride in a private railroad car, you are not likely to be drawn into a life of voluntary poverty. But if your mother opens your home to the poor three days each week and your father spends half an hour each evening in prayer, it is not impossible that you will devote your life to the poor and give away millions of dollars. Katharine Drexel did that.

She was born in Philadelphia in 1858. She had an excellent education and traveled widely. As a rich girl, she had a grand debut into society. But when she nursed her stepmother through a three-year terminal illness, she saw that all the Drexel money could not buy safety from pain or death, and her life took a profound turn.

She had always been interested in the plight of the Indians, having been appalled by reading Helen Hunt Jackson's *A Century of Dishonor.* While on a European tour, she met Pope Leo XIII and asked him to send more missionaries to Wyoming for her friend Bishop James O'Connor. The pope replied, "Why don't you become a missionary?" His answer shocked her into considering new possibilities.

Back home, she visited the Dakotas, met the Sioux leader Red Cloud, and began her systematic aid to Native American missions.

She could easily have married. But after much discussion with Bishop O'Connor, she wrote in 1889, "The feast of Saint Joseph brought me the grace to give the remainder of my life to the Indians and the Colored." Newspaper headlines screamed "Gives Up Seven Million!"

After three and a half years of training, she and her first band of nuns (Sisters of the Blessed Sacrament for Indians and Colored) opened a boarding school in Santa Fe. A string of foundations followed. By 1942 she had a system of Black Catholic schools in thirteen states, plus forty mission centers and twenty-three rural schools. Segregationists harassed her work, even burning a school in Pennsylvania. In all, she established fifty missions for Native Americans in sixteen states.

Two saints met when she was advised by Mother Frances Cabrini (November 13) about the "politics" of getting her order's Rule approved in Rome. Her crowning achievement was the founding of Xavier University in New Orleans, the first Catholic university in the United States for African Americans.

At seventy-seven, she suffered a heart attack and was forced to retire. Her life of service seemed over. But then came almost twenty years of quiet, intense prayer from a small room overlooking the sanctuary. Small notebooks and slips of paper record her various prayers, ceaseless aspirations, and meditation. She died at ninety-six and was canonized in 2000.

COMMENT: Saints have always said the same thing: Pray, be humble, accept the cross, love, and forgive. But it is good to hear these things in the American idiom from one who, for instance, had her ears pierced as a teenager, who resolved to have "no cake, no preserves," who wore a watch, was interviewed by the press, traveled by train, and could concern herself with the proper size of pipe for a new mission. These are obvious reminders that holiness can be lived in today's culture as well as in that of Jerusalem or Rome.

QUOTE: "The patient and humble endurance of the cross—whatever nature it may be—is the highest work we have to do." "Oh, how far I am at eighty-four years of age from being an image of Jesus in his sacred life on earth!" (St. Katharine Drexel).

• • •

MARCH 4 + OPTIONAL

Casimir

KING (1458–1483)

A teenage conscientious objector is the patron saint of Poland and Lithuania. Casimir, born of kings and in line (third among thirteen children) to be a king himself, was filled with exceptional values and learning by a great teacher, John Dlugosz. Even his critics could not say that his conscientious objection indicated softness. Even as a teenager, Casimir lived a highly disciplined, even severe life, sleeping on the ground, spending a great part of the night in prayer, and dedicating himself to lifelong celibacy.

When nobles in Hungary became dissatisfied with their king, they prevailed upon Casimir's father, the king of Poland, to send his son to take over the country. Casimir obeyed his father, as many young men over the centuries have obeyed their government. The army he was supposed to lead was clearly outnumbered by the enemy; some of his troops were deserting because they were not paid. At the advice of his officers, Casimir decided to return home. His father was irked at the failure and confined his fifteen-year-old son for three months. The lad made up his mind never again to become involved in the wars of his day, and no amount of persuasion could change his mind. He returned to prayer and study, maintaining his decision to remain celibate even under pressure to marry the emperor's daughter. He reigned briefly as king of Poland during his father's absence. He died of lung trouble at twenty-three while visiting Lithuania, of which he was also Grand Duke. He was buried in Vilnius, Lithuania.

COMMENT: For many years Poland and Lithuania faded into the gray prison on the other side of the Iron Curtain. Despite repression, the Poles and Lithuanians remained firm in the faith that has become synonymous with their name. Their youthful patron reminds us: Peace is not won by war; sometimes a comfortable peace is not even won by virtue, but Christ's peace can penetrate every government repression of religion.

STORY: Casimir had great love of the Mother of God; in particular he loved the great Marian Latin hymn, *Omni die dic Mariae* (translated, not literally, as "Daily, daily, sing to Mary"). He asked that a copy of it be buried with him.

* * *

MARCH 7 + MEMORIAL
Perpetua and Felicity
MARTYRS (D. 203?)

"When my father in his affection for me was trying to turn me from my purpose by arguments and thus weaken my faith, I said to him, 'Do you see this vessel—waterpot or whatever it may be? Can it be called by any other name than what it is?' 'No,' he replied. 'So also I cannot call myself by any other name than what I am—a Christian.'"

So writes Perpetua, young, beautiful, well-educated, a noblewoman of Carthage in North Africa, mother of an infant son, and chronicler of the persecution of the Christians by Emperor Septimius Severus.

Despite threats of persecution and death, Perpetua, Felicity (a slave and expectant mother), and three companions, Revocatus, Secundulus, and Saturninus, refused to renounce their Christian faith. For their unwillingness, all were sent to the public games in the amphitheater. There, Perpetua and Felicity were beheaded, and the others were killed by beasts.

Perpetua's mother was a Christian and her father a pagan. He continually pleaded with her to deny her faith. She refused and was imprisoned at twenty-two.

In her diary, Perpetua describes her period of captivity:

> What a day of horror! Terrible heat, owing to the crowds! Rough treatment by the soldiers! To crown all, I was tormented with anxiety for my baby…. Such anxieties I suffered for many days, but I obtained leave for my baby to remain in the prison with me, and being relieved of my trouble and anxiety for him, I at once recovered my health, and my prison became a palace to me and I would rather have been there than anywhere else.

Felicity gave birth to a girl a few days before the games commenced.

Perpetua's record of her trial and imprisonment ends the day before the games. "Of what was done in the games themselves, let him write who will." The diary was finished by an eyewitness.

COMMENT: Persecution for religious beliefs is not confined to Christians in ancient times. Consider Anne Frank, the Jewish girl who, with her family, was forced into hiding and later died in Bergen-Belsen, one of Hitler's death camps during World War II. Anne, like Perpetua and Felicity, endured hardship and suffering and finally death because she committed herself to God. In her diary Anne writes, "It's twice as hard for us young ones to hold our ground, and maintain our opinions, in a time when all ideals are being shattered and destroyed, when people are showing their worst side, and do not know whether to believe in truth and right and God."

QUOTE: Perpetua, unwilling to renounce Christianity, comforted her father in his grief over her decision, "It shall happen as God shall choose, for assuredly we depend not on our own power but on the power of God."

• • •

MARCH 8 + OPTIONAL
John of God
RELIGIOUS (1495–1550)

Having given up active Christian belief while a soldier, John was forty before the depth of his sinfulness began to dawn on him. He decided to give the rest of his life to God's service and headed at once for Africa, where he hoped to free captive Christians and, possibly, be martyred.

He was soon advised that his desire for martyrdom was not spiritually well-based and returned to Spain and the relatively prosaic activity of a religious goods store. Yet he was still not settled. Moved initially by a sermon of St. John of Avila (May 10), he one day engaged in a public beating of himself, begging mercy and wildly repenting for his past life.

Committed to a mental hospital for these actions, John was visited by St. John, who advised him to be more actively involved in tending to the needs of others rather than in enduring personal hardships. John gained peace of heart and, shortly, after left the hospital to begin work among the poor.

He established a house where he wisely tended to the needs of the sick poor, at first doing his own begging. But excited by the saint's great work and inspired by his devotion, many people began to back him up with money and provisions. Among them were the archbishop and marquis of Tarifa.

Behind John's outward acts of total concern and love for Christ's sick poor was a deep interior prayer life which was reflected in his spirit of humility. These qualities attracted helpers who, twenty years after John's death, formed the Brothers Hospitallers, now a worldwide religious order.

John became ill after ten years of service but tried to disguise his poor health. He began to put the hospital's administrative work into order and appointed a leader for his helpers. He died under the care of a spiritual friend and admirer, Lady Ana Ossorio.

COMMENT: The utter humility of John of God, which led to a totally selfless dedication to others, is most impressive. Here is a man who realized his nothingness in the face of God. The Lord blessed him with the gifts of prudence, patience, courage, enthusiasm, and the ability to influence and inspire others. He saw that in his early life he had turned away from the Lord, and, moved to receive his mercy, John began his new commitment to love others in openness to God's love.

STORY: The archbishop called John of God to him in response to a complaint that he was keeping tramps and immoral women in his hospital. In submission John fell on his knees and said: "The Son of Man came for sinners, and we are bound to seek their conversion. I am unfaithful to my vocation because I neglect this, but I confess that I know of no bad person in my hospital except myself alone, who am indeed unworthy to eat the bread of the poor." The archbishop could only trust in John's sincerity and humility, and dismissed him with deep respect.

• • •

MARCH 9 + OPTIONAL
Frances of Rome
RELIGIOUS (1384–1440)

Frances's life combines aspects of secular and religious life. A devoted and loving wife, she longed for a lifestyle of prayer and service, so she organized a group of women to minister to the needs of Rome's poor.

Born of wealthy parents, Frances found herself attracted to the religious life during her youth. But her parents objected, and a young nobleman was selected to be her husband.

As she became acquainted with her new relatives, Frances soon discovered that the wife of her husband's brother also wished to live a life of service and prayer. So the two, Frances and Vannozza, set out together—with their husbands' blessings—to help the poor.

Frances fell ill for a time, but this apparently only deepened her commitment to the suffering people she met. The years passed, and Frances gave birth to two sons and a daughter. With the new responsibilities of family life, the young mother turned her attention more to the needs of her own household. The family flourished under Frances's care, but within a few years a great plague began to sweep across Italy. It struck Rome with devastating cruelty and left Frances's second son dead. In an effort to help alleviate some of the suffering, Frances used all her money and sold her possessions to buy whatever the sick might possibly need. When all the resources had been exhausted, Frances and Vannozza went door to door begging. Later, Frances's daughter died, and the saint opened a section of her house as a hospital.

Frances became more and more convinced that this way of life was so necessary for the world, and it was not long before she requested and was given permission to found a society of women bound by no vows. They simply offered themselves to God and to the service of the poor. Once the society was established, Frances chose not to live at the community residence, but rather at home with her husband. She did this for seven years, until her husband passed away, and then came to live the remainder of her life with the society—serving the poorest of the poor.

COMMENT: Looking at the exemplary life of fidelity to God and devotion to her fellow human beings that Frances of Rome was blessed to lead, one cannot help but be reminded of Blessed Mother Teresa of Kolkata (September 5), who loved Jesus Christ in prayer and also in the poor. The life of Frances of Rome calls each of us not only to look deeply for God in prayer, but also to carry our devotion to Jesus living in the suffering of our world. Frances shows us that this life need not be restricted to those bound by vows.

QUOTE: Malcolm Muggeridge's book *Something Beautiful for God* contains this quote from Mother Teresa about each sister in her community: "Let Christ radiate and live his life in her and through her in the slums. Let the poor seeing her be drawn to Christ and invite him to enter their homes and lives." Says Frances of Rome: "It is most laudable in a married woman to be devout, but she must never forget that she is a housewife. And sometimes she must leave God at the altar to find Him in her housekeeping" (*Butler's Lives of the Saints*).

* * *

MARCH 17 + OPTIONAL

Patrick

BISHOP (415?–493?)

Legends about Patrick abound, but truth is best served by our seeing two solid qualities in him: He was humble and he was courageous. The determination to accept suffering and success with equal indifference guided the life of God's instrument for winning most of Ireland for Christ.

Details of his life are uncertain. Current research places his dates of birth and death a little later than earlier accounts. Patrick may have been born in Dunbarton, Scotland, Cumberland, England, or northern Wales. He called himself both a Roman and a Briton. At sixteen, he and a large number of his father's slaves and vassals were captured by Irish raiders and sold as slaves in Ireland. Forced to work as a shepherd, he suffered greatly from hunger and cold.

After six years, Patrick escaped, probably to France, and later returned to Britain at the age of twenty-two. His captivity had meant spiritual conversion. He may have studied at Lerins, off the French coast. He spent years at Auxerre, France, and was consecrated bishop at the age of forty-three. His great desire was to proclaim the Good News to the Irish.

In a dream vision it seemed "all the children of Ireland from their mothers' wombs were stretching out their hands" to him. He understood the vision to be a call to do mission work in pagan Ireland. Despite opposition from those who felt his education had been defective, he was sent to carry out the task. He went to the West and North, where the faith had never been preached, obtained the protection of local kings, and made numerous converts.

Because of the island's pagan background, Patrick was emphatic in encouraging widows to remain chaste and young women to consecrate their virginity to Christ. He ordained many priests, divided the country into dioceses, held Church councils, founded several monasteries, and continually urged his people to greater holiness in Christ.

He suffered much opposition from pagan druids, and was criticized in both England and Ireland for the way he conducted his mission.

In a relatively short time, the island had experienced deeply the Christian spirit and was prepared to send out missionaries whose efforts were greatly responsible for Christianizing Europe.

Patrick was a man of action, with little inclination toward learning. He had a rocklike belief in his vocation, in the cause he had espoused.

One of his few certainly authentic writings is his *Confessio*, above all an act of homage to God for having called Patrick, an unworthy sinner, to the apostolate.

There is hope rather than irony in the fact that his burial place is said to be in strife-torn Ulster, in County Down.

COMMENT: What distinguishes Patrick is the durability of his efforts. When one considers the state of Ireland when he began his mission work, the vast extent of his labors (all of Ireland), and how the seeds he planted continued to grow and flourish, one can only admire the kind of man Patrick must have been. The holiness of a person is known only by the fruits of his or her work.

QUOTE: "Christ shield me this day: Christ with me, Christ before me, Christ behind me, Christ in me, Christ beneath me, Christ above me, Christ on my right, Christ on my left, Christ when I lie down, Christ when I arise, Christ in the heart of every person who thinks of me, Christ in the eye that sees me, Christ in the ear that hears me" (from "The Breastplate of St. Patrick").

• • •

MARCH 18 + OPTIONAL
Cyril of Jerusalem
BISHOP AND DOCTOR (315?–386)

The crises that the Church faces may seem minor when compared with the threat posed by the Arian heresy, which denied the divinity of Christ and almost overcame Christianity in the fourth century. Cyril was to be caught up in the controversy, accused (later) of Arianism by St. Jerome (September 30), and ultimately vindicated both by the men of his own time and by being declared a Doctor of the Church in 1822.

Raised in Jerusalem, well-educated, especially in the Scriptures, he was ordained a priest by the bishop of Jerusalem and given the task of catechizing during Lent those preparing for baptism and during the Easter season the newly baptized. His *Catecheses* remain valuable as examples of the ritual and theology of the Church in the mid-fourth century.

There are conflicting reports about the circumstances of his becoming bishop of Jerusalem. It is certain that he was validly consecrated by bishops of the province. Since one of them was an Arian, Acacius, it may have been expected that his "cooperation" would follow. Conflict soon rose between Cyril and Acacius, bishop of the nearby rival see of Caesarea. Cyril was summoned to a council, accused of insubordination, and of selling Church property to relieve the poor. Probably, however, a theological difference was also involved. He was condemned, driven from Jerusalem, and later vindicated, not without some association and help of Semi-Arians. Half his episcopate was spent in exile (his first experience was repeated twice). He finally returned to find Jerusalem torn with heresy, schism, and strife, and wracked with crime. Even St. Gregory of Nyssa, sent to help, left in despair.

They both went to the (second ecumenical) Council of Constantinople, where an amended form of the Nicene Creed was promulgated in 381. Cyril accepted the word *consubstantial* (that is, of Christ and the Father). Some said it was an act of repentance, but the bishops of the Council praised him as a champion of orthodoxy against the Arians. Though not friendly with the greatest defender of orthodoxy against the Arians, Cyril may be counted among those whom Athanasius called "brothers, who mean what we mean, and differ only about the word [*consubstantial*]."

COMMENT: Those who imagine that the lives of saints are simple and placid, untouched by the vulgar breath of controversy, are rudely shocked by history. Yet it should be no surprise that saints, indeed all Christians, will experience the same difficulties as their Master. The definition of truth is an endless, complex pursuit, and good men and women have suffered the pain of both controversy and error. Intellectual, emotional, and political roadblocks may slow up people like Cyril for a time. But their lives taken as a whole are monuments to honesty and courage.

QUOTE: "It is not only among us, who are marked with the name of Christ, that the dignity of faith is great; all the business of the world, even of those outside the Church, is accomplished by faith. By faith, marriage laws join in union persons who were strangers to one another. By faith, agriculture is sustained; for a man does not endure the toil involved unless he believes he will reap a harvest. By faith, seafaring men, entrusting themselves to a tiny wooden craft, exchange the solid element of the land for the unstable motion of the waves. Not only among us does this hold true but also, as I have said, among those outside the fold. For though they do not accept the Scriptures but advance certain doctrines of their own, yet even these they receive on faith" (Cyril, *Catechesis V*).

• ◦ •

MARCH 19 + SOLEMNITY

Joseph

HUSBAND OF MARY

The Bible pays Joseph the highest compliment: he was a "just" man. The quality meant a lot more than faithfulness in paying debts.

When the Bible speaks of God justifying someone, it means that God, the all-holy or righteous One, so transforms a person that the individual shares somehow in God's own holiness, and hence it is really right for God to love him or her. In other words, God is not playing games, acting as if we were lovable when we are not.

By saying Joseph was "just," the Bible means that he was one who was completely open to all that God wanted to do for him. He became holy by opening himself totally to God.

The rest we can easily surmise. Think of the kind of love with which he wooed and won Mary, and the depth of the love they shared during their marriage.

It is no contradiction of Joseph's manly holiness that he decided to divorce Mary when she was found to be with child. The important words of the Bible are that he planned to do this "quietly" because he was "a righteous man, yet unwilling to expose her to shame" (Matthew 1:19).

The just man was simply, joyfully, wholeheartedly obedient to God—in marrying Mary, in naming Jesus, in shepherding the precious pair to Egypt, in bringing them to Nazareth, in the undetermined number of years of quiet faith and courage.

COMMENT: The Bible tells us nothing of Joseph in the years after the return to Nazareth except the incident of finding Jesus in the Temple (see Luke 2:41–51). Perhaps this can be taken to mean that God wants us to realize that the holiest family was like every other family, that the circumstances of life for the holiest family were like those of every family, so that when Jesus's mysterious nature began to appear, people couldn't believe that he came from such humble beginnings: "Is he not the carpenter's son? Is not his mother named Mary?" (Matthew 13:55a). It was almost as indignant as "Can anything good come from Nazareth?" (John 1:46b).

QUOTE: "He was chosen by the eternal Father as the trustworthy guardian and protector of his greatest treasures, namely, his divine Son and Mary, Joseph's wife. He carried out this vocation with complete fidelity until at last God called him, saying: 'Good and faithful servant, enter into the joy of your Lord' " (St. Bernardine of Siena).

• • •

MARCH 23 + OPTIONAL
Turibius of Mogrovejo
BISHOP (1538–1606)

Together with Rose of Lima (August 23), Turibius is the first known saint of the New World, serving the Lord in Peru, South America, for twenty-six years.

Born in Spain and educated for the law, he became so brilliant a scholar that he was made professor of law at the University of Salamanca and eventually became chief judge of the Inquisition at Granada. He succeeded too well. But he was not a sharp enough lawyer to prevent a surprising sequence of events.

When the archdiocese of Lima in Peru required a new leader, Turibius was chosen to fill the post: He was the one person with the strength of character and holiness of spirit to heal the scandals that had infected that area.

He cited all the canons that forbade giving laymen ecclesiastical dignities, but he was overruled. He was ordained priest and bishop and sent to Peru, where he found colonialism at its worst. The Spanish conquerors were guilty of every sort of oppression of the native population. Abuses among the clergy were flagrant, and he devoted his energies (and suffering) to this area first.

He began the long and arduous visitation of an immense archdiocese, studying the language, staying two or three days in each place, often with neither bed nor food. He confessed every morning to his chaplain and celebrated Mass with intense fervor. Among those to whom he gave the sacrament of confirmation was St. Rose of Lima, and possibly St. Martin de

Porres (November 3). After 1590 he had the help of another great missionary, St. Francis Solanus.

His people, though very poor, were sensitive, dreading to accept public charity from others. Turibius solved the problem by helping them anonymously.

COMMENT: The Lord indeed writes straight with crooked lines. Against his will, and from the unlikely springboard of an Inquisition tribunal, this man became the Christ-like shepherd of a poor and oppressed people. God gave him the gift of loving others as they needed it.

STORY: When Turibius undertook the reform of the clergy as well as unjust officials, he naturally suffered opposition. Some tried, in human fashion, to explain God's law in such a way as to sanction their accustomed way of life. He answered them in the words of Tertullian, "Christ said, 'I am the truth'; he did not say, 'I am the custom.'"

* * *

MARCH 25 + SOLEMNITY
Annunciation of the Lord

The feast of the Annunciation was first celebrated in the fourth or fifth century. Its central focus is the Incarnation: God has become one of us. From all eternity God had decided that the Second Person of the Blessed Trinity should become human. Now, as Luke 1:26–38 tells us, the decision is being realized. The God-Man embraces all humanity, indeed all creation, to bring it to God in one great act of love. Because human beings have rejected God, Jesus will accept a life of suffering and an agonizing death: "No one has greater love than this, to lay down one's life for one's friends" (John 15:13).

Mary has an important role to play in God's plan. From all eternity God destined her to be the mother of Jesus and closely related to him in the creation and redemption of the world. We could say that God's decrees of creation and redemption are joined in the decree of Incarnation. Because Mary is God's instrument in the Incarnation, she has a role to play with Jesus in creation and redemption. It is a God-given role. It is God's grace from beginning to end. Mary becomes the eminent figure she is only by God's grace. She is the empty space where God could act. Everything she is she owes to the Trinity.

She is the virgin-mother who fulfills Isaiah 7:14 in a way that Isaiah could not have imagined. She is united with her son in carrying out the will of God (see Psalm 40:8–9; Hebrews 10:7–9; Luke 1:38).

Together with Jesus, the privileged and graced Mary is the link between heaven and earth. She is the human being who, after Jesus, best exemplifies the possibilities of human existence. She received into her lowliness the infinite love of God. She shows how an ordinary human being can reflect God in the ordinary circumstances of life. She exemplifies what the Church and every member of the Church are meant to become. She is the ultimate product of the creative and redemptive power of God. She manifests what the Incarnation is meant to accomplish for all of us.

COMMENT: Sometimes spiritual writers are accused of putting Mary on a pedestal and thereby discouraging ordinary humans from imitating her. Perhaps such an observation is misguided. God did put Mary on a pedestal and has put all human beings on a pedestal. We have scarcely begun to realize the magnificence of divine grace, the wonder of God's freely given love. The marvel of Mary—even in the midst of her very ordinary life—is God's shout to us to wake up to the marvelous creatures that we all are by divine design.

QUOTE: "Enriched from the first instant of her conception with the splendor of an entirely unique holiness, the virgin of Nazareth is hailed by the heralding angel, by divine command, as 'full of grace' (cf. Luke 1:28). To the heavenly messenger she replies: 'Behold the handmaid of the Lord; be it done to me according to thy word' (Luke 1:38). Thus the daughter of Adam, Mary, consenting to the word of God, became the Mother of Jesus. Committing herself wholeheartedly and impeded by no sin to God's saving will, she devoted herself totally, as a handmaid of the Lord, to the person and work of her Son, under and with him, serving the mystery of redemption, by the grace of Almighty God" (Dogmatic Constitution on the Church, 56).

• • •

APRIL 2 + OPTIONAL

Francis of Paola

HERMIT (1416–1507)

Francis of Paola was a man who deeply loved contemplative solitude and wished only to be the "least in the household of God." Yet, when the Church called him to active service in the world, he became a miracle-worker and influenced the course of nations.

After accompanying his parents on a pilgrimage to Rome and Assisi, he began to live as a contemplative hermit in a remote cave near Paola, on Italy's southern coast. Before he was twenty, he received the first followers who had come to imitate his way of life. Seventeen years later, when his disciples had grown in number, Francis established a Rule for his austere community and sought Church approval. This was the founding of the Hermits of St. Francis of Assisi, who were approved by the Holy See in 1474.

In 1492, Francis changed the name of his community to "Minims" because he wanted them to be known as the least (*minimi*) in the household of God. Humility was to be the hallmark of the brothers as it had been in Francis's personal life. Besides the vows of poverty, chastity, and obedience, Francis enjoined upon his followers the fourth obligation of a perpetual Lenten fast. He felt that heroic mortification was necessary as a means for spiritual growth.

It was Francis's desire to be a contemplative hermit, yet he believed that God was calling him to the apostolic life. He began to use the gifts he had received, such as the gifts of miracles and prophecy, to minister to the people of God. A defender of the poor and oppressed, Francis incurred the wrath of King Ferdinand of Naples for the admonitions he directed toward the king and his sons.

Following the request of Pope Sixtus IV, Francis traveled to Paris to help Louis XI of France prepare for his death. While ministering to the king, Francis was able to influence the course of national politics. He helped to restore peace between France and Brittany by advising a marriage between the ruling families and between France and Spain by persuading Louis XI to return some disputed land. Francis died while at the French court.

COMMENT: The life of Francis of Paola speaks plainly to an overactive world. He was a contemplative man called to active ministry and must have felt keenly the tension between prayer and service. Yet in Francis's life it was a productive tension, for he clearly utilized the fruits of contemplation in his ministry, which came to involve the workings of nations. He responded so readily and so well to the call of the Church because of a solid foundation in prayer and mortification. When he went out to the world, it was not he who worked but Christ working through him—"the least in the household of God."

STORY: The King of France, Louis XI, was slowly dying after an apoplectic seizure. He sent a messenger to Italy to beg Francis to come and heal him, making many promises to assist him and his order. Francis refused, until the king appealed to the pope, who ordered Francis to go. Louis fell on his knees and begged Francis to heal him. The saint replied that the lives of kings are in the hands of God and have their appointed limits: Prayer should be addressed to God.

Many meetings followed. Though Francis was an unlearned man, those who heard him testified that his words were so full of wisdom that all present were convinced the Holy Spirit was speaking through him. By prayer and example he brought about a change of heart in the king, who died peacefully in his arms.

• • •

APRIL 4 + OPTIONAL

Isidore of Seville

BISHOP AND DOCTOR (560?–636)

The seventy-six years of Isidore's life were a time of conflict and growth for the Church in Spain. The Visigoths had invaded the land a century and a half earlier and, shortly before Isidore's birth, they set up their own capital. They were Arians—Christians who said Christ was not God. Thus Spain was split in two: One people (Catholic Romans) struggled with another (Arian Goths).

Isidore reunited Spain, making it a center of culture and learning, a teacher and guide for other European countries whose culture was also threatened by barbarian invaders.

Born in Cartagena of a family that included three other saints, he was educated (severely) by his elder brother, whom he succeeded as bishop of Seville.

An amazingly learned man, he was sometimes called the "Schoolmaster of the Middle Ages" because the encyclopedia he wrote was used as a textbook for nine centuries. He required seminaries to be built in every diocese, wrote a rule for religious orders, and founded schools that taught every branch of learning. Isidore wrote numerous books, including a dictionary, an encyclopedia, a history of the Goths, and a history of the world—beginning with creation! He completed the Mozarabic liturgy, which is still in use in Toledo, Spain.

He continued his austerities even as he approached eighty. During the last six months of his life, he increased his charities so much that his house was crowded from morning till night with the poor of the countryside.

COMMENT: Our society can well use Isidore's spirit of combining learning and holiness. Loving, understanding knowledge can heal and bring a broken people back together. We are not barbarians like the invaders of Isidore's Spain. But people who are swamped by riches and overwhelmed by scientific and technological advances can lose much of their understanding love for one another. So vast was Isidore's knowledge that some have proposed him as the patron of Internet users.

STORY: Once, when Isidore was a boy, he ran away from home and from school. His brother Leander, some twenty years older than he, was his teacher, and a very demanding one. While Isidore sat by himself out in the woods, loafing, he watched some drops of water falling on a rock. Then he noticed that the dripping water had worn a hole in the hard rock! The thought came to him that he could do what the little drops of water did.

Little by little, by sticking to it, he could learn all his brother demanded, and maybe even more.

. . .

APRIL 5 + OPTIONAL
Vincent Ferrer
PRIEST (1350?–1419)

The polarization in the Church today is a mild breeze compared with the tornado that ripped the Church apart during the lifetime of this saint. If any saint is a patron of reconciliation, Vincent Ferrer is.

Despite parental opposition, at nineteen he entered the Dominican Order in his native Spain. After brilliant studies, he was ordained a priest by Cardinal Peter de Luna—who would figure tragically in his life.

Of a very ardent nature, Vincent practiced the austerities of his order with great energy. He was chosen prior of the Dominican house in Valencia shortly after his ordination.

The Western Schism divided Christianity first between two, then three, popes. Clement VII lived at Avignon in France, Urban VI in Rome. Vincent was convinced the election of Urban was invalid (though Catherine of Siena [April 29] was equally as devoted a supporter of the Roman pope). In the service of Cardinal de Luna, Vincent worked to persuade Spaniards to follow Clement. When Clement died, Cardinal de Luna was elected at Avignon and became Benedict XIII.

Vincent worked for him as apostolic penitentiary and Master of the Sacred Palace. But the new pope did not resign as all candidates in the conclave had sworn to do. He remained stubborn despite being deserted by the French king and nearly all of the cardinals.

Vincent became disillusioned and very ill, but finally took up the work of simply "going through the world preaching Christ," though he felt that any renewal in the Church depended on healing the schism. An eloquent and fiery preacher, he spent the last twenty years of his life spreading the Good News in Spain, France, Switzerland, the Low Countries, and Lombardy, stressing the need of repentance and the fear of coming judgment. (He became known as the "Angel of the Judgment.")

He tried, unsuccessfully, in 1408 and 1415, to persuade his former friend to resign. He finally concluded that Benedict was not the true pope. Though very ill, he mounted the pulpit before an assembly over which Benedict himself was presiding and thundered his denunciation of the man who had ordained him a priest. Benedict fled for his life, abandoned by those who had formerly supported him. Strangely, Vincent had no part in the Council of Constance, which ended the schism.

COMMENT: The split in the Church at the time of Vincent Ferrer should have been fatal—thirty-six long years of having two "heads." We cannot imagine what condition the Church today would be in if, for that length of time, half the world followed a succession of popes in Rome, and half, an equally "official" number of popes in, say, Rio de Janeiro. It is an ongoing miracle that the Church has not long since been shipwrecked on the rocks of pride and ignorance, greed and ambition. Contrary to poet Robert Lowell's words, "Truth forever on the scaffold, wrong forever on the throne," we believe that "truth is mighty, and it shall prevail"—but it sometimes takes a long time.

QUOTE: "You strengthen [the Church] by the example of his holy life, teach her by the words of preaching, and keep her safe in answer to his prayers" (*Roman Missal*, Preface for Holy Pastors).

· · ·

APRIL 7 + MEMORIAL
John Baptist de la Salle
PRIEST (1651–1719)

Complete dedication to what he saw as God's will for him dominated the life of John Baptist de la Salle. In 1950, Pope Pius XII named him patron of schoolteachers for his efforts in upgrading school instruction. As a young seventeenth-century Frenchman, John had everything going for him: scholarly bent, good looks, noble family background, money, and a refined upbringing. At the age of eleven, he received the tonsure and started preparation for the priesthood, to which he was ordained at twenty-seven. He seemed assured then of a life of dignified ease and a high position in the Church.

But God had other plans for John, which were gradually revealed to him in the next several years. During a chance meeting with M. Nyel of Raven, he became interested in the creation of schools for poor boys in Raven, where he was stationed. Though the work was extremely distasteful to him at first, he became more involved in working with the deprived youths.

Once convinced that this was his divinely appointed mission, John threw himself wholeheartedly into the work, left home and family, abandoned his position as canon at Rheims, gave away his fortune, and reduced himself to the level of the poor to whom he devoted his entire life.

The remainder of his life was closely entwined with the community of religious men he founded, the Brothers of the Christian Schools (Christian Brothers, or De La Salle Brothers). This community grew rapidly and was successful in educating boys of poor families, using methods designed by John. It prepared teachers in the first training college for teachers and also set up homes and schools for young delinquents of wealthy families. The motivating element in all these endeavors was the desire to become a good Christian.

Yet even in his success, John did not escape experiencing many trials: heartrending disappointment and defections among his disciples, bitter opposition from the secular schoolmasters who resented his new and fruitful methods, and persistent opposition from the Jansenists of his time, whose moral rigidity and pessimism about the human condition John resisted vehemently all his life.

Afflicted with asthma and rheumatism in his last years, he died on Good Friday at sixty-eight and was canonized in 1900.

COMMENT: Complete dedication to one's calling by God, whatever it may be, is a rare quality. Jesus asks us to "love the Lord your God with *all* your heart, with *all* your soul, with *all* your mind, and with *all* your strength" (Mark 12:30b, emphasis added). Paul gives similar advice: "Whatever you do, do from the heart" (Colossians 3:23).

QUOTE: "What is nobler than to mold the character of the young? I consider that he who knows how to form the youthful mind is truly greater than all painters, sculptors, and all others of that sort" (St. John Chrysostom).

● ● ●

APRIL 11 + MEMORIAL
Stanislaus
BISHOP AND MARTYR (1030–1079)

Anyone who reads the history of Eastern Europe cannot help but chance on the name of Stanislaus, the saintly but tragic bishop of Kraków, patron of Poland. He is remembered with Sts. Thomas More (June 22) and Thomas Becket (December 29) for vigorous opposition to the evils of an unjust government.

Born in Szczepanow near Kraków on July 26, 1030, he was ordained a priest after being educated in the cathedral schools of Gniezno, then capital of Poland, and at Paris. He was appointed preacher and archdeacon to the bishop of Kraków, where his eloquence and example brought about real conversion in many of his penitents, both clergy and laity. He became bishop of Kraków in 1072.

During an expedition against the Grand Duchy of Kiev, Stanislaus became involved in the political situation of Poland. Known for his outspokenness, he aimed his attacks at the evils of the peasantry and the king, especially the unjust wars and immoral acts of King Boleslaus II.

The king first excused himself, then made a show of penance, then relapsed into his old ways. Stanislaus continued his open opposition in spite of charges of treason and threats of death, finally excommunicating the king. The latter, enraged, ordered soldiers to kill the bishop. When they refused, the king killed him with his own hands.

Forced to flee to Hungary, Boleslaus supposedly spent the rest of his life as a penitent in the Benedictine abbey in Osiak.

COMMENT: John the Baptist, Thomas Becket, Thomas More, and Stanislaus are a few of the prophets who dared to denounce corruption in high places. They follow in the footsteps of Jesus himself, who pointed out the moral corruption in the religious leadership of his day. It is a risky business: "Let the one among you who is without sin be the first to throw a stone" (John 8:7b).

QUOTE: "Men desire authority for its own sake that they may bear a rule, command and control other men, and live uncommanded and uncontrolled themselves" (St. Thomas More, *A Dialogue of Comfort*).

• • •

APRIL 13 + OPTIONAL
Martin I
POPE AND MARTYR (D. 655)

When Martin I became pope in 649, Constantinople was the capital of the Byzantine Empire, and the patriarch of Constantinople was the most influential Church leader in the Eastern Christian world. The struggles that existed within the Church at that time were magnified by the close cooperation of emperor and patriarch.

A teaching, strongly supported in the East, held that Christ had no human will. Twice emperors had officially favored this position, Heraclius by publishing a formula of faith and Constans II by silencing the issue of one or two wills in Christ.

Shortly after assuming the office of the papacy (which he did without first being confirmed by the emperor), Martin held a council at the Lateran in which the imperial documents were censured, and in which the patriarch of Constantinople and two of his predecessors were condemned. Constans II, in response, tried first to turn bishops and people against the pope.

Failing in this and in an attempt to kill the pope, the emperor sent troops to Rome to seize Martin and to bring him back to Constantinople. Already in poor health, Martin offered no resistance, returned with the exarch Calliopas and was then submitted to various imprisonments, tortures, and hardships.

Although condemned to death and with some of the torture imposed already carried out, Martin was saved from execution by the pleas of a repentant Paul, patriarch of Constantinople, who was himself gravely ill.

Martin died shortly thereafter, tortures and cruel treatment having taken their toll. He is the last of the early popes to be venerated as a martyr.

COMMENT: The real significance of the word *martyr* comes not from the dying but from the witnessing, which the word means in its derivation. People who are willing to give up everything, their most precious possessions, their very lives, put a supreme value on the cause or belief for which they sacrifice. Martyrdom, dying for the faith, is an incidental extreme to which some have had to go to manifest their belief in Christ. A living faith, a life that exemplifies Christ's teaching throughout, and that in spite of difficulties, is required of all Christians. Martin refused to cut corners as a way of easing his lot, to make some accommodations with the civil rulers.

QUOTE: The breviary of the Orthodox Church pays tribute to Martin: "Glorious definer of the Orthodox Faith…sacred chief of divine dogmas, unstained by error…true reprover of heresy…foundation of bishops, pillar of the Orthodox faith, teacher of religion…. Thou didst adorn the divine see of Peter, and since from this divine Rock, thou didst immovably defend the Church, so now thou art glorified with him."

• • •

APRIL 21 + OPTIONAL
Anselm
BISHOP AND DOCTOR (1033–1109)

Indifferent toward religion as a young man, Anselm became one of the Church's greatest theologians and leaders. He received the title "Father of Scholasticism" for his attempt to analyze and illumine the truths of faith through the aid of reason.

At fifteen, Anselm wanted to enter a monastery, but was refused acceptance because of his father's opposition. Twelve years later, after careless disinterest in religion and years of worldly living, he finally fulfilled his desire to be a monk. He entered the monastery of Bec in Normandy, three years later was elected prior, and fifteen years later was unanimously chosen abbot.

Considered an original and independent thinker, Anselm was admired for his patience, gentleness, and teaching skill. Under his leadership, the abbey of Bec became a monastic school, influential in philosophical and theological studies.

During these years, at the community's request, Anselm began publishing his theological works, comparable to those of St. Augustine (August 28). Anselm's best-known work is the book *Cur Deus Homo* ("Why God Became Man").

At sixty, against his will, Anselm was appointed archbishop of Canterbury in 1093. His appointment was opposed at first by England's King William Rufus and later accepted. Rufus persistently refused to cooperate with efforts to reform the Church.

Anselm finally went into voluntary exile until Rufus died in 1100. He was then recalled to England by Rufus's brother and successor, Henry I. Disagreeing fearlessly with Henry over the king's insistence on investing England's bishops, Anselm spent another three years in exile in Rome.

His care and concern extended to the very poorest people; he opposed the slave trade. Anselm obtained from the national council at Westminster the passage of a resolution prohibiting the sale of human beings.

COMMENT: Anselm, like every true follower of Christ, had to carry his cross, especially in the form of opposition and conflict with those in political control. Though personally a mild and gentle man and a lover of peace, he would not back off from conflict and persecution when principles were at stake.

QUOTE: "No one will have any other desire in heaven than what God wills; and the desire of one will be the desire of all; and the desire of all and of each one will also be the desire of God" (St. Anselm, Letter 112).

• • •

Adalbert of Prague
BISHOP AND MARTYR (956–997)

Opposition to the Good News of Jesus did not discourage Adalbert, who is now remembered with great honor in the Czech Republic, Poland, Hungary, and Germany.

Born to a noble family in Bohemia, he received part of his education from St. Adalbert of Magdeburg. At the age of twenty-seven, he was chosen as bishop of Prague. Those who resisted his program of clerical reform forced him into exile eight years later.

In time, the people of Prague requested his return as their bishop. Within a short time, however, he was exiled a second time after excommunicating those who violated the right of sanctuary by dragging a woman accused of adultery from a church and murdering her.

After a short ministry in Hungary, he went to preach the Good News to people living near the Baltic Sea. He and two companions were martyred by pagan priests in that region. Adalbert's body was immediately ransomed and buried in Gniezno Cathedral (Poland). In the mid-eleventh century his relics were moved to St. Vitus Cathedral in Prague.

COMMENT: Preaching the Good News can be dangerous work whether the audience is already baptized or not. Adalbert fearlessly preached Jesus's Gospel and received a martyr's crown for his efforts. Similar zeal has created modern martyrs in many places, especially in Central and South America. Some of those martyrs grew up in areas once evangelized by Adalbert.

QUOTE: "O God, [you] bestowed the crown of martyrdom upon the Bishop St. Adalbert, as he burned with zeal for souls, grant, we pray, by his prayers, that the obedience of the flock may never fail the shepherds, nor the care of the shepherds ever be lacking to the flock" (adapted from the Common of a Martyr in the Easter Season).

• • •

APRIL 23 + OPTIONAL

George

MARTYR (D. 303?)

If Mary Magdalene (July 22) was the victim of misunderstanding, George is the object of a vast amount of imagination. There is every reason to believe that he was a real martyr who suffered at Lydda in Palestine, probably before the time of Constantine. The Church adheres to his memory, but not to the legends surrounding his life.

That he was willing to pay the supreme price to follow Christ is what the Church believes. And it is enough.

The story of George slaying the dragon, rescuing the king's daughter, and converting Libya is a twelfth-century Italian fable.

George was a favorite patron saint of crusaders, as well as of Eastern soldiers in earlier times. He is a patron saint of England, Portugal, Germany, Aragon, Catalonia, Genoa, and Venice.

COMMENT: Human nature seems unable to be satisfied with mere cold historical data. Americans have Washington and Lincoln, but we somehow need Paul Bunyan, too. The life of St. Francis of Assisi is inspiring enough, but for centuries the Italians have found his spirit in the legends of the *Fioretti*, too. Santa Claus is the popular extension of the spirit of St. Nicholas. Both fact and legend are human ways of illumining the mysterious truth about the One who alone is holy.

QUOTE: "When we look at the lives of those who have faithfully followed Christ, we are inspired with a new reason for seeking the city which is to come" (Dogmatic Constitution on the Church, 50).

* * *

Fidelis of Sigmaringen
PRIEST AND MARTYR (1577–1622)

If a poor man needed some clothing, Fidelis would often give the man the clothes right off his back. Complete generosity to others characterized this saint's life.

Born in 1577, Mark Rey (Fidelis was his religious name) became a lawyer who constantly upheld the causes of the poor and oppressed people. Nicknamed "the poor man's lawyer," Fidelis soon grew disgusted with the corruption and injustice he saw among his colleagues. He left his law career to become a priest, joining his brother George as a member of the Capuchin Order. His wealth was divided between needy seminarians and the poor.

As a follower of Francis, Fidelis continued his devotion to the weak and needy. Once, during a severe epidemic in a city where he was guardian of a friary, Fidelis cared for and cured many sick soldiers.

He was appointed head of a group of Capuchins sent to preach against the Calvinists and Zwinglians in Switzerland. Almost certain violence threatened. Those who observed the mission felt that success was more attributable to the prayer of Fidelis during the night than to his sermons and instructions.

He was accused of opposing the peasants' national aspirations for independence from Austria. While he was preaching at Seewis, to which he had gone against the advice of his friends, a gun was fired at him, but he escaped unharmed. A Protestant offered to shelter Fidelis, but he declined, saying his life was in God's hands. On the road back, he was set upon by a group of armed men and killed.

He was canonized in 1746. Fifteen years later, the Congregation for the Propagation of the Faith, which was established in 1622, recognized him as its first martyr.

COMMENT: Fidelis's constant prayer was that he be kept completely faithful to God and not give in to any lukewarmness or apathy. He was often heard to exclaim, "Woe to me if I should prove myself but a halfhearted soldier in the service of my thorn-crowned Captain." His prayer against apathy, and his concern for the poor and weak make him a saint whose example is valuable today. The modern Church is calling us to follow the example of "the poor man's lawyer" by sharing ourselves and our talents with those less fortunate and by working for justice in the world.

QUOTE: "Action on behalf of justice and participation in the transformation of the world fully appear to us as a constitutive dimension of the preaching of the Gospel, or, in other words, of the Church's mission for the redemption of the human race and its liberation from every oppressive situation" (*Justice in the World,* 1971 World Synod of Bishops).

* * *

APRIL 25 + FEAST
Mark
EVANGELIST

Most of what we know about Mark comes directly from the New Testament. He is usually identified with the Mark of Acts 12:12. (The verse states that when Peter escaped from prison, he went to the home of Mark's mother.)

Paul and Barnabas took him along on the first missionary journey, but for some reason Mark returned alone to Jerusalem. It is evident, from Paul's refusal to let Mark accompany him on the second journey despite Barnabas's insistence, that Mark had displeased Paul. Later, Paul asks Mark to visit him in prison, so we may assume the trouble did not last long.

The oldest and the shortest of the four Gospels, the Gospel of Mark emphasizes Jesus's rejection by humanity while being God's triumphant envoy. Probably written for Gentile converts in Rome—after the death of Peter and Paul sometime between A.D. 60 and 70—Mark's Gospel is the gradual manifestation of a "scandal": a crucified Messiah.

Evidently a friend of Mark (Peter called him "my son"), Peter is only one of the Gospel sources, others being the church in Jerusalem (Jewish roots) and the church at Antioch (largely Gentile).

Like one other Gospel writer, Luke, Mark was not one of the twelve apostles. We cannot be certain whether he knew Jesus personally. Some scholars feel that the evangelist is speaking of himself when describing the arrest of Jesus in Gethsemane: "Now a young man followed him wearing nothing but a linen cloth about his body. They seized him, but he left the cloth behind and ran off naked" (Mark 14:51–52).

Others hold Mark to be the first bishop of Alexandria, Egypt. Venice, famous for the Piazza San Marco, claims Mark as its patron saint; the large basilica there is believed to contain his remains.

A winged lion is Mark's symbol. The lion derives from Mark's description of John the Baptist as a "voice of one crying out in the desert" (Mark 1:3), which artists compared to a roaring lion. The wings come from the application of Ezekiel's vision of four winged creatures (Ezekiel 1) to the evangelists.

COMMENT: Mark fulfilled in his life what every Christian is called to do: Proclaim to all people the Good News that is the source of salvation. In particular, Mark's way was by writing. Others may proclaim the Good News by music, drama, poetry, or by teaching children around a family table.

QUOTE: There is very little in Mark that is not in the other Gospels—only four passages. One is: "This is how it is with the kingdom of God; it is as if a man were to scatter seed on the land and would sleep and rise night and day and the seed would sprout and grow, he knows not how. Of its own accord the land yields fruit, first the blade, then the ear, then the full grain in the ear. And when the grain is ripe, he wields the sickle at once, for the harvest has come" (Mark 4:26–29).

•   •   •

APRIL 25 + OPTIONAL
Pedro de San José Betancur
FOUNDER (1626–1667)

Pedro very much wanted to become a priest, but God had other plans. Born of a poor family on Tenerife in the Canary Islands, Pedro was a shepherd until 1650 when he left for Guatemala, where he had a relative in government service. He got as far as Havana when his money ran out. After he had earned more money, he went to Honduras and then in 1651 to Guatemala City. When he arrived he was so poor that he frequented the breadline run by the Franciscans.

Pedro enrolled in the local Jesuit college in hopes of studying for the priesthood. No matter how hard he tried, however, he could not succeed at his studies and so had to withdraw. In 1655 he joined the Secular Franciscan Order.

Three years later he opened a hospital for the convalescent poor; a shelter for the homeless and a school for the poor soon followed. Not wanting to neglect the rich of Guatemala City, Pedro began walking through their part of town, ringing a bell and inviting them to repent.

Other men came to share in Pedro's work. Out of this group came the Bethlehemite Congregation, which won papal approval after Pedro's death. A Bethlehemite sisters' community, similarly founded after Pedro's death, was inspired by his life of prayer and compassion.

He is sometimes credited with originating the pre-Christmas *posadas* procession in which people representing Mary and Joseph seek a night's lodging from their neighbors. The custom soon spread to Mexico and other Central American countries. Beatified in 1980, Pedro was canonized by Pope John Paul II in Guatemala City on July 30, 2002.

COMMENT: Fervent prayer and various works of mercy were equally important for Pedro, who was nicknamed "the man who was charity." Responding to God's love calls for ever-expanding generosity such as Pedro had. Saints are simply people who, with God's grace, have tried to find the most generous way of living out God's love.

QUOTE: During his homily at the canonization Mass, Pope John Paul II, speaking about the new saint's deep prayer, said: "An intensely devout life always bears abundant fruit. Brother Pedro modeled his spirituality in this way, particularly in contemplation of the mysteries of Bethlehem and of the Cross. If, in the birth and childhood of Jesus, he immersed himself deeply in the fundamental event of the Incarnation of the Word—which led him to discover spontaneously, as it were, the face of God in [people]—then in meditating on the Cross, he found the strength to practice mercy heroically with the lowliest and most deprived."

* * *

APRIL 28 + OPTIONAL

Louis Mary de Montfort
PRIEST (1673–1716)

Louis's life is inseparable from his efforts to promote genuine devotion to Mary, the mother of Jesus and mother of the Church. *Totus tuus* ("completely yours") was Louis's personal motto; Karol Wojtyla (Blessed John Paul II, October 22) chose it as his episcopal motto.

Born in the Breton village of Montfort, close to Rennes (France), as an adult Louis identified himself by the place of his baptism instead of his family name, Grignion. After being educated by the Jesuits and the Sulpicians, he was ordained as a diocesan priest in 1700.

Soon he began preaching parish missions throughout western France. His years of ministering to the poor prompted him to travel and live very simply, sometimes getting him into trouble with Church authorities. In his preaching, which attracted thousands of people back to the faith, Fr. Louis recommended frequent, even daily, Holy Communion (not the custom then!) and imitation of the Virgin Mary's ongoing acceptance of God's will for her life.

Louis founded the Missionaries of the Company of Mary (for priests and brothers) and the Daughters of Wisdom, who cared especially for the sick. His book *True Devotion to the Blessed Virgin* has become a classic explanation of Marian devotion.

Louis died in Saint-Laurent-sur-Sèvre, where a basilica has been erected in his honor. He was canonized in 1947.

COMMENT: Like Mary, Louis experienced challenges in his efforts to follow Jesus. Opposed at times in his preaching and in his other ministries, Louis knew with St. Paul, "Neither the one who plants nor the one who waters is anything, but only God, who causes the growth" (1 Corinthians 3:7). Any attempt to succeed by worldly standards runs the risk of betraying the Good News of Jesus. Mary is "the first and most perfect disciple," as Raymond Brown, S.S., described her.

QUOTE: "Mary is the fruitful Virgin, and in all the souls in which she comes to dwell she causes to flourish purity of heart and body, rightness of intention and abundance of good works. Do not imagine that Mary, the most fruitful of creatures who gave birth to a God, remains barren in a faithful soul. It will be she who makes the soul live incessantly for Jesus Christ, and will make Jesus live in the soul" (St. Louis de Montfort, *True Devotion to the Blessed Virgin*).

· · ·

APRIL 28 + OPTIONAL

Peter Chanel

PRIEST AND MARTYR (1803–1841)

Anyone who has worked in loneliness, with great adaptation required and with little apparent success, will find a kindred spirit in Peter Chanel.

As a young priest he revived a parish in a "bad" district by the simple method of showing great devotion to the sick. Wanting to be a missionary, he joined the Society of Mary (Marists) at twenty-eight. Obediently, he taught in the seminary for five years. Then, as superior of seven Marists, he traveled to Western Oceania where he was entrusted with an apostolic vicariate (term for a region that may later become a diocese). The bishop accompanying the missionaries left Peter and a brother on Futuna Island in the New Hebrides, promising to return in six months. He was gone five years.

Meanwhile Peter struggled with this new language and mastered it, making the difficult adjustment to life with whalers, traders, and warring natives. Despite little apparent success and severe want, he maintained a serene and gentle spirit and endless patience and courage. A few natives had been baptized, a few more were being instructed. When the chieftain's son asked to be baptized, persecution by the chieftain reached a climax. Fr. Chanel was clubbed to death, his body cut to pieces.

Within two years after his death, the whole island became Catholic and has remained so. Peter Chanel is the first martyr of Oceania and is its patron.

COMMENT: Suffering for Christ means suffering because we are like Christ. Very often the opposition we meet is the result of our own selfishness or imprudence. We are not martyrs when we are "persecuted" by those who merely treat us as we treat them. A Christian martyr is one who, like Christ, is simply a witness to God's love, and brings out of human hearts the good or evil that is already there.

QUOTE: "No one is a martyr for a conclusion, no one is a martyr for an opinion; it is faith that makes martyrs" (John Newman, *Discourses to Mixed Congregations*).

* * *

APRIL 28 + OPTIONAL
Gianna Beretta Molla
WIFE AND MOTHER (1922–1962)

In less than forty years, Gianna Beretta Molla became a pediatric physician, a wife, a mother, and a saint!

She was born in Magenta (near Milan) as the tenth of Alberto and Maria's thirteen children. An active member of the St. Vincent de Paul Society, Gianna earned degrees in medicine and surgery from the University of Pavia and opened a clinic in Mesero. Gianna also enjoyed skiing and mountain climbing.

Shortly before her 1955 marriage to Peter Molla, Gianna wrote to him: "Love is the most beautiful sentiment that the Lord has put into the soul of men and women." She and Peter had three children: Pierluigi, Maria Zita, and Laura.

Early in the pregnancy for her fourth child, doctors discovered that Gianna had both a child and a tumor in her uterus. She allowed the surgeons to remove the tumor but not to perform the complete hysterectomy that they recommended. Seven months later, Gianna Emanuela was born. On April 28, 1962, Gianna Beretta Molla died in Monza of complications from childbirth. She is buried in Mesero.

Gianna Emanuela went on to become a physician herself. Gianna Beretta Molla was beatified in 1994 and canonized ten years later.

COMMENT: With great faith and courage, Gianna made the choice that enabled her daughter to be born. We can often wish that we were in different circumstances, but holiness frequently comes from making difficult choices in bad situations.

QUOTE: In his homily at the canonization Mass, Pope John Paul II said: "Gianna Beretta Molla was a simple, but more than ever, significant messenger of divine love…. Following the example of Christ, who 'having loved his own…loved them to the end' [John 13:1], this holy mother of a family remained heroically faithful to the commitment she made on the day of her marriage. The extreme sacrifice she sealed with her life testifies that only those who have the courage to give of themselves totally to God and to others are able to fulfill themselves."

• • •

APRIL 29 + MEMORIAL
Catherine of Siena
VIRGIN AND DOCTOR (1347–1380)

The value Catherine makes central in her short life and which sounds clearly and consistently through her experience is complete surrender to Christ. What is most impressive about her is that she learns to view her surrender to her Lord as a goal to be reached through time.

She was the twenty-third child of Jacopo and Lapa Benincasa and grew up as an intelligent, cheerful, and intensely religious person. Catherine disappointed her mother by cutting off her hair as a protest against being overly encouraged to improve her appearance in order to attract a husband. Her father ordered her to be left in peace and she was given a room of her own for prayer and meditation.

She entered the Dominican Third Order at eighteen and spent the next three years in seclusion, prayer, and austerity. Gradually a group of followers gathered around her—men and women, priests, and religious. An active public apostolate grew out of her contemplative life. Her letters, mostly for spiritual instruction and encouragement of her followers, began to take more and more note of public affairs. Opposition and slander resulted from her mixing fearlessly with the world and speaking with the candor and authority of one completely committed to Christ. She was cleared of all charges at the Dominican General Chapter of 1374.

Her public influence reached great heights because of her evident holiness, her membership in the Dominican Third Order, and the deep impression she made on the pope. She worked tirelessly for the crusade against the Turks and for peace between Florence and the pope.

In 1378, the Great Schism began, splitting the allegiance of Christendom between two, then three, popes and putting even saints on opposing sides (see St. Vincent Ferrer, April 5). Catherine spent the last two years of her life in Rome, in prayer and pleading on behalf of the cause of Urban VI and the unity of the Church. She offered herself as a victim for the Church in its agony. She died surrounded by her "children" and was canonized in 1461.

Catherine ranks high among the mystics and spiritual writers of the Church. In 1939 she and Francis of Assisi were declared co-patrons of Italy. Paul VI named her and Teresa of Avila as Doctors of the Church in 1970. Her spiritual testament is found in *The Dialogue*.

COMMENT: Though she lived her faith experience and spirituality in a time far different from our own, Catherine of Siena stands as a companion with us on the Christian journey in her undivided effort to invite the Lord to take flesh in her own life. Events that might seem strange to us fill her biographies: a mystical experience at six, childhood betrothal to Christ, stories of harsh asceticism, her frequent ecstatic visions. Still, Catherine lived in an age that did not know the rapid change of twenty-first–century America. The value of her life for us today lies in her recognition of holiness as a goal to be sought over the course of a lifetime.

QUOTE: Catherine's book *The Dialogue* contains four treatises—her testament of faith to the spiritual world. She wrote: "No one should judge that he has greater perfection because he performs great penances and gives himself in excess to the staying of the body than he who does less, inasmuch as neither virtue nor merit consists therein; for otherwise he would be an evil case, who for some legitimate reason was unable to do actual penance. Merit consists in the virtue of love alone, flavored with the light of true discretion without which the soul is worth nothing."

● ● ●

APRIL 30 + OPTIONAL
Pius V
POPE (1504–1572)

This is the pope whose job was to implement the historic Council of Trent. If we think popes had difficulties in implementing Vatican Council II, Pius V had even greater problems after that historic council more than four centuries ago.

During his papacy (1566–1572), Pius V was faced with the almost overwhelming responsibility of getting a shattered and scattered Church back on its feet. The family of God had been shaken by corruption, by the Reformation, by the constant threat of Turkish invasion, and by the bloody bickering of young nation-states. In 1545 a previous pope convened the Council of Trent in an attempt to deal with all these pressing problems. Off and on over eighteen years, the Church Fathers discussed, condemned, affirmed, and decided upon a course of action. The Council closed in 1563.

Pius V was elected in 1566 and was charged with the task of implementing the sweeping reforms called for by the Council. He ordered the founding of seminaries for the proper training of priests. He published a new missal, a new breviary, a new catechism, and established the Confraternity of Christian Doctrine (CCD) classes for the young. Pius zealously enforced legislation against abuses in the Church. He patiently served the sick and the poor by building hospitals, providing food for the hungry, and giving money customarily used for the papal banquets to poor Roman converts. His decision to keep wearing his Dominican habit led to the custom of the pope wearing a white cassock.

In striving to reform both Church and state, Pius encountered vehement opposition from England's Queen Elizabeth and the Roman Emperor Maximilian II. Problems in France and in the Netherlands also hindered Pius's hopes for a Europe united against the Turks. Only at the last minute was he able to organize a fleet that won a decisive victory in the Gulf of Lepanto, off Greece, on October 7, 1571.

Pius's ceaseless papal quest for a renewal of the Church was grounded in his personal life as a Dominican friar. He spent long hours with his God in prayer, fasted rigorously, deprived himself of many customary papal luxuries, and faithfully observed the spirit of the Dominican Rule that he had professed.

COMMENT: In their personal lives and in their actions as popes, Pius V and Venerable Paul VI (d. 1978) both led the family of God in the process of interiorizing and implementing the new birth called for by the Spirit in major councils. With zeal and patience, Pius and Paul pursued the changes urged by the Council Fathers. Like Pius and Paul, we, too, are called to constant change of heart and life.

QUOTE: "In this universal assembly, in this privileged point of time and space, there converge together the past, the present, and the future. The past: for here, gathered in this spot, we have the Church of Christ with her tradition, her history, her councils, her doctors, her saints; the present: we are taking leave of one another to go out toward the world of today with its miseries, its sufferings, its sins, but also with its prodigious accomplishments, values, and virtues; and the future is here in the urgent appeal of the peoples of the world for more justice, in their will for peace, in their conscious or unconscious thirst for a higher life, that life precisely which the Church of Christ can give and wishes to give to them" (from Pope Paul's closing message at Vatican II).

• • •

MAY 1 + OPTIONAL
Joseph the Worker

Apparently in response to the "May Day" celebrations for workers sponsored by communists, Pius XII instituted the feast of St. Joseph the Worker in 1955. But the relationship between Joseph and the cause of workers has a much longer history.

In a constantly necessary effort to keep Jesus from being removed from ordinary human life, the Church has from the beginning proudly emphasized that Jesus was a carpenter, obviously trained by Joseph in both the satisfactions and the drudgery of that vocation. Humanity is like God not only in thinking and loving, but also in creating. Whether we make a table or a cathedral, we are called to bear fruit with our hands and mind, ultimately for the building up of the Body of Christ.

COMMENT: "The Lord God then took the man and settled him in the Garden of Eden, to cultivate and care for it" (Genesis 2:15). The Father created all and asked humanity to continue the work of creation. We find our dignity in our work, in raising a family, in participating in the life of the Father's creation. Joseph the Worker was able to help participate in the deepest mystery of creation. Pius XII emphasized this when he said, "The spirit flows to you and to all men from the heart of the God-Man, Savior of the world, but certainly, no worker was ever more completely and profoundly penetrated by it than the foster father of Jesus, who lived with Him in closest intimacy and community of family life and work. Thus, if you wish to be close to Christ, we again today repeat, 'Go to Joseph' " (see Genesis 41:44).

QUOTE: In *Brothers of Men,* René Voillaume of the Little Brothers of Jesus speaks about ordinary work and holiness: "Now this holiness (of Jesus) became a reality in the most ordinary circumstances of life, those of work, of the family and the social life of a village, and this is an emphatic affirmation of the fact that the most obscure and humdrum human activities are entirely compatible with the perfection of the Son of God...in relation to this mystery, involves the conviction that the evangelical holiness proper to a child of God is possible in the ordinary circumstances of someone who is poor and obliged to work for his living."

•   •   •

Athanasius

BISHOP AND DOCTOR (295?–373)

Athanasius led a tumultuous but dedicated life of service to the Church. He was the great champion of the faith against the widespread heresy of Arianism, which denied Christ's divinity. The vigor of his writings earned him the title of Doctor of the Church.

Born of a Christian family in Alexandria, Egypt, and given a classical education, Athanasius became secretary to Alexander, the bishop of Alexandria, entered the priesthood, and was eventually named bishop himself. His predecessor, Alexander, had been an outspoken critic of a new movement growing in the East—Arianism.

When Athanasius assumed his role as bishop of Alexandria, he continued the fight against Arianism. At first it seemed that the battle would be easily won and that Arianism would be condemned. Such, however, did not prove to be the case. The Council of Tyre was called and for several reasons that are still unclear, the Emperor Constantine exiled Athanasius to northern Gaul. This was to be the first in a series of travels and exiles reminiscent of the life of St. Paul.

After Constantine died, his son restored Athanasius as bishop. This lasted only a year, however, for he was deposed once again by a coalition of Arian bishops. Athanasius took his case to Rome, and Pope Julius I called a synod to review the case and other related matters.

Five times Athanasius was exiled for his defense of the doctrine of Christ's divinity. During one period of his life, he enjoyed ten years of relative peace—reading, writing, and promoting the Christian life along the lines of the monastic ideal to which he was greatly devoted. His dogmatic and historical writings are almost all polemic, directed against every aspect of Arianism. Among his ascetical writings, his *Life of St. Anthony* (January 17) achieved astonishing popularity and contributed greatly to the establishment of monastic life throughout the Western Christian world.

COMMENT: Athanasius suffered many trials while he was bishop of Alexandria. He was given the grace to remain strong against what probably seemed at times to be insurmountable opposition. Athanasius lived his office as bishop completely. He defended the true faith for his flock, regardless of the cost to himself. In today's world we are experiencing this same call to remain true to our faith, no matter what.

QUOTE: The hardships Athanasius suffered in exile, hiding, fleeing from place to place remind us of what Paul said of his own life: "On frequent journeys, in dangers from rivers, dangers from robbers, dangers from my own race, dangers from Gentiles, dangers in the city, dangers in the wilderness, dangers at sea, dangers among false brothers; in toil and hardship, through many sleepless nights, through hunger and thirst, through frequent fastings, through cold and exposure. And apart from these things, there is the daily pressure upon me of my anxiety for all the churches" (2 Corinthians 11:26–28).

• • •

MAY 3 + FEAST

Philip and James

APOSTLES

James, Son of Alphaeus. We know nothing of this man except his name, and of course the fact that Jesus chose him to be one of the twelve pillars of the New Israel, his Church. He is not the James of Acts, son of Clopas, "brother" of Jesus and later bishop of Jerusalem and the traditional author of the Letter of James. James, son of Alphaeus, is also known as James the Lesser to avoid confusing him with James the son of Zebedee, also an apostle and known as James the Greater.

Philip. Philip came from the same town as Peter and Andrew, Bethsaida in Galilee. Jesus called him directly, whereupon he sought out Nathanael and told him of the "one about whom Moses wrote" (John 1:45).

Like the other apostles, Philip took a long time coming to realize who Jesus was. On one occasion, when Jesus saw the great multitude following him and wanted to give them food, he asked Philip where they should buy bread for the people to eat. St. John comments, "[Jesus] said this to test him, because he himself knew what he was going to do" (John 6:6). Philip answered, "Two hundred days' wages worth of food would not be enough for each of them to have a little [bit]" (John 6:7).

John's story is not a put-down of Philip. It was simply necessary for these men who were to be the foundation stones of the Church to see the clear distinction between humanity's total helplessness apart from God and the human ability to be a bearer of divine power by God's gift.

On another occasion, we can almost hear the exasperation in Jesus's voice. After Thomas had complained that they did not know where Jesus was going, Jesus said, "I am the way.... If you know me, then you will also know my Father. From now on you do know him and have seen him" (John 14:6a, 7). Then Philip said, "Master, show us the Father, and that will be enough for us" (John 14:8). Enough! Jesus answered, "Have I been with you for so long a time and you still do not know me, Philip? Whoever has seen me has seen the Father" (John 14:9a).

Possibly because Philip bore a Greek name or because he was thought to be close to Jesus, some Gentile proselytes came to him and asked him to introduce them to Jesus. Philip went to Andrew, and Andrew went to Jesus. Jesus's reply in John's Gospel is indirect; Jesus says that now his hour has come, that in a short time he will give his life for Jew and Gentile alike.

COMMENT: As in the case of the other apostles, we see in James and Philip human men who became foundation stones of the Church, and we are reminded again that holiness and its consequent apostolate are entirely the gift of God, not a matter of human achieving. All power is God's power, even the power of human freedom to accept his gifts. "You will be clothed with power from on high," Jesus told Philip and the others. Their first commission had been to expel unclean spirits, heal diseases, and announce the kingdom. They learned, gradually, that these externals were sacraments of an even greater miracle inside their persons—the divine power to love like God.

QUOTE: "He sent them...so that as sharers in his power they might make all peoples his disciples, sanctifying and governing them.... They were fully confirmed in this mission on the day of Pentecost (cf. Acts 2:1–26) in accordance with the Lord's promise: 'You shall receive power when the Holy Spirit comes upon you, and you shall be witnesses for me...even to the very ends of the earth' (Acts 1:8). By everywhere preaching the gospel (cf. Mark 16:20), which was accepted by their hearers under the influence of the Holy Spirit, the apostles gathered together the universal Church, which the Lord established on the apostles and built upon blessed Peter, their chief, Christ Jesus himself remaining the supreme cornerstone" (Dogmatic Constitution on the Church, 19).

* * *

MAY 10 + OPTIONAL (U.S.A.)

Damien de Veuster of Molokai

PRIEST (1840–1889)

When Joseph de Veuster was born in Tremelo, Belgium, in 1840, few people in Europe had any firsthand knowledge of leprosy (Hansen's disease). By the time he died at the age of forty-nine, people all over the world knew about this disease because of him. They knew that human compassion could soften the ravages of this disease.

Forced to quit school at age thirteen to work on the family farm, six years later Joseph entered the Congregation of the Sacred Hearts of Jesus and Mary, taking the name of a fourth-century physician and martyr. When his brother Pamphile, a priest in the same congregation, fell ill and was unable to go to the Hawaiian Islands as assigned, Damien quickly volunteered in his place. In May 1864, two months after arriving in his new mission, Damien was ordained a priest in Honolulu and assigned to the island of Hawaii.

In 1873, he went to the Hawaiian government's leper colony on the island of Molokai, set up seven years earlier. Part of a team of four chaplains taking that assignment for three months each year, Damien soon volunteered to remain permanently, caring for the people's physical, medical and spiritual needs. In time, he became their most effective advocate to obtain promised government support.

Soon the settlement had new houses and a new church, school, and orphanage. Morale improved considerably. A few years later he succeeded in getting the Franciscan Sisters of Syracuse, led by Blessed Marianne Cope (January 23), to help staff this colony in Kalaupapa.

Damien contracted Hansen's disease and died of its complications. As requested, he was buried in Kalaupapa, but in 1936 the Belgian government succeeded in having his body moved to Belgium. Part of Damien's body was returned to his beloved Hawaiian brothers and sisters after his beatification in 1995. He was canonized in 2009.

When Hawaii became a state in 1959, it selected Damien's image as one of its two representatives in the Statuary Hall at the U.S. Capitol.

COMMENT: Some people thought Damien was a hero for going to Molokai and others thought he was crazy. When a Protestant clergyman wrote that Damien was guilty of immoral behavior, Robert Louis Stevenson vigorously defended him in an "Open Letter to Dr. Hyde."

QUOTE: During the canonization homily, Pope Benedict XVI said: "Let us remember before this noble figure that it is charity which makes unity, brings it forth and makes it desirable. Following in St. Paul's footsteps, St. Damien prompts us to choose the good warfare (1 Timothy 1:18), not the kind that brings division but the kind that gather people together. He invites us to open our eyes to the forms of leprosy that disfigure the humanity of our brethren and still today call for the charity of our presence as servants, beyond that of our generosity."

• • •

MAY 10 + OPTIONAL
John of Avila
PRIEST AND DOCTOR (1500-1569)

Born in the Castile region of Spain, John was sent at the age of fourteen to the University of Salamanca to study law. He later moved to Alcalá, where he studied philosophy and theology before his ordination as a diocesan priest.

After John's parents died and left him as their sole heir to a considerable fortune, he distributed his money to the poor. In 1527, he traveled to Seville, hoping to become a missionary in Mexico. The archbishop of that city persuaded him to stay and spread the faith in Andalusia (southwestern Spain). During nine years of work there, John developed a reputation as an engaging preacher, a perceptive spiritual director, and a wise confessor.

Because he was not afraid to denounce vice in high places, John was investigated by the Inquisition but was cleared in 1533. He later worked in Cordoba and then in Granada, where he organized the University of Baeza, the first of several colleges run by diocesan priests who dedicated themselves to teaching and giving spiritual direction to young people.

He was friends with Sts. Francis Borgia, Ignatius of Loyola (July 31), John of God (March 8), John of the Cross (December 14), Peter of Alcantara, and Teresa of Avila (October 15). John of Avila worked closely with members of the Society of Jesus and helped their growth within Spain and its colonies. John's mystical writings have been translated into several languages.

He was beatified in 1894, canonized in 1970, and declared a Doctor of the Church on October 7, 2012.

COMMENT: St. John of Avila knew that the lives of Christians can contradict the Good News of Jesus Christ, implicitly encouraging Christians to live their faith halfheartedly and causing obstacles to non-Christians who might be considering baptism. In sixteenth-century Spain, those who advocated reforming the Church were often suspected of heresy. John of Avila held his ground and was eventually recognized as a very reliable teacher about the Christian faith.

QUOTE: At the October 2012 Mass after John of Avila and Hildegard of Bingen (December 17) were declared Doctors of the Church, Pope Benedict XVI described John as "a profound expert on the sacred Scripture...gifted with an ardent missionary spirit." The pope continued: "He knew how to penetrate in a uniquely profound way the mysteries of the redemption worked by Christ for humanity. A man of God, he united constant prayer to apostolic action. He dedicated himself to preaching and to the more frequent practice of the sacraments, concentrating his commitment on improving the formation of candidates for the priesthood, of religious and of laypeople, with a view to a fruitful reform of the Church."

* * *

MAY 12 + OPTIONAL
Nereus and Achilleus
MARTYRS (FIRST CENTURY?)

Devotion to these two saints goes back to the fourth century, though almost nothing is known of their lives. They were praetorian soldiers of the Roman army who became Christians and were removed to the island of Terracina, where they were martyred. Their bodies were buried in a family vault, later known as the cemetery of Domitilla. Excavations by De Rossi in 1896 resulted in the discovery of their empty tomb in the underground church built by Pope Siricius in 390.

Two hundred years after their death, Pope Gregory the Great delivered his twenty-eighth homily on the occasion of their feast. "These saints, before whom we are assembled, despised the world and trampled it under their feet when peace, riches, and health gave it charms."

COMMENT: As in the case of many early martyrs, the Church clings to its memories though the events are clouded in the mists of history. It is a heartening thing for all Christians to know that they have a noble heritage. Our brothers and sisters in Christ have stood in the same world in which we live—militarist, materialist, cruel, and cynical —yet transfigured from within by the presence of the Living One. Our own courage is enlivened by the heroes and heroines who have gone before us marked by the sign of faith and the wounds of Christ.

QUOTE: Pope Damasus wrote an epitaph for Nereus and Achilleus in the fourth century. The text is known from travelers who read it while the slab was still entire, but the broken fragments found by De Rossi are sufficient to identify it: "The martyrs Nereus and Achilleus had enrolled themselves in the army and exercised the cruel office of carrying out the orders of the tyrant, being ever ready, through the constraint of fear, to obey his will. O miracle of faith! Suddenly they cease from their fury, they become converted, they fly from the camp of their wicked leader; they throw away their shields, their armor and their blood-stained javelins. Confessing the faith of Christ, they rejoice to bear testimony to its triumph. Learn now from the words of Damasus what great things the glory of Christ can accomplish."

• • •

MAY 12 + OPTIONAL
Pancras
MARTYR (D. 304?)

St. Pancras Railway Station in London got its name from an early Christian martyr about whom we have little information. He is said to have been martyred at fourteen during the persecution of Diocletian. He was buried in a cemetery that later was named after him. Pope Gregory the Great built a monastery for Benedictines and, when Augustine of Canterbury (a Benedictine) came to England, he named the first church he erected after Pancras—hence the name of the railway station.

Pancras (Pancratius) appears in fictionalized form in Cardinal Wiseman's novel *Fabiola*. German farmers had a saying that three saints whose names are similar—Pancras, Servatz, and Bonifatz—were the "ice men" because it was often unseasonably chilly on their feast days, May 12, 13, and 14.

COMMENT: Again we have a saint about whom almost nothing is known, but whose life and death are cherished in the Church's memory. Details fall away or are mixed with legend. But a single, powerful fact remains: He died for Christ, and his heroism sent a wave of inspiration through the Church of his day. It is good for us to share that feeling.

QUOTE: "They will seize and persecute you, they will hand you over to the synagogues and to prisons, and they will have you led before kings and governors because of my name. It will lead to your giving testimony. Remember, you are not to prepare your defense beforehand, for I myself shall give you a wisdom in speaking that all your adversaries will be powerless to resist or refute" (Luke 21:12–15).

* * *

MAY 13 + OPTIONAL
Our Lady of Fatima

Between May 13 and October 13, 1917, three Portuguese children received apparitions of Our Lady at Cova da Iria, near Fatima, a city 110 miles north of Lisbon. (See February 20 entry for Blesseds Jacinta and Francisco Marto) Mary asked the children to pray the rosary for world peace, for the end of World War I, for sinners, and for the conversion of Russia. The third visionary, Lucia dos Santos, became a Carmelite nun and died in 2005 at the age of ninety-seven.

Mary gave the children three secrets. Since Francisco died in 1919 and Jacinta the following year, Lucia revealed the first secret in 1927, concerning devotion to the Immaculate Heart of Mary. The second secret was a vision of hell.

Pope John Paul II directed the Holy See's Secretary of State to reveal the third secret in 2000; it spoke of a "bishop in white" who was shot by a group of soldiers who fired bullets and arrows into him. Many people linked this to the assassination attempt against Blessed John Paul II in St. Peter's Square on May 13, 1981.

The feast of Our Lady of Fatima was approved by the local bishop in 1930; it was added to the Church's worldwide calendar in 2002.

COMMENT: The message of Fatima is simple: Pray. Unfortunately, some people—not Sister Lucia—have distorted these revelations, making them into an apocalyptic prophecy for which they are now the only reliable interpreters. They have, for example, claimed that Mary's request that the world be consecrated to her has been ignored. Sister Lucia has agreed that Pope John Paul II's public consecration in St. Peter's Square on March 25, 1984, fulfilled Mary's request. The Congregation for the Doctrine of the Faith prepared a June 26, 2000, document explaining the "third secret" (available at www.vatican.va).

Mary is perfectly honored when people generously imitate her response "Let it be done to me as you say" (Luke 1:38). Mary can never be seen as a rival to Jesus nor to the Church's teaching authority, as exercised by the college of bishops united with the bishop of Rome.

QUOTE: "Throughout history there have been supernatural apparitions and signs which go to the heart of human events and which, to the surprise of believers and non-believers alike, play their part in the unfolding of history. These manifestations can never contradict the content of faith, and must therefore have their focus in the core of Christ's proclamation: the Father's love which leads men and women to conversion and bestows the grace required to abandon oneself to him with filial devotion. This too is the message of Fatima which, with its urgent call to conversion and penance, draws us to the heart of the Gospel" (*The Message of Fatima*, Congregation for the Doctrine of the Faith, 2000).

• • •

MAY 14 + FEAST
Matthias
APOSTLE

According to Acts 1:15–26, during the days after the Ascension, Peter stood up in the midst of the brothers (about 120 of Jesus's followers). Now that Judas had betrayed his ministry, it was necessary, Peter said, to fulfill the scriptural recommendation that another take his office. "Therefore, it is necessary that one of the men who accompanied us the whole time the Lord Jesus came and went among us, beginning from the baptism of John until the day on which he was taken up from us, become with us a witness to his resurrection" (Acts 1:21–22).

They nominated two men: Joseph Barsabbas and Matthias. They prayed and drew lots. The choice fell upon Matthias, who was added to the eleven.

Matthias is not mentioned by name anywhere else in the New Testament.

COMMENT: What was the holiness of Matthias? Obviously he was suited for apostleship by the experience of being with Jesus from his baptism to his ascension. He must also have been suited personally, or he would not have been nominated for so great a responsibility. Must we not remind ourselves that the fundamental holiness of Matthias was his receiving gladly the relationship with the Father offered him by Jesus and completed by the Holy Spirit? If the apostles are the foundations of our faith by their witness, they must also be reminders, if only implicitly, that holiness is entirely a matter of God's giving, and it is offered to all, in the everyday circumstances of life. We receive, and even for this, God supplies the power of freedom.

QUOTE: Jesus speaks of the apostles' function of being judges, that is, rulers. He said, "Amen, I say to you that you who have followed me, in the new age, when the Son of Man is seated on his throne of glory, will yourselves sit on twelve thrones, judging the twelve tribes of Israel" (Matthew 19:28).

* * *

MAY 15 + OPTIONAL (U.S.A.)
Isidore the Farmer
HUSBAND (1070–1130)

Isidore has become the patron of farmers and rural communities. In particular he is the patron of Madrid, Spain, and of the United States National Rural Life Conference.

When he was barely old enough to wield a hoe, Isidore entered the service of John de Vergas, a wealthy landowner from Madrid, and worked faithfully on his estate outside the city for the rest of his life. He married a young woman as simple and upright as himself who also became a saint—Maria de la Cabeza. They had one son, who died as a child.

Isidore had deep religious instincts. He rose early in the morning to go to church and spent many a holiday devoutly visiting the churches of Madrid and surrounding areas. All day long, as he walked behind the plow, he communed with God. His devotion, one might say, became a problem, for his fellow workers sometimes complained that he often showed up late because of lingering in church too long.

He was known for his love of the poor, and there are accounts of Isidore's supplying them miraculously with food. He had a great concern for the proper treatment of animals.

He died May 15, 1130, and was declared a saint in 1622 with Ignatius of Loyola, Francis Xavier, Teresa of Avila, and Philip Neri. Together, the group is known in Spain as "the five saints."

COMMENT: Many implications can be found in a simple laborer achieving sainthood: Physical labor has dignity; sainthood does not stem from status; contemplation does not depend on learning; the simple life is conducive to holiness and happiness. Legends about angel helpers and mysterious oxen indicate that his work was not neglected, and his duties did not go unfulfilled. Perhaps the truth that emerges is this: If you have your spiritual self in order, your earthly commitments will fall into order also. "Seek first the kingdom [of God] and his righteousness," said the carpenter from Nazareth, "and all these things will be given you besides" (Matthew 6:33).

QUOTE: "God blessed them, saying: 'Be fertile and multiply; fill the earth and subdue it…. See, I give you every seed-bearing plant all over the earth and every tree that has seed-bearing fruit on it to be your food; and to all the animals of the land, all the birds of the air, and all the living creatures that crawl on the ground, I give all the green plants for food' " (Genesis 1:28a, 29–30a).

. . .

John I

POPE AND MARTYR (D. 526)

Pope John I inherited the Arian heresy, which denied the divinity of Christ. Italy had been ruled for thirty years by an emperor who accepted the heresy, though he treated the empire's Catholics with toleration. His policy changed at about the time the young John was elected pope.

When the Eastern emperor began imposing severe measures on the Arians of his area, the Western emperor forced John to head a delegation to the East to soften the measures against the heretics. Little is known of the manner or outcome of the negotiations—designed to secure continued toleration of Catholics in the West.

When John returned to Rome, he found that the emperor had begun to suspect his friendship with his Eastern rival.

On his way home, John was imprisoned when he reached Ravenna because the emperor suspected a conspiracy against his throne. Shortly after his imprisonment, John died, apparently from the treatment he had received.

COMMENT: We cannot choose the issues for which we have to suffer and perhaps die. John I suffered because of a power-conscious emperor. Jesus suffered because of the suspicions of those who were threatened by his freedom, openness, and powerlessness. "If you find that the world hates you, know it has hated me before you" (John 15:18).

QUOTE: "Martyrdom makes disciples like their Master, who willingly accepted death for the salvation of the world, and through it they are made like him by the shedding of blood. Therefore, the Church considers it the highest gift and supreme test of love. And while it is given to few, all however must be prepared to confess Christ before humanity and to follow him along the way of the cross amid the persecutions which the Church never lacks" (Dogmatic Constitution on the Church, 42).

• • •

Bernardine of Siena
PRIEST (1380–1444)

Most of the saints suffer great personal opposition, even persecution. Bernardine, by contrast, seems more like a human dynamo who simply took on the needs of the world.

He was the greatest preacher of his time, journeying across Italy, calming strife-torn cities, attacking the paganism he found rampant, attracting crowds of thirty thousand, following St. Francis's admonition to preach about "vice and virtue, punishment and glory."

Compared with St. Paul by the pope, Bernardine had a keen intuition of the needs of the time, along with solid holiness and boundless energy and joy. He accomplished all this despite having a very weak and hoarse voice, miraculously improved later because of his devotion to Mary.

When he was twenty, the plague was at its height in his hometown, Siena. Sometimes as many as twenty people died in one day at the hospital. Bernardine offered to run the hospital and, with the help of other young men, nursed patients there for four months. He escaped the plague but was so exhausted that a fever confined him for several months. He spent another year caring for a beloved aunt (her parents had died when he was a child) and at her death began to fast and pray to know God's will for him.

At twenty-two, he entered the Franciscan Order and was ordained two years later. For almost a dozen years he lived in solitude and prayer, but his gifts ultimately caused him to be sent to preach. He always traveled on foot, sometimes speaking for hours in one place, then doing the same in another town.

Especially known for his devotion to the Holy Name of Jesus, Bernardine devised a symbol—IHS, the first three letters of the name of Jesus in Greek, in Gothic letters on a blazing sun (see entry for January 3). This was to displace the superstitious symbols of the day, as well as the insignia of factions (for example, of the warring Guelphs and Ghibellines). The devotion spread, and the symbol began to appear in churches, homes, and public buildings. Opposition arose from those who thought it a dangerous innovation. Three attempts were made to have the pope take action against him, but Bernardine's holiness, orthodoxy, and intelligence were evidence of his faithfulness.

General of a branch of the Franciscan Order, the Friars of the Strict Observance, he strongly emphasized scholarship and further study of theology and canon law. When he started there were three hundred friars in the community; when he died there were four thousand. He returned to preaching the last two years of his life, dying while traveling.

COMMENT: Another dynamic saint once said, "I will not be a burden, for I want not what is yours, but you.... I will most gladly spend and be utterly spent for your sakes" (2 Corinthians 12:14–15). There is danger that we see only the whirlwind of activity in the Bernardines of faith—taking care of the sick, preaching, studying, administering, always driving—and forget the source of their energy. We should not say that Bernardine could have been a great contemplative if he had had the chance. He had the chance, every day, and he took it.

STORY: At Bologna, Bernardine preached mightily against the evils of gambling. As was the custom, a huge bonfire was made in the public square, to be a holocaust consuming all the instruments of the vice—playing cards, dice, and the like. A manufacturer of playing cards complained that Bernardine was taking away his livelihood. The saint told him to start making the symbol IHS, and he made more money than ever before.

● ● ●

MAY 21 + OPTIONAL
Cristóbal Magallanes and Companions
PRIEST AND MARTYR; MARTYRS (1915–1928)

Like Blessed Miguel Agustín Pro, S.J. (November 23), Cristóbal and his twenty-four companion martyrs lived under a very anti-Catholic government in Mexico, one determined to weaken the Catholic faith of its people. Churches, schools, and seminaries were closed; foreign clergy were expelled. Cristóbal established a clandestine seminary at Totatiche, Jalisco. Magallanes and the other priests were forced to minister secretly to Catholics during the presidency of Plutarco Calles (1924–1928).

All of these martyrs except three were diocesan priests. David, Manuel, and Salvador were laymen who died with their parish priest, Luis Batis. All of these martyrs belonged to the Cristero movement, pledging their allegiance to Christ and to the Church that he established to spread the Good News in society—even if Mexico's leaders once made it a crime to receive baptism or celebrate the Mass.

These martyrs did not die as a single group but in eight Mexican states, with Jalisco and Zacatecas having the largest number. They were beatified in 1992 and canonized eight years later.

COMMENT: Every martyr realizes how to avoid execution but refuses to pay the high price of doing so. A clear conscience was more valuable than a long life. We may be tempted to compromise our faith while telling ourselves that we are simply being realistic, dealing with situations as we find them. Is survival really the ultimate value? Do our concrete, daily choices reflect our deepest values, the ones that allow us to tick the way we do?

Anyone can imagine situations in which being a follower of Jesus is easier than the present situation. Saints remind us that our daily choices, especially in adverse circumstances, form the pattern of our lives.

QUOTE: During his homily at the canonization Mass on May 21, 2000, Blessed John Paul II addressed the Mexican men, women, and children present in Rome and said: "After the harsh trials that the Church endured in Mexico during those turbulent years, today Mexican Christians, encouraged by the witness of these witnesses to the faith, can live in peace and harmony, contribute the wealth of Gospel values to society. The Church grows and advances, since she is the crucible in which many priestly and religious vocations are born, where families are formed according to God's plan, and where young people, a substantial part of the Mexican population, can grow with the hope of a better future. May the shining example of Cristóbal

Magallanes and his companion martyrs help you to make a renewed commitment of fidelity to God, which can continue to transform Mexican society so that justice, fraternity, and harmony will prevail among all."

* * *

MAY 21 + OPTIONAL (CANADA)

Eugene de Mazenod

BISHOP (1782–1861)

Born into a noble family in Aix-en-Provence, Eugene spent part of his childhood in Italy because his family went there to escape the French Revolution. He returned to France at age twenty, feeling depressed and abandoned. While looking at the cross one Good Friday, Eugene realized that Jesus really loved him, despite his circumstances or failings. After his ordination as a diocesan priest in 1811, Eugene soon organized missionaries to go to rural parts of Provence, using the local dialect to instruct the people whose religious training had been disrupted during and after the French Revolution.

Eugene began the Missionary Oblates of Mary Immaculate (OMI) in 1816, obtaining papal approval for them ten years later. Dedicated to their motto, "He has sent me to evangelize the poor," they soon moved into running seminaries to improve the quality of the clergy. Their first foreign mission was in Canada in 1841; soon they were in Africa, Asia, Australia, and Latin America.

In 1837 Eugene followed his uncle as archbishop of Marseilles, encouraging his Oblate sons, his diocesan clergy, and laypeople to search out and assist the spiritually, materially, and educationally poor. He focused his energies on Church renewal and reform while vigorously defending the Church's right to spread the Good News.

His congregation of priests and brothers has grown to become one of the largest in the Church, serving in over sixty countries. And like St. Eugene, they do not do this alone, but call on men and women of all ages to help bring the Good News of God's unconditional love to those most in need.

At Eugene's canonization in 1998, Pope John Paul II praised his vision, perseverance, and conformity to God's will.

COMMENT: Eugene de Mazenod allowed the grace of God to bear rich fruit in his life. That required a certain amount of flexibility as well as courage to face the problems every growing group encounters. We look to saints like Eugene not to borrow their courage and zeal but, with God's grace, to discover our own, always seeking first God's kingdom (see Matthew 6:33).

QUOTE: "We must lead people to act like human beings, first of all, and then like Christians and finally, we must help them to become saints." (Eugene de Mazenod, Preface to 1825 OMI Rule).

• • •

MAY 22 + OPTIONAL
Rita of Cascia
RELIGIOUS (1381–1457)

Like Elizabeth Ann Seton (January 4), Rita of Cascia was a wife, mother, widow, and member of a religious community. Her holiness was reflected in each phase of her life.

Born at Roccaporena in central Italy, Rita wanted to become a nun but was pressured at a young age into marrying a harsh and cruel man. During her eighteen-year marriage, she bore and raised two sons. After her husband was killed in a brawl and her sons had died, Rita tried to join the Augustinian nuns in Cascia. Unsuccessful at first because she was a widow, Rita eventually succeeded.

Over the years, her austerity, prayerfulness, and charity became famous. When she developed wounds on her forehead, people quickly associated them with the wounds from Christ's crown of thorns. She meditated frequently on Christ's passion. Her care for the sick nuns was legendary. She also counseled laypeople who came to her monastery.

Beatified in 1626, Rita was not canonized until 1900. She has acquired the reputation, together with St. Jude, as a saint of impossible cases. Many people visit her tomb each year.

COMMENT: Although we can easily imagine an ideal world in which to live out our baptismal vocation, such a world does not exist. An "If only…" approach to holiness never quite gets underway, never produces the fruit that God has a right to expect.

Rita became holy because she made choices that reflected her baptism and her growth as a disciple of Jesus. Her overarching, lifelong choice was to cooperate generously with God's grace, but many small choices were needed to make that happen.

Few of those choices were made in ideal circumstances—not even when Rita became an Augustinian nun.

QUOTE: For the baptism of adults and for all the baptized at the Easter Vigil, three questions are asked: "Do you reject sin so as to live in the freedom of God's children? Do you reject the glamour of evil, and refuse to be mastered by sin? Do you reject Satan, father of sin and prince of darkness?"

* * *

MAY 25 + OPTIONAL
Bede the Venerable
PRIEST AND DOCTOR (672?–735)

Bede is one of the few saints honored as such even during his lifetime. His writings were filled with such faith and learning that even while he was still alive, a Church council ordered them to be read publicly in the churches.

At an early age, Bede was entrusted to the care of the abbot of the Monastery of St. Paul in Jarrow, England. The happy combination of genius and the instruction of scholarly, saintly monks produced a saint and an extraordinary scholar, perhaps the most outstanding one of his day. He was deeply versed in all the sciences of his times: natural philosophy, the philosophical principles of Aristotle, astronomy, arithmetic, grammar, ecclesiastical history, the lives of the saints, and, especially, Holy Scripture.

From the time of his ordination to the priesthood at thirty (he had been ordained deacon at nineteen) till his death, he was ever occupied with learning, writing, and teaching. Besides the many books that he copied, he composed forty-five of his own, including thirty commentaries on books of the Bible.

Although eagerly sought by kings and other notables, even Pope Sergius, Bede managed to remain in his own monastery till his death. Only once did he leave for a few months in order to teach in the school of the archbishop of York.

Bede died in 735 praying his favorite prayer: "Glory be to the Father, and to the Son, and to the Holy Spirit. As in the beginning, so now, and forever."

His *Ecclesiastical History of the English People* is commonly regarded as of decisive importance in the art and science of writing history. A unique era was coming to an end at the time of Bede's death: It had fulfilled its purpose of preparing Western Christianity to assimilate the non-Roman barbarian North. Bede recognized the opening to a new day in the life of the Church even as it was happening.

COMMENT: Though his *History* is the greatest legacy Bede has left us, his work in all the sciences (especially in Scripture) should not be overlooked. During his last Lent, he worked on a translation of the Gospel of St. John into English, completing it the day he died. But of this work "to break the word to the poor and unlearned" nothing remains today.

QUOTE: "We have not, it seems to me, amid all our discoveries, invented as yet anything better than the Christian life which Bede lived, and the Christian death which he died" (C. Plummer, editor of Bede's *Ecclesiastical History*).

• • •

MAY 25 + OPTIONAL
Gregory VII
POPE (1020–1085)

The tenth century and the first half of the eleventh were dark days for the Church, partly because the papacy was the pawn of various Roman families. In 1049, things began to change when Pope Leo IX, a reformer, was elected.

He brought a young monk named Hildebrand to Rome as his counselor and special representative on important missions. He was to become Gregory VII.

Three evils plagued the Church then: simony (the buying and selling of sacred offices and things), the unlawful marriage of the clergy, and lay investiture (kings and nobles controlling the appointment of Church officials). To all of these Hildebrand directed his reformer's attention, first as counselor to the popes and later (1073–1085) as pope himself.

Gregory's papal letters stress the role of bishop of Rome as the vicar of Christ and the visible center of unity in the Church. He is well known for his long dispute with Holy Roman Emperor Henry IV over who should control the selection of bishops and abbots.

Gregory fiercely resisted any attack on the liberty of the Church. For this he suffered and finally died in exile. He said, "I have loved justice and hated iniquity; therefore I die in exile." Thirty years later the Church finally won its struggle against lay investiture.

COMMENT: The Gregorian Reform, a milestone in the history of Christ's Church, was named after this man who tried to extricate the papacy and the whole Church from undue control by civil rulers. Against an unhealthy Church nationalism in some areas, Gregory reasserted the unity of the whole Church based on Christ and expressed in the bishop of Rome, the successor of St. Peter.

QUOTE: Gregory's words still ring true today when civil or national religion is making subtle demands: "In every country, even the poorest of women is permitted to take a lawful husband according to the law of the land and by her own choice; but, through the desires and evil practices of the wicked, Holy Church, the bride of God and mother of us all, is not permitted lawfully to cling to her spouse on earth in accordance with divine law and her own will" (Pope St. Gregory VII, *A Call to the Faithful*).

• • •

MAY 25 + OPTIONAL

Mary Magdalene de' Pazzi

VIRGIN (1566–1607)

Mystical ecstasy is the elevation of the spirit to God in such a way that the person is aware of this union with God while both internal and external senses are detached from the sensible world. Mary Magdalene de Pazzi received this special gift of God so completely that she is called the "ecstatic saint."

She was born into a noble family in Florence in 1566, when Florence was a great city and its first families had influence. The normal course would have been for Catherine de' Pazzi to marry nobly and enjoy comfort. But she hardly followed the normal course. At nine she learned to meditate from the family confessor. She made her First Communion at the then early age of ten and made a vow of virginity one month later. When sixteen, she entered the Carmelite convent in Florence because she could receive Communion daily there.

Catherine had taken the name Mary Magdalene and had been a novice for a year when she became critically ill. Death seemed near so her superiors let her make her profession of vows from a cot in the chapel in a private ceremony. Immediately after, she fell into an ecstasy that lasted about two hours. This was repeated after Communion on the following forty mornings. These ecstasies were rich experiences of union with God and contained marvelous insights into divine truths.

As a safeguard against deception and to preserve the revelations, her confessor asked Mary Magdalene to dictate her experiences to sister secretaries. Over the next six years, five large volumes were filled. The first three books record ecstasies from May 27, 1584, through Pentecost week of 1585. This week was a preparation for a severe five-year trial. The fourth book records that trial and the fifth is a collection of letters concerning reform and renewal. Another book, *Admonitions*, is a collection of her sayings arising from her experiences in the formation of religious.

The extraordinary was ordinary for this saint. She read the thoughts of others and predicted future events. During her lifetime, she appeared to several persons in distant places and cured a number of sick people.

It would be easy to dwell on the ecstasies and pretend that Mary Magdalene only had spiritual highs. This is far from true. It seems that God permitted her this special closeness to prepare her for the five years of desolation that followed when she experienced spiritual dryness. She was plunged into a state of darkness in which she saw nothing but what was horrible in herself and all around her. She had violent temptations and endured great physical suffering. She died in 1607 at forty-one and was canonized in 1669.

COMMENT: Intimate union, God's gift to mystics, is a reminder to all of us of the eternal happiness of union he wishes to give us. The cause of mystical ecstasy in this life is the Holy Spirit, working through spiritual gifts. The ecstasy occurs because of the weakness of the body and its powers to withstand the divine illumination, but as the body is purified and strengthened, ecstasy no longer occurs. On various aspects of ecstasy, see Teresa of Avila, "Sixth Mansion," *Interior Castle*, and John of the Cross, *Dark Night of the Soul*, 2:1–2.

QUOTE: There are many people today who see no purpose in suffering. Mary Magdalene de' Pazzi discovered saving grace in suffering. When she entered religious life, she was filled with a desire to suffer during the rest of her life for Christ. The more she suffered, the greater her desire for it grew. Her dying words to her fellow sisters were: "The last thing I ask of you—and I ask it in the name of our Lord Jesus Christ—is that you love him alone, that you trust implicitly in him and that you encourage one another continually to suffer for the love of him."

• • •

MAY 26 + MEMORIAL

Philip Neri

PRIEST (1515–1595)

Philip Neri was a sign of contradiction, combining popularity with piety against the background of a corrupt Rome and a disinterested clergy, the whole post-Renaissance malaise.

At an early age, he abandoned the chance to become a businessman, moved to Rome from Florence, and devoted his life and individuality to God. After three years of philosophy and theology studies, he gave up any thought of ordination. The next thirteen years were spent in a vocation unusual at the time—that of a layperson actively engaged in prayer and the apostolate.

As the Council of Trent (1545–1563) was reforming the Church on a doctrinal level, Philip's appealing personality was winning him friends from all levels of society, from beggars to cardinals. He rapidly gathered around himself a group of laypersons won over by his audacious spirituality. Initially they met as an informal prayer and discussion group, and also served poor people in Rome.

At the urging of his confessor, he was ordained priest and soon became an outstanding confessor, gifted with the knack of piercing the pretenses and illusions of others, though always in a charitable manner and often with a joke. He arranged talks, discussions, and prayers for his penitents in a room above the church. He sometimes led "excursions" to other churches, often with music and a picnic on the way.

Some of his followers became priests and lived together in community. This was the beginning of the Oratory, the religious institute he founded. A feature of their life was a daily afternoon service of four informal talks, with vernacular hymns and prayers. Giovanni Palestrina was one of Philip's followers, and composed music for the services.

The Oratory was finally approved after suffering through a period of accusations of being an assembly of heretics, where laypersons preached and sang vernacular hymns! (Cardinal Newman founded the first English-speaking house of the Oratory.)

Philip's advice was sought by many of the prominent figures of his day. He is one of the influential figures of the Counter-Reformation, mainly for converting to personal holiness many of the influential people within the Church itself. His characteristic virtues were humility and gaiety.

COMMENT: Many people wrongly feel that such an attractive and jocular personality as Philip's cannot be combined with an intense spirituality. Philip's life melts our rigid, narrow views of piety. His approach to sanctity was truly catholic, all-embracing, and accompanied by a good laugh. Philip always wanted his followers to become not less but more human through their striving for holiness.

QUOTE: Philip Neri prayed, "Let me get through today, and I shall not fear tomorrow."

* * *

MAY 27 + OPTIONAL
Augustine of Canterbury
BISHOP (D. 605?)

In the year 596, some forty monks set out from Rome to evangelize the Anglo-Saxons in England. Leading the group was Augustine, the prior of their monastery in Rome. Hardly had he and his men reached Gaul (France) when they heard stories of the ferocity of the Anglo-Saxons and of the treacherous waters of the English Channel. Augustine returned to Rome and to the pope who had sent them—St. Gregory the Great (September 3)—only to be assured by him that their fears were groundless.

Augustine again set out and this time the group crossed the English Channel and landed in the territory of Kent, ruled by King Ethelbert, a pagan married to a Christian, Bertha. Ethelbert received them kindly, set up a residence for them in Canterbury and, within the year, on Pentecost Sunday, 597, was himself baptized. After being consecrated a bishop in France, Augustine returned to Canterbury, where he founded his see. He constructed a church and monastery near where the present cathedral, begun in 1070, now stands. As the faith spread, additional sees were established at London and Rochester.

Work was sometimes slow and Augustine did not always meet with success. Attempts to reconcile the Anglo-Saxon Christians with the original Briton Christians (who had been driven into western England by Anglo-Saxon invaders) ended in dismal failure. Augustine failed to convince the Britons to give up certain Celtic customs at variance with Rome and to forget their bitterness, helping him evangelize their Anglo-Saxon conquerors.

Laboring patiently, Augustine wisely heeded the missionary principles— quite enlightened for the times—suggested by Pope Gregory the Great: purify rather than destroy pagan temples and customs, let pagan rites and festivals be transformed into Christian feasts, retain local customs as far as possible. The limited success Augustine achieved in England before his death in 605, a short eight years after he arrived in England, would eventually bear fruit long after in the conversion of England. Truly Augustine of Canterbury can be called the "Apostle of England."

COMMENT: Augustine of Canterbury comes across today as a very human saint, one who could suffer like many of us from a failure of nerve. For example, his first venture to England ended in a big U-turn back to Rome. He made mistakes and met failure in his peacemaking attempts with the Briton Christians. He often wrote to Rome for decisions on matters he could have decided on his own had he been more self-assured. He even received mild warnings against pride from Pope Gregory, who cautioned him to "fear lest, amidst the wonders that are done, the weak mind be puffed up by self-esteem." Augustine's perseverance amidst obstacles and only partial success teaches today's apostles and pioneers to struggle on despite frustrations and be satisfied with gradual advances.

QUOTE: In a letter to Augustine, Pope Gregory the Great wrote: "He who would climb to a lofty height must go by steps, not leaps."

• • •

MAY 30 + OPTIONAL
Joan of Arc
MARTYR (1412–1431)

Burned at the stake as a heretic after a politically motivated trial, Joan was beatified in 1909 and canonized in 1920.

She was born of a fairly well-to-do peasant couple in Domremy-Greux (southeast of Paris). Joan was only twelve when she experienced a vision and heard voices that she later identified as Sts. Michael the Archangel (September 29), Catherine of Alexandria (November 25), and Margaret of Antioch.

During the Hundred Years' War, she led French troops against the English and recaptured the cities of Orléans and Troyes. This enabled Charles VII to be crowned as king in Reims in 1429. Captured near Compiegne the following year, she was sold to the English and placed on trial for heresy and witchcraft. Professors at the University of Paris supported Bishop Pierre Cauchon of Beauvis, the judge at her trial; Cardinal Henry Beaufort of Winchester, England, participated in the questioning of Joan in prison. In the end, she was condemned for wearing men's clothes.

On May 30, 1431, she was burned at the stake in Rouen, and her ashes were scattered in the Seine River. A second Church trial twenty-five years later nullified the earlier verdict, which was reached under political pressure, primarily because the English resented France's military success, to which Joan contributed by her efforts.

Remembered by most people for her military exploits, Joan had a great love for the sacraments, which strengthened her compassion toward the poor. Popular devotion to her increased greatly in nineteenth-century France and later among French soldiers during World War I. Theologian George Tavard writes that her life "offers a perfect example of the conjunction of contemplation and action" because her spiritual insight is that there should be a "unity of heaven and earth."

Joan of Arc has been the subject of many books, plays, operas, and movies.

COMMENT: As she was bring burned at the stake, Joan called on Jesus.

QUOTE: "Joan of Arc is like a shooting star across the landscape of French and English history, amid the stories of the Church's saints and into our consciousness. Women identify with her; men admire her courage. She challenges us in fundamental ways. Despite the fact that more than five hundred years have passed since she lived, her issues of mysticism, calling, identity, trust and betrayal, conflict and focus are our issues still." (Barbara Beckwith, *Joan of Arc: God's Warrior*).

• • •

MAY 31 + FEAST

Visitation

This is a fairly late feast, going back only to the thirteenth or fourteenth century. It was established widely throughout the Church to pray for unity. The present date of celebration was set in 1969 in order to follow the Annunciation of the Lord (March 25) and precede the birthday of John the Baptist (June 24).

Like most feasts of Mary, it is closely connected with Jesus and his saving work. The more visible actors in the visitation drama (see Luke 1:39–45) are Mary and Elizabeth. However, Jesus and John the Baptist steal the scene in a hidden way. Jesus makes John leap with joy—the joy of messianic salvation. Elizabeth, in turn, is filled with the Holy Spirit and addresses words of praise to Mary—words that echo down through the ages.

It is helpful to recall that we do not have a journalist's account of this meeting. Rather, Luke, speaking for the Church, gives a prayerful poet's rendition of the scene. Elizabeth's praise of Mary as "the mother of my Lord" can be viewed as the earliest Church's devotion to Mary. As with all authentic devotion to Mary, Elizabeth's (the Church's) words first praise God for what God has done to Mary. Only secondly does she praise Mary for trusting God's words.

Then comes the Magnificat (Luke 1:46–55). Here Mary herself (like the Church) traces all her greatness to God.

COMMENT: One of the invocations in Mary's litany is "Ark of the Covenant." Like the Ark of the Covenant of old, Mary brings God's presence into the lives of other people. As David danced before the Ark, John the Baptist leaps for joy. As the Ark helped to unite the twelve tribes of Israel by being placed in David's capital, so Mary has the power to unite all Christians in her son. At times, devotion to Mary may have occasioned some divisiveness, but we can hope that authentic devotion will lead all to Christ and therefore to one another.

QUOTE: "Moved by charity, therefore, Mary goes to the house of her kinswoman.... While every word of Elizabeth's is filled with meaning, her final words would seem to have a fundamental importance: 'And blessed is she who believed that there would be a fulfillment of what had been spoken to her from the Lord' (Luke 1:45). These words can be linked with the title 'full of grace' of the angel's greeting. Both of these texts reveal an essential Mariological content, namely the truth about Mary, who has become really present in the mystery of Christ precisely because she 'has believed.' The fullness of grace announced by the angel means the gift of God himself. Mary's faith, proclaimed by Elizabeth at the visitation, indicates how the Virgin of Nazareth responded to this gift" (Blessed John Paul II, *The Mother of the Redeemer*, 12).

● ● ●

FRIDAY AFTER CORPUS CHRISTI + SOLEMNITY
Sacred Heart

Devotion to the heart pierced on Calvary is nearly as old as Christianity, but it has undergone many changes over the centuries. Patristic writers saw in the blood and water issuing from the crucified Lord's side (John 19:34) the fulfillment of his promise to give living water (John 4:13–14; 7:37), the fountain from which the Spirit flows upon the Church. Medieval piety placed less emphasis on Jesus's heart as the source of grace and moved toward more personal and sentimental devotion.

The public cult celebrated today began in the seventeenth century, when St. John Eudes (August 19) pressed for a liturgy (Mass and Office) of the Sacred Heart. Toward the end of that century St. Mary Margaret Alacoque (October 16) received visions of the Lord exposing his heart and urging public devotion. Her apparitions gave impetus to the devotion and shape to its purpose: to promote greater use of the sacrament of penance to offset indifference to the Blessed Sacrament.

Pius VI saw the devotion as a means of refuting Jansenism, which rejected the doctrine that Christ died for all people. Clement XIII first granted the petition for a liturgical observance to the Polish bishops and the Roman Archconfraternity of the Sacred Heart in 1765. Pius IX extended the observance to the universal Church in 1856 and, late in the nineteenth century, Leo XIII raised its rank to a feast.

Popular devotion includes the nine First Fridays and the enthronement of an image of the Sacred Heart in homes as a sign that love is the Christian way of life.

COMMENT: A Jewish midrash on the Exodus account of Moses's encounter with God compares the burning bush to the human heart: the only created thing which can burn without being consumed. Yet nothing seems to be harder for human beings to believe in than unconditional love—love that is neither deserved nor earned. The Sacred Heart of Jesus, aflame with an unquenchable fire, stands today against lingering traces of Jansenism as a powerful symbol of Christ's unquenchable love for the whole human race.

QUOTE: "Whoever does not love does not know God. Why? Because God is Love. What more can be said, my Brothers? If one did not find one word in praise of love through this epistle, nor the least word throughout all the other pages of Scripture, and we heard only this one word from the voice of the Spirit of God: Because 'God is Love,' we should seek for nothing more" (St. Augustine, *Homily on the First Epistle of St. John*).

• • •

SATURDAY AFTER CORPUS CHRISTI + OPTIONAL
Immaculate Heart of Mary

In the seventeenth century, St. John Eudes promoted devotion to the hearts of Jesus and Mary. He even composed an Office and Mass in honor of the Heart of Mary. It became a feast of the universal Church only in the twentieth century and is celebrated on the day after the feast of the Sacred Heart of Jesus.

The New Testament mentions Mary's heart only twice. Luke 2:19 says, "Mary kept all these things, reflecting on them in her heart." Luke 2:51 has a similar text.

Both in Scripture and in later reflections on Mary's heart, it is obvious that the usage is symbolic. The physical heart stands for the inner reaches of the human personality. It includes or connotes the mind, the soul, the will, the spirit, the core of one's being. It is the place where a person thinks, remembers, feels, desires, makes decisions.

Medieval saints such as Mechtild, Gertrude (November 16) and Bridget (July 23) promoted devotion to the heart of Mary. Franciscan and Jesuit theologians made their contributions. St. Francis de Sales (January 24) dedicated his *Treatise on the Love of God* to Mary's heart. But it was St. John Eudes (August 19) who wrote extensively about this theme. He says that the divine Word printed on Mary's heart a perfect likeness of the divine attributes and a share in the properties of each person of the Trinity.

Perhaps this devotion came into its own in the twentieth century. It is a special theme of Fatima. In 1942 Pius XII consecrated the world to the Immaculate Heart of Mary and established the feast for the universal Church.

COMMENT: To honor Mary's heart is to honor her total dedication to God. As she pondered in her heart the mysteries of Jesus's infancy and childhood (Luke 2:19, 51), she must have done the same for all the mysteries of his life, death, and resurrection. This feast suggests that Mary is the greatest of the mystics—totally wrapped up in God and committed to God's will. Her spirituality is a model for all the members of the Church.

QUOTE: "We can say that the mystery of the redemption took shape beneath the heart of the Virgin of Nazareth when she pronounced her 'fiat.' From then on, under the special influence of the Holy Spirit, this heart, the heart of both a virgin and a mother, has always followed the work of her Son and has gone out to all those whom Christ has embraced and continues to embrace with inexhaustible love. For that reason her heart must have the inexhaustibility of a mother" (Blessed John Paul II, *Redeemer of Man*, 22).

* * *

JUNE 1 + MEMORIAL
Justin
MARTYR (D. 165)

Justin never ended his quest for religious truth even when he converted to Christianity after years of studying various pagan philosophies.

As a young man, he was principally attracted to the school of Plato. However, he found that the Christian religion answered the great questions about life and existence better than the philosophers.

Upon his conversion he continued to wear the philosopher's mantle, and became the first Christian philosopher. He combined the Christian religion with the best elements in Greek philosophy. In his view, philosophy was a pedagogue of Christ, an educator leading others to Christ.

Justin is known as an apologist, one who defends in writing the Christian religion against the attacks and misunderstandings of the pagans. Two of his apologies have come down to us; they are addressed to the Roman emperor and to the senate.

For his staunch adherence to the Christian religion, Justin was beheaded in Rome in 165.

COMMENT: As patron of philosophers, Justin may inspire us to use our natural powers (especially our power to know and understand) in the service of Christ and to build up the Christian life within us. Since we are prone to error, especially in reference to the deep questions concerning life and existence, we should also be willing to correct and check our natural thinking in light of religious truth. Thus we will be able to say with the learned saints of the Church: I believe in order to understand, and I understand in order to believe.

QUOTE: "Philosophy is the knowledge of that which exists, and a clear understanding of the truth; and happiness is the reward of such knowledge and understanding" (Justin, *Dialogue with Trypho*, 3).

• • •

Marcellinus and Peter
MARTYRS (D. 304)

Marcellinus and Peter were prominent enough in the memory of the Church to be included among the saints of the Roman Canon. Mention of their names is optional in our present Eucharistic Prayer I.

Marcellinus was a priest and Peter was an exorcist, that is, someone authorized by the Church to deal with cases of demonic possession. They were beheaded during the persecution of Emperor Diocletian. Pope Damasus wrote an epitaph apparently based on the report of their executioner, and Constantine erected a basilica over the crypt in which they were buried in Rome. Numerous legends sprang from an early account of their death.

COMMENT: Why are these men included in our Eucharistic Prayer, and given their own feast day, in spite of the fact that almost nothing is known about them? Probably because the Church respects its collective memory. They once sent an impulse of encouragement through the whole Church. They made the ultimate step of faith.

QUOTE: "The Church has always believed that the apostles, and Christ's martyrs who had given the supreme witness of faith and charity by the shedding of their blood, are quite closely joined with us in Christ" (Dogmatic Constitution on the Church, 50).

• • •

Charles Lwanga and Companions
MARTYRS (D. 1886)

One of twenty-two Ugandan martyrs, Charles Lwanga is the patron of youth and Catholic Action in most of tropical Africa. He protected his fellow pages (aged thirteen to thirty) from the sexual demands of the Bagandan ruler,

Mwanga, and encouraged and instructed them in the Catholic faith during their imprisonment for refusing the ruler's demands.

For his own unwillingness to submit to the immoral acts and his efforts to safeguard the faith of his friends, Charles was burned to death at Namugongo on June 3, 1886, by Mwanga's order.

Charles first learned of Christ's teachings from two retainers in the court of Chief Mawulugungu. While a catechumen, he entered the royal household as assistant to Joseph Mukaso, head of the court pages.

On the night of Mukaso's martyrdom for encouraging the African youths to resist Mwanga, Charles requested and received baptism. Imprisoned with his friends, Charles's courage and belief in God inspired them to remain chaste and faithful.

When Pope Paul VI canonized these twenty-two martyrs on October 18, 1964, he referred to the Anglican pages martyred for the same reason.

COMMENT: Like Charles Lwanga, we are all teachers and witnesses to Christian living by the examples of our own lives. We are all called upon to spread the Word of God, whether by word or deed. By remaining courageous and unshakable in our faith during times of great moral and physical temptation, we live as Christ lived.

QUOTE: On his African tour in 1969, Pope Paul VI told twenty-two young Ugandan converts that "being a Christian is a fine thing but not always an easy one."

• • •

JUNE 5 + MEMORIAL
Boniface
BISHOP AND MARTYR (672?–754)

Boniface, known as the apostle of the Germans, was an English Benedictine monk who gave up being elected abbot to devote his life to the conversion of the Germanic tribes. Two characteristics stand out: his Christian orthodoxy and his fidelity to the pope of Rome.

How absolutely necessary this orthodoxy and fidelity were is borne out by the conditions he found on his first missionary journey in 719 at the request of Pope Gregory II. Paganism was a way of life. What Christianity he did find had either lapsed into paganism or was mixed with error. The clergy were mainly responsible for these latter conditions since they were in many instances uneducated, lax, and questionably obedient to their bishops. In particular instances their very ordination was questionable.

These are the conditions that Boniface was to report in 722 on his first return visit to Rome. The Holy Father instructed him to reform the German church. The pope sent letters of recommendation to religious and civil leaders. Boniface later admitted that his work would have been unsuccessful, from a human viewpoint, without a letter of safe conduct from Charles Martel, the powerful Frankish ruler, grandfather of Charlemagne. Boniface was finally made a regional bishop and authorized to organize the whole German church. He was eminently successful.

In the Frankish kingdom, he met great problems because of lay interference in bishops' elections, the worldliness of the clergy, and lack of papal control.

During a final mission to the Frisians, he and fifty-three companions were massacred while he was preparing converts for confirmation.

In order to restore the Germanic church to its fidelity to Rome and to convert the pagans, he had been guided by two principles. The first was to restore the obedience of the clergy to their bishops in union with the pope of Rome. The second was the establishment of many houses of prayer, which took the form of Benedictine monasteries. A great number of Anglo-Saxon monks and nuns followed him to the continent. He introduced Benedictine nuns to the active apostolate of education.

COMMENT: Boniface bears out the Christian rule: To follow Christ is to follow the way of the cross. For Boniface, it was not only physical suffering or death, but the painful, thankless, bewildering task of Church reform. Missionary glory is often thought of in terms of bringing new persons to Christ. It seems—but is not—less glorious to heal the household of the faith.

STORY: Boniface literally struck a blow for Christianity in his attempt to destroy pagan superstitions. On a day previously announced, in the presence of a tense crowd, he attacked Donar's sacred oak on Mount Gudenburg with an axe. The huge tree crashed, splitting into four parts. The people waited for the gods to strike Boniface dead—then realized their gods were powerless, nonexistent. He used planks from the tree to build a chapel.

• • •

JUNE 6 + OPTIONAL

Norbert

BISHOP (1080?–1134)

In the twelfth century in the French region of Premontre, St. Norbert founded a religious order known as the Premonstratensians or the Norbertines.

Norbert's founding of the order was truly a monstrous task: combating rampant heresies (particularly regarding the Blessed Sacrament), revitalizing many of the faithful who had grown indifferent and dissolute, plus effecting peace and reconciliation among enemies.

Norbert entertained no pretensions about his own ability to accomplish these difficult tasks. Even with the aid of a goodly number of men who joined his order, he realized that nothing could be effectively done without God's power. Finding this help especially in devotion to the Blessed Sacrament, he and his Norbertines praised God for success in converting heretics, reconciling numerous enemies, and rebuilding faith in indifferent believers. Many of them lived in central houses during the week and served in parishes on the weekends.

Reluctantly, Norbert became archbishop of Magdeburg in central Germany, a territory half pagan and half Christian. In this position he zealously and courageously continued his work for the Church until his death on June 6, 1134.

COMMENT: A different world cannot be built by indifferent people. The same is true in regard to the Church. The indifference of vast numbers of nominal faithful and their indifference to ecclesiastical authority and essential doctrines of the faith weakens the Church's witness. Unswerving loyalty to the Church and fervent devotion to the Eucharist, as practiced by Norbert, will help keep the people of God close to the heart of Christ.

QUOTE: On the occasion of his ordination to the priesthood, Norbert said, "O Priest! You are not yourself because you are God's. You are not of yourself because you are the servant and minister of Christ. You are not your own because you are the spouse of the Church. You are not yourself because you are the mediator between God and man. You are not from yourself because you are nothing. What then are you? Nothing and everything. O Priest! Take care lest what was said to Christ on the cross be said to you: 'He saved others, himself he cannot save!'"

• • •

JUNE 9 + OPTIONAL
Ephrem
DEACON AND DOCTOR (306?–373)

Poet, teacher, orator, and defender of the faith, Ephrem is the only Syrian recognized as a Doctor of the Church. He took upon himself the special task of opposing the many false doctrines rampant at his time, always remaining a true and forceful defender of the Catholic Church.

Born in Nisibis, Mesopotamia, he was baptized as a young man and became famous as a teacher in his native city. When the Christian emperor had to cede Nisibis to the Persians, Ephrem, along with many Christians, fled as a refugee to Edessa. He is credited with attracting great glory to the biblical school there. He was ordained a deacon but declined becoming a priest (and was said to have avoided episcopal consecration by feigning madness!).

He had a prolific pen and his writings best illumine his holiness. Although he was not a man of great scholarship, his works reflect deep insight and knowledge of the Scriptures. In writing about the mysteries of humanity's redemption, Ephrem reveals a realistic and humanly sympathetic spirit and a great devotion to the humanity of Jesus. It is said that his poetic account of the last judgment inspired Dante.

It is surprising to read that he wrote hymns against the heretics of his day. He would take the popular songs of the heretical groups and, using their melodies, compose beautiful hymns embodying orthodox doctrine. Ephrem became one of the first to introduce song into the Church's public worship as a means of instruction for the faithful. His many hymns have earned him the title "Harp of the Holy Spirit."

He preferred a simple, austere life, living in a small cave overlooking the city of Edessa. It was here he died around 373.

COMMENT: Many Catholics still find singing in Church a problem, probably because of the rather individualistic piety that they inherited. Yet singing has been a tradition of both the Old and the New Testament. It is an excellent way of expressing and creating a community spirit of unity as well as joy. Ephrem's hymns, an ancient historian testifies, "lent luster to the Christian assemblies." We need some modern Ephrems—and cooperating singers—to do the same for our Christian assemblies today.

QUOTE: "Lay me not with sweet spices, For this honor avails me not, Nor yet use incense and perfumes, For the honor befits me not. Burn yet the incense in the holy place; As for me, escort me only with your prayers, Give ye your incense to God, And over me send up hymns. Instead of perfumes and spices, Be mindful of me in your intercessions" (From *The Testament of St. Ephrem*).

● ● ●

JUNE 11 + MEMORIAL
Barnabas
APOSTLE

Barnabas, a Jew of Cyprus, comes as close as anyone outside the twelve to being a full-fledged apostle. He was closely associated with St. Paul (he introduced Paul to Peter and the other apostles) and served as a kind of mediator between the former persecutor and the still-suspicious Jewish Christians.

When a Christian community developed at Antioch, Barnabas was sent as the official representative of the church of Jerusalem to incorporate them into the fold. He and Paul instructed in Antioch for a year, after which they took relief contributions to Jerusalem.

Later, Paul and Barnabas, now clearly seen as charismatic leaders, were sent by Antioch officials to preach to the Gentiles. Enormous success crowned their efforts. After a miracle at Lystra, the people wanted to offer sacrifice to them as gods—Barnabas being Zeus, and Paul, Hermes—but the two said, "We are of the same nature as you, human beings. We proclaim to you good news that you should turn from these idols to the living God" (see Acts 14:8–18).

But all was not peaceful. They were expelled from one town, they had to go to Jerusalem to clear up the ever-recurring controversy about circumcision, and even the best of friends can have differences. When Paul wanted to revisit the places they had evangelized, Barnabas wanted to take along John Mark (April 25), his cousin, author of the Gospel, but Paul insisted that, since Mark had deserted them once, he was not fit to take along now. The disagreement that followed was so sharp that Barnabas and Paul separated, Barnabas taking Mark to Cyprus, Paul taking Silas to Syria. Later, they were reconciled—Paul, Barnabas, and Mark.

When Paul stood up to Peter for not eating with Gentiles for fear of his Jewish friends, we learn that "even Barnabas was carried away by their hypocrisy" (see Galatians 2:1–13).

COMMENT: Barnabas is spoken of simply as one who dedicated his life to the Lord. He was a man "filled with the Holy Spirit and faith. Thereby large numbers were added to the Lord." Even when he and Paul were expelled from Antioch in Pisidia (in modern-day Turkey), they were "filled with joy and the Holy Spirit."

STORY: Barnabas is mentioned by name as one of the generous members of the idyllic and extremely poor church in Jerusalem: "The community of believers was of one heart and mind, and no one claimed that any of his possessions was his own, but they had everything in common.... There was no needy person among them, for those who owned property or houses would sell them, bring the proceeds of the sale, and put them at the feet of the apostles, and they were distributed to each according to need.

"Thus Joseph, also named by the apostles Barnabas (which is translated 'son of encouragement'), a Levite, a Cypriot by birth, sold a piece of property that he owned, then brought the money and put it at the feet of the apostles" (Acts 4:32, 34–37).

• • •

JUNE 13 + MEMORIAL
Anthony of Padua
PRIEST AND DOCTOR (1195–1231)

The Gospel call to leave everything and follow Christ was the rule of Anthony's life. Over and over again God called him to something new in his plan. Every time, Anthony responded with renewed zeal and self-sacrificing to serve his Lord Jesus more completely.

His journey began when as a young man he decided to join the Augustinians in Lisbon, giving up a future of wealth and power to be a servant of God. Later, when the bodies of the first Franciscan martyrs went through the Portuguese city where he was stationed, he was again filled with an intense longing to be one of those closest to Jesus himself: those who die for the Good News.

So Anthony entered the Franciscan Order and set out to preach to the Moors. But an illness prevented him from achieving that goal. He went to Italy and was stationed in a small hermitage where he spent most of his time praying, reading the Scriptures, and doing menial tasks.

The call of God came again at an ordination where no one was prepared to speak. The humble and obedient Anthony hesitantly accepted the task. The years of searching for Jesus in prayer, of reading sacred Scripture, and of serving him in poverty, chastity, and obedience had prepared Anthony to allow the Spirit to use his talents. Anthony's sermon was astounding to those who expected an unprepared speech and knew not the Spirit's power to give people words.

Recognized as a great man of prayer and a great Scripture and theology scholar, Anthony became the first friar to teach theology to the other friars. Soon he was called from that post to preach to the Albigensians in France, using his profound knowledge of Scripture and theology to convert and reassure those who had been misled by their denial of Christ's humanity and of the sacraments.

After he led the friars in northern Italy for three years, Anthony made his headquarters in the city of Padua. He resumed his preaching and began writing sermon notes to help other preachers.

COMMENT: Anthony should be the patron of those who find their lives completely uprooted and set in a new and unexpected direction. Like all saints, he is a perfect example of turning one's life completely over to Christ. God did with Anthony as God pleased—and what God pleased was a life of spiritual power and brilliance that still attracts admiration today. He whom popular devotion has nominated as finder of lost objects found himself by losing himself totally to the providence of God.

QUOTE: In his sermon notes, Anthony writes: "The saints are like the stars. In his providence Christ conceals them in a hidden place that they may not shine before others when they might wish to do so. Yet they are always ready to exchange the quiet of contemplation for the works of mercy as soon as they perceive in their heart the invitation of Christ."

* * *

JUNE 19 + OPTIONAL
Romuald
ABBOT (950?–1027)

After a wasted youth, Romuald saw his father kill a relative in a duel over property. In horror he fled to a monastery near Ravenna in Italy. After three years some of the monks found him to be uncomfortably holy and eased him out.

He spent the next thirty years going about Italy, founding monasteries and hermitages. He longed to give his life to Christ in martyrdom and got the pope's permission to preach the Gospel in Hungary. But he was struck with illness as soon as he arrived, and the illness recurred as often as he tried to proceed.

During another period of his life, he suffered great spiritual dryness. One day as he was praying Psalm 32 ("I will instruct you and show you the way you should walk"), he was given an extraordinary light and spirit that never left him.

At the next monastery where he stayed, he was accused of a scandalous crime by a young nobleman he had rebuked for a dissolute life. Amazingly, his fellow monks believed the accusation. He was given a severe penance, forbidden to offer Mass, and excommunicated, an unjust sentence he endured in silence for six months.

The most famous of the monasteries he founded was that of the Camaldoli (Campus Maldoli, name of the owner) in Tuscany. Here he founded the order of the Camaldolese Benedictines, uniting a monastic and hermit life.

His father later became a monk, wavered, and was kept faithful by the encouragement of his son.

COMMENT: Christ is a gentle leader, but he calls us to total holiness. Now and then men and women are raised up to challenge us by the absoluteness of their dedication, the vigor of their spirit, the depth of their conversion. The fact that we cannot duplicate their lives does not change the call to us to be totally open to God in our own circumstances.

STORY: A Polish duke had a son in the monastery where Romuald was living. On behalf of his father, the son presented Romuald with a fine horse. Romuald exchanged it for a donkey, saying that he felt closer to Jesus Christ on such a mount.

• • •

JUNE 21 + MEMORIAL
Aloysius Gonzaga
RELIGIOUS (1568–1591)

The Lord can make saints anywhere, even amid the brutality and license of Renaissance life. Florence was the "mother of piety" for Aloysius Gonzaga despite his exposure to a "society of fraud, dagger, poison, and lust." As a son of a princely family, he grew up in royal courts and army camps. His father wanted Aloysius to be a military hero.

At age seven he experienced a profound spiritual quickening. His prayers included the Office of Mary, the psalms, and other devotions. At age nine he came from his hometown of Castiglione to Florence to be educated; by age eleven he was teaching catechism to poor children, fasting three days a week, and practicing great austerities. When he was thirteen years old he traveled with his parents and the empress of Austria to Spain and acted as a page in the court of Philip II. The more Aloysius saw of court life, the more disillusioned he became, seeking relief in learning about the lives of saints.

A book about the experience of Jesuit missionaries in India suggested to him the idea of entering the Society of Jesus, and in Spain his decision became final. Now began a four-year contest with his father. Eminent churchmen and laypeople were pressed into service to persuade him to remain in his "normal" vocation. Finally he prevailed, was allowed to renounce his right to succession, and was received into the Jesuit novitiate.

Like other seminarians, Aloysius was faced with a new kind of penance— that of accepting different ideas about the exact nature of penance. He was obliged to eat more and to take recreation with the other students. He was forbidden to pray except at stated times. He spent four years in the study of philosophy and had St. Robert Bellarmine (September 17) as his spiritual adviser.

In 1591 a plague struck Rome. The Jesuits opened a hospital of their own. The general himself and many other Jesuits rendered personal service. Because he nursed patients, washing them and making their beds, Aloysius caught the disease himself. A fever persisted after his recovery and he was so weak he could scarcely rise from bed. Yet, he maintained his great discipline of prayer, knowing that he would die within the octave of Corpus Christi, three months later, at the age of twenty-three.

COMMENT: As a saint who fasted, scourged himself, sought solitude and prayer, and did not look on the faces of women, Aloysius seems an unlikely patron of youth in a society where asceticism is confined to the training camps of athletes and sexual permissiveness has little left to permit. Can an overweight and air-conditioned society deprive itself of anything? It will when it discovers a reason, as Aloysius did. The motivation for letting God purify us is the experience of God loving us, in prayer.

QUOTE: "When we stand praying, beloved brethren, we ought to be watchful and earnest with our whole heart, intent on our prayers. Let all carnal and worldly thoughts pass away, nor let the soul at that time think on anything except the object of its prayer" (St. Cyprian, *On the Lord's Prayer*, 31).

* * *

JUNE 22 + OPTIONAL
Paulinus of Nola
BISHOP (354?–431)

Anyone who is praised in the letters of six or seven saints undoubtedly must be of extraordinary character. Such a person was Paulinus of Nola, correspondent and friend of Sts. Augustine (August 28), Jerome (September 30), Melania, Martin of Tours (November 11), Gregory (September 3), and Ambrose (December 7).

Born near Bordeaux, he was the son of the Roman prefect of Gaul, who had extensive property in both Gaul and Italy. Paulinus became a distinguished lawyer, holding several public offices in the Roman Empire. With his Spanish wife, Therasia, he retired at an early age to a life of cultured leisure.

The two were baptized by the saintly bishop of Bordeaux and moved to Therasia's estate in Spain. After many childless years, they had a son who died a week after birth. This occasioned their beginning a life of great austerity and charity, giving away most of their Spanish property. Possibly as a result of this great example, Paulinus was rather unexpectedly ordained a priest at Christmas by the bishop of Barcelona.

He and his wife then moved to Nola, near Naples. He had a great love for St. Felix of Nola and spent much effort in promoting devotion to this saint. Paulinus gave away most of his remaining property (to the consternation of his relatives) and continued his work for the poor. Supporting a host of debtors, the homeless, and other needy people, he lived a monastic life in another part of his home. By popular demand he was made bishop of Nola and guided that diocese for twenty-one years.

His last years were saddened by the invasion of the Huns. Among his few writings is the earliest extant Christian wedding song.

COMMENT: Many of us are tempted to "retire" early in life, after an initial burst of energy. Christ's work is waiting to be done all around us. Paulinus's life had scarcely begun when he thought it was over, while he took his ease on that estate in Spain. "Man proposes, but God disposes."

STORY: An eyewitness described Paulinus's last days: A priest came to him three days before his death, saying that forty pieces of silver were needed for the poor. Paulinus smiled and said that someone would pay the debt of the poor. Almost immediately a messenger came with a gift of fifty silver pieces. On his last day, when the lamps were being lighted for Vespers, after having said nothing for a long time, he stretched out his hands and said, "I have prepared a lamp for my Christ."

* * *

John Fisher
BISHOP AND MARTYR (1469–1535)

John Fisher is usually associated with Erasmus, Thomas More (June 22), and other Renaissance humanists. His life, therefore, did not have the external simplicity found in the lives of some saints. Rather, he was a man of learning, associated with the intellectuals and political leaders of his day. He was interested in the contemporary culture and eventually became chancellor at Cambridge. He had been made a bishop at thirty-five, and one of his interests was raising the standard of preaching in England. Fisher himself was an accomplished preacher and writer. His sermons on the penitential psalms were reprinted seven times before his death. With the coming of Lutheranism, he was drawn into controversy. His eight books against heresy gave him a leading position among European theologians.

In 1521 he was asked to study the problem of Henry VIII's marriage. He incurred Henry's anger by defending the validity of the king's marriage to Catherine of Aragon and later by rejecting Henry's claim to be the supreme head of the Church in England.

In an attempt to be rid of him, Henry first had him accused of not reporting all the "revelations" of the nun of Kent, Elizabeth Barton. John was summoned, in feeble health, to take the oath to the new Act of Succession. He and Thomas More refused because the act presumed the legality of Henry's divorce and his claim to be head of the English Church. They were sent to the Tower of London, where Fisher remained fourteen months without trial. They were finally sentenced to life imprisonment and loss of goods.

When the two were called to further interrogations, they remained silent. Fisher was tricked, on the supposition he was speaking privately as a priest, and declared again that the king was not supreme head of the Church. The king, further angered that the pope had made John Fisher a cardinal, had him brought to trial on the charge of high treason. He was condemned and executed, his body left to lie all day on the scaffold and his head hung on London Bridge. More was executed two weeks later.

COMMENT: Today many questions are raised about Christians' and priests' active involvement in social issues. John Fisher remained faithful to his calling as a bishop. He strongly upheld the teachings of the Church; the very cause of his martyrdom was his loyalty to Rome. He was involved in the cultural enrichment circles as well as in the political struggles of his time. This involvement caused him to question the moral conduct of the leadership of his country. "The Church has the right, indeed the duty, to proclaim justice on the social, national and international level, and to denounce instances of injustice, when the fundamental rights of man and his very salvation demand it" (*Justice in the World*, 1971 World Synod of Bishops).

QUOTE: Erasmus said of John Fisher: "He is the one man at this time who is incomparable for uprightness of life, for learning, and for greatness of soul."

• • •

JUNE 22 + OPTIONAL
Thomas More
MARTYR (1478–1535)

His belief that no lay ruler has jurisdiction over the Church of Christ cost Thomas More his life.

Beheaded on Tower Hill, London, July 6, 1535, he steadfastly refused to approve Henry VIII's divorce and remarriage and the establishment of the Church of England.

Described as "a man for all seasons," More was a literary scholar, eminent lawyer, gentleman, father of four children, and chancellor of England. An intensely spiritual man, he would not support the king's divorce from Catherine of Aragon and marriage to Anne Boleyn. Nor would he acknowledge Henry as supreme head of the Church in England, breaking with Rome and denying the pope as head.

More was committed to the Tower of London to await trial for treason: not swearing to the Act of Succession and the Oath of Supremacy. Upon conviction, More declared that he had all the councils of Christendom and not just the council of one realm to support him in the decision of his conscience.

COMMENT: Four hundred years later, in 1935, Thomas More was canonized a saint of God. Few saints are more relevant to our time. In fact, in 2000, Blessed John Paul II named him patron of political leaders. The supreme diplomat and counselor, Thomas More did not compromise his own moral values in order to please the king, knowing that true allegiance to authority is not blind acceptance of everything that authority wants. Henry himself realized this and tried desperately to win his chancellor to his side because he knew More was a man whose approval counted, a man whose personal integrity no one questioned. But when Thomas resigned as chancellor, unable to approve the two matters that meant most to Henry, the king felt he had to get rid of Thomas.

STORY: When the executioner offered to blindfold him, More said that he would do this himself. But after he had stretched his head over the low block—it was merely a log of wood—he made a signal to the man to wait a moment. Then he made his last joke: His beard was lying on the block and he would like to remove it. At least that had committed no treason. The heavy axe went slowly up, hung a moment in the air and fell.

● ● ●

JUNE 24 + SOLEMNITY
Birth of John the Baptist

Jesus called John the greatest of all those who had preceded him: "I tell you, among those born of women, no one is greater than John…." But John would have agreed completely with what Jesus added: "Yet the least in the kingdom of God is greater than he" (Luke 7:28).

John spent his time in the desert, an ascetic. He began to announce the coming of the kingdom and to call everyone to a fundamental reformation of life.

His purpose was to prepare the way for Jesus. His baptism, he said, was for repentance. But One would come who would baptize with the Holy Spirit and fire. John is not worthy even to carry his sandals. His attitude toward Jesus was: "He must increase; I must decrease" (John 3:30).

John was humbled to find among the crowd of sinners who came to be baptized the one whom he already knew to be the Messiah. "I need to be baptized by you" (Matthew 3:14b). But Jesus insisted, "Allow it now, for thus it is fitting for us to fulfill all righteousness" (Matthew 3:15b). Jesus, true and humble human as well as eternal God, was eager to do what was required of any good Jew. John thus publicly entered the community of those awaiting the Messiah. But making himself part of that community, he made it truly messianic.

The greatness of John, his pivotal place in the history of salvation, is seen in the great emphasis Luke gives to the announcement of his birth and the event itself—both made prominently parallel to the same occurrences in the life of Jesus. John attracted countless people ("all Judea") to the banks of the Jordan, and it occurred to some people that he might be the Messiah. But he constantly deferred to Jesus, even to sending away some of his followers to become the first disciples of Jesus.

Perhaps John's idea of the coming of the kingdom of God was not being perfectly fulfilled in the public ministry of Jesus. For whatever reason, he sent his disciples (when he was in prison) to ask Jesus if he was the Messiah. Jesus's answer showed that the Messiah was to be a figure like that of the Suffering Servant in Isaiah (chapters forty-nine through fifty-three). John himself would share in the pattern of messianic suffering, losing his life to the revenge of Herodias.

COMMENT: John challenges us Christians to the fundamental attitude of Christianity—total dependence on the Father, in Christ. Except for the Mother of God, no one had a higher function in the unfolding of salvation. Yet the least in the kingdom, Jesus said, is greater than he, for the pure gift that the Father gives. The attractiveness as well as the austerity of John, his fierce courage in denouncing evil—all stem from his fundamental and total placing of his life within the will of God.

QUOTE: "And this is not something which was only true once, long ago in the past. It is always true, because the repentance that he preached always remains the way into the kingdom that he announced. He is not a figure that we can forget now that Jesus, the true light, has appeared. John is always relevant because he calls for a preparation that all people need to make. Hence every year there are four weeks in the life of the Church in which it listens to the voice of the Baptist. These are the weeks of Advent" (*A New Catechism: Catholic Faith for Adults*).

• • •

Cyril of Alexandria
BISHOP AND DOCTOR (376?–444)

Saints are not born with halos around their heads. Cyril, recognized as a great teacher of the Church, began his career as archbishop of Alexandria, Egypt, with impulsive, often violent, actions. He pillaged and closed the churches of the Novatian heretics (who required those who denied the faith to be rebaptized), participated in the deposing of St. John Chrysostom (September 13), and confiscated Jewish property, expelling the Jews from Alexandria in retaliation for their attacks on Christians.

Cyril opposed the heresy of Nestorius, who taught that in Christ there were two persons, one human and one divine.

The controversy centered around the two natures in Christ. Nestorius would not agree to the title "God-bearer" for Mary. He preferred "Christ-bearer," saying there are two distinct persons in Christ (divine and human) joined only by a moral union. He said Mary was not the mother of God but only of the man Christ, whose humanity was only a temple of God. Nestorianism implied that the humanity of Christ was a mere disguise.

Presiding as the pope's representative at the Council of Ephesus (431), Cyril condemned Nestorianism and proclaimed Mary truly the "God-bearer" (the mother of the one Person who is truly God and truly human). In the confusion that followed, Cyril was deposed and imprisoned for three months, after which he was welcomed back to Alexandria as a second Athanasius (the champion against Arianism).

Besides needing to soften some of his opposition to those who had sided with Nestorius, Cyril had difficulties with some of his own allies, who thought he had gone too far, sacrificing not only language but orthodoxy. Until his death, his policy of moderation kept his extreme partisans under control. On his deathbed, despite pressure, he refused to condemn the teacher of Nestorius, who taught that in Christ there were two persons, one divine and one human.

COMMENT: Lives of the saints are valuable not only for the virtue they reveal but also for the less admirable qualities that also appear. Holiness is a gift of God to us as human beings. Life is a process. We respond to God's gift, but sometimes with a lot of zigzagging. If Cyril had been more patient and diplomatic, the Nestorian church might not have risen and maintained power so long. But even saints must grow out of immaturity, narrowness, and selfishness. It is because they—and we—do grow, that we are truly saints, persons who live the life of God.

QUOTE: Cyril's theme: "Only if it is one and the same Christ who is consubstantial with the Father and with men can he save us, for the meeting ground between God and man is the flesh of Christ. Only if this is God's own flesh can man come into contact with Christ's divinity through his humanity. Because of our kinship with the Word made flesh we are sons of God. The Eucharist consummates our kinship with the word, our communion with the Father, our sharing in the divine nature—there is very real contact between our body and that of the Word" (*New Catholic Encyclopedia*).

• • •

JUNE 28 + MEMORIAL

Irenaeus
BISHOP AND MARTYR (130?–220)

The Church is fortunate that Irenaeus was involved in many of its controversies in the second century. He was a student, well trained, no doubt, with great patience in investigating, tremendously protective of apostolic teaching, but prompted more by a desire to win over his opponents than to prove them in error.

As bishop of Lyons he was especially concerned with the Gnostics, who took their name from the Greek word for knowledge. Claiming access to secret knowledge imparted by Jesus to only a few disciples, their teaching was attracting and confusing many Christians. After thoroughly investigating the various Gnostic sects and their "secret," Irenaeus showed to what logical conclusions their tenets led. These he contrasted with the teaching of the apostles and the text of Holy Scripture, giving us, in five books, a system of theology of great importance to subsequent times. Moreover, his work, widely used and translated into Latin and Armenian, gradually ended the influence of the Gnostics.

The circumstances and details about his death, like those of his birth and early life in Asia Minor, are not at all clear.

COMMENT: A deep and genuine concern for other people will remind us that the discovery of truth is not to be a victory for some and a defeat for others. Unless all can claim a share in that victory, truth itself will continue to be rejected by the losers because it will be regarded as inseparable from the yoke of defeat. And so, confrontation and controversy might yield to a genuine united search for God's truth and how it can best be served.

STORY: A group of Christians in Asia Minor had been excommunicated by Pope Victor I because of their refusal to accept the Western Church's date for celebrating Easter. Irenaeus, the "lover of peace" as his name indicates, interceded with the pope to lift the ban, suggesting that this was not an essential matter and that these people were merely following an old tradition, one that men such as St. Polycarp (February 23) and Pope Anicetus had not seen as divisive. The pope responded favorably, and the rift was healed. Some one hundred years later, the Western practice was voluntarily adopted.

● ● ●

JUNE 29 + SOLEMNITY

Peter and Paul

APOSTLES

Peter (d. 64?). St. Mark ends the first half of his Gospel with a triumphant climax. He has recorded doubt, misunderstanding, and the opposition of many to Jesus. Now Peter makes his great confession of faith: "You are the Messiah" (Mark 8:29b).

It was one of the many glorious moments in Peter's life, beginning with the day he was called from his nets along the Sea of Galilee to become a fisher of men for Jesus.

The New Testament clearly shows Peter as the leader of the apostles, chosen by Jesus to have a special relationship with him. With James and John, Peter was privileged to witness the Transfiguration, the raising of a dead child to life, and the agony in Gethsemane. His mother-in-law was cured by Jesus. He was sent with John to prepare for the last Passover before Jesus's death. His name is first on every list of apostles.

And to Peter alone did Jesus say, "Blessed are you, Simon son of Jonah. For flesh and blood has not revealed this to you, but my heavenly Father. And so I say to you, you are Peter, and upon this rock I will build my church, and the gates of the netherworld shall not prevail against it. I will give you the keys to the kingdom of heaven. Whatever you bind on earth shall be bound in heaven; and whatever you loose on earth shall be loosed in heaven" (Matthew 16:17b–19).

But the Gospels prove their own trustworthiness by the unflattering details they include about Peter. He clearly had no public-relations person. It is a great comfort for ordinary mortals to know that Peter also has his human weakness, even in the presence of Jesus.

He generously gave up all things, yet he can ask in childish self-regard, "What are we going to get for all this?" (see Matthew 19:27). He receives the full force of Christ's anger when he objects to the idea of a suffering Messiah: "Get behind me, Satan! You are an obstacle to me. You are thinking not as God does, but as human beings do" (Matthew 16:23b).

Peter is willing to accept Jesus's doctrine of forgiveness, but suggests a limit of seven times. He walks on the water in faith, but sinks in doubt. He refuses to let Jesus wash his feet, and then wants his whole body cleansed. He swears at the Last Supper that he will never deny Jesus, and then swears to a servant maid that he has never known the man. He loyally resists the first attempt to arrest Jesus by cutting off Malchus's ear, but in the end he runs away with the others. Because of the depth of Peter's sorrow, Jesus looks on him and forgives him, and Peter goes away to shed bitter tears. The Risen Jesus tells Peter to feed his lambs and his sheep (John 21:15–17).

COMMENT: We would probably go to confession to Peter sooner than to any of the other apostles. He is perhaps a more striking example of the simple fact of holiness. Jesus says to us as he said, in effect, to Peter: "It is not you who have chosen me, but I who have chosen you. Peter, it is not human wisdom that makes it possible for you to believe, but my Father's revelation. I, not you, build my Church."

QUOTE: "So humble yourselves under the mighty hand of God, that he may exalt you in due time. Cast all your worries upon him because he cares for you.

"Be sober and vigilant. Your opponent the devil is prowling around like a roaring lion looking for [someone] to devour. Resist him, steadfast in faith, knowing that your fellow believers throughout the world undergo the same sufferings. The God of all grace who called you to his eternal glory through Christ will himself restore, confirm, strengthen, and establish you after you have suffered a little" (1 Peter 5:6–10).

Paul (d. 64?). If the most well-known preacher today suddenly began preaching that the United States should adopt Marxism and not rely on the Constitution, the angry reaction would help us understand Paul's life when he started preaching that Christ alone can save us. He had been the strictest of Pharisees, the most legalistic of Mosaic lawyers. Now he suddenly appears to other Jews as a heretical welcomer of Gentiles, a traitor, and an apostate.

Paul's central conviction was simple and absolute: Only God can save humanity. No human effort—even the most scrupulous observance of the Law—can create a human good that we can bring to God as reparation for sin and payment for grace. To be saved from themselves, from sin, from the devil and from death, people must open themselves completely to the saving power of Jesus.

Paul never lost his love for his Jewish family, though he carried on a lifelong debate with them about the uselessness of the Law without Christ. He reminded the Gentiles that they were grafted onto the parent stock of the Jews, who were still God's chosen people, the children of the promise.

COMMENT: Paul's experience of the Risen Jesus on the road to Damascus was the driving force that made him one of the most zealous, dynamic, and courageous ambassadors of Christ the Church has ever had. But persecution, humiliation, and weakness became his day-by-day carrying of the cross, material for further transformation. The dying Christ was in him; the living Christ was his life.

QUOTE: Paul talks about his sufferings: "Five times at the hands of the Jews I received forty lashes minus one. Three times I was beaten with rods, once I was stoned, three times I was shipwrecked, I passed a night and a day on the deep; on frequent journeys, in dangers from rivers, dangers from robbers, dangers from my own race, dangers from Gentiles, dangers in the city, dangers in the wilderness, dangers at sea, dangers among false brothers; in toil and hardship, through many sleepless nights, through hunger and thirst, through frequent fastings, through cold and exposure.... I am content with weaknesses, insults, hardships, persecutions, and constraints, for the sake of Christ; for when I am weak, then I am strong" (2 Corinthians 11:24–27; 12:10).

• • •

JUNE 30 + OPTIONAL
First Martyrs of the Church of Rome
(A.D. 64)

There were Christians in Rome within a dozen or so years after the death of Jesus, though they were not the converts of the "Apostle of the Gentiles" (see Romans 15:20). Paul had not yet visited them at the time he wrote his great letter in A.D. 57–58.

There was a large Jewish population in Rome. Probably as a result of controversy between Jews and Jewish Christians, the Emperor Claudius expelled all Jews from Rome in A.D. 49–50. The historian Suetonius says that the expulsion was due to disturbances in the city "caused by the certain Chrestus" [Christ]. Perhaps many came back after Claudius's death in A.D.

54. Paul's letter was addressed to a church with members from Jewish and Gentile backgrounds.

In July of A.D. 64, more than half of Rome was destroyed by fire. Rumor blamed the tragedy on Nero, who wanted to enlarge his palace. He shifted the blame by accusing the Christians. According to the historian Tacitus, many Christians were put to death because of their "hatred of the human race." Peter and Paul were probably among the victims.

Threatened by an army revolt and condemned to death by the senate, Nero committed suicide in A.D. 68 at the age of thirty-one.

COMMENT: Wherever the Good News of Jesus was preached, it met the same opposition as Jesus did, and many of those who began to follow him shared his suffering and death. But no human force could stop the power of the Spirit unleashed upon the world. The blood of the martyrs has always been, and will always be, the seed of Christianity.

QUOTE: Pope Clement I, third successor of St. Peter, writes: "It was through envy and jealousy that the greatest and most upright pillars of the Church were persecuted and struggled unto death.... First of all, Peter, who because of unreasonable jealousy suffered not merely once or twice but many times, and, having thus given his witness, went to the place of glory that he deserved. It was through jealousy and conflict that Paul showed the way to the prize for perseverance. He was put in chains seven times, sent into exile, and stoned; a herald both in the east and the west, he achieved a noble fame by his faith....

"Around these men with their holy lives there are gathered a great throng of the elect, who, though victims of jealousy, gave us the finest example of endurance in the midst of many indignities and tortures. Through jealousy women were tormented, like Dirce or the daughters of Danaus, suffering terrible and unholy acts of violence. But they courageously finished the course of faith and despite their bodily weakness won a noble prize."

• • •

JULY 1 + OPTIONAL (U.S.A.)
Blessed Junipero Serra
PRIEST (1713–1784)

In 1776, when the American Revolution was beginning in the East, another part of the future United States was being born in California. That year a gray-robed Franciscan founded Mission San Juan Capistrano, now famous for its annually returning swallows. San Juan was the seventh of nine missions established under the direction of this indomitable Spaniard.

Born in Spain's island of Mallorca, Serra entered the Franciscan Order, taking the name of St. Francis's childlike companion, Brother Juniper. Until he was thirty-five, he spent most of his time in the classroom—first as a student of theology and then as a professor. He also became famous for his preaching. Suddenly he gave it all up and followed the yearning that had begun years before when he heard about the missionary work of St. Francis Solanus in South America. Junipero's desire was to convert native peoples in the New World.

Arriving by ship at Vera Cruz, Mexico, he and a companion walked the 250 miles to Mexico City. On the way Junipero's left leg became infected by an insect bite and would remain a cross—sometimes life-threatening—the rest of his life. For eighteen years he worked in central Mexico and in the Baja Peninsula. He became president of the missions there.

Enter politics: the threat of a Russian invasion south from Alaska. Charles III of Spain ordered an expedition to beat Russia to the territory. So the last two *conquistadores*—one military, one spiritual—began their quest. José de Galvez persuaded Junipero to set out with him for present-day Monterey, California. The first mission founded after the nine-hundred-mile journey north was San Diego (1769). That year a shortage of food almost canceled the expedition. Vowing to stay with the local people, Junipero and another friar began a novena in preparation for St. Joseph's Day, March 19, the scheduled day of departure. On that day, the relief ship arrived.

Other missions followed: Monterey/Carmel (1770); San Antonio and San Gabriel (1771); San Luís Obispo (1772); San Francisco and San Juan Capistrano (1776); Santa Clara (1777); and San Buenaventura (1782). Twelve more were founded after Serra's death.

Junipero made the long trip to Mexico City to settle great differences with the military commander. He arrived at the point of death. The outcome was substantially what Junipero sought: the famous "Regulation" protecting the Indians and the missions. It was the basis for the first significant legislation in California, a "Bill of Rights" for Native Americans.

Because the Native Americans were living a subhuman life (from the Spanish point of view), the friars were made their legal guardians. The Native Americans were kept at the mission after baptism lest they be "corrupted" in their former haunts—a move that many today recognize as unjust.

Junipero's missionary life was a long battle with cold and hunger, with unsympathetic military commanders, and even with danger of death from non-Christian native peoples. Through it all, his unquenchable zeal was fed by prayer each night, often from midnight until dawn. He baptized over six thousand people and confirmed five thousand. His travels would have circled the globe. He brought the Native Americans not only the gift of faith but also a decent standard of living. He won their love, as witnessed especially by their grief at his death. He is buried at Mission San Carlo Borromeo, Carmel, California, and was beatified in 1988.

COMMENT: The word that best describes Junipero is *zeal*. It was a spirit that came from his deep prayer and dauntless will. "Always forward, never back" was his motto. His work bore fruit for fifty years after his death as the rest of the missions were founded in a kind of Christian communal living by the Native Americans. When both Mexican and American greed caused the secularization of the missions, the Chumash people went back to what they had been—God again writing straight with crooked lines.

QUOTE: During his homily at Serra's beatification, Blessed John Paul II said: "Relying on the divine power of the message he proclaimed, Fr. Serra led the native peoples to Christ. He was well aware of their heroic virtues—as exemplified in the life of [Saint] Kateri Tekakwitha [July 14]—and he sought to further their authentic human development on the basis of their newfound faith as persons created and redeemed by God. He also had to admonish the powerful, in the spirit of our second reading from James, not to abuse and exploit the poor and the weak."

• • •

JULY 3 + FEAST

Thomas
APOSTLE

Poor Thomas! He made one remark and has been branded as "Doubting Thomas" ever since. But if he doubted, he also believed. He made what is certainly the most explicit statement of faith in the New Testament: "My Lord and my God!" (see John 20:24–28) and, in so expressing his faith, gave Christians a prayer that will be said till the end of time. He also occasioned a compliment from Jesus to all later Christians: "Have you come to believe because you have seen me? Blessed are those who have not seen and have believed" (John 20:29).

Thomas should be equally well known for his courage. Perhaps what he said was impetuous—since he ran, like the rest, at the showdown—but he can scarcely have been insincere when he expressed his willingness to die with Jesus. The occasion was when Jesus proposed to go to Bethany after Lazarus had died. Since Bethany was near Jerusalem, this meant walking into the very midst of his enemies and to almost certain death. Realizing this, Thomas said to the other apostles, "Let us also go to die with him" (John 11:16b).

COMMENT: Thomas shares the lot of Peter the impetuous, James and John, the "sons of thunder," Philip and his foolish request to see the Father—indeed all the apostles in their weakness and lack of understanding. We must not exaggerate these facts, however, for Christ did not pick worthless men. But their human weakness again points out the fact that holiness is a gift of God, not a human creation. It is given to ordinary men and women with weaknesses. It is God who gradually transforms the weaknesses into the image of Christ, the courageous, trusting, and loving one.

QUOTE: "Prompted by the Holy Spirit, the Church must walk the same road which Christ walked: a road of poverty and obedience, of service and self-sacrifice to the death.... For thus did all the apostles walk in hope. On behalf of Christ's Body, which is the Church, they supplied what was wanting in the sufferings of Christ by their own trials and sufferings [cf. Colossians 1:24]" (Decree on the Church's Missionary Activity, 5).

● ● ●

JULY 5 + OPTIONAL
Anthony Zaccaria
PRIEST (1502–1539)

At the same time that Martin Luther was attacking abuses in the Church, a reformation within the Church was already being attempted. Among the early movers of the Counter-Reformation was Anthony Zaccaria. His mother became a widow at eighteen and devoted herself to the spiritual education of her son. He received a medical doctorate at twenty-two and, while working among the poor of his native Cremona in Italy, was attracted to the religious apostolate. He renounced his rights to any future inheritance, worked as a catechist, and was ordained a priest at the age of twenty-six. Called to Milan in a few years, he laid the foundations of two religious congregations, one for men and one for women, plus an association of married couples. Their aim was the reform of the decadent society of their day, beginning with the clergy, religious, and laypeople.

Greatly inspired by St. Paul (his congregation is named the Barnabites, after the companion of that saint), Anthony preached with great vigor in church and street, conducted popular missions, and was not ashamed of doing public penance.

He encouraged such innovations as the collaboration of the laity in the apostolate, frequent Communion, the Forty Hours devotion, and the ringing of church bells at 3:00 P.M. on Fridays.

His holiness moved many to reform their lives but, as with all saints, it also moved many to oppose him. Twice his community had to undergo official religious investigation, and twice it was exonerated.

While on a mission of peace, he became seriously ill and was brought home for a visit to his mother. He died at Cremona at the age of thirty-six.

COMMENT: The austerity of Anthony's spirituality and the Pauline ardor of his preaching would probably alienate many people today. When even some psychiatrists complain that people lack a sense of sin, we might acknowledge that not all evil is explained by emotional disorder, subconscious and unconscious drives, and parental influence. The old-time "hell and damnation" mission sermons have given way to positive, encouraging, biblical homilies. We do indeed need assurance of forgiveness and relief from existential anxiety and future shock. But we still need prophets to stand up and tell us, "If we say 'We are without sin,' we deceive ourselves and the truth is not in us" (1 John 1:8).

QUOTE: "I charge you in the presence of God and of Christ Jesus, who will judge the living and the dead, and by his appearing and his kingly power: proclaim the word; be persistent whether it is convenient or inconvenient; convince, reprimand, encourage through all patience and teaching. For the time will come when people will not tolerate sound doctrine but, following their own desires and insatiable curiosity, will accumulate teachers and will stop listening to the truth and will be diverted to myths" (2 Timothy 4:1–4).

• • •

JULY 5 + OPTIONAL (U.S.A.)

Elizabeth of Portugal
WIFE AND MOTHER (1271–1336)

Elizabeth is usually depicted in royal garb with a dove or an olive branch. At her birth in 1271, her father, Pedro III, future king of Aragon, was reconciled with his father, James, the reigning monarch. This proved to be a portent of things to come. Under the healthful influences surrounding her early years, she quickly learned self-discipline and acquired a taste for spirituality. Thus fortunately prepared, she was able to meet the challenge when, at the age of twelve, she was given in marriage to Denis, king of Portugal. She was able to establish for herself a pattern of life conducive to growth in God's love, not merely through her exercises of piety, including daily Mass, but also through her exercise of charity, by which she was able to befriend and help pilgrims, strangers, the sick, the poor—in a word, all those whose need came to her notice. At the same time she remained devoted to her husband, whose infidelity to her was a scandal to the kingdom.

He, too, was the object of many of her peace endeavors. She long sought peace for him with God, and was finally rewarded when he gave up his life of sin. She repeatedly sought and effected peace between the king and their rebellious son, Alfonso, who thought that he was passed over to favor the king's illegitimate children. She acted as peacemaker in the struggle between Ferdinand, king of Aragon, and his cousin James, who claimed the crown. And finally from Coimbra, where she had retired as a Franciscan tertiary to the monastery of the Poor Clares after the death of her husband, she set out and was able to bring about a lasting peace between her son Alfonso, now king of Portugal, and his son-in-law, the king of Castile.

COMMENT: The work of promoting peace is anything but a calm and quiet endeavor. It takes a clear mind, a steady spirit, and a brave soul to intervene between people whose emotions are so aroused that they are ready to destroy one another. This was all the more true of a woman in the early fourteenth century. But Elizabeth had a deep and sincere love and sympathy for people, almost a total lack of concern for herself, and an abiding confidence in God. These were the tools of her success.

STORY: Elizabeth was not well enough to undertake her final peacemaking journey, made all the more difficult by the oppressive heat of the season. She would not, however, permit herself to be dissuaded from it. She answered that there was no better way to give of her life and her health than by averting the miseries and destruction of war. By the time she had successfully brought about peace, she was so sick that death was imminent. After her death in 1336, her body was returned to the monastery at Coimbra for burial.

●　●　●

JULY 6 + OPTIONAL
Maria Goretti
VIRGIN AND MARTYR (1890–1902)

One of the largest crowds ever assembled for a canonization—250,000—symbolized the reaction of millions touched by the simple story of Maria Goretti.

She was the daughter of a poor Italian tenant farmer, had no chance to go to school, and never learned to read or write. When she made her First Communion not long before her death, she was one of the larger and somewhat backward members of the class.

On a hot afternoon in July, Maria was sitting at the top of the stairs of her house, mending a shirt. She was not quite twelve years old, but physically mature. A cart stopped outside, and a neighbor, Alessandro Serenelli, eighteen years old, ran up the stairs. He seized her and pulled her into a bedroom. She struggled and tried to call for help, gasping that she would be killed rather than submit. "No, God does not wish it. It is a sin. You would go to hell for it." Alessandro began striking at her blindly with a long dagger.

She was taken to a hospital. Her last hours were marked by the usual simple compassion of the good—concern about where her mother would sleep, forgiveness of her murderer (she had been in fear of him, but did not say anything lest she cause trouble to his family), and her devout welcoming of Viaticum, her last Holy Communion. She died about twenty-four hours after the attack.

Her murderer was sentenced to thirty years in prison. For a long time he was unrepentant and surly. One night he had a dream or vision of Maria, gathering flowers and offering them to him. His life changed. When he was released after twenty-seven years, his first act was to go to beg the forgiveness of Maria's mother.

Devotion to the young martyr grew, miracles were worked, and in less than half a century she was canonized. At her beatification in 1947, her mother (then eighty-two), two sisters, and a brother appeared with Pope Pius XII on the balcony of St. Peter's. Three years later, at her canonization, a sixty-six-year-old Alessandro Serenelli knelt among the quarter-million and cried tears of joy.

COMMENT: Maria may have had trouble with learning her catechism, but she had no trouble with faith. God's will was holiness, decency, respect for one's body, absolute obedience, total trust. In a complex world, her faith was simple: It is a privilege to be loved by God and to love him—at any cost. As the virtue of chastity dies the death of a thousand qualifications, she is a breath of sweet fresh air.

QUOTE: "Even if she had not been a martyr, she would still have been a saint, so holy was her everyday life" (Cardinal Salotti).

• • •

JULY 9 + OPTIONAL

Augustine Zhao Rong and Companions
PRIEST AND MARTYR; MARTYRS
(17TH–20TH CENTURIES)

Christianity arrived in China by way of Syria in the fifth century A.D. Depending on China's relations with the outside world, Christianity over the centuries was free to grow or was forced to operate secretly.

The 120 martyrs remembered on this day died between 1648 and 1930. Most of them (eighty-seven) were born in China and were children, parents, catechists, or laborers, ranging from nine years of age to seventy-two. This group includes four Chinese diocesan priests.

The thirty-three foreign-born martyrs were mostly priests or women religious, especially from the Order of Preachers, the Paris Foreign Mission Society, the Friars Minor, Jesuits, Salesians, and Franciscan Missionaries of Mary.

Augustine Zhao Rong was a Chinese soldier who accompanied Bishop John Gabriel Taurin Dufresse (of the Paris Foreign Mission Society) to his martyrdom in Beijing. Augustine was baptized and not long after was ordained a diocesan priest. He was martyred in 1815.

Beatified in groups at various times, these 120 martyrs were canonized in Rome on October 1, 2000.

COMMENT: The People's Republic of China and the Roman Catholic Church each have well over a billion members, but there are only twelve million Catholics in China. The reasons for the relatively small number of Catholics are better explained by historical conflicts than by a wholesale rejection of the Good News of Jesus Christ. The Chinese-born martyrs honored by today's feast were regarded by their persecutors as dangerous because they were considered allies of enemy Catholic countries. The martyrs born outside China often tried to distance themselves from European political struggles relating to China, but their persecutors saw them as Westerners and therefore, by definition, anti-Chinese.

The Good News of Jesus Christ is intended to benefit all peoples; today's martyrs knew that. May twenty-first–century Christians live in such a way that Chinese women and men will be attracted to hearing that Good News and embracing it.

QUOTE: A year after these martyrs were canonized, Blessed John Paul II addressed a group of Chinese and Western scholars, gathered in Rome for a symposium honoring the four hundredth anniversary of the arrival in Beijing of Matteo Ricci, a Jesuit scholar and Chinese intellectual.

After noting the positive contributions that Christianity had made to China, especially in health care and education, Pope John Paul II continued: "History, however, reminds us of the unfortunate fact that the work of members of the Church in China was not always without error, the bitter fruit of their personal limitations and of the limits of their action. Moreover, their action was often conditioned by difficult situations connected with complex historical events and conflicting political interests. Nor were theological disputes lacking, which caused bad feelings and created serious difficulties in preaching the Gospel....

"I feel deep sadness for these errors and limits of the past, and I regret that in many people these failings may have given the impression of a lack of respect and esteem for the Chinese people on the part of the Catholic Church, making them feel that the Church was motivated by feelings of hostility toward China. For all of this I ask the forgiveness and understanding of those who may have felt hurt in some way by such actions on the part of Christians."

* * *

JULY 11 + MEMORIAL

Benedict

ABBOT (480?–543)

It is unfortunate that no contemporary biography was written of a man who has exercised the greatest influence on monasticism in the West. Benedict is well recognized in the later *Dialogues* of St. Gregory (September 3), but these are sketches to illustrate miraculous elements of his career.

Benedict was born of a distinguished family in central Italy, studied at Rome, and, early in life, was drawn to the monastic life. At first he became a hermit, leaving a depressing world—with pagan armies on the march, the Church torn by schism, people suffering from war, and morality at a low ebb.

He soon realized that he could not live a hidden life in a small town any better than in a large city, so he withdrew to a cave high in the mountains for three years. Some monks chose him as their leader for a while, but found his strictness not to their taste. Still, the shift from hermit to community life had begun for him. He had an idea of gathering various families of monks into one "grand monastery" to give them the benefit of unity, fraternity, permanent worship in one house. Finally he began to build what was to become one of the most famous monasteries in the world—Monte Cassino, commanding three narrow valleys running toward the mountains north of Naples.

The Rule that he gradually developed prescribed a life of liturgical prayer, study, manual labor, and living together in community under a common father (abbot). Benedictine asceticism is known for its moderation, and Benedictine charity has always shown concern for the people in the surrounding countryside. In the course of the Middle Ages, all monasticism in the West was gradually brought under the Rule of St. Benedict.

Today the Benedictine family is represented by two branches: the Benedictine Federation and the Cistercians.

The feast of Benedict's sister, Scholastica, is celebrated February 10.

COMMENT: The Church has been blessed through Benedictine devotion to the liturgy, not only in its actual celebration with rich and proper ceremony in the great abbeys, but also through the scholarly studies of many of its members. Liturgy is sometimes confused with guitars or choirs, Latin or Bach. We should be grateful to those who both preserve and adapt the genuine tradition of worship in the Church.

QUOTE: "Rightly, then, the liturgy is considered as an exercise of the priestly office of Jesus Christ. In the liturgy the sanctification of man is manifested by signs perceptible to the senses...; in the liturgy full public worship is performed by the Mystical Body of Jesus Christ, that is, by the Head and his members.

"From this it follows that every liturgical celebration, because it is an action of Christ the priest and of his Body the Church, is a sacred action, surpassing all others" (Constitution on the Sacred Liturgy, 7).

●   ●   ●

JULY 13 + OPTIONAL
Henry
KING (972–1024)

As German king and Holy Roman Emperor, Henry was a practical man of affairs. He was energetic in consolidating his rule. He crushed rebellions and feuds. On all sides he had to deal with drawn-out disputes so as to protect his frontiers. This involved him in a number of battles, especially in the south in

Italy. He also helped Pope Benedict VIII quell disturbances in Rome. Always his ultimate purpose was to establish a stable peace in Europe.

According to eleventh-century custom, Henry took advantage of his position and appointed as bishops men loyal to him. In his case, however, he avoided the pitfalls of this practice and actually fostered the reform of ecclesiastical and monastic life. He was canonized in 1146.

COMMENT: All in all, this saint was a man of his times. From our standpoint, he may have been too quick to do battle and too ready to use power to accomplish reforms. But, granted such limitations, he shows that holiness is possible in a busy secular life. It is in doing our job that we become saints.

QUOTE: "We deem it opportune to remind our children of their duty to take an active part in public life and to contribute toward the attainment of the common good of the entire human family as well as to that of their own political community. They should endeavor, therefore, in the light of their Christian faith and led by love, to insure that the various institutions— whether economic, social, cultural, or political in purpose—should be such as not to create obstacles, but rather to facilitate or render less arduous man's perfecting of himself in both the natural order and the supernatural.... Every believer in this world of ours must be a spark of light, a center of love, a vivifying leaven amidst his fellow men. And he will be this all the more perfectly, the more closely he lives in communion with God in the intimacy of his own soul" (Blessed Pope John XXIII, *Peace on Earth*, 146, 164).

• • •

JULY 14 + MEMORIAL (U.S.A.)
Kateri Tekakwitha
VIRGIN (1656–1680)

The blood of the martyrs is the seed of the Church. Nine years after Jesuits Isaac Jogues and Jean de Brébeuf (October 19) were killed by Iroquois warriors, a baby girl was born near the place of their martyrdom, Auriesville, New York. Her mother was a Christian Algonquin, taken captive by the Iroquois and given as wife to the chief of the Mohawk clan, the boldest and fiercest of the Five Nations. When she was four, Kateri lost her parents and little brother in a smallpox epidemic that left her disfigured and half blind. She was adopted by an uncle, who succeeded her father as chief. He hated the coming of the Blackrobes (Jesuit missionaries), but could do nothing to them because a peace treaty with the French required their presence in villages with Christian captives. She was moved by the words of three Blackrobes who lodged with her uncle, but fear of him kept her from seeking instruction. She refused to marry a Mohawk man and at nineteen finally had the courage to take the step of converting. She was baptized with the name Kateri (Catherine) on Easter Sunday.

Now she would be treated as a slave. Because she would not work on Sunday, she received no food that day. Her life in grace grew rapidly. She told a missionary that she often meditated on the great dignity of being baptized. She was powerfully moved by God's love for human beings and saw the dignity of each of her people. She was always in danger, for her conversion and holy life created great opposition. On the advice of a priest, she stole away one night and began a two-hundred-mile walking journey to a Christian Native American village at Sault St. Louis, near Montreal.

For three years she grew in holiness under the direction of a priest and an older Iroquois woman, giving herself totally to God in long hours of prayer, in charity, and in strenuous penance. At twenty-three, she took a vow of virginity, an unprecedented act for a Native American woman, whose future depended on being married. She found a place in the woods where she could pray an hour a day—and was accused of meeting a man there! Her dedication to virginity was instinctive: She did not know about religious life for women until she visited Montreal. Inspired by this, she and two friends wanted to start a community, but the local priest dissuaded her. She humbly accepted an "ordinary" life. She practiced severe fasting as penance for the conversion of her nation. She died the afternoon before Holy Thursday. Witnesses said her emaciated face changed color and became like that of a healthy child. The lines of suffering, even the pockmarks, disappeared, and the hint of a smile came upon her lips. She was beatified in 1980 and canonized in 2012.

COMMENT: We like to think that our proposed holiness is thwarted by our situation. If only we could have more solitude, less opposition, better health. Kateri repeats the example of the saints: Holiness thrives on the cross, anywhere. Yet she did have what Christians—all people—need: the support of a community. She had a good mother, helpful priests, and Christian friends. These were present in what we call primitive conditions, and blossomed in the Christian triad of prayer, fasting, and almsgiving: union with God in Jesus and the Spirit, self-discipline and often suffering, and charity for her brothers and sisters.

QUOTE: Kateri said: "I am not my own; I have given myself to Jesus. He must be my only love. The state of helpless poverty that may befall me if I do not marry does not frighten me. All I need is a little food and a few pieces of clothing. With the work of my hands I shall always earn what is necessary and what is left over I'll give to my relatives and to the poor. If I should become sick and unable to work, then I shall be like the Lord on the cross. He will have mercy on me and help me, I am sure."

• • •

Bonaventure

BISHOP AND DOCTOR (1221–1274)

Bonaventure, Franciscan, theologian, Doctor of the Church, was both learned and holy. Because of the spirit that filled him and his writings, he was at first called the Devout Doctor, but in more recent centuries he has been known as the Seraphic Doctor after the "Seraphic Father," Francis, because of the truly Franciscan spirit he possessed.

Born in Bagnoregio, a town in central Italy, he was cured of a serious illness as a boy through the prayers of Francis of Assisi. Later, he studied liberal arts in Paris. Inspired by Francis and the example of the friars, especially of his master in theology, Alexander of Hales, he entered the Franciscan Order and became in turn a teacher of theology in the university. Chosen as minister general of the order in 1257, he was God's instrument in bringing it back

SAINT OF THE DAY

to a deeper love of the way of St. Francis, both through the biography of Francis, which he wrote at the behest of the brothers, and through other works that defended the order or explained its ideals and way of life.

COMMENT: Bonaventure so united holiness and theological knowledge that he rose to the heights of mysticism while yet remaining an active preacher and teacher, one beloved by all who met him. To know him was to love him; to read him is still for us today to meet a true Franciscan and a gentleman.

STORY: The morning of the fifteenth of July, 1274, in the midst of the Second Council of Lyons, Pope Gregory X and the Fathers of the Council were shocked to learn that toward dawn Brother Bonaventure, bishop of Albano, had sickened and died. An unknown chronicler provides his impression of the Franciscan cardinal: "A man of eminent learning and eloquence, and of outstanding holiness, he was known for his kindness, approachableness, gentleness, and compassion. Full of virtue, he was beloved of God and man. At his funeral Mass that same day, many were in tears, for the Lord had granted him this grace, that whoever came to know him was forthwith drawn to a deep love of him."

• • •

JULY 16 + OPTIONAL
Our Lady of Mount Carmel

Hermits lived on Mount Carmel near the Fountain of Elijah (northern Israel) in the twelfth century. They had a chapel dedicated to Our Lady. By the thirteenth century they became known as "Brothers of Our Lady of Mount Carmel." They soon celebrated a special Mass and Office in honor of Mary. In 1726 it became a celebration of the universal Church under the title of Our Lady of Mount Carmel. For centuries the Carmelites have seen themselves as specially related to Mary. Their great saints and theologians have promoted devotion to her and often championed the mystery of her Immaculate Conception.

St. Teresa of Avila (October 15) called Carmel "the Order of the Virgin." St. John of the Cross (December 14) credited Mary with saving him from drowning as a child, leading him to Carmel, and helping him escape from prison. St. Thérèse of the Child Jesus (October 1) believed that Mary cured her from illness. On her First Communion, she dedicated her life to Mary. During the last days of her life she frequently spoke of Mary.

There is a tradition (which may not be historical) that Mary appeared to St. Simon Stock, a leader of the Carmelites, and gave him a scapular, telling him to promote devotion to it. The scapular is a modified version of Mary's own garment. It symbolizes her special protection and calls the wearers to consecrate themselves to her in a special way. The scapular reminds us of the Gospel call to prayer and penance—a call that Mary models in a splendid way.

COMMENT: The Carmelites were known from early on as "Brothers of Our Lady of Mount Carmel." The title suggests that they saw Mary not only as "mother," but also as "sister." The word *sister* is a reminder that Mary is very close to us. She is a daughter of God and therefore can help us be authentic daughters and sons of God. She also can help us grow in appreciation of being sisters and brothers to one another. She leads us to a new realization that all human beings belong to the family of God. When such a conviction grows, there is hope that the human race can find its way to peace.

QUOTE: "The various forms of piety toward the Mother of God, which the Church has approved within the limits of sound and orthodox doctrine, according to the dispositions and understanding of the faithful, ensure that while the mother is honored, the Son through whom all things have their being (cf. Colossians 1:15–16) and in whom it has pleased the Father that all fullness should dwell (cf. Colossians 1:19) is rightly known, loved and glorified and his commandments are observed" (Dogmatic Constitution on the Church, 66).

• • •

Camillus de Lellis
PRIEST (1550–1614)

Humanly speaking, Camillus was not a likely candidate for sainthood. His mother died when he was a child, his father neglected him, and he grew up with an excessive love for gambling. At seventeen he was afflicted with a disease of his leg that remained with him for life. In Rome, he entered the San Giacomo hospital for incurables as both patient and servant, but was dismissed after nine months because he quarreled so much. He served in the Venetian army for three years. Then, in the winter of 1574, when he was twenty-four, he gambled away everything he had—savings, weapons, literally down to his shirt. He accepted work in the Capuchin friary at Manfredonia, and was one day so moved by a sermon of the superior that he began a conversion that changed his whole life. He entered the Capuchin novitiate, but was dismissed because of the apparently incurable sore on his leg. After another stint of service at San Giacomo, he came back to the Capuchins, only to be dismissed again for the same reason.

Back at San Giacomo for the third time, his dedication was rewarded by his being made superintendent. He devoted the rest of his life to the care of the sick, and has been named, along with St. John of God, patron of hospitals, nurses, and the sick. On the advice of his friend St. Philip Neri (May 26), he studied for the priesthood and was ordained at the age of thirty-four. Contrary to the advice of his friend, he left San Giacomo and founded a congregation of his own. As superior, he devoted much of his time to the care of the sick.

Charity was his first concern, but the physical aspects of the hospital received his diligent attention. He insisted on cleanliness and the technical competence of those who served the sick. The members of his community bound themselves to serve prisoners and persons infected by the plague as well as those dying in private homes. Some of his men were with troops fighting in Hungary and Croatia in 1595, forming the first recorded military field ambulance. In Naples, he and his men went onto the galleys that were not allowed to land because some of the crew had the plague. He discovered that there were people being buried alive, and ordered his brothers to continue the prayers for the dying fifteen minutes after apparent death.

He suffered from the disease of his leg throughout his life. In his last illness he left his own bed to see if other patients in the hospital needed help.

COMMENT: Saints are created by God. Parents must indeed nurture the faith in their children; husbands and wives must cooperate to deepen their baptismal grace; friends must support each other. But all human effort is only the dispensing of divine power. We must all try as if everything depended on us. But only the power of God can fulfill the plan of God—to make us like himself.

STORY: A doctor in Philadelphia is a modern Camillus. An AP news story reports that the thirty-one-year-old bachelor does not have an office and gave up a lucrative health center job to treat the chronically ill in the inner city who cannot get to a clinic. He limits his practice to house calls in that neighborhood.

* * *

JULY 20 + OPTIONAL
Apollinaris
BISHOP AND MARTYR

According to tradition, St. Peter sent Apollinaris to Ravenna, Italy, as its first bishop. His preaching of the Good News was so successful that the pagans there beat him and drove him from the city. He returned, however, and was exiled a second time. After preaching in the area surrounding Ravenna, he entered the city again. After being cruelly tortured, he was put on a ship heading to Greece. Pagans there caused him to be expelled to Italy, where he went to Ravenna for a fourth time. He died from wounds received during a savage beating at Classis, a suburb of Ravenna. A beautiful basilica honoring him was built there in the sixth century.

COMMENT: Following Jesus involves risks—sometimes even the risk of life itself. Martyrs are people who would rather accept the risk of death than deny the cornerstone of their whole life: faith in Jesus Christ. Everyone will die eventually—the persecutors and those persecuted. The question is what kind of a conscience people will bring before the Lord for judgment. Remembering the witness of past and present martyrs can help us make the often small sacrifices that following Jesus today may require.

QUOTE: During his remarks before the *Regina Caeli* noontime prayer on May 7, 2000, Blessed John Paul II noted that later that day at Rome's Colosseum he would participate in an ecumenical service honoring twentieth-century martyrs. He said, "It is the same paschal light that shines in them. Indeed, it is from Christ's resurrection that the disciples receive the strength to follow the Master in their hour of trial." What the pope said of those martyrs is true of all martyrs for Christ, including today's saint.

● ● ●

JULY 21 + OPTIONAL
Lawrence of Brindisi
PRIEST AND DOCTOR (1559–1619)

At first glance, perhaps the most remarkable quality of Lawrence of Brindisi is his outstanding gift of languages. In addition to a thorough knowledge of his native Italian, he had complete reading and speaking ability in Latin, Hebrew, Greek, German, Bohemian, Spanish, and French.

He was born on July 22, 1559, and died exactly sixty years later in 1619. His parents, William and Elizabeth Russo, gave him the name of Julius Caesar, "Caesare" in Italian. After the early deaths of his parents, he was educated by his uncle at the College of St. Mark in Venice.

When he was just sixteen he entered the Capuchin Franciscan Order in Venice and received the name of Lawrence. He completed his studies of philosophy and theology at the University of Padua and was ordained a priest at twenty-three.

With his facility for languages, he was able to study the Bible in its original texts. At the request of Pope Clement VIII, he spent much time preaching to the Jews in Italy. So excellent was his knowledge of Hebrew, the rabbis felt sure he was a Jew who had become a Christian.

In 1956 the Capuchins completed a fifteen-volume edition of his writings. Eleven of these fifteen contain his sermons, each of which relies chiefly on scriptural quotations to illustrate his teaching.

Lawrence's sensitivity to the needs of people—a character trait perhaps unexpected in such a talented scholar—began to surface. He was elected major superior of the Capuchin Franciscan province of Tuscany at the age of thirty-one. He had the combination of brilliance, human compassion, and administrative skill needed to carry out his duties. In rapid succession he was promoted by his fellow Capuchins and was elected minister general in 1602. In this position he was responsible for great growth and geographical expansion of the order.

Lawrence was appointed papal emissary and peacemaker, a job that took him to a number of foreign countries. An effort to achieve peace in his native kingdom of Naples took him on a journey to Lisbon to visit the king of Spain. Serious illness in Lisbon took his life in 1619.

COMMENT: His constant devotion to Scripture, coupled with great sensitivity to the needs of people, presents a lifestyle that appeals to Christians today. Lawrence had a balance in his life that blended self-discipline with a keen appreciation for the needs of those he was called to serve.

QUOTE: "God is love, and all his operations proceed from love. Once he wills to manifest that goodness by sharing his love outside himself, then the Incarnation becomes the supreme manifestation of his goodness and love and glory. So, Christ was intended before all other creatures and for his own sake. For him all things were created and to him all things must be subject, and God loves all creatures in and because of Christ. Christ is the firstborn of every creature, and the whole of humanity as well as the created world finds its foundation and meaning in him. Moreover, this would have been the case even if Adam had not sinned" (*St. Lawrence of Brindisi: Doctor of the Universal Church*, Capuchin Educational Conference).

• • •

Mary Magdalene
HOLY WOMAN

Except for the mother of Jesus, few women are more honored in the Bible than Mary Magdalene. Yet she could well be the patron of the slandered, since there has been a persistent legend in the Church that she is the unnamed sinful woman who anointed the feet of Jesus in Luke 7:36–50.

Most Scripture scholars today point out that there is no scriptural basis for confusing the two women. Mary Magdalene, that is, "of Magdala," was the one from whom Christ cast out "seven demons" (Luke 8:2)—an indication, at the worst, of extreme demonic possession or, possibly, severe illness.

Fr. Wilfrid J. Harrington, O.P., writing in the *New Catholic Commentary*, says that "seven demons" "does not mean that Mary had lived an immoral life—a conclusion reached only by means of a mistaken identification with the anonymous woman of Luke 7:36." Fr. Edward Mally, S.J., writing in the *Jerome Biblical Commentary*, agrees that she "is not...the same as the sinner of Luke 7:37, despite the later Western romantic tradition about her."

Mary Magdalene was one of the many "who were assisting them [Jesus and the twelve] out of their means." She was one of those who stood by the cross of Jesus with his mother. And, of all the "official" witnesses that might have been chosen for the first awareness of the resurrection, she was the one to whom that privilege was given. She is known as the "Apostle to the Apostles."

COMMENT: Mary Magdalene has been smiling at her "mistaken identity" for over twenty centuries. Yet she would no doubt insist that it makes no difference. We are all sinners in need of the saving power of God, whether our sins have been lurid or not. More importantly, we are all, with her, "unofficial" witnesses of the resurrection.

STORY: Today's Gospel (John 20:1–2, 11–18) shows Mary at first not recognizing the Risen Jesus in the garden, then knowing him as he spoke her name. Her great love bursts forth, echoing the First Reading for today, "I took hold of him and would not let him go" (Song 3:4b). Jesus says, "Stop holding on to me, for I have not yet ascended to the Father" (John 20:17a). The meaning probably is that there is an entirely new relationship now—a much deeper one, resting in faith rather than the former relationship that was possible because of his visible body. St. John may also be stressing the fact that Jesus's exaltation at the right hand of the Father is the completion of the resurrection.

At first, the apostles did not believe Mary. Christ's followers, even today, meet disbelief in their witness to the resurrection.

● ● ●

JULY 23 + OPTIONAL

Bridget

RELIGIOUS (1303?–1373)

From age seven on, Bridget had visions of Christ crucified. Her visions formed the basis for her activity—always with the emphasis on charity rather than spiritual favors.

She lived her married life in the court of the Swedish king Magnus II. Mother of eight children (the second eldest was St. Catherine of Sweden), she lived the strict life of a penitent after her husband's death.

Bridget constantly strove to exert her good influence over Magnus; while never fully reforming, he did give her land and buildings to found a monastery for men and women. This group eventually expanded into an order known as the Brigittines, still in existence.

In 1350, a year of jubilee, Bridget braved a plague-stricken Europe to make a pilgrimage to Rome. Although she never returned to Sweden, her years in Rome were far from happy, being hounded by debts and by opposition to her work against Church abuses.

A final pilgrimage to the Holy Land, marred by shipwreck and the death of her son Charles, eventually led to her death in 1373. In 1999, she, St. Catherine of Siena (April 29), and St. Teresa Benedicta (Edith Stein, August 9) were named copatrons of Europe.

COMMENT: Bridget's visions, rather than isolating her from the affairs of the world, involved her in many contemporary issues, whether they be royal policy or the years that the legitimate bishop of Rome lived in Avignon, France. She saw no contradiction between mystical experience and secular activity, and her life is a testimony to the possibility of a holy life in the marketplace.

QUOTE: Despite the hardships of life and wayward children (not all became saints), Margery Kempe of Lynn says Bridget was "kind and meek to every creature," and "she had a laughing face."

* * *

JULY 24 + OPTIONAL
Sharbel Makhluf
PRIEST (1828–1898)

Although this saint never traveled far from the Lebanese village of Beka-Karfa, where he was born, his influence has spread widely.

Joseph Zaroun Makhlouf was raised by an uncle because his father, a mule driver, died when Joseph was only three. At the age of twenty-three, Joseph joined the Monastery of St. Maron at Annaya, Lebanon, and took the name Sharbel in honor of a second-century martyr. He professed his final vows in 1853 and was ordained six years later.

Following the example of the fifth-century St. Maron, Sharbel lived as a hermit from 1875 until his death. His reputation for holiness prompted people to seek him to receive a blessing and to be remembered in his prayers. He followed a strict fast and was very devoted to the Blessed Sacrament. When his superiors occasionally asked him to administer the sacraments to nearby villages, Sharbel did so gladly.

He died in the late afternoon on Christmas Eve. Christians and non-Christians soon made his tomb a place of pilgrimage and of cures. Pope Paul VI beatified him in 1965 and canonized him twelve years later.

COMMENT: Blessed John Paul II often said that the Church has two lungs (East and West) and it must learn to breathe using both of them. Remembering saints like Sharbel helps the Church to appreciate both the diversity and unity present in the Catholic Church. Like all the saints, Sharbel points us to God and invites us to cooperate generously with God's grace, no matter what our situation in life may be. As our prayer life becomes deeper and more honest, we become more ready to make that generous response.

QUOTE: When Sharbel was canonized in 1977, Bishop Francis Zayek, head of the U.S. Diocese of St. Maron, wrote a pamphlet entitled *A New Star of the East*. Bishop Zayek wrote: "St. Sharbel is called the second St. Anthony of the Desert, the Perfume of Lebanon, the first Confessor of the East to be raised to the Altars according to the actual procedure of the Catholic Church, the honor of our Aramaic Antiochian Church, and the model of spiritual values and renewal. Sharbel is like a Cedar of Lebanon standing in eternal prayer, on top of a mountain."

The bishop noted that Sharbel's canonization plus other beatification cases prove "that the Aramaic Maronite Antiochian Church is indeed a living branch of the Catholic Church and is intimately connected with the trunk, who is Christ, our Savior, the beginning and the end of all things."

● ● ●

JULY 25 + FEAST

James

APOSTLE

This James is the brother of John the Evangelist. The two were called by Jesus as they worked with their father in a fishing boat on the Sea of Galilee. Jesus had already called another pair of brothers from a similar occupation: Peter and Andrew. "He walked along a little farther and saw James, the son of Zebedee, and his brother John. They too were in a boat mending their nets. Then he called them. So they left their father Zebedee in the boat along with the hired men and followed him" (Mark 1:19–20).

James was one of the favored three who had the privilege of witnessing the transfiguration, the raising to life of the daughter of Jairus and the agony in Gethsemane.

Two incidents in the Gospels describe the temperament of this man and his brother. St. Matthew tells that their mother came (Mark says it was the brothers themselves) to ask that they have the seats of honor (one on the right, one on the left of Jesus) in the kingdom. "Jesus said in reply, 'You do not know what you are asking. Can you drink the cup that I am going to drink?' They said to him, 'We can' " (Matthew 20:22). Jesus then told them they would indeed drink the cup and share his baptism of pain and death, but that sitting at his right hand or left was not his to give—it "is for those for whom it has been prepared by my Father" (Matthew 20:23b). It remained to be seen how long it would take to realize the implications of their confident "We can!"

The other disciples became indignant at the ambition of James and John. Then Jesus taught them all the lesson of humble service: The purpose of authority is to serve. They are not to impose their will on others, or lord it over them. This is the position of Jesus himself. He was the servant of all; the service imposed on him was the supreme sacrifice of his own life.

On another occasion, James and John gave evidence that the nickname Jesus gave them—"sons of thunder"—was an apt one. The Samaritans would not welcome Jesus because he was on his way to hated Jerusalem. "When the disciples James and John saw this they asked, 'Lord, do you want us to call down fire from heaven to consume them?' Jesus turned and rebuked them…" (Luke 9:54–55).

James was apparently the first of the apostles to be martyred. "About that time King Herod laid hands upon some members of the Church to harm them. He had James, the brother of John, killed by the sword, and when he saw that this was pleasing to the Jews he proceeded to arrest Peter also" (Acts 12:1–3a).

This James, sometimes called James the Greater, is not to be confused with James the Lesser (May 3) or with the author of the Letter of James and the leader of the Jerusalem community.

COMMENT: The way the Gospels treat the apostles is a good reminder of what holiness is all about. There is very little about their virtues as static possessions, entitling them to heavenly reward. Rather, the great emphasis is on the kingdom, on God's giving them the power to proclaim the Good News. As far as their personal lives are concerned, there is much about Jesus's purifying them of narrowness, pettiness, fickleness.

QUOTE: "Christ the Lord, in whom the entire revelation of the most high God is summed up (see 2 Corinthians 1:20; 3:16—4:6), having fulfilled in his own person and promulgated with his own lips the Gospel promised by the prophets, commanded the apostles to preach it to everyone as the source of all saving truth and moral law, communicating God's gifts to them. This was faithfully done: it was done by the apostles who handed on, by oral preaching, by their example, by their dispositions, what they themselves had received—whether from the lips of Christ, from his way of life and his works, or by coming to know it through the prompting of the Holy Spirit" (Constitution on Divine Revelation, 7).

* * *

JULY 26 + MEMORIAL
Joachim and Anne
PARENTS OF MARY

In the Scriptures, Matthew and Luke furnish a legal family history of Jesus, tracing ancestry to show that Jesus is the culmination of great promises. Not only is his mother's family neglected, we also know nothing factual about them except that they existed. Even the names Joachim and Anne come from a legendary source written more than a century after Jesus died.

The heroism and holiness of these people, however, is inferred from the whole family atmosphere around Mary in the Scriptures. Whether we rely on the legends about Mary's childhood or make guesses from the information in the Bible, we see in her a fulfillment of many generations of prayerful persons, herself steeped in the religious traditions of her people.

The strong character of Mary in making decisions, her continuous practice of prayer, her devotion to the laws of her faith, her steadiness at moments of crisis, and her devotion to her relatives—all indicate a close-knit, loving family that looked forward to the next generation even while retaining the best of the past.

Joachim and Anne—whether these are their real names or not—represent that entire quiet series of generations who faithfully perform their duties, practice their faith, and establish an atmosphere for the coming of the Messiah, but remain obscure.

COMMENT: This is the "feast of grandparents." It reminds grandparents of their responsibility to establish a tone for generations to come: They must make the traditions live and offer them as a promise to little children. But the feast has a message for the younger generation as well. It reminds the young that older people's greater perspective, depth of experience, and appreciation of life's profound rhythms are all part of a wisdom not to be taken lightly or ignored.

QUOTE: "The family is the foundation of society. In it the various generations come together and help one another to grow wise and to harmonize personal rights with the other requirements of social life" (Pastoral Constitution on the Church in the Modern World, 52).

• • •

JULY 29 + MEMORIAL
Martha
HOLY WOMAN

Martha, Mary, and their brother Lazarus were evidently close friends of Jesus. He came to their home simply as a welcomed guest, rather than as one celebrating the conversion of a sinner like Zacchaeus or one unceremoniously received by a suspicious Pharisee. The sisters feel free to call on Jesus at their brother's death, even though a return to Judea at that time seems almost certain death.

No doubt Martha was an active sort of person. On one occasion (see Luke 10:38–42) she prepares the meal for Jesus and possibly his fellow guests and forthrightly states the obvious: All hands should pitch in to help with the dinner.

Yet, as biblical scholar Fr. John McKenzie points out, she need not be rated as an "unrecollected activist." The evangelist is emphasizing what our Lord said on several occasions about the primacy of the spiritual: "Do not worry about your life, what you will eat [or drink], or about your body, what you will wear.... But seek first the kingdom [of God] and his righteousness" (Matthew 6:25b, 33a); "One does not live by bread alone" (Luke 4:4b); "Blessed are they who hunger and thirst for righteousness" (Matthew 5:6a).

Martha's great glory is her simple and strong statement of faith in Jesus after her brother's death. "Jesus told her, 'I am the resurrection and the life; whoever believes in me, even if he dies, will live, and everyone who lives and believes in me will never die. Do you believe this?' She said to him, 'Yes, Lord. I have come to believe that you are the Messiah, the Son of God, the one who is coming into the world' " (John 11:25–27).

COMMENT: Scripture commentators point out that in writing his account of the raising of Lazarus, St. John intends that we should see Martha's words to Mary before Lazarus was raised as a summons that every Christian must obey. In her saying "The teacher is here and is asking for you," Jesus is calling every one of us to resurrection—now in baptismal faith, forever in sharing his victory over death. And all of us, as well as these three friends, are in our own unique way called to special friendship with him.

QUOTE: "...[E]ncouraged by so great a cloud of witnesses, we may run as victors in the race before us and win with them the imperishable crown of glory through Christ our Lord" (Preface of Saints).

* * *

JULY 30 + OPTIONAL

Peter Chrysologus
BISHOP AND DOCTOR (406–450?)

A man who vigorously pursues a goal may produce results far beyond his expectations and his intentions. Thus it was with Peter of the Golden Words, as he was called, who as a young man became bishop of Ravenna, the capital of the empire in the West. At the time there were abuses and vestiges of paganism evident in his diocese, and these he was determined to battle and overcome. His principal weapon was the short sermon, and many of them have come down to us. They do not contain great originality of thought. They are, however, full of moral applications, sound in doctrine, and historically significant in that they reveal Christian life in fifth-century Ravenna. So authentic were the contents of his sermons that, some thirteen centuries later, he was declared a Doctor of the Church by Pope Benedict XIII. He who had earnestly sought to teach and motivate his own flock was recognized as a teacher of the universal Church.

In addition to his zeal in the exercise of his office, Peter Chrysologus was distinguished by a fierce loyalty to the Church, not only in its teaching, but in its authority as well. He looked upon learning not as a mere opportunity but as an obligation for all, both as a development of God-given faculties and as a solid support for the worship of God.

Some time before his death, St. Peter returned to Imola, his birthplace, where he died around A.D. 450.

COMMENT: Quite likely, it was St. Peter Chrysologus's attitude toward learning that gave substance to his exhortations. Next to virtue, learning, in his view, was the greatest improver of the human mind and the support of true religion. Ignorance is not a virtue, nor is anti-intellectualism. Knowledge is neither more nor less a source of pride than physical, administrative, or financial prowess. To be fully human is to expand our knowledge—whether sacred or secular—according to our talent and opportunity.

STORY: Eutyches, the leader of the heresy denying the humanity of Christ, sought support from Church leaders, Peter Chrysologus among them, after his condemnation in A.D. 448. Peter frankly told him: "In the interest of peace and the faith, we cannot judge in matters of faith without the consent of the Roman bishop." He further exhorted Eutyches to accept the mystery of the Incarnation in simple faith. Peter reminded him that if the peace of the Church causes joy in heaven, then divisions must give birth to grief.

* * *

Ignatius of Loyola
P R I E S T   (1 4 9 1 – 1 5 5 6)

The founder of the Jesuits was on his way to military fame and fortune when a cannonball shattered his leg. Because there were no novels on hand during his convalescence, he whiled away the time reading a life of Christ and lives of the saints. His conscience was deeply touched and a long, painful turning to Christ began. Having seen the Mother of God in a vision, he made a pilgrimage to her shrine at Montserrat (near Barcelona). He remained for almost a year at nearby Manresa, sometimes with the Dominicans, sometimes in a pauper's hospice, often in a cave in the hills praying. After a period of great peace of mind, he went through a harrowing trial of scruples. There was no comfort in anything—prayer, fasting, sacraments, penance. At length, his peace of mind returned.

It was during this year of conversion that he began to write down material that later became his greatest work, the *Spiritual Exercises*.

He finally achieved his purpose of going to the Holy Land, but could not remain as he had planned, because of the hostility of the Turks. He spent the next eleven years in various European universities, studying with great difficulty, beginning almost as a child. Like many others, he fell victim twice to the suspicions of the time, and he was twice jailed for brief periods.

In 1534, at the age of forty-three, he and six others (one of whom was St. Francis Xavier, December 3) vowed to live in poverty and chastity and to go to the Holy Land. If this became impossible, they vowed to offer themselves to the apostolic service of the pope. The latter became the only choice. Four years later, Ignatius made the association permanent. The new Society of Jesus was approved by Paul III, and Ignatius was elected to serve as the first general.

When companions were sent on various missions by the pope, Ignatius remained in Rome, consolidating the new venture but still finding time to found homes for orphans, catechumens, and penitents. He founded the

Roman College, intended to be the model of all other colleges of the Society.

Ignatius was a true mystic. He centered his spiritual life on the essential foundations of Christianity—the Trinity, Christ, the Eucharist. His spirituality is expressed in the Jesuit motto, *ad majorem Dei gloriam*—"for the greater glory of God." In his concept, obedience was to be the prominent virtue, to assure the effectiveness and mobility of his men. All activity was to be guided by a true love of the Church and unconditional obedience to the Holy Father, for which reason all professed members took a fourth vow to go wherever the pope should send them for the salvation of souls.

COMMENT: Luther nailed his theses to the church door at Wittenberg in 1517. Seventeen years later, Ignatius founded the Society that was to play so prominent a part in the Catholic Reformation. He was an implacable foe of Protestantism. Yet the seeds of ecumenism may be found in his words: "Great care must be taken to show forth orthodox truth in such a way that if any heretics happen to be present they may have an example of charity and Christian moderation. No hard words should be used nor any sort of contempt for their errors be shown." One of the greatest twentieth-century ecumenists was Cardinal Bea, a Jesuit.

QUOTE: Ignatius recommended this prayer to penitents: "Receive, Lord, all my liberty, my memory, my understanding and my whole will. You have given me all that I have, all that I am, and I surrender all to your divine will, that you dispose of me. Give me only your love and your grace. With this I am rich enough, and I have no more to ask."

• • •

AUGUST 1 + MEMORIAL

Alphonsus Liguori

BISHOP AND DOCTOR (1696–1787)

Moral theology, according to Vatican II, should be more thoroughly nourished by Scripture and show the nobility of the Christian vocation of the faithful and their obligation to bring forth fruit in charity for the life of the world. Alphonsus, declared patron of moral theologians by Pius XII in 1950, would rejoice in that statement.

In his day, Alphonsus fought for the liberation of moral theology from the rigidity of Jansenism. His moral theology, which went through sixty editions in the century following him, concentrated on the practical and concrete problems of pastors and confessors. If a certain legalism and minimalism crept into moral theology, it should not be attributed to this model of moderation and gentleness.

At the University of Naples he received, at the age of sixteen, a doctorate in both canon and civil law by acclamation, but he soon gave up the practice of law for apostolic activity. He was ordained a priest and concentrated his pastoral efforts on popular (parish) missions, hearing confessions, and forming Christian groups.

He founded the Redemptorist congregation in 1732. It was an association of priests and brothers living a common life, dedicated to the imitation of Christ, and working mainly in popular missions for peasants in rural areas. Almost as an omen of what was to come later, he found himself deserted, after a while, by all his original companions except one lay brother. But the congregation managed to survive and was formally approved seventeen years later, though its troubles were not over.

Alphonsus's great pastoral reforms were in the pulpit and confessional— replacing the pompous oratory of the time with simplicity, and the rigorism of Jansenism with kindness. His great fame as a writer has somewhat eclipsed the fact that for twenty-six years he traveled up and down the Kingdom of Naples, preaching popular missions.

He was made bishop (after trying to reject the honor) at sixty-six and at once instituted a thorough reform of his diocese.

His greatest sorrow came toward the end of his life. The Redemptorists, precariously continuing after the suppression of the Jesuits in 1773, had difficulty in getting their Rule approved by the Kingdom of Naples. Alphonsus acceded to the condition that they possess no property in common, but a royal official, with the connivance of a high Redemptorist official, changed the Rule substantially. Alphonsus, old, crippled and with very bad sight, signed the document, unaware that he had been betrayed. The Redemptorists in the Papal States then put themselves under the pope, who withdrew those in Naples from the jurisdiction of Alphonsus. It was only after his death that the branches were united.

At seventy-one he was afflicted with rheumatic pains which left incurable bending of his neck; until it was straightened a little, the pressure of his chin caused a raw wound on his chest. He suffered a final eighteen months of "dark night" scruples, fears, and temptations against every article of faith and every virtue interspersed with intervals of light and relief, when ecstasies were frequent.

Alphonsus is best known for his moral theology, but he also wrote well in the field of spiritual and dogmatic theology. His *Glories of Mary* is one of the great works on that subject, and his book *Visits to the Blessed Sacrament* went through forty editions in his lifetime, greatly influencing the practice of this devotion in the Church.

COMMENT: St. Alphonsus was known above all as a practical man who dealt in the concrete rather than the abstract. His life is indeed a practical model for the everyday Christian who has difficulty recognizing the dignity of Christian life amid the swirl of problems, pain, misunderstanding, and failure. Alphonsus suffered all these things. He is a saint because he was able to maintain an intimate sense of the presence of the suffering Christ through it all.

QUOTE: Someone once remarked, after a sermon by Alphonsus, "It is a pleasure to listen to your sermons; you forget yourself and preach Jesus Christ."

• • •

Peter Julian Eymard

PRIEST (1811–1868)

Born in La Mure d'Isère in southeastern France, Peter Julian's faith journey drew him from being a priest in the Diocese of Grenoble (1834) to joining the Marists (1839) to founding the Congregation of the Blessed Sacrament (1856).

In addition to those changes, Peter Julian coped with poverty, his father's initial opposition to Peter's vocation, serious illness, a Jansenistic overemphasis on sin, and the difficulties of getting diocesan and later papal approval for his new religious community.

His years as a Marist, including service as a provincial leader, saw the deepening of his Eucharistic devotion, especially through his preaching of Forty Hours in many parishes.

The Congregation of the Blessed Sacrament began working with children in Paris to prepare them to receive their first Communion. It also reached out to non-practicing Catholics, inviting them to repent and begin receiving Holy Communion again. He was a tireless proponent of frequent Holy Communion, an idea given more authoritative backing by Pope Pius X in 1905.

Inspired at first by the idea of reparation for indifference to the Eucharist, Peter Julian was eventually attracted to a more positive spirituality of Christ-centered love. Members of the men's community, which Peter founded, alternated between an active apostolic life and the contemplation of Jesus in the Eucharist. He and Marguerite Guillot founded the women's Congregation of the Servants of the Blessed Sacrament.

Peter Julian Eymard was beatified in 1925 and canonized in 1962, one day after Vatican II's first session ended.

COMMENT: In every century, sin has been painfully real in the life of the Church. It is easy to give in to despair, to speak so strongly of human failings that people may forget the immense and self-sacrificing love of Jesus, as his death on the cross and his gift of the Eucharist make evident. Peter Julian knew that the Eucharist was central to helping Catholics live out their baptism and preach by word and example the Good News of Jesus Christ.

QUOTE: "The Eucharist is the life of the people. The Eucharist gives them a center of life. All can come together without the barriers of race or language in order to celebrate the feast days of the Church. It gives them a law of life, that of charity, of which it is the source; thus it forges between them a common bond, a Christian kinship" (Peter Julian Eymard).

* * *

AUGUST 2 + OPTIONAL
Eusebius of Vercelli
BISHOP (283?–371)

Someone has said that if there had been no Arian heresy denying Christ's divinity, it would be very difficult to write the lives of many early saints. Eusebius is another of the defenders of the Church during one of its most trying periods.

Born on the isle of Sardinia, he became a member of the Roman clergy and is the first recorded bishop of Vercelli in Piedmont in northwest Italy. He is also the first to link the monastic life with that of the clergy, establishing a community of his diocesan clergy on the principle that the best way to sanctify his people was to have them see a clergy formed in solid virtue and living in community.

He was sent by Pope Liberius to persuade the emperor to call a council to settle Catholic-Arian troubles. When it was called at Milan, Eusebius went reluctantly, sensing that the Arian block would have its way, although the Catholics were more numerous. He refused to go along with the condemnation of Athanasius (May 2); instead, he laid the Nicene Creed on the table and insisted that all sign it before taking up any other matter. The emperor put pressure on him, but Eusebius insisted on Athanasius's innocence and reminded the emperor that secular force should not be used to influence Church decisions. At first the emperor threatened to kill him, but later sent him into exile in Palestine. There the Arians dragged him through the streets and shut him up in a little room, releasing him only after his four-day hunger strike. They resumed their harassment shortly after.

His exile continued in Asia Minor and Egypt, until the new emperor permitted him to be welcomed back to his see in Vercelli. He attended the Council of Alexandria with Athanasius and approved the leniency shown to bishops who had wavered. He also worked with St. Hilary of Poitiers (January 13) against the Arians.

He died peacefully in his own diocese at an advanced age.

COMMENT: Catholics in the U.S. have sometimes felt penalized by an unwarranted interpretation of the principle of separation of Church and state, especially in the matter of Catholic schools. Be that as it may, the Church is happily free today from the tremendous pressure put on it after it became an established Church under Constantine. We are happily rid of such things as a pope asking an emperor to call a Church council, Pope John I being sent by the emperor to negotiate in the East, and the pressure of kings on papal elections. The Church cannot be a prophet if it's in someone's pocket.

QUOTE: "To render the care of souls more efficacious, community life for priests is strongly recommended, especially for those attached to the same parish. While this way of living encourages apostolic action, it also affords an example of charity and unity to the faithful" (Decree on the Office of Bishops, 30).

• ◦ •

AUGUST 4 + MEMORIAL
John Vianney
PRIEST (1786–1859)

A man with vision overcomes obstacles and performs deeds that seem impossible. John Vianney was a man with vision: He wanted to become a priest. But he had to overcome his meager formal schooling, which inadequately prepared him for seminary studies.

His failure to comprehend Latin lectures forced him to discontinue. But his vision of being a priest urged him to seek private tutoring. After a lengthy battle with the books, John was ordained.

Situations calling for "impossible" deeds followed him everywhere. As pastor of the parish at Ars, John encountered people who were indifferent and quite comfortable with their style of living. His vision led him through severe fasts and short nights of sleep. (Some devils can only be cast out by prayer and fasting.)

With Catherine Lassagne and Benedicta Lardet, he established La Providence, a home for girls. Only a man of vision could have such trust that God would provide for the spiritual and material needs of all those who came to make La Providence their home.

His work as a confessor is John Vianney's most remarkable accomplishment. In the winter months, he was to spend eleven to twelve hours daily reconciling people with God. In the summer months, this time was increased to sixteen hours. Unless a man was dedicated to his vision of a priestly vocation, he could not have endured this giving of self day after day.

Many people look forward to retirement and taking it easy, doing the things they always wanted to do but never had the time. But John Vianney had no thoughts of retirement. As his fame spread, more hours were consumed in serving God's people. Even the few hours he would allow himself for sleep were disturbed frequently by the devil.

Who, but a man with vision, could keep going with ever-increasing strength? In 2009, Pope Benedict XVI named him the patron of all priests worldwide.

COMMENT: Indifference toward religion, coupled with a love for material comfort, seem to be common signs of our times. A person from another planet observing us would not likely judge us to be pilgrim people, on our way to somewhere else. John Vianney, on the other hand, was a man on a journey with his goal before him at all times.

QUOTE: Recommending liturgical prayer, John Vianney would say, "Private prayer is like straw scattered here and there: If you set it on fire, it makes a lot of little flames. But gather these straws into a bundle and light them, and you get a mighty fire, rising like a column into the sky; public prayer is like that."

• • •

AUGUST 5 + OPTIONAL

Dedication of St. Mary Major

First raised at the order of Pope Liberius in the mid-fourth century, the Liberian basilica was rebuilt by Pope Sixtus III shortly after the Council of Ephesus affirmed Mary's title as Mother of God in 431. Rededicated at that time to the Mother of God, St. Mary Major is the largest church in the world honoring God through Mary. Standing atop one of Rome's seven hills, the Esquiline, it has survived many restorations without losing its character as an early Roman basilica. Its interior retains three naves divided by colonnades in the style of Constantine's era. Fifth-century mosaics on its walls testify to its antiquity.

St. Mary Major is one of the four Roman basilicas known as patriarchal cathedrals in memory of the first centers of the Church. St. John Lateran (November 9) represents Rome, the See of Peter; St. Paul Outside the Walls, the See of Alexandria, allegedly the see presided over by Mark (April 25); St. Peter, the See of Constantinople; and St. Mary, the See of Antioch, where Mary is supposed to have spent most of her life.

One legend, unreported before the year 1000, gives another name to this feast: Our Lady of the Snows. According to that story, a wealthy Roman couple pledged their fortune to the Mother of God. In affirmation, she produced a miraculous summer snowfall and told them to build a church on the site. The legend was long celebrated by releasing a shower of white rose petals from the basilica's dome every August 5.

COMMENT: Theological debate over Christ's nature as God and man reached fever pitch in Constantinople in the early fifth century. The chaplain of Bishop Nestorius began preaching against the title *Theotokos,* "Mother of God," insisting that the Virgin was mother only of the human Jesus.

Nestorius agreed, decreeing that Mary would henceforth be named "Mother of Christ" in his see. The people of Constantinople virtually revolted against their bishop's refutation of a cherished belief. When the Council of Ephesus refuted Nestorius, believers took to the streets, enthusiastically chanting, *"Theotokos! Theotokos!"*

QUOTE: "From the earliest times the Blessed Virgin is honored under the title of Mother of God, in whose protection the faithful take refuge together in prayer in all their perils and needs. Accordingly, following the Council of Ephesus, there was a remarkable growth in the cult of the People of God towards Mary, in veneration and love, in invocation and imitation" (Dogmatic Constitution on the Church, 66).

●   ●   ●

AUGUST 6 + FEAST

Transfiguration of the Lord

All three Synoptic Gospels tell the story of the Transfiguration (Matthew 17:1–8; Mark 9:2–9; Luke 9:28–36). With remarkable agreement, all three place the event shortly after Peter's confession of faith that Jesus is the Messiah and Jesus's first prediction of his passion and death. Peter's eagerness to erect tents or booths on the spot suggests it occurred during the Jewish weeklong fall Feast of Booths.

In spite of the texts' agreement, it is difficult to reconstruct the disciples' experience, according to Scripture scholars, because the Gospels draw heavily on Old Testament descriptions of the Sinai encounter with God and prophetic visions of the Son of Man. Certainly Peter, James, and John had a glimpse of Jesus's divinity strong enough to strike fear into their hearts. Such an experience defies description, so they drew on familiar religious language to describe it. And certainly Jesus warned them that his glory and his suffering were to be inextricably connected—a theme John highlights throughout his Gospel.

Tradition names Mt. Tabor as the site of the revelation. A church first raised there in the fourth century was dedicated on August 6. A feast in honor of the transfiguration was celebrated in the Eastern Church from about that time. Western observance began in some localities about the eighth century.

On July 22, 1456, Crusaders defeated the Turks at Belgrade. News of the victory reached Rome on August 6, and Pope Callistus III placed the feast on the Roman calendar the following year.

COMMENT: One of the transfiguration accounts is read on the second Sunday of Lent each year, proclaiming Christ's divinity to catechumens and baptized alike. The Gospel for the first Sunday of Lent, by contrast, is the story of the temptation in the desert—affirmation of Jesus's humanity. The two distinct but inseparable natures of the Lord were a subject of much theological argument at the beginning of the Church's history; it remains hard for believers to grasp.

QUOTE: "At his Transfiguration Christ showed his disciples the splendor of his beauty, to which he will shape and color those who are his: 'He will reform our lowness configured to the body of his glory' (Philippians 3:21)" (St. Thomas Aquinas, *Summa Theologiae*).

• • •

AUGUST 7 + OPTIONAL
Sixtus II and Companions
POPE AND MARTYR; MARTYRS (D. 258)

Freedom to assemble has always been one of the first liberties that dictators deny to subjects (and one highly prized by our American forebears). The emperor Valerian published his first decree against Christians in 257 and forbade them to hold assemblies. Pope Sixtus had been pope for only one year when he was murdered while presiding at the Eucharist in one of the underground caverns used as cemeteries (catacombs). He and four deacons were seized and beheaded. Two other deacons were probably martyred the same day, and St. Lawrence (August 10) four days later.

During his year in office, Sixtus had to deal with the controversy about the validity of baptism by heretics. He supported the positive view but was tolerant toward the practice of the Eastern Church, which rebaptized those who had received the sacrament from heretics. The negative view was shared by St. Cyprian (September 16), to whom Sixtus sent messengers for discussion. Sixtus was asked to be patient with those in error, and contented himself with a strong recommendation of the truth. Other popes did the same, until the error was finally condemned.

COMMENT: What are we willing to suffer to practice our faith? In times of persecution Christians have always dared to come together to celebrate the Eucharist—huddled in a corner of the prison, risking life and possessions— in Ireland, for example, by providing "priest's holes." Those of us who live in Christian lands can scarcely comprehend the possibility: Does the Eucharist mean so much to us that, under government persecution, we would gather at night in one of our homes to celebrate the mystery of the Body and Blood of Jesus, risking that fatal knock on the door?

QUOTE: "Baptism, of itself, is only a beginning, a point of departure, for it is wholly directed toward the acquiring of fullness of life in Christ. Baptism is thus oriented toward a complete profession of faith, a complete incorporation into the system of salvation such as Christ himself willed it to be, and finally, toward a complete participation in Eucharistic communion" (Decree on Ecumenism, 22).

· · ·

AUGUST 7 + OPTIONAL

Cajetan
PRIEST (1480–1557)

Like most of us, Cajetan seemed headed for an ordinary life—first as a lawyer, then as a priest engaged in the work of the Roman Curia.

His life took a characteristic turn when he joined the Oratory of Divine Love in Rome, a group devoted to piety and charity, shortly after his ordination at thirty-six. When he was forty-two he founded a hospital for incurables at Venice. At Vicenza, he joined a "disreputable" religious community that consisted only of men of the lowest stations of life—and was roundly censured by his friends, who thought his action was a reflection on his family. He sought out the sick and poor of the town and served them.

The greatest need of the time was the reformation of a church that was "sick in head and members." Cajetan and three friends decided that the best road to reformation lay in reviving the spirit and zeal of the clergy. (One of them later became Paul IV.) Together they founded a congregation known as the Theatines (from Teate [*Chieti*] where their first superior-bishop had his see). They managed to escape to Venice after their house in Rome was wrecked when Emperor Charles V's troops sacked Rome in 1527. The Theatines were outstanding among the Catholic reform movements that took shape before the Protestant Reformation.

He founded a *monte de pietà* ("mountain [or fund] of piety") in Naples—one of many charitable, nonprofit credit organizations that lent money on the security of pawned objects. The purpose was to help the poor and protect them against usurers. Cajetan's little organization, with great changes in policy, ultimately became the Bank of Naples.

COMMENT: If Vatican II had been summarily stopped after its first session in 1962, many Catholics would have felt that a great blow had been dealt to the growth of the Church. Cajetan had the same feeling about the Council of Trent (1545–1563). But, as he said, God is the same in Naples as in Venice, with or without Trent or Vatican II. We open ourselves to God's power in whatever circumstances we find ourselves, and God's will is done. God's standards of success differ from ours.

STORY: When Cajetan was sent to establish a house of his congregation in Naples, a count tried to prevail upon him to accept an estate in lands. He refused. The count pointed out that he would need the money, for the people of Naples were not as generous as the people of Venice. "That may be true," replied Cajetan, "but God is the same in both cities."

• • •

AUGUST 8 + MEMORIAL

Dominic

PRIEST (1170–1221)

If he hadn't taken a trip with his bishop, Dominic would probably have remained within the structure of contemplative life; after the trip, he spent the rest of his life being a contemplative in active apostolic work.

Born in old Castile, Spain, he was trained for the priesthood by a priest-uncle, studied the arts and theology, and became a canon of the cathedral at Osma, where there was an attempt to revive the apostolic common life described in Acts of the Apostles.

On a journey through France with his bishop, he came face to face with the then-virulent Albigensian heresy at Languedoc. The Albigensians (Cathari, "the pure") held to two principles—one good, one evil—in the world. All matter is evil—hence they denied the Incarnation and sacraments. On the same principle, they abstained from procreation and took a minimum of food and drink. The inner circle led what some people regarded as a heroic life of purity and asceticism not shared by ordinary followers.

Dominic sensed the need for the Church to combat this heresy and was commissioned to be part of the preaching crusade against it. He saw immediately why the preaching was not succeeding: The ordinary people admired and followed the ascetical heroes of the Albigensians. Understandably, they were not impressed by the Catholic preachers who traveled with horse and retinue, stayed at the best inns and had servants. Dominic therefore, with three Cistercians, began itinerant preaching according to the Gospel ideal. He continued this work for ten years, being successful with the ordinary people but not with the leaders.

His fellow preachers gradually became a community, and in 1215 he founded a religious house at Toulouse, the beginning of the Order of Preachers (Dominicans).

His ideal, and that of his order, was to link organically a life with God, study and prayer in all forms, with a ministry of salvation to people by the word of God. His ideal: *contemplata tradere:* "to pass on the fruits of contemplation" or "to speak only of God or with God."

COMMENT: The Dominican ideal, like that of all religious communities, is for the imitation, not merely the admiration, of the rest of the Church. The effective combining of contemplation and activity is the vocation of truck driver Smith as well as theologian Aquinas. Acquired contemplation is the tranquil abiding in the presence of God and is an integral part of any full human life. It must be the wellspring of all Christian activity.

STORY: Legend has it that Dominic saw the sinful world threatened by God's anger but saved by the intercession of Mary, who pointed out to her Son two figures: One was Dominic himself, the other a stranger. In Church the next day he saw a ragged beggar enter—the man in the vision. He went up to him, embraced him and said, "You are my companion and must walk with me. If we hold together, no earthly power can withstand us." The beggar was Francis of Assisi. The meeting of the two founders is commemorated twice a year, when on their respective feast days Dominicans and Franciscans celebrate Mass in each other's churches and afterward sit at the same table "to eat the bread which for seven centuries has never been wanting" (*Butler's Lives of the Saints*).

● ● ●

AUGUST 8 + OPTIONAL
Mary MacKillop
VIRGIN (1842–1909)

If St. Mary MacKillop were alive today, she would be a household name. It's not that she sought the limelight. On the contrary, she simply wanted to serve the poor wherever she found them in her native Australia. But along the way, she managed to rouse the ire of some rather powerful churchmen. One even excommunicated her for a time.

Born in Melbourne in 1842 to parents who had emigrated from Scotland, Mary grew up in a family that faced constant financial struggles. As a young woman she was drawn to religious life but could not find an existing order of sisters that met her needs. In 1860 she met Fr. Julian Woods, who became her spiritual director. Together they founded a community of women—the Sisters of St. Joseph of the Sacred Heart, also known as the Josephite Sisters. Its members were to staff schools, especially for poor children, as well as orphanages, and engage in other works of charity.

As the congregation grew, so did Mary MacKillop's problems. Her priest-friend proved unreliable in many ways, and he was removed from his responsibilities for the direction of the sisters. Meanwhile, Mary had the support of some local bishops as she and her sisters went about their work. But the bishop in South Australia, aging and relying on others for advice, briefly excommunicated Mary—charging her with disobedience— and dispensed fifty of her sisters from their vows. In truth, the bishop's quarrel was about power and who had authority over whom. He ultimately rescinded his order of excommunication.

Mary insisted that her congregation should be governed by an elected mother general answerable to Rome, not to the local bishop. (There were also disputes about whether the congregation could own property.) In the end, Rome proved to be Mary's best source of support. After a long wait, official approval of the congregation—and how it was to be governed— came from Pope Leo XIII.

Despite her struggles with Church authorities, Mary MacKillop and her sisters were able to offer social services that few, if any, government agencies in Australia could. They served Protestants and Catholics alike, and worked among the aborigines. They taught in schools and orphanages and served unmarried mothers.

Money, actually the lack of it, was a constant worry. But the sisters, who begged from door to door, were bolstered by faith and by the conviction that their struggles were opportunities to grow closer to God.

By the time Mary was approaching the end of her life, the congregation was thriving. She died in 1909 at the age of sixty-seven. Blessed John Paul II beatified her in 1995, and in 2010, Pope Benedict XVI canonized her, making her Australia's first saint.

COMMENT: It is sometimes easier to suffer for the Church than at the hands of the Church. Sts. Mary MacKillop and Joan of Arc are examples of this. In the end, it is enough that God knows the truth about a person's beliefs, practices, and motivations.

QUOTE: In 1890, Sister Mary MacKillop said, "Have courage no matter what your crosses are."

* * *

AUGUST 9 + OPTIONAL

Teresa Benedicta of the Cross

MARTYR (1891–1942)

A brilliant philosopher who stopped believing in God when she was fourteen, Edith Stein was so captivated by reading the autobiography of Teresa of Avila (October 15) that she began a spiritual journey that led to her baptism in 1922. Twelve years later she imitated Teresa by becoming a Carmelite, taking the name Teresa Benedicta of the Cross.

Born into a prominent Jewish family in Breslau (now Wroclaw, Poland), Edith abandoned Judaism in her teens. As a student at the University of Göttingen, she became fascinated by phenomenology, an approach to philosophy. Excelling as a protégé of Edmund Husserl, one of the leading phenomenologists, Edith earned a doctorate in philosophy in 1916. She continued as a university teacher until 1922 when she moved to a Dominican school in Speyer. Her appointment as lecturer at the Educational Institute of Munich ended under pressure from the Nazis.

After living in the Cologne Carmel (1934–1938), she moved to the Carmelite monastery in Echt, Netherlands. The Nazis occupied that country in 1940. In retaliation for being denounced by the Dutch bishops, the Nazis arrested all Dutch Jews who had become Christians. Teresa Benedicta and her sister Rosa, also a Catholic, died in a gas chamber in Auschwitz on August 9, 1942.

Blessed John Paul II beatified Teresa Benedicta in 1987 and canonized her twelve years later.

COMMENT: The writings of Edith Stein fill seventeen volumes, many of which have been translated into English. A woman of integrity, she followed the truth wherever it led her. After becoming a Catholic, Edith continued to honor her mother's Jewish faith. Sister Josephine Koeppel, O.C.D., translator of several of Edith's books, sums up this saint with the phrase, "Learn to live at God's hands."

QUOTE: In his homily at the canonization Mass, Pope John Paul II said: "Because she was Jewish, Edith Stein was taken with her sister Rosa and many other Catholics and Jews from the Netherlands to the concentration camp in Auschwitz, where she died with them in the gas chambers. Today we remember them all with deep respect. A few days before her deportation, the woman religious had dismissed the question about a possible rescue: 'Do not do it! Why should I be spared? Is it not right that I should gain no advantage from my baptism? If I cannot share the lot of my brothers and sisters, my life, in a certain sense, is destroyed.'"

Addressing himself to the young people gathered for the canonization, the pope said: "Your life is not an endless series of open doors! Listen to your heart! Do not stay on the surface but go to the heart of things! And when the time is right, have the courage to decide! The Lord is waiting for you to put your freedom in his good hands."

• • •

AUGUST 9 + OPTIONAL
Blessed Franz Jägerstätter
LAYMAN AND MARTYR (1907–1943)

Called to serve his country as a Nazi solider, Franz eventually refused and this husband and father of three daughters (Rosalie, Marie, and Aloisia) was executed because of it.

Born in St. Radegund in Upper Austria, Franz lost his father during World War I and was adopted after Heinrich Jägerstätter married Rosalia Huber. As a young man, he loved to ride his motorcycle and was the natural leader of a gang whose members were arrested for brawling in 1934. For three years he worked in the mines in another city and then returned to St. Radegund, where he became a farmer, married Franziska, and lived his faith with quiet but intense conviction.

In 1938 he publicly opposed the German *Anschluss* (annexation) of Austria. The next year he was drafted into the Austrian army, trained for seven months, and then received a deferment. In 1940 he was called up again but allowed to return home at the request of the town's mayor. He was in active service between October 1940 and April 1941 but was again deferred. His pastor, other priests and the bishop of Linz urged him not to refuse to serve if drafted.

In February 1943 he was called up again and reported to army officials in Enns, Austria. When he refused to take the oath of loyalty to Hitler, he was imprisoned in Linz. Later he volunteered to serve in the medical corps but was not assigned there.

During Holy Week he wrote to his wife: "Easter is coming and, if it should be God's will that we can never again in this world celebrate Easter together in our intimate family circle, we can still look ahead in the happy confidence that, when the eternal Easter morning dawns, no one in our family circle shall be missing—so we can then be permitted to rejoice together forever." In May, he was transferred to a prison in Berlin.

Challenged by his attorney that other Catholics were serving in the army, Franz responded, "I can only act on my own conscience. I do not judge anyone. I can only judge myself." He continued, "I have considered my family. I have prayed and put myself and my family in God's hands. I know that, if I do what I think God wants me to do, he will take care of my family."

On August 8, 1943, he wrote to Fransizka: "Dear wife and mother, I thank you once more from my heart for everything that you have done for me in my lifetime, for all the sacrifices that you have borne for me. I beg you to forgive me if I have hurt or offended you, just as I have forgiven everything.... My heartfelt greetings for my dear children. I will surely beg the dear God, if I am permitted to enter heaven soon, that he will set aside a little place in heaven for all of you."

Franz was beheaded and cremated the following day. In 1946 his ashes were reburied in St. Radegund near a memorial inscribed with his name and the names of almost sixty village men who died during their military service. He was beatified in Linz on October 26, 2007. His "spiritual testament" is now in Rome's St. Bartholomew Church as part of a shrine to twentieth-century martyrs for their faith.

COMMENT: Franz Jägerstätter followed his conscience and paid the highest price possible. In December 2008 his widow and three daughters were introduced to Pope Benedict XVI in connection with the presentation of a new biography, *Christ or Hitler? The Life of Blessed Franz Jägerstätter*. Many people first learned about him from Gordon Zahn's book *In Solitary Witness: The Life and Death of Franz Jägerstätter*.

QUOTE: In his homily at the beatification Mass, Cardinal José Saraiva Martins quoted Giorgio La Pira, a twentieth-century mayor of Florence, who wrote: "The holiness of our century will have this characteristic: It will be a holiness of laypeople. We encounter on the streets those who within fifty years may be on the altars—along the streets, in factories, in parliament and in university classrooms." Cardinal Martins noted that after long internal struggles, Franz arrived at an extraordinary life of Christian witness. "Saints and blesseds have always given an example of what it means and signifies to be Christians, even in particular, concrete historical moments."

• • •

AUGUST 10 + FEAST
Lawrence
DEACON AND MARTYR (D. 258?)

The esteem in which the Church holds Lawrence is seen in the fact that today's celebration ranks as a feast. We know very little about his life. He is one of those whose martyrdom made a deep and lasting impression on the early Church. Celebration of his feast day spread rapidly.

He was a Roman deacon under Pope St. Sixtus II (August 7). Four days after this pope was put to death, Lawrence and four clerics suffered martyrdom, probably during the persecution of the Emperor Valerian.

Legendary details of his death were known to Damasus (December 11), Prudentius, Ambrose (December 7), and Augustine (August 28). The church built over his tomb became one of the seven principal churches in Rome and a favorite place for Roman pilgrimages.

COMMENT: Once again we have a saint about whom almost nothing is known, yet one who has received extraordinary honor in the Church since the fourth century. Almost nothing—yet the greatest fact of his life is certain: He died for Christ. We who are hungry for details about the lives of the saints are again reminded that their holiness was, after all, a total response to Christ, expressed perfectly by a death like this.

STORY: A well-known legend has persisted from earliest times. As deacon in Rome, Lawrence was charged with the responsibility for the material goods of the Church and the distribution of alms to the poor. When Lawrence knew he would be arrested like the pope, he sought out the poor, widows and orphans of Rome and gave them all the money he had on hand, selling even the sacred vessels to increase the sum. When the prefect of Rome heard of this, he imagined that the Christians must have considerable treasure. He sent for Lawrence and said, "You Christians say we are cruel to you, but that is not what I have in mind. I am told that your priests offer in gold, that the sacred blood is received in silver cups, that you have golden candlesticks at your evening services. Now, your doctrine says you must render to Caesar what is his. Bring these treasures—the emperor needs them to maintain his forces. God does not cause money to be counted: He brought none of it into the world with him—only words. Give me the money, therefore, and be rich in words."

Lawrence replied that the Church was indeed rich. "I will show you a valuable part. But give me time to set everything in order and make an inventory." After three days he gathered a great number of blind, lame, maimed, leprous, orphaned, and widowed persons and put them in rows. When the prefect arrived, Lawrence simply said, "These are the treasure of the Church."

The prefect was so angry he told Lawrence that he would indeed have his wish to die—but it would be by inches. He had a great gridiron prepared, with coals beneath it, and had Lawrence's body placed on it. After the martyr had suffered the pain for a long time, the legend concludes, he made his famous cheerful remark, "It is well done. Turn me over!"

• • •

AUGUST 11 + MEMORIAL

Clare

VIRGIN (1194–1253)

One of the more sugary movies made about Francis of Assisi (October 4) pictures Clare as a golden-haired beauty floating through sun-drenched fields, a sort of one-woman counterpart to the new Franciscan Order.

The beginning of her religious life was indeed movie material. Having refused to marry at fifteen, she was moved by the dynamic preaching of Francis. He became her lifelong friend and her spiritual guide.

At eighteen, she escaped one night from her father's home, was met on the road by friars carrying torches, and in the poor little chapel called the Portiuncula received a rough woolen habit, exchanged her jeweled belt for a common rope with knots in it, and sacrificed the long tresses to Francis's scissors. He placed her in a Benedictine convent, which her uncles immediately stormed in rage. She clung to the altar of the church, threw aside her veil to show her cropped hair and remained adamant.

End of movie material. Sixteen days later her sister Agnes joined her. Others came. They lived a simple life of great poverty, austerity, and complete seclusion from the world, according to a rule that Francis gave them as a Second Order (Poor Clares). Francis obliged her under obedience at age twenty-one to accept the office of abbess, one she exercised until her death.

The nuns went barefoot, slept on the ground, ate no meat, and observed almost complete silence. (Later Clare, like Francis, persuaded her sisters to moderate this rigor: "Our bodies are not made of brass.") The greatest emphasis, of course, was on Gospel poverty. They possessed no property, even in common, subsisting on daily contributions. When even the pope tried to persuade her to mitigate this practice, she showed her characteristic firmness: "I need to be absolved from my sins, but I do not wish to be absolved from the obligation of following Jesus Christ."

Contemporary accounts glow with admiration of her life in the convent of San Damiano in Assisi. She served the sick, waited on table, washed the feet of the begging nuns. She came from prayer, it was said, with her face so shining it dazzled those about her. She suffered serious illness for the last twenty-seven years of her life. Her influence was such that popes, cardinals, and bishops often came to consult her—she never left the walls of San Damiano.

Francis always remained her great friend and inspiration. She was always obedient to his will and to the great ideal of Gospel life that he was making real.

A well-known story concerns her prayer and trust. She had the Blessed Sacrament placed on the walls of the convent when it faced attack by invading Saracens. "Does it please you, O God, to deliver into the hands of these beasts the defenseless children I have nourished with your love? I beseech you, dear Lord, protect these whom I am now unable to protect." To her sisters she said, "Don't be afraid. Trust in Jesus." The Saracens fled.

COMMENT: The forty-one years of Clare's religious life are a scenario of sanctity: an indomitable resolve to lead the simple, literal Gospel life as Francis taught her; courageous resistance to the ever-present pressure to dilute the ideal; a passion for poverty and humility; an ardent life of prayer; and a generous concern for her sisters.

STORY: On her deathbed, Clare was heard to say to herself: "Go forth in peace, for you have followed the good road. Go forth without fear, for he who created you has made you holy, has always protected you, and loves you as a mother. Blessed be you, my God, for having created me."

• • •

AUGUST 12 + OPTIONAL

Jane Frances de Chantal

RELIGIOUS (1562–1641)

Jane Frances was wife, mother, nun, and founder of a religious community. Her mother died when Jane was eighteen months old, and her father, head of parliament at Dijon, France, became the main influence on her education. She developed into a woman of beauty and refinement, lively and cheerful in temperament. At twenty-one she married Baron de Chantal, by whom she had six children, three of whom died in infancy. At her castle she restored the custom of daily Mass, and was seriously engaged in various charitable works.

Jane's husband was killed after seven years of marriage, and she sank into deep dejection for four months at her family home. Her father-in-law threatened to disinherit her children if she did not return to his home. He was then seventy-five, vain, fierce, and extravagant. Jane Frances managed to remain cheerful in spite of him and his insolent housekeeper.

When she was thirty-two, she met St. Francis de Sales (January 24) who became her spiritual director, softening some of the severities imposed by her former director. She wanted to become a nun, but he persuaded her to defer this decision. She took a vow to remain unmarried and to obey her director.

After three years Francis told her of his plan to found an institute of women that would be a haven for those whose health, age, or other considerations barred them from entering the already established communities. There would be no cloister, and they would be free to undertake spiritual and corporal works of mercy. They were primarily intended to exemplify the virtues of Mary at the Visitation (hence their name, the Visitation nuns): humility and meekness.

The usual opposition to women in active ministry arose, and Francis de Sales was obliged to make it a cloistered community following the Rule of St. Augustine. Francis wrote his famous *Treatise on the Love of God* for them.

The congregation (three women) began when Jane Frances was forty-five. She underwent great sufferings: Francis de Sales died; her son was killed; a plague ravaged France; her daughter-in-law and son-in-law died. She encouraged the local authorities to make great efforts for the victims of the plague, and she put all her convent's resources at the disposal of the sick.

During a part of her religious life, she had to undergo great trials of the spirit—interior anguish, darkness, and spiritual dryness. She died while on a visitation of convents of the community.

COMMENT: It may strike some as unusual that a saint should be subject to spiritual dryness, darkness, interior anguish. We tend to think that such things are the usual condition of ordinary sinful people. Some of our lack of spiritual liveliness may indeed be our fault. But the life of faith is still one that is lived in trust, and sometimes the darkness is so great that trust is pressed to its limit.

QUOTE: St. Vincent de Paul (September 27) said of Jane Frances: "She was full of faith, yet all her life had been tormented by thoughts against it. While apparently enjoying the peace and easiness of mind of souls who have reached a high state of virtue, she suffered such interior trials that she often told me her mind was so filled with all sorts of temptations and abominations that she had to strive not to look within herself.... But for all that suffering her face never lost its serenity, nor did she once relax in the fidelity God asked of her. And so I regard her as one of the holiest souls I have ever met on this earth" (*Butler's Lives of the Saints*).

* * *

AUGUST 13 + OPTIONAL
Pontian and Hippolytus
POPE AND MARTYR; PRIEST AND MARTYR (D. 235)
Two men died for the faith after harsh treatment and exhaustion in the mines of Sardinia. One had been pope for five years, the other an antipope for eighteen. They died reconciled.

Pontian. Pontian was a Roman who served as pope from 230 to 235. During his reign he held a synod that confirmed the excommunication of the great theologian Origen in Alexandria. Pontian was banished to exile by the Roman emperor in 235, and resigned so that a successor could be elected in Rome. He was sent to the "unhealthy" island of Sardinia, where he died of harsh treatment in 235. With him was Hippolytus with whom he was reconciled. The bodies of both men were brought back to Rome and buried with solemn rites as martyrs.

Hippolytus. As a priest in Rome, Hippolytus (the name means "a horse turned loose") was at first "holier than the Church." He censured the pope for not coming down hard enough on a certain heresy—calling him a tool in the hands of one Callistus, a deacon—and coming close to advocating the opposite heresy himself. When Callistus (October 14) was elected pope, Hippolytus accused him of being too lenient with penitents and had himself elected antipope by a group of followers. He felt that the Church must be composed of pure souls uncompromisingly separated from the world; Hippolytus evidently thought that his group fit the description. He remained in schism through the reigns of three popes. In 235 he was also banished to the island of Sardinia. Shortly before or after this event, he was reconciled to the Church and died with Pope Pontian in exile.

Hippolytus was a rigorist, a vehement and intransigent man for whom even orthodox doctrine and practice were not purified enough. He is, nevertheless, the most important theologian and prolific religious writer before the age of Constantine. His writings are the fullest source of our knowledge of the Roman liturgy and the structure of the Church in the second and third centuries. His works include many Scripture commentaries, polemics against heresies, and a history of the world. A marble statue, dating from the third century, representing the saint sitting in a chair, was found in 1551. On one side is inscribed his table for computing the date of Easter, on the other a list of how the system works out until the year 224. Blessed John XXIII installed the statue in the Vatican library.

COMMENT: Hippolytus was a strong defender of orthodoxy and admitted his excesses by his humble reconciliation. He was not a formal heretic, but an overzealous disciplinarian. What he could not learn in his prime as a reformer and purist, he learned in the pain and desolation of imprisonment. It was a fitting symbolic event that Pope Pontian shared his martyrdom.

QUOTE: "Christ, like a skillful physician, understands the weakness of men. He loves to teach the ignorant and the erring he turns again to his own true way. He is easily found by those who live by faith; and to those of pure eye and holy heart, who desire to knock at the door, he opens immediately. He does not disdain the barbarian, nor does he set the eunuch aside as no man. He does not hate the female on account of the woman's act of disobedience in the beginning, nor does he reject the male on account of the man's transgression. But he seeks all, and desires to save all, wishing to make all the children of God, and calling all the saints unto one perfect man" (Hippolytus, *Treatise on Christ and Antichrist*).

• • •

AUGUST 14 + MEMORIAL
Maximilian Mary Kolbe
PRIEST AND MARTYR (1894–1941)

"I don't know what's going to become of you!" How many parents have said that? Maximilian Mary Kolbe's reaction was, "I prayed very hard to Our Lady to tell me what would happen to me. She appeared, holding in her hands two crowns, one white, one red. She asked if I would like to have them— one was for purity, the other for martyrdom. I said, 'I choose both.' She smiled and disappeared." After that he was not the same.

He entered the minor seminary of the Conventual Franciscans in Lvív (then in Poland, now in the Ukraine), near his birthplace and at sixteen became a novice. Though he later achieved doctorates in philosophy and theology, he was deeply interested in science, even drawing plans for rocket ships.

Ordained at twenty-four, he saw religious indifference as the deadliest poison of the day. His mission was to combat it. He had already founded the Militia of the Immaculata, whose aim was to fight evil with the witness of the good life, prayer, work, and suffering. He dreamed of and then founded *Knight of the Immaculata*, a religious magazine under Mary's protection to preach the Good News to all nations. For the work of publication he established a "City of the Immaculata"—Niepokalanow—which housed seven hundred of his Franciscan brothers. He later founded one in Nagasaki, Japan. Both the Militia and the magazine ultimately reached the one-million mark in members and subscribers. His love of God was daily filtered through devotion to Mary.

In 1939 Nazi panzers overran Poland with deadly speed. Niepokalanow was severely bombed. Kolbe and his friars were arrested then released in less than three months on the feast of the Immaculate Conception.

In 1941 he was arrested again. The Nazis' purpose was to liquidate the select ones, the leaders. The end came quickly, in Auschwitz three months later, after terrible beatings and humiliations.

A prisoner had escaped. The commandant announced that ten men would die. He relished walking along the ranks. "This one. That one." As they were being marched away to the starvation bunkers, Number 16670 dared to step from the line. "I would like to take that man's place. He has a wife and children." "Who are you?" "A priest." No name, no mention of fame. Silence. The commandant, dumbfounded, perhaps with a fleeting thought of history, kicked Sergeant Francis Gajowniczek out of line and ordered Fr. Kolbe to go with the nine. In the "block of death," they were ordered to strip naked and their slow starvation began in darkness. But there was no screaming—the prisoners sang. By the eve of the Assumption, four were left alive. The jailer came to finish Kolbe off as he sat in a corner praying. He lifted his fleshless arm to receive the bite of the hypodermic needle. It was filled with carbolic acid. They burned his body with all the others. He was beatified in 1971 and canonized eleven years later.

COMMENT: Fr. Kolbe's death was not a sudden, last-minute act of heroism. His whole life had been a preparation. His holiness was a limitless, passionate desire to convert the whole world to God. And his beloved Immaculata was his inspiration.

QUOTE: "Courage, my sons. Don't you see that we are leaving on a mission? They pay our fare in the bargain. What a piece of good luck! The thing to do now is to pray well in order to win as many souls as possible. Let us, then, tell the Blessed Virgin that we are content, and that she can do with us anything she wishes" (Maximilian Mary Kolbe, when first arrested).

*   *   *

AUGUST 15 + SOLEMNITY
Assumption

On November 1, 1950, Pius XII defined the Assumption of Mary to be a dogma of faith: "We pronounce, declare and define it to be a divinely revealed dogma that the immaculate Mother of God, the ever Virgin Mary, having completed the course of her earthly life, was assumed body and soul to heavenly glory." The pope proclaimed this dogma only after a broad consultation of bishops, theologians, and laity. There were few dissenting voices. What the pope solemnly declared was already a common belief in the Catholic Church.

We find homilies on the Assumption going back to the sixth century. In following centuries the Eastern Churches held steadily to the doctrine, but some authors in the West were hesitant. However, by the thirteenth century there was universal agreement. The feast was celebrated under various names (Commemoration, Dormition, Passing, Assumption) from at least the fifth or sixth century.

Scripture does not give an account of Mary's assumption into heaven. Nevertheless, chapter twelve of Revelation speaks of a woman who is caught up in the battle between good and evil. Many see this woman as God's people. Since Mary best embodies the people of both Old and New Testament, her assumption can be seen as an exemplification of the woman's victory.

Furthermore, in 1 Corinthians 15:20 Paul speaks of Christ's resurrection as the firstfruits of those who have fallen asleep. Since Mary is closely associated with all the mysteries of Jesus's life, it is not surprising that the Holy Spirit has led the Church to belief in Mary's share in his glorification. So close was she to Jesus on earth, she must be with him body and soul in heaven.

COMMENT: In the light of the assumption of Mary, it is easy to pray her Magnificat (Luke 1:46–55) with new meaning. In her glory she proclaims the greatness of the Lord and finds joy in God her savior. God has done marvels to her and she leads others to recognize God's holiness. She is the lowly handmaid who deeply reverenced her God and has been raised to the heights. From her position of strength she will help the lowly and the poor find justice on earth, and she will challenge the rich and powerful to distrust wealth and power as a source of happiness.

QUOTE: "In the bodily and spiritual glory which she possesses in heaven, the Mother of Jesus continues in this present world as the image and first flowering of the Church as she is to be perfected in the world to come. Likewise, Mary shines forth on earth, until the day of the Lord shall come (cf. 2 Peter 3:10), as a sign of certain hope and comfort for the pilgrim People of God" (Dogmatic Constitution on the Church, 68).

. . .

AUGUST 16 + OPTIONAL
Stephen of Hungary
HUSBAND AND FATHER (975–1038)

The Church is universal, but its expression is always affected—for good or ill—by local culture. There are no "generic" Christians; there are Mexican Christians, Polish Christians, Filipino Christians. This fact is evident in the life of Stephen, national hero and spiritual patron of Hungary.

Born a pagan, he was baptized around the age of ten, together with his father, chief of the Magyars, a group who migrated to the Danube area in the ninth century. At twenty he married Gisela, sister to the future emperor, St. Henry (July 13). When he succeeded his father, Stephen adopted a policy of Christianization of the country for both political and religious reasons. He suppressed a series of revolts by pagan nobles and welded the Magyars into a strong national group. He asked the pope to provide for the Church's organization in Hungary—and also requested that the pope confer the title of king upon him. He was crowned on Christmas day in 1001.

Stephen established a system of tithes to support churches and pastors and to relieve the poor. Out of every ten towns, one had to build a church and support a priest. He abolished pagan customs with a certain amount of violence and commanded all to marry, except clergy and religious. He was easily accessible to all, especially the poor.

In 1031 his son Emeric died, and the rest of Stephen's days were embittered by controversy over his successor. His nephews attempted to kill him. He died in 1038 and was canonized, along with his son, in 1083.

COMMENT: God's gift of holiness is a Christ-like love of God and humanity. Love must sometimes bear a stern countenance for the sake of ultimate good. Christ attacked hypocrites among the Pharisees, but died forgiving them. Paul excommunicated the incestuous man at Corinth "that his spirit may be saved." Some Christians fought the Crusades with noble zeal, in spite of the unworthy motives of others. Today, after senseless wars, and with a deeper understanding of the complex nature of human motives, we shrink from any use of violence, physical or "silent." This wholesome development continues as people debate whether it is possible for a Christian to be an absolute pacifist or whether evil must sometimes be repelled by force.

QUOTE: "Although the Church has contributed much to the development of culture, experience shows that, because of circumstances, it is sometimes difficult to harmonize culture with Christian teaching.

"These difficulties do not necessarily harm the life of faith. Indeed they can stimulate the mind to a more accurate and penetrating grasp of the faith. For recent studies and findings of science, history and philosophy raise new questions which influence life and demand new theological investigations" (Pastoral Constitution on the Church in the Modern World, 62).

• • •

AUGUST 19 + OPTIONAL
John Eudes
PRIEST (1601–1680)

How little we know where God's grace will lead. Born on a farm in northern France, John died at seventy-nine in the next "county" or department. In that time he was a religious, a parish missionary, a founder of two religious communities, and a great promoter of the devotion to the Sacred Heart and the Immaculate Heart of Mary.

He joined the religious community of the Oratorians and was ordained a priest at twenty-four. During severe plagues in 1627 and 1631, he volunteered to care for the stricken in his own diocese. Lest he infect his fellow religious, he lived in a huge cask in the middle of a field during the plague.

At age thirty-two, John became a parish missionary. His gifts as preacher and confessor won him great popularity. He preached over one hundred parish missions, some lasting from several weeks to several months.

In his concern with the spiritual improvement of the clergy, he realized that the greatest need was for seminaries. He had permission from his general superior, the bishop and even Cardinal Richelieu to begin this work, but the succeeding general superior disapproved. After prayer and counsel, John decided it was best to leave the religious community. The same year he founded a new one, ultimately called the Eudists (Congregation of Jesus and Mary), devoted to the formation of the clergy by conducting diocesan seminaries. The new venture, while approved by individual bishops, met with immediate opposition, especially from Jansenists and some of his former associates. John founded several seminaries in Normandy, but was unable to get approval from Rome (partly, it was said, because he did not use the most tactful approach).

In his parish mission work, John was disturbed by the sad condition of prostitutes who sought to escape their miserable life. Temporary shelters were found, but arrangements were not satisfactory. A certain Madeleine

Lamy, who had cared for several of the women, one day said to him, "Where are you off to now? To some church, I suppose, where you'll gaze at the images and think yourself pious. And all the time what is really wanted of you is a decent house for these poor creatures." The words, and the laughter of those present, struck deeply within him. The result was another new religious community, called the Sisters of Charity of the Refuge.

He is probably best known for the central theme of his writings: Jesus as the source of holiness, Mary as the model of the Christian life. John's devotion to the Sacred Heart and to the Immaculate Heart of Mary led Pius XI to declare him the father of the liturgical cult of the Hearts of Jesus and Mary.

COMMENT: Holiness is the wholehearted openness to the love of God. It is visibly expressed in many ways, but the variety of expression has one common quality: concern for the needs of others. In John's case, those who were in need were plague-stricken people, ordinary parishioners, those preparing for the priesthood, prostitutes, and all Christians called to imitate the love of Jesus and his mother.

QUOTE: "Our wish, our object, our chief preoccupation must be to form Jesus in ourselves, to make his spirit, his devotion, his affections, his desires and his disposition live and reign there. All our religious exercises should be directed to this end. It is the work which God has given us to do unceasingly" (St. John Eudes, *The Life and Reign of Jesus in Christian Souls*).

• • •

AUGUST 20 + MEMORIAL
Bernard
ABBOT AND DOCTOR (1091–1153)

Man of the century! Woman of the century! You see such terms applied to so many today—"golfer of the century," "composer of the century," "right tackle of the century"—that the line no longer has any punch. But Western Europe's "man of the twelfth century," without doubt or controversy, has to be Bernard of Clairvaux. Adviser of popes, preacher of the Second Crusade, defender of the faith, healer of a schism, reformer of a monastic order, Scripture scholar, theologian, and eloquent preacher: any one of these titles would distinguish an ordinary man. Yet Bernard was all of these—and he still retained a burning desire to return to the hidden monastic life of his younger days.

In the year 1111, at the age of twenty, Bernard left his home to join the monastic community of Citeaux. His five brothers, two uncles, and some thirty young friends followed him into the monastery. Within four years a dying community had recovered enough vitality to establish a new house in the nearby valley of Wormwoods, with Bernard as abbot. The zealous young man was quite demanding, though more on himself than others. A slight breakdown of health taught him to be more patient and understanding. The valley was soon renamed Clairvaux, the valley of light.

His ability as arbitrator and counselor became widely known. More and more he was lured away from the monastery to settle long-standing disputes. On several of these occasions he apparently stepped on some sensitive toes in Rome. Bernard was completely dedicated to the primacy of the Roman see. But to a letter of warning from Rome, he replied that the good fathers in Rome had enough to do to keep the Church in one piece. If any matters arose that warranted their interest, he would be the first to let them know.

Shortly thereafter it was Bernard who intervened in a full-blown schism and settled it in favor of the Roman pontiff against the antipope.

The Holy See prevailed on Bernard to preach the Second Crusade throughout Europe. His eloquence was so overwhelming that a great army was assembled, and the success of the crusade seemed assured. The ideals of the men and their leaders, however, were not those of Abbot Bernard, and the project ended as a complete military and moral disaster.

Bernard felt responsible in some way for the degenerative effects of the crusade. This heavy burden possibly hastened his death, which came August 20, 1153.

COMMENT: Bernard's life in the Church was more active than we can imagine possible today. His efforts produced far-reaching results. But he knew that they would have availed little without the many hours of prayer and contemplation that brought him strength and heavenly direction. His life was characterized by a deep devotion to the Blessed Mother. His sermons and books about Mary are still the standard of Marian theology.

QUOTE: "In dangers, in doubts, in difficulties, think of Mary, call upon Mary. Let not her name depart from your lips, never suffer it to leave your heart. And that you may more surely obtain the assistance of her prayer, neglect not to walk in her footsteps. With her for guide, you shall never go astray; while invoking her, you shall never lose heart; so long as she is in your mind, you are safe from deception; while she holds your hand, you cannot fall; under her protection you have nothing to fear; if she walks before you, you shall not grow weary; if she shows you favor, you shall reach the goal" (St. Bernard).

● ● ●

AUGUST 21 + MEMORIAL
Pius X
POPE (1835–1914)

Pope Pius X is perhaps best remembered for his encouragement of the frequent reception of Holy Communion, especially by children.

The second of ten children in a poor Italian family, Joseph Sarto became Pius X at sixty-eight, one of the twentieth century's greatest popes.

Ever mindful of his humble origin, he stated, "I was born poor, I lived poor, I will die poor." He was embarrassed by some of the pomp of the papal court. "Look how they have dressed me up," he said in tears to an old friend. To another, "It is a penance to be forced to accept all these practices. They lead me around surrounded by soldiers like Jesus when he was seized in Gethsemane."

Interested in politics, he encouraged Italian Catholics to become more politically involved. One of his first papal acts was to end the supposed right of governments to interfere by veto in papal elections —a practice that reduced the freedom of the 1903 conclave that had elected him.

In 1905, when France renounced its agreement with the Holy See and threatened confiscation of Church property if governmental control of Church affairs were not granted, Pius X courageously rejected the demand.

While he did not author a famous social encyclical as his predecessor had done, he denounced the ill treatment of indigenous peoples on the plantations of Peru, sent a relief commission to Messina after an earthquake, and sheltered refugees at his own expense.

On the eleventh anniversary of his election as pope, Europe was plunged into World War I. Pius had foreseen it, but it killed him. "This is the last affliction the Lord will visit on me. I would gladly give my life to save my poor children from this ghastly scourge." He died a few weeks after the war began and was canonized in 1954.

COMMENT: His humble background was no obstacle in relating to a personal God and to people whom he loved genuinely. He gained his strength, his gentleness, and his warmth for people from the source of all gifts, the Spirit of Jesus. In contrast, we often feel embarrassed by our backgrounds. Shame makes us prefer to remain aloof from people whom we perceive as superior. If we are in a superior position, on the other hand, we often ignore simpler people. Yet we, too, have to help "restore all things in Christ," especially the wounded people of God.

QUOTE: Describing Pius X, a historian wrote that he was "a man of God who knew the unhappiness of the world and the hardships of life, and in the greatness of his heart wanted to comfort everyone."

• • •

Queenship of Mary

Pius XII established this feast in 1954. But Mary's queenship has roots in Scripture. At the annunciation, Gabriel announced that Mary's Son would receive the throne of David and rule forever. At the visitation, Elizabeth calls Mary "mother of my Lord." As in all the mysteries of Mary's life, Mary is closely associated with Jesus: Her queenship is a share in Jesus's kingship.

We can also recall that in the Old Testament the mother of the king has great influence in court.

In the fourth century St. Ephrem (June 9) called Mary "Lady" and "Queen." Later Church fathers and doctors continued to use the title. Hymns of the eleventh to thirteenth centuries address Mary as queen: "Hail, Holy Queen," "Hail, Queen of Heaven," "Queen of Heaven." The Dominican rosary and the Franciscan crown as well as numerous invocations in Mary's litany celebrate her queenship.

The feast is a logical follow-up to the assumption and is now celebrated on the octave day of that feast. In his 1954 encyclical *To the Queen of Heaven*, Pius XII points out that Mary deserves the title because she is Mother of God, because she is closely associated as the New Eve with Jesus's redemptive work, because of her preeminent perfection and because of her intercessory power.

COMMENT: As St. Paul suggests in Romans 8:28–30, God has predestined human beings from all eternity to share the image of his Son. All the more was Mary predestined to be the mother of Jesus. As Jesus was to be king of all creation, Mary, in dependence on Jesus, was to be queen. All other titles to queenship derive from this eternal intention of God. As Jesus exercised his kingship on earth by serving his Father and his fellow human beings, so did Mary exercise her queenship. As the glorified Jesus remains with us as our king till the end of time (Matthew 28:20), so does Mary, who was assumed into heaven and crowned queen of heaven and earth.

QUOTE: "Let the entire body of the faithful pour forth persevering prayer to the Mother of God and Mother of men. Let them implore that she who aided the beginnings of the Church by her prayers may now, exalted as she is in heaven above all the saints and angels, intercede with her Son in the fellowship of all the saints. May she do so until all the peoples of the human family, whether they are honored with the name of Christian or whether they still do not know their Savior, are happily gathered together in peace and harmony into the one People of God, for the glory of the Most Holy and Undivided Trinity" (Dogmatic Constitution on the Church, 69).

• • •

AUGUST 23 + OPTIONAL
Rose of Lima
VIRGIN (1586–1617)

The first canonized saint of the New World has one characteristic of all saints—the suffering of opposition—and another characteristic that is more for admiration than for imitation—excessive practice of mortification.

She was born to parents of Spanish descent in Lima, Peru, at a time when South America was in its first century of evangelization. She seems to have taken Catherine of Siena (April 29) as a model, in spite of the objections and ridicule of parents and friends.

The saints have so great a love of God that what seems bizarre to us, and is indeed sometimes imprudent, is simply a logical carrying out of a conviction that anything that might endanger a loving relationship with God must be rooted out. So, because her beauty was so often admired, Rose used to rub her face with pepper to produce disfiguring blotches. Later, she wore a thick circlet of silver on her head, studded on the inside, like a crown of thorns.

When her parents fell into financial trouble, she worked in the garden all day and sewed at night. Ten years of struggle against her parents began when they tried to make Rose marry. They refused to let her enter a convent, and out of obedience she continued her life of penance and solitude at home as a member of the Third Order of St. Dominic. So deep was her desire to live the life of Christ that she spent most of her time at home in solitude.

During the last few years of her life, Rose set up a room in the house where she cared for homeless children, the elderly, and the sick. This was a beginning of social services in Peru. Though secluded in life and activity, she was brought to the attention of Inquisition interrogators, who could only say that she was influenced by grace.

What might have been a merely eccentric life was transfigured from the inside. If we remember some unusual penances, we should also remember the greatest thing about Rose: a love of God so ardent that it withstood ridicule from without, violent temptation, and lengthy periods of sickness.

When she died at thirty-one, the city turned out for her funeral. Prominent men took turns carrying her coffin.

COMMENT: It is easy to dismiss excessive penances of the saints as the expression of a certain culture or temperament. But a woman wearing a crown of thorns may at least prod our consciences. We enjoy the most comfort-oriented life in human history. We eat too much, drink too much, use a million gadgets, and fill our eyes and ears with everything imaginable. Commerce thrives on creating useless needs on which to spend our money. It seems that when we have become most like slaves, there is the greatest talk of "freedom." Are we willing to discipline ourselves in such an atmosphere?

QUOTE: "If your hand or your foot causes you to sin, cut it off and throw it away. It is better for you to enter into life maimed or crippled than with two hands or two feet to be thrown into eternal fire. And if your eye causes you to sin, tear it out and throw it away. It is better for you to enter into life with one eye than with two eyes to be thrown into fiery Gehenna" (Matthew 18:8–9).

• • •

AUGUST 24 + FEAST
Bartholomew
APOSTLE

In the New Testament, Bartholomew is mentioned only in the lists of the apostles. Some scholars identify him with Nathanael, a man of Cana in Galilee who was summoned to Jesus by Philip. Jesus paid him a great compliment: "Here is a true Israelite. There is no duplicity in him" (John 1:47b). When Nathanael asked how Jesus knew him, Jesus said, "I saw you under the fig tree" (John 1:48b). Whatever amazing revelation this involved, it brought Nathanael to exclaim, "Rabbi, you are the Son of God; you are the King of Israel" (John 1:49b). But Jesus countered with, "Do you believe because I told you that I saw you under the fig tree? You will see greater things than this" (John 1:50b).

Nathanael did see greater things. He was one of those to whom Jesus appeared on the shore of the Sea of Tiberias after his resurrection (see John 21:1–14). They had been fishing all night without success. In the morning, they saw someone standing on the shore though no one knew it was Jesus. He told them to cast their net again, and they made so great a catch that they could not haul the net in. Then John cried out to Peter, "It is the Lord."

When they brought the boat to shore, they found a fire burning, with some fish laid on it and some bread. Jesus asked them to bring some of the fish they had caught and invited them to come and eat their meal. John relates that although they knew it was Jesus, none of the apostles presumed to inquire who he was. This, John notes, was the third time Jesus appeared to the apostles.

COMMENT: Bartholomew or Nathanael? We are confronted again with the fact that we know almost nothing about most of the apostles. Yet the unknown ones were also foundation stones, the twelve pillars of the new Israel whose twelve tribes now encompass the whole earth. Their personalities were secondary (without thereby being demeaned) to their great office of bearing tradition from their firsthand experience, speaking in the name of Jesus, putting the Word made flesh into human words for the enlightenment of the world. Their holiness was not an introverted contemplation of their status before God. It was a gift that they had to share with others. The Good News was that all are called to the holiness of being Christ's members, by the gracious gift of God.

The simple fact is that humanity is totally meaningless unless God is its total concern. Then humanity, made holy with God's own holiness, becomes the most precious creation of God.

QUOTE: "Like Christ himself, the apostles were unceasingly bent upon bearing witness to the truth of God. They showed special courage in speaking 'the word of God with boldness' (Acts 4:31) before the people and their rulers. With a firm faith they held that the gospel is indeed the power of

God unto salvation for all who believe.... They followed the example of the gentleness and respectfulness of Christ" (Declaration on Religious Freedom, 11).

* * *

AUGUST 25 + OPTIONA

Louis

HUSBAND AND FATHER (1214–1270)

At his coronation as king of France, Louis bound himself by oath to behave as God's anointed, as the father of his people and feudal lord of the King of Peace. Other kings had done the same, of course. Louis was different in that he actually interpreted his kingly duties in the light of faith. After the violence of two previous reigns, he brought peace and justice.

He was crowned king at twelve, at his father's death. His mother, Blanche of Castile, ruled during his minority. When he was nineteen (and his bride twelve), he was married to Marguerite of Provence. It was a loving marriage, despite her arrogant and restless nature. They had eleven children.

Louis "took the cross" for a crusade when he was thirty. His army seized Damietta in Egypt but not long after, weakened by dysentery and without support, they were surrounded and captured. Louis obtained the release of the army by giving up the city of Damietta in addition to paying a ransom. He stayed in Syria four years.

He is admired as a crusader, but perhaps he deserves greater credit for his extending justice in civil administration. His regulations for royal officials became the first of a series of reform laws. He replaced trial by battle with a form of examination of witnesses and encouraged the use of written records in court.

Louis was always respectful of the papacy but defended royal interests against the popes and refused to acknowledge Innocent IV's sentence against Emperor Frederick II.

Louis was devoted to his people, founding hospitals, visiting the sick, and, like his patron St. Francis (October 4), caring even for people with leprosy. (He is one of the patrons of the Secular Franciscan Order.) Louis united France—lords and townsfolk, peasants and priests and knights—by the force of his personality and holiness. For many years the nation was at peace.

Disturbed by new Muslim advances in Syria, he led another crusade in 1267, at the age of forty-one. His crusade was diverted to Tunis for his brother's sake. The army was decimated by disease within a month, and Louis himself died on foreign soil at the age of forty-four. He was canonized twenty-seven years later.

COMMENT: Louis was strong-willed, strong-minded. His word was trusted utterly, and his courage in action was remarkable. What was most remarkable was his sense of respect for anyone with whom he dealt, especially the "humble folk of the Lord." To care for his people he built cathedrals, churches, libraries, hospitals, and orphanages. He dealt with princes honestly and equitably. He hoped to be treated the same way by the King of Kings, to whom he gave his life, his family and his country.

STORY: Every day Louis had thirteen special guests from among the poor to eat with him, and a large number of poor were served meals near his palace. During Advent and Lent, all who presented themselves were given a meal, and Louis often served them in person. He kept lists of needy people, whom he regularly relieved, in every province of his dominion.

• • •

AUGUST 25 + OPTIONAL
Joseph Calasanz
PRIEST (1556–1648)

From Aragon, where he was born in 1556, to Rome, where he died ninety-two years later, fortune alternately smiled and frowned on the work of Joseph Calasanz. A priest with university training in canon law and theology, respected for his wisdom and administrative expertise, he put aside his career because he was deeply concerned with the need for education of poor children.

When he was unable to get other institutes to undertake this apostolate at Rome, he and several companions personally provided a free school for deprived children. So overwhelming was the response that there was a constant need for larger facilities to house their effort. Soon Pope Clement VIII gave support to the school, and this aid continued under Pope Paul V. Other schools were opened; other men were attracted to the work, and in 1621 the community (for so the teachers lived) was recognized as a religious community, the Clerks Regular of Religious Schools (Piarists or Scolopi). Not long after, Joseph was appointed superior for life.

A combination of various prejudices and political ambition and maneuvering caused the institute much turmoil. Some did not favor educating the poor, for education would leave the poor dissatisfied with their lowly tasks for society! Others were shocked that some of the Piarists were sent for instruction to Galileo (a friend of Joseph) as superior, thus dividing the members into opposite camps. Repeatedly investigated by papal commissions, Joseph was demoted; when the struggle within the institute persisted, the Piarists were suppressed. Only after Joseph's death were they formally recognized as a religious community.

COMMENT: No one knew better than Joseph the need for the work he was doing; no one knew better than he how baseless were the charges brought against him. Yet if he were to work within the Church, he realized that he must submit to its authority, that he must accept a setback if he was unable to convince authorized investigators. While the prejudice, the scheming, and the ignorance of men often keep the truth from emerging for a long period of time, Joseph was convinced, even under suppression, that his institute would again be recognized and authorized. With this trust he joined exceptional patience and a genuine spirit of forgiveness.

QUOTE: Even after his own demotion, Joseph protected his persecutors against his enraged partisans. When the community was suppressed, he stated with Job, to whom he was often compared: "The Lord gave and the Lord has taken away; / blessed be the name of the Lord!" (Job 1:21b).

• • •

AUGUST 27 + MEMORIAL

Monica

WIFE AND MOTHER (322?–387)

The circumstances of St. Monica's life could have made her a nagging wife, a bitter daughter-in-law, and a despairing parent, yet she did not give way to any of these temptations. Although she was a Christian, her parents gave her in marriage to a pagan, Patricius, who lived in her hometown of Tagaste in North Africa. Patricius had some redeeming features, but he had a violent temper and was licentious. Monica also had to bear with a cantankerous mother-in-law who lived in her home. Patricius criticized his wife because of her charity and piety, but always respected her. Monica's prayers and example finally won her husband and mother-in-law to Christianity. Her husband died in 371, one year after his baptism.

Monica had at least three children who survived infancy. The oldest, Augustine (August 28), is the most famous. At the time of his father's death, Augustine was seventeen and a rhetoric student in Carthage. Monica was distressed to learn that her son had accepted the Manichean heresy (all flesh is evil) and was living an immoral life. For a while, she refused to let him eat or sleep in her house. Then one night she had a vision that assured her Augustine would return to the faith. From that time on, she stayed close to her son, praying and fasting for him. In fact, she often stayed much closer than Augustine wanted.

When he was twenty-nine, Augustine decided to go to Rome to teach rhetoric. Monica was determined to go along. One night he told his mother that he was going to the dock to say good-bye to a friend. Instead, he set sail for Rome. Monica was heartbroken when she learned of Augustine's trick, but she still followed him. She arrived in Rome only to find that he had left for Milan. Although travel was difficult, Monica pursued him to Milan.

In Milan, Augustine came under the influence of the bishop, St. Ambrose (December 7), who also became Monica's spiritual director. She accepted his advice in everything and had the humility to give up some practices that had become second nature to her. Monica became a leader of the devout women in Milan as she had been in Tagaste.

She continued her prayers for Augustine during his years of instruction. At Easter, 387, St. Ambrose baptized Augustine and several of his friends. Soon after, his party left for Africa. Although no one else was aware of it, Monica knew her life was near the end. She told Augustine, "Son, nothing in this world now affords me delight. I do not know what there is now left for me to do or why I am still here, all my hopes in this world being now fulfilled." She became ill shortly after and suffered severely for nine days before her death.

Almost all we know about St. Monica is in the writings of St. Augustine, especially his *Confessions*.

COMMENT: Today, with Internet searches, e-mail, text messages, tweets, online shopping, and instant credit, we have little patience for things that take time. Likewise, we want instant answers to our prayers. Monica is a model of patience. Her long years of prayer, coupled with a strong, well-disciplined character, finally led to the conversion of her hot-tempered husband, her cantankerous mother-in-law, and her brilliant but wayward son, Augustine.

QUOTE: When Monica moved from North Africa to Milan, she found religious practices new to her and also that some of her former customs, such as a Saturday fast, were not common there. She asked St. Ambrose which customs she should follow. His classic reply was: "When I am here, I do not fast on Saturday, but I fast when I am in Rome; do the same and always follow the custom and discipline of the church as it is observed in the particular locality in which you find yourself."

• • •

AUGUST 28 + MEMORIAL

Augustine

BISHOP AND DOCTOR (354–430)

A Christian at thirty-three, a priest at thirty-six, a bishop at forty-four: Many people are familiar with the biographical sketch of Augustine of Hippo, sinner turned saint. But really to get to know the man is a rewarding experience.

There quickly surfaces the intensity with which he lived his life, whether his path led away from or toward God. The tears of his mother, Monica (August 27), the instructions of Ambrose (December 7), and, most of all, God himself speaking to him in the Scriptures redirected Augustine's love of life to a life of love.

Having been so deeply immersed in creature-pride of life in his early days and having drunk deeply of its bitter dregs, it is not surprising that Augustine should have turned, with a holy fierceness, against the many demon-thrusts rampant in his day. His times were truly decadent—politically, socially, morally. He was both feared and loved, like the Master. The perennial criticism leveled against him: a fundamental rigorism.

In his day, he providentially fulfilled the office of prophet. Like Jeremiah and other greats, he was hard-pressed but could not keep quiet. "I say to myself, I will not mention him, / I will speak in his name no more. / But then it becomes like fire burning in my heart, / imprisoned in my bones; / I grow weary holding it in, / I cannot endure it" (Jeremiah 20:9).

COMMENT: Augustine is still acclaimed and condemned in our day. He is a prophet for today, trumpeting the need to scrap escapisms and stand face-to-face with personal responsibility and dignity.

QUOTE: "Too late have I loved you, O Beauty of ancient days, yet ever new! Too late I loved you! And behold, you were within, and I abroad, and there I searched for you; I was deformed, plunging amid those fair forms, which you had made. You were with me, but I was not with you. Things held me far from you—things which, if they were not in you, were not at all. You called, and shouted, and burst my deafness. You flashed and shone, and scattered my blindness. You breathed odors and I drew in breath—and I pant for you. I tasted, and I hunger and thirst. You touched me, and I burned for your peace" (St. Augustine, *Confessions*).

• • •

AUGUST 29 + MEMORIAL

Martyrdom of John the Baptist

The drunken oath of a king with a shallow sense of honor, a seductive dance, and the hateful heart of a queen combined to bring about the martyrdom of John the Baptist. The greatest of prophets suffered the fate of so many Old Testament prophets before him: rejection and martyrdom. The "voice crying in the desert" did not hesitate to accuse the guilty, did not hesitate to speak the truth. But why? What possesses a man to give up his very life?

This great religious reformer was sent by God to prepare the people for the Messiah. His vocation was one of selfless giving. The only power that he claimed was the Spirit of God. "I am baptizing you with water, for repentance, but the one who is coming after me is mightier than I. I am not worthy to carry his sandals. He will baptize you with the holy Spirit and fire" (Matthew 3:11). Scripture tells us that many people followed John, looking to him for hope, perhaps in anticipation of some great messianic power. John never allowed himself the false honor of receiving these people for his own glory. He knew his calling was one of preparation. When the time came, he led his disciples to Jesus: "The next day John was there again with two of his disciples, and as he watched Jesus walk by, he said, 'Behold, the Lamb of God.' The two disciples heard what he said and followed Jesus" (John 1:35–37).

It is John the Baptist who has pointed the way to Christ. John's life and death were a giving over of self for God and other people. His simple style of life was one of complete detachment from earthly possessions. His heart was centered on God and the call that he heard from the Spirit of God speaking to his heart. Confident of God's grace, he had the courage to speak words of condemnation, repentance, and salvation.

COMMENT: Each of us has a calling to which we must listen. No one will ever repeat the mission of John, and yet all of us are called to that very mission. It is the role of the Christian to witness to Jesus. Whatever our position in this world, we are called to be disciples of Christ. By our words and deeds, others should realize that we live in the joy of knowing that Jesus is Lord. We do not have to depend upon our own limited resources, but can draw strength from the vastness of Christ's saving grace.

QUOTE: "So they came to John and said to him, 'Rabbi, the one who was with you across the Jordan, to whom you testified, here he is baptizing and everyone is coming to him.' John answered and said, 'No one can receive anything except what has been given him from heaven. You yourselves can testify that I said [that] I am not the Messiah, but that I was sent before him. The one who has the bride is the bridegroom; the best man, who stands and listens for him, rejoices greatly at the bridegroom's voice. So this joy of mine has been made complete. He must increase; I must decrease' " (John 3:26–30).

• • •

AUGUST 30 + OPTIONAL
Jeanne Jugan
VIRGIN (1792–1879)

Born in northern France during the French Revolution—a time when congregations of women and men religious were being suppressed by the national government, Jeanne would eventually be highly praised in the French Academy for her community's compassionate care of elderly poor people.

When Jeanne was three and a half years old, her father, a fisherman, was lost at sea. Her widowed mother was hard-pressed to raise her eight children (four died young) alone. At the age of fifteen or sixteen, Jeanne became a kitchen maid for a generous family that not only cared for its own members, but also served poor, elderly people nearby. Ten years later, Jeanne became a nurse at the hospital in Le Rosais. Soon thereafter she joined a third order group founded by St. John Eudes (August 19).

After six years she became a servant and friend of a woman she met through the third order. They prayed, visited the poor, and taught catechism to children. After her friend's death, Jeanne and two other women continued a similar life in the city of Saint-Sevran. In 1839 they brought in their first permanent guest. They began an association, received more members and more guests. Mother Marie of the Cross, as Jeanne was now known, founded six more houses for the elderly by the end of 1849, all staffed by members of her association—the Little Sisters of the Poor. By 1853 the association numbered five hundred and had houses as far away as England.

Abbé Le Pailleur, a chaplain, had prevented Jeanne's reelection as superior in 1843. Nine years later, he had her assigned to duties within the congregation, but would not allow her to be recognized as its founder. He was removed from office by the Holy See in 1890.

By the time Pope Leo XIII gave final approval to the community's constitutions in 1879, there were 2,400 Little Sisters of the Poor. Jeanne died later that same year, on August 30. Her cause was introduced in Rome in 1970; she was beatified in 1982 and canonized in 2009.

COMMENT: Jeanne Jugan saw Christ in what Blessed Mother Teresa of Kolkata would describe as his "distressing disguises." With great confidence in God's providence and the intercession of St. Joseph, she begged willingly for the many homes that she opened, relying on the good example of the sisters and the generosity of benefactors who knew the good that the sisters were doing. They now work in thirty countries, "With the eye of faith, we must see Jesus in our old people—for they are God's mouthpiece," Jeanne once said. No matter what the difficulties, she was always able to praise God and move ahead.

QUOTE: In his homily at the canonization Mass, Pope Benedict XVI said: "In the Beatitudes, Jeanne Jugan found the source of the spirit of hospitality and fraternal love, founded on unlimited trust in Providence, which illuminated her whole life. This evangelical dynamism is continued today across the world in the Congregation of the Little Sisters of the Poor, which she founded and which testifies, after her example, to the mercy of God and the compassionate love of the Heart of Jesus for the lowliest."

• • •

Gregory the Great
POPE AND DOCTOR (540?–604)

Coming events cast their shadows before: Gregory was the prefect of Rome before he was thirty. After five years in office, he resigned, founded six monasteries on his Sicilian estate, and became a Benedictine monk in his own home at Rome.

Ordained a priest, he became one of the pope's seven deacons and also served six years in the East as papal representative in Constantinople. He was recalled to become abbot and at the age of fifty was elected pope by the clergy and people of Rome.

He was direct and firm. He removed unworthy priests from office, forbade taking money for many services, and emptied the papal treasury to ransom prisoners of the Lombards in northern Italy and to care for persecuted Jews, as well as victims of plague and famine. He was very concerned about the conversion of England, sending forty monks from his own monastery. He is known for his reform of the liturgy, for strengthening respect for doctrine. Whether he was largely responsible for the revision of "Gregorian" chant is disputed.

Gregory lived in a time of perpetual strife with invading Lombards and difficult relations with the East. When Rome itself was under attack, he interviewed the Lombard king.

An Anglican historian has written: "It is impossible to conceive what would have been the confusion, the lawlessness, the chaotic state of the Middle Ages without the medieval papacy; and of the medieval papacy, the real father is Gregory the Great."

His book *Pastoral Care* on the duties and qualities of a bishop, was read for centuries after his death. He described bishops as physicians whose duties were preaching and the enforcement of discipline. In his own preaching, Gregory was skilled at applying the daily Gospel reading to the needs of his listeners.

Called "the Great," Gregory has been given a place with Augustine (August 28), Ambrose (December 7), and Jerome (September 30) as one of the four key Doctors of the Western Church.

COMMENT: Gregory was content to be a monk, but he willingly served the Church in other ways when asked. He sacrificed his own preferences in many ways, especially when he was called to be bishop of Rome. Once he was called to public service, Gregory gave his considerable energies completely to this work.

QUOTE: "Perhaps it is not after all so difficult for a man to part with his possessions, but it is certainly most difficult for him to part with himself. To renounce what one has is a minor thing; but to renounce what one is, that is asking a lot" (St. Gregory, *Homilies on the Gospels*).

* * *

SEPTEMBER 5 + OPTIONAL
Blessed Teresa of Kolkata
VIRGIN (1910–1997)

Mother Teresa of Kolkata, the tiny woman recognized throughout the world for her work among the poorest of the poor, was beatified October 19, 2003. Among those present were hundreds of Missionaries of Charity, the order she founded in 1950 as a diocesan religious community. Today the congregation also includes contemplative sisters and brothers and a community of priests.

Born to Albanian parents in what is now Skopje, Macedonia (then part of the Ottoman Empire), Gonxha (Agnes) Bojaxhiu was the youngest of the three children who survived. For a time, the family lived comfortably, and her father's construction business thrived. But life changed overnight following his unexpected death.

During her years in public school, Agnes participated in a Catholic sodality and showed a strong interest in the foreign missions. At age eighteen she entered the Loreto Sisters in Dublin. It was 1928 when she said goodbye to her mother for the final time and made her way to a new land and a new life. The following year she was sent to the Loreto novitiate in Darjeeling,

India. There she chose the name Teresa and prepared for a life of service. She was assigned to a high school for girls in Calcutta, where she taught history and geography to the daughters of the wealthy. But she could not escape the realities around her—the poverty, the suffering, the overwhelming numbers of destitute people.

In 1946 while riding a train to Darjeeling to make a retreat, Sister Teresa heard what she later explained as "a call within a call. The message was clear. I was to leave the convent and help the poor while living among them." She also heard a call to give up her life with the Sisters of Loreto and, instead, to "follow Christ into the slums to serve him among the poorest of the poor."

After receiving permission to leave Loreto, establish a new religious community, and undertake her new work, she took a nursing course for several months. She returned to Kolkata, where she lived in the slums and opened a school for poor children. Dressed in a white sari and sandals (the ordinary dress of an Indian woman), she soon began getting to know her neighbors—especially the poor and sick—and getting to know their needs through visits.

The work was exhausting, but she was not alone for long. Volunteers who came to join her in the work, some of them former students, became the core of the Missionaries of Charity. Others helped by donating food, clothing, supplies, the use of buildings. In 1952 the city of Kolkata gave Mother Teresa a former hostel, which became a home for the dying and the destitute. As the congregation expanded, services were offered to orphans, abandoned children, those suffering from alcoholism, the aging, and street people.

For the next four decades, Mother Teresa worked tirelessly on behalf of the poor. Her love knew no bounds. Nor did her energy, as she crisscrossed the globe, pleading for support and inviting others to see the face of Jesus in the poorest of the poor. In 1979 she was awarded the Nobel Peace Prize. On September 5, 1997, God called her home.

COMMENT: Mother Teresa's beatification, just over six years after her death, was part of an expedited process put into effect by Pope John Paul II. Like so many others around the world, he found her love for the Eucharist, for prayer and for the poor a model for all to emulate.

QUOTE: Speaking in a strained, weary voices at the 2003 beatification Mass, Pope John Paul II declared her blessed, prompting waves of applause before the three hundred thousand pilgrims in St. Peter's Square. In his homily, read by an aide for the aging pope, the Holy Father called Mother Teresa "one of the most relevant personalities of our age" and "an icon of the Good Samaritan." Her life, he said, was "a bold proclamation of the Gospel."

* * *

SEPTEMBER 7 + OPTIONAL
Blessed Frédéric Ozanam
HUSBAND AND FATHER (1815–1853)

A man convinced of the inestimable worth of each human being, Frédéric served the poor of Paris well and drew others into serving the poor of the world. Through the St. Vincent de Paul Society, his work continues to the present day.

Frédéric was the fifth of Jean and Marie Ozanam's fourteen children, one of only three to reach adulthood. As a teenager he began having doubts about his religion. Reading and prayer did not seem to help, but long walking discussions with Fr. Noirot of the Lyons College clarified matters a great deal.

Although his father, a doctor, wanted him to become a lawyer, Frédéric wanted to study literature. Yielding to his father's wishes, he began studying law at the University of the Sorbonne in 1831. When some professors mocked Catholic teaching in their lectures, Frédéric defended the Church.

A discussion club he organized sparked the turning point in Frédéric's life. In this club Catholics, atheists, and agnostics debated the issues of the day. After Frédéric once spoke eloquently about Christianity's role in civilization, a club member responded: "Let us be frank, Mr. Ozanam; let us also be very particular. What do you do besides talk to prove the faith you claim is in you?"

Stung by that question, Frédéric soon decided to ground his words in action. He and a friend began visiting Paris tenements and offering assistance as best they could. Soon the St. Vincent de Paul Society was born.

Feeling that the Catholic faith needed an excellent speaker to explain its teachings, Frédéric convinced the archbishop of Paris to appoint Fr. Lacordaire, France's greatest living preacher, to begin a Lenten series in Notre Dame Cathedral. The series was well attended and became an annual tradition in Paris.

After Frédéric earned his law degree, he taught law at the University of Lyons. He also earned a doctorate in literature. In 1841 he married Amelie Soulacroix and returned to the Sorbonne to teach literature. A well-respected lecturer, Frédéric worked to bring out the best in each student. Meanwhile, the St. Vincent de Paul Society grew throughout Europe. Paris alone counted twenty-five conferences.

The revolution of 1848 left many needy Parisians in its wake; 275,000 people were unemployed. The government asked Frédéric and his coworkers to supervise government aid to the poor. Vicentians throughout Europe came to the aid of Paris.

He began *The New Era*, a newspaper dedicated to securing justice for the poor and the working classes. Not all Catholics were happy with what Frédéric wrote! Describing the poor man as "the nation's priest," Frédéric said that the hunger and sweat of the poor formed a sacrifice which could redeem the people's humanity.

In 1852, poor health forced him to seek a cure in Italy with his wife and their daughter. He returned to France and died on September 8, 1853. In his sermon at the funeral, Lacordaire described Frédéric as "one of those privileged creatures who came direct from the hand of God in whom God joins tenderness to genius in order to enkindle the world." He was beatified during the 1997 World Youth Day celebration in Paris.

COMMENT: Frédéric Ozanam always respected the poor while offering whatever service he could. Each man, woman, and child was too precious to suffer the indignity of uncharitable pity. Serving the poor taught Frédéric something about God that he could not have learned elsewhere.

QUOTE: In his homily at the beatification Mass in Notre Dame Cathedral, Blessed John Paul II mentioned that before World War II, he belonged to the St. Vincent de Paul Society. He noted that Frédéric Ozanam "observed the real situation of the poor and sought to be more and more effective in helping them in their human development. He understood that charity must lead to efforts to remedy injustice. Charity and justice go together."

• • •

SEPTEMBER 8 + FEAST
Birth of the Blessed Virgin Mary

The Church has celebrated Mary's birth since at least the sixth century. A September birth was chosen because the Eastern Church begins its liturgical year with September. The September 8 date helped determine the date for the feast of the Immaculate Conception on December 8 (nine months earlier).

Scripture does not give an account of Mary's birth. However, the apocryphal *Protoevangelium of James* fills in the gap. This work has no historical value, but it does reflect the development of Christian piety. According to this account, Anne and Joachim are infertile but pray for a child. They receive the promise of a child that will advance God's plan of salvation for the world. Such a story (like many biblical counterparts) stresses the special presence of God in Mary's life from the beginning.

St. Augustine (August 28) connects Mary's birth with Jesus's saving work. He tells the earth to rejoice and shine forth in the light of her birth. "She is the flower of the field from whom bloomed the precious lily of the valley. Through her birth the nature inherited from our first parents is changed." The opening prayer at Mass speaks of the birth of Mary's Son as the dawn of our salvation and asks for an increase of peace.

COMMENT: We can see every human birth as a call for new hope in the world. The love of two human beings has joined with God in his creative work. The loving parents have shown hope in a world filled with travail. The new child has the potential to be a channel of God's love and peace to the world.

This is all true in a magnificent way in Mary. If Jesus is the perfect expression of God's love, Mary is the foreshadowing of that love. If Jesus has brought the fullness of salvation, Mary is its dawning.

Birthday celebrations bring happiness to the celebrant as well as to family and friends. Next to the birth of Jesus, Mary's birth offers the greatest possible happiness to the world. Each time we celebrate her birth, we can confidently hope for an increase of peace in our hearts and in the world at large.

QUOTE: "Today the barren Anna claps her hands for joy, the earth radiates with light, kings sing their happiness, priests enjoy every blessing, the entire universe rejoices, for she who is queen and the Father's immaculate bride buds forth from the stem of Jesse" (adapted from *Byzantine Daily Worship*).

• • •

SEPTEMBER 9 + MEMORIAL (U.S.A.)
Peter Claver
PRIEST (1581–1654)

A native of Spain, Peter Claver left his homeland forever in 1610 to be a Jesuit missionary in the New World. He sailed into Cartagena (now in Colombia), a rich port city washed by the Caribbean. He was ordained there in 1615.

By this time the slave trade had been established in America for nearly one hundred years, and Cartagena was a chief center for it. Ten thousand slaves poured into the port each year after crossing the Atlantic from West Africa under conditions so foul and inhuman that an estimated one-third of the passengers died in transit. Although the practice of slave trading was condemned by Pope Paul III, it continued to flourish.

Peter Claver's predecessor, Jesuit Fr. Alfonso de Sandoval, had devoted himself to the service of the slaves for forty years before Claver arrived to continue his work, declaring himself "the slave of the Negroes forever."

As soon as a slave ship entered the port, Peter Claver moved into its infested hold to minister to the ill-treated and exhausted passengers. After the slaves were herded out of the ship like chained animals and shut up in nearby yards to be gazed at by the crowds, Claver plunged in among them with medicines, food, bread, brandy, lemons, and tobacco. With the help of interpreters, he gave basic instructions and assured his brothers and sisters of their human dignity and God's saving love. During the forty years of his ministry, Claver instructed and baptized an estimated three hundred thousand slaves.

His apostolate extended beyond his care for slaves. He became a moral force, indeed, the apostle of Cartagena. He preached in the city square, gave missions to sailors and traders as well as country missions, during which he avoided, when possible, the hospitality of the planters and owners and lodged in the slave quarters instead.

After four years of sickness, which forced the saint to remain inactive and largely neglected, he died on September 8, 1654. The city magistrates, who had previously frowned at his solicitude for outcasts, ordered that he should be buried at public expense and with great pomp.

He was canonized in 1888, and Pope Leo XIII declared him the worldwide patron of missionary work among black slaves.

COMMENT: The Holy Spirit's might and power is manifested in the striking decisions and bold actions of Peter Claver. A decision to leave one's homeland never to return reveals a gigantic act of will, difficult for us to imagine. Peter's determination to serve forever the most abused, rejected and lowly of all people is stunningly heroic. When we measure our lives against such a man's, we become aware of our own barely used potential and of our need to open ourselves more to the jolting power of Jesus's Spirit.

QUOTE: Peter Claver understood that concrete service like the distributing of medicine, food, or brandy to his brothers and sisters could be as effective a communication of the word of God as *verbal* preaching. As Peter Claver often said, "We must speak to them with our hands before we try to speak to them with our lips."

• • •

Most Holy Name of the Blessed Virgin Mary

This feast is a counterpart to the feast of the Holy Name of Jesus (January 3); both have the possibility of uniting people easily divided on other matters.

The feast of the Most Holy Name of Mary began in Spain in 1513 and in 1671 was extended to all of Spain and the Kingdom of Naples. In 1683, John Sobieski, king of Poland, brought an army to the outskirts of Vienna to stop the advance of Muslim armies loyal to Mohammed IV in Constantinople. After Sobieski entrusted himself to the Blessed Virgin Mary, he and his soldiers thoroughly defeated the Muslims. Pope Innocent XI extended this feast to the entire Church.

COMMENT: Mary always points us to God, reminding us of God's infinite goodness. She helps us to open our hearts to God's ways, wherever those may lead us. Honored under the title "Queen of Peace," Mary encourages us to cooperate with Jesus in building a peace based on justice, a peace that respects the fundamental human rights (including religious rights) of all peoples.

QUOTE: "Lord our God, when your Son was dying on the altar of the cross, he gave us as our mother the one he had chosen to be his own mother, the Blessed Virgin Mary; grant that we who call upon the holy name of Mary, our mother, with confidence in her protection may receive strength and comfort in all our needs" (Marian Sacramentary, Mass for the Holy Name of the Blessed Virgin Mary).

• • •

John Chrysostom
BISHOP AND DOCTOR (D. 407)

The ambiguity and intrigue surrounding John, the great preacher (his name means "golden-mouthed") from Antioch, are characteristic of the life of any great man in a capital city. Brought to Constantinople after a dozen years of priestly service in Syria, John found himself the reluctant victim of an imperial ruse to make him bishop in the greatest city of the empire. Ascetic, unimposing but dignified, and troubled by stomach ailments from his desert days as a monk, John became a bishop under the cloud of imperial politics.

If his body was weak, his tongue was powerful. The content of his sermons and his exegesis of Scripture were never without a point. Sometimes the point stung the high and mighty. Some sermons lasted up to two hours.

His lifestyle at the imperial court was not appreciated by many courtiers. He offered a modest table to episcopal sycophants hanging around for imperial and ecclesiastical favors. John deplored the court protocol that accorded him precedence before the highest state officials. He would not be a kept man.

His zeal led him to decisive action. Bishops who bribed their way into office were deposed. Many of his sermons called for concrete steps to share wealth with the poor. The rich did not appreciate hearing from John that private property existed because of Adam's fall from grace—any more than married men liked to hear that they were bound to marital fidelity just as much as their wives were. When it came to justice and charity, John acknowledged no double standards.

Aloof, energetic, outspoken, especially when he became excited in the pulpit, John was a sure target for criticism and personal trouble. He was accused of gorging himself secretly on rich wines and fine foods. His faithfulness as spiritual director to the rich widow, Olympia, provoked much gossip attempting to prove him a hypocrite where wealth and chastity were concerned. His actions against unworthy bishops in Asia Minor were viewed by other ecclesiastics as a greedy, uncanonical extension of his authority.

Theophilus, archbishop of Alexandria, and Empress Eudoxia were determined to discredit John. Theophilus feared the growth in importance of the bishop of Constantinople and took occasion to charge John with fostering heresy. Theophilus and other angered bishops were supported by Eudoxia. The empress resented John's sermons contrasting Gospel values with the excesses of imperial court life. Whether intended or not, sermons mentioning the lurid Jezebel (1 Kings 9:1—21:23) and impious Herodias (Mark 6:17–29) were associated with the empress, who finally did manage to have John exiled. He died in exile in 407.

COMMENT: John Chrysostom's preaching, by word and example, exemplifies the role of the prophet to comfort the afflicted and to afflict the comfortable. For his honesty and courage, he paid the price of a turbulent ministry as bishop, personal vilification, and exile.

QUOTE: Bishops "should set forth the ways by which are to be solved very grave questions concerning the ownership, increase, and just distribution of material goods, peace and war, and brotherly relations among all people" (Decree on the Pastoral Office of Bishops, 12).

• • •

SEPTEMBER 14 + FEAST
Exaltation of the Holy Cross

Early in the fourth century, St. Helena, mother of the Roman Emperor Constantine, went to Jerusalem in search of the holy places of Christ's life. She razed the second-century temple of Aphrodite, which tradition held was built over the Savior's tomb, and her son built the Basilica of the Holy Sepulcher over it. During the excavation, workers found three crosses. Legend has it that the one on which Jesus died was identified when its touch healed a dying woman.

The cross immediately became an object of veneration. At a Good Friday celebration in Jerusalem toward the end of the fourth century, according to an eyewitness, the wood was taken out of its silver container and placed on a table together with the inscription Pilate ordered placed above Jesus's head. Then "all the people pass through one by one; all of them bow down, touching the cross and the inscription, first with their foreheads, then with their eyes; and, after kissing the cross, they move on."

To this day the Eastern Churches, Catholic and Orthodox alike, celebrate the Exaltation of the Holy Cross on the September anniversary of the basilica's dedication. The feast entered the Western calendar in the seventh century after Emperor Heraclius recovered the cross from the Persians, who had carried it off in 614, fifteen years earlier. According to the story, the emperor intended to carry the cross back into Jerusalem himself, but was unable to move forward until he put off his imperial garb and became a barefoot pilgrim.

COMMENT: The cross is today the universal image of Christian belief. Countless generations of artists have turned it into a thing of beauty to be carried in procession or worn as jewelry. To the eyes of the first Christians, it had no beauty. It stood outside too many city walls, decorated only with decaying corpses, as a threat to anyone who defied Roman authority— including Christians who refused sacrifice to Roman gods. Although believers spoke of the cross as the instrument of salvation, it seldom appeared in Christian art unless disguised as an anchor or the *chi-rho* until after Constantine's Edict of Toleration (313).

QUOTE: "How splendid the cross of Christ! It brings life, not death; light, not darkness; Paradise, not its loss. It is the wood on which the Lord, like a great warrior, was wounded in hands and feet and side, but healed thereby our wounds. A tree has destroyed us, a tree now brought us life" (Theodore of Studios).

- - -

SEPTEMBER 15 + MEMORIAL
Our Lady of Sorrows

For a while there were two feasts in honor of the Sorrowful Mother: one going back to the fifteenth century, the other to the seventeenth century. For a while both were celebrated by the universal Church: one on the Friday before Palm Sunday, the other in September.

The principal biblical references to Mary's sorrows are in Luke 2:35 and John 19:26–27. The Lucan passage is Simeon's prediction about a sword piercing Mary's soul; the Johannine passage relates Jesus's words to Mary and to the beloved disciple.

Many early Church writers interpret the sword as Mary's sorrows, especially as she saw Jesus die on the cross. Thus, the two passages are brought together as prediction and fulfillment.

St. Ambrose (December 7) in particular sees Mary as a sorrowful yet powerful figure at the cross. Mary stood fearlessly beneath the cross while others fled. Mary looked on her Son's wounds with pity but saw in them the salvation of the world. As Jesus hung on the cross, Mary did not fear to be killed but offered herself to her persecutors.

COMMENT: John's account of Jesus's death is highly symbolic. When Jesus gives the beloved disciple to Mary, we are invited to appreciate Mary's role in the Church: She symbolizes the Church; the beloved disciple represents all believers. As Mary mothered Jesus, she is now mother to all his followers. Furthermore, as Jesus died, he handed over his Spirit. Mary and the Spirit cooperate in begetting new children of God—almost an echo of Luke's account of Jesus's conception. Christians can trust that they will continue to experience the caring presence of Mary and Jesus's Spirit throughout their lives and throughout history.

QUOTE "At the cross her station keeping, / Stood the mournful mother weeping, / Close to Jesus to the last. / Through her heart, his sorrow sharing, / All his bitter anguish bearing, / Now at length the sword has passed" (*Stabat Mater*).

• • •

SEPTEMBER 16 + MEMORIAL
Cornelius and Cyprian
POPE AND MARTYR; BISHOP AND MARTYR

Cornelius (d. 253). There was no pope for fourteen months after the martyrdom of St. Fabian (January 20) because of the intensity of the persecution of the Church. During the interval, the Church was governed by a college of priests. St. Cyprian, a friend of Cornelius, writes that Cornelius was elected pope "by the judgment of God and of Christ, by the testimony of most of the clergy, by the vote of the people, with the consent of aged priests and of good men."

The greatest problem of Cornelius's two-year term as pope involved the sacrament of penance and centered on the readmission of Christians who had denied their faith during the time of persecution. Two extremes were finally both condemned. Cyprian, primate of North Africa, appealed to the pope to confirm his stand that the relapsed could be reconciled only by the decision of the bishop.

In Rome, however, Cornelius met with the opposite view. After his election, a priest named Novatian (one of those who had governed the Church) had himself consecrated a rival bishop of Rome—one of the first antipopes. He denied that the Church had any power to reconcile not only the apostates, but also those guilty of murder, adultery, fornication, or second marriage! Cornelius had the support of most of the Church (especially of Cyprian of Africa) in condemning Novatianism, though the sect persisted for several centuries. Cornelius held a synod at Rome in 251 and ordered the "relapsed" to be restored to the Church with the usual "medicines of repentance."

The friendship of Cornelius and Cyprian was strained for a time when one of Cyprian's rivals made accusations about him. But the problem was cleared up.

A document from Cornelius shows the extent of organization in the Church of Rome in the mid-third century: forty-six priests, seven deacons, seven subdeacons. It is estimated that the number of Christians totaled about fifty thousand.

Cornelius died as a result of the hardships of his exile in what is now Civitavecchia (near Rome).

COMMENT: It seems fairly true to say that almost every possible false doctrine has been proposed at some time or other in the history of the Church. The third century saw the resolution of a problem we scarcely consider—the penance to be done before reconciliation with the Church after mortal sin. Men like Cornelius and Cyprian were God's instruments in helping the Church find a prudent path between extremes of rigorism and laxity. They are part of the Church's ever-living stream of tradition, ensuring the continuance of what was begun by Christ, and evaluating new experiences through the wisdom and experience of those who have gone before.

QUOTE: "There is one God and one Christ and but one episcopal chair, originally founded on Peter, by the Lord's authority. There cannot, therefore, be set up another altar or another priesthood. Whatever any man in his rage or rashness shall appoint, in defiance of the divine institution, must be a spurious, profane and sacrilegious ordinance" (St. Cyprian, *The Unity of the Catholic Church*).

Cyprian (d. 258). Cyprian is important in the development of Christian thought and practice in the third century, especially in northern Africa.

Highly educated, a famous orator, he became a Christian as an adult. He distributed his goods to the poor, and amazed his fellow citizens by making a vow of chastity before his baptism. Within two years he had been ordained priest and was chosen, against his will, as bishop of Carthage (near modern Tunis).

Cyprian complained that the peace that the Church enjoyed had weakened the spirit of many Christians and had opened the door to converts who did not have the true spirit of faith. When Emperor Decian's persecution began, many Christians easily abandoned the Church. It was their reinstatement that caused the great controversies of the third century and helped the Church progress in its understanding of the sacrament of penance.

Novatus, a priest who had opposed Cyprian's election, set himself up in Cyprian's absence (he had fled to a hiding place from which to direct the Church, bringing criticism on himself) and received back all apostates without imposing any canonical penance. Ultimately he was condemned. Cyprian held a middle course, holding that those who had actually sacrificed to idols could receive Holy Communion only at death, whereas those who had only bought certificates saying they had sacrificed could be admitted after a more or less lengthy period of penance. Even this was relaxed during a new persecution.

During a plague in Carthage, Cyprian urged Christians to help everyone, including their enemies and persecutors.

A friend of Pope Cornelius, he opposed the following pope, Stephen. He and the other African bishops would not recognize the validity of baptism conferred by heretics and schismatics. This was not the universal view of the Church, but Cyprian was not intimidated even by Stephen's threat of excommunication.

He was exiled by the emperor and then recalled for trial. He refused to leave the city, insisting that his people should have the witness of his martyrdom.

Cyprian was a mixture of kindness and courage, vigor and steadiness. He was cheerful and serious, so that people did not know whether to love or respect him more. He waxed warm during the baptismal controversy; his feelings must have concerned him, for it was at this time that he wrote his treatise on patience. St. Augustine (August 28) remarks that Cyprian atoned for his anger by his glorious martyrdom.

COMMENT: The controversies about baptism and penance in the third century remind us that the early Church had no ready-made solutions from the Holy Spirit. The leaders and members of the Church of that day had to make the best judgments they could, following the entire teaching of Christ without being diverted by exaggerations to the right or left.

QUOTE: "You cannot have God for your Father if you do not have the Church for your mother…. God is one and Christ is one, and his Church is one; one is the faith, and one is the people cemented together by harmony into the strong unity of a body…if we are the heirs of Christ, let us abide in the peace of Christ; if we are the sons of God, let us be lovers of peace" (St. Cyprian, *The Unity of the Catholic Church*).

. . .

Robert Bellarmine
BISHOP AND DOCTOR (1542–1621)

When Robert Bellarmine was ordained in 1570, the study of Church history and the Fathers of the Church was in a sad state of neglect. A promising scholar from his youth in Tuscany, he devoted his energy to these two subjects, as well as to Scripture in order to systematize Church doctrine against the attacks of Protestant reformers. He was the first Jesuit to become a professor at Louvain (in Belgium).

His most famous work is his three-volume *Disputations on the Controversies of the Christian Faith*. Particularly noteworthy are the sections on the temporal power of the pope and the role of the laity. He incurred the anger of monarchists in England and France by showing the divine-right-of-kings theory untenable. He developed the theory of the indirect power of the pope in temporal affairs. Although he was defending the pope against the Scottish philosopher Barclay, he also incurred the ire of Pope Sixtus V.

Bellarmine was made a cardinal by Pope Clement VIII on the grounds that "he had not his equal for learning." While he occupied apartments in the Vatican, Bellarmine relaxed none of his former austerities. He limited his household expenses to what was barely essential, eating only the food available to the poor. He was known to have ransomed a soldier who had deserted from the army, and Bellarmine used the hangings of his rooms to clothe poor people, remarking, "The walls won't catch cold."

Among many activities, he became theologian to Pope Clement VIII, preparing two catechisms that have had great influence in the Church.

The last major controversy of Bellarmine's life came in 1616 when he had to admonish his friend Galileo, whom he admired. Bellarmine delivered the admonition on behalf of the Holy Office, which had decided that the heliocentric theory of Copernicus (the sun as stationary) was contrary to Scripture. The admonition amounted to a caution against putting forward—

other than as a hypothesis—theories not yet fully proved. This shows that saints are not infallible.

Bellarmine died on September 17, 1621. The process for his canonization was begun in 1627 but was delayed until 1930 for political reasons, stemming from his writings. In 1930, Pius XI canonized him and the next year declared him a Doctor of the Church.

COMMENT: The renewal in the Church sought by Vatican II was difficult for many Catholics. In the course of change, many felt a lack of firm guidance from those in authority. They yearned for the stone columns of orthodoxy and an iron command with clearly defined lines of authority.

Vatican II assures us in the *Pastoral Constitution on the Church*, "There are many realities which do not change and which have their ultimate foundation in Christ, who is the same yesterday and today, yes, and forever" (10, quoting Hebrews 13:8).

Robert Bellarmine devoted his life to the study of Scripture and Catholic doctrine. His writings help us understand that not only is the content of our faith important, it is Jesus's living person—as revealed by his life, death, and resurrection—that is the source of revelation.

The real source of our faith is not merely a set of doctrines but rather the person of Christ still living in the Church today. When he left his apostles, Jesus assured them of his living presence: "When the Spirit of truth comes, he will lead you to the complete truth" (John 16:30).

QUOTE: "Sharing in solicitude for all the churches, bishops exercise this episcopal office of theirs, received through episcopal consecration, in communion with and under the authority of the Supreme Pontiff. All are united in a college or body with respect to teaching the universal Church of God and governing her as shepherds" (Decree on the Pastoral Office of Bishops, 3).

• • •

SEPTEMBER 19 + OPTIONAL

Januarius

BISHOP AND MARTYR (D. 305?)

Little is known about the life of Januarius. He is believed to have been martyred in the persecution of Emperor Diocletian in 305. Legend has it that after he was thrown to the bears in the amphitheater of Pozzuoli, he was beheaded, and his blood ultimately brought to Naples.

COMMENT: It is defined Catholic doctrine that miracles can happen and can be recognized—hardly a mind-boggling statement to anyone who believes in God. Problems arise, however, when we must decide whether an occurrence is unexplainable in natural terms or only unexplained. We do well to avoid an excessive credulity, which may be a sign of insecurity. On the other hand, when even scientists speak about "probabilities" rather than "laws" of nature, it is something less than imaginative for Christians to think that God is too "scientific" to work extraordinary miracles to wake us up to the everyday miracles of sparrows and dandelions, raindrops and snowflakes.

QUOTE: "A dark mass that half fills a hermetically sealed four-inch glass container, and is preserved in a double reliquary in the Naples cathedral as the blood of St. January, liquefies eighteen times during the year.... This phenomenon goes back to the fourteenth century.... Tradition connects it with a certain Eusebia, who had allegedly collected the blood after the martyrdom.... The ceremony accompanying the liquefaction is performed by holding the reliquary close to the altar on which is located what is believed to be the martyr's head. While the people pray, often tumultuously, the priest turns the reliquary up and down in the full sight of the onlookers until the liquefaction takes place.... Various experiments have been applied, but the phenomenon eludes natural explanation. There are, however, similar miraculous claims made for the blood of John the Baptist, Stephen, Pantaleon, Patricia, Nicholas of Tolentino and Aloysius Gonzaga—nearly all in the neighborhood of Naples" (*Catholic Encyclopedia*).

• • •

SEPTEMBER 20 + MEMORIAL
Andrew Kim Taegon, Paul Chong Hasang, and Companions
PRIEST AND MARTYR; MARTYRS (1821–1846)

This first native Korean priest was the son of Korean converts. His father, Ignatius Kim, was martyred during the persecution of 1839 and was beatified in 1925. After baptism at the age of fifteen, Andrew traveled thirteen hundred miles to the seminary in Macao, China. After six years he managed to return to his country through Manchuria. That same year he crossed the Yellow Sea to Shanghai and was ordained a priest. Back home again, he was assigned to arrange for more missionaries to enter by a water route that would elude the border patrol. He was arrested, tortured and finally beheaded at the Han River near Seoul, the capital. Paul Chong Hasang was a lay apostle and married man, aged forty-five.

Christianity came to Korea during the Japanese invasion in 1592 when some Koreans were baptized, probably by Christian Japanese soldiers. Evangelization was difficult because Korea refused all contact with the outside world except for bringing taxes to Beijing annually. On one of these occasions, around 1777, Christian literature obtained from Jesuits in China led educated Korean Christians to study. A home church began. When a Chinese priest managed to enter secretly a dozen years later, he found four thousand Catholics, none of whom had ever seen a priest. Seven years later there were ten thousand Catholics. Religious freedom came in 1883.

When Pope John Paul II visited Korea in 1984, he canonized Andrew, Paul, ninety-eight Koreans, and three French missionaries who had been martyred between 1839 and 1867. Among them were bishops and priests, but for the most part they were laypersons: forty-seven women, forty-five men.

Among the martyrs in 1839 was Columba Kim, an unmarried woman of twenty-six. She was put in prison, pierced with hot awls and seared with burning coals. She and her sister Agnes were disrobed and kept for two days in a cell with condemned criminals, but they were not molested. After Columba complained about the indignity, no more women were subjected to it. The two were beheaded. A boy of thirteen, Peter Ryou, had his flesh so badly torn that he could pull off pieces and throw them at the judges. He was killed by strangulation. Protase Chong, a forty-one-year-old noble, apostatized under torture and was freed. Later he came back, confessed his faith and was tortured to death.

Today there are almost 5.1 million Catholics in South Korea.

COMMENT: We marvel at the fact that the Korean Church was strictly a lay church for a dozen years after its birth. How did they survive without the Eucharist? It is no belittling of this and other sacraments to realize that there must be a living faith before there can be a truly beneficial celebration of the Eucharist. The sacraments are signs of God's initiative and response to faith already present. The sacraments increase grace and faith, but only if there is something ready to be increased.

QUOTE: "The Korean Church is unique because it was founded entirely by laypeople. This fledgling Church, so young and yet so strong in faith, withstood wave after wave of fierce persecution. Thus, in less than a century, it could boast of ten thousand martyrs. The death of these martyrs became the leaven of the Church and led to today's splendid flowering of the Church in Korea. Even today their undying spirit sustains the Christians in the Church of silence in the north of this tragically divided land" (Blessed John Paul II, speaking at the 1984 canonization).

• • •

Matthew
APOSTLE AND EVANGELIST

Matthew was a Jew who worked for the occupying Roman forces, collecting taxes from other Jews. The Romans were not scrupulous about what the "tax farmers" got for themselves. Hence the latter, known as "publicans," were generally hated as traitors by their fellow Jews. The Pharisees lumped them with "sinners" (Matthew 9:11–13). So it was shocking to them to hear Jesus call such a man to be one of his intimate followers.

Matthew got Jesus in further trouble by having a sort of going-away party at his house. His Gospel tells us that "many" tax collectors and "those known as sinners" came to the dinner. What business did the supposedly great teacher have associating with such immoral people? The Pharisees were even more shocked by Jesus's answer, "Those who are well do not need a physician, but the sick do. Go and learn the meaning of the words, 'I desire mercy, not sacrifice.' I did not come to call the righteous but sinners" (Matthew 9:12b–13). Jesus is not setting aside ritual and worship; he is saying that loving others is even more important.

No other particular incidents about Matthew are found in the New Testament.

COMMENT: From such an unlikely situation, Jesus chose one of the foundations of the Church, a man whom others, judging from his job, thought was not holy enough for the position. But he was honest enough to admit that he was one of the sinners Jesus came to call. He was open enough to recognize truth when he saw him. "And he got up and followed him" (Matthew 9:9b).

STORY: We imagine Matthew, after the terrible events surrounding the death of Jesus, going to the mountain to which the Risen Lord had summoned them. "When they saw him, they worshiped, but they doubted. Then Jesus approached and said to them [we think of him looking at each one in turn,

Matthew listening and excited with the rest], 'All power in heaven and on earth has been given to me. Go, therefore, and make disciples of all nations, baptizing them in the name of the Father, and of the Son, and of the holy Spirit, teaching them to observe all that I have commanded you. And behold, I am with you always, until the end of the age' " (Matthew 28:17–20).

Matthew would never forget that day. He proclaimed the Good News by his life and by his word. Our faith rests upon his witness and that of his fellow apostles.

* * *

SEPTEMBER 23 + MEMORIAL
Pio of Pietrelcina
PRIEST (1887–1968)

According to one estimate, over 325 people since the time of Francis of Assisi (October 4) have received the stigmata, that is, all or some of the wounds of Christ's passion. Few of those stigmatics have had a more difficult life than Padre Pio.

Francesco Forgione joined the Capuchin Franciscans at age fifteen, taking the name Pio. Ordained in 1910, he served for a short time in the Italian army during World War I. In 1917 he was assigned to the friary in San Giovanni Rotondo, seventy-five miles from Bari on Italy's Adriatic coast.

A year later, while making his thanksgiving after Mass, he had a vision of Jesus, and when it was over Padre Pio had the stigmata on his hands, feet, and side.

After undergoing various medical and Church investigations, for a short time he was not permitted to celebrate Mass publicly or hear confessions. Although he wrote nothing after 1924, unscrupulous people sometimes presented him as the author of prophecies they wrote.

In time, busloads of men and women came to his 5:00 A.M. Mass and to his confessional, which he occupied up to ten hours a day. During his mid-morning break, he blessed the sick.

Faith must lead to action, to works of compassion. In 1946, ground was broken on nearby Mount Gargano for the "House for the Alleviation of Suffering," a 350-bed facility financed by Padre Pio's benefactors.

COMMENT: At Padre Pio's canonization Mass in 2002, Blessed John Paul II referred to that day's Gospel (Matthew 11:25–30) and said: "The Gospel image of 'yoke' evokes the many trials that the humble Capuchin of San Giovanni Rotondo endured. Today we contemplate in him how sweet is the 'yoke' of Christ and indeed how light the burden whenever someone carries these with faithful love. The life and mission of Padre Pio testify that difficulties and sorrows, if accepted with love, transform themselves into a privileged journey of holiness, which opens the person toward a greater good, known only to the Lord."

QUOTE: "The life of a Christian is nothing but a perpetual struggle against self; there is no flowering of the soul to the beauty of its perfection except at the price of pain" (saying of Padre Pio).

• • •

SEPTEMBER 26 + OPTIONAL
Cosmas and Damian
MARTYRS (D. 303?)

Nothing is known of their lives except that they suffered martyrdom in Syria during the persecution of Emperor Diocletian.

A church erected on the site of their burial place was enlarged by Emperor Justinian. Devotion to the two saints spread rapidly in both East and West. A famous basilica was erected in their honor in Constantinople. Their names were placed in the canon of the Mass (now Eucharistic Prayer I), probably in the sixth century.

Legend says that they were twin brothers born in Arabia, who became skilled doctors. They were among those who are venerated in the East as the "moneyless ones" because they did not charge a fee for their services. It was impossible that such prominent persons would escape unnoticed in time of persecution: They were arrested and beheaded.

Nine centuries later, Francis of Assisi (October 4) rebuilt the dilapidated San Damiano chapel outside Assisi.

COMMENT: For a long time, it seems, we have been very conscious of Jesus's miracles as proofs of his divinity. What we sometimes overlook is Jesus's consuming interest in simply healing people's sickness, whatever other meaning his actions had. The power that "went out from him" was indeed a sign that God was definitively breaking into human history in final fulfillment of his promises; but the love of God was also concrete in a very human heart that was concerned about the suffering of his brothers and sisters. It is a reminder to Christians that salvation is for the whole person, the unique body-spirit unity.

QUOTE: In the Preface of Martyrs, the Church acknowledges that a martyr's blood shows God's "marvelous works, by which in our weakness you perfect your power and on the feeble bestow strength to bear you witness, through Christ our Lord."

. . .

SEPTEMBER 27 + MEMORIAL
Vincent de Paul
PRIEST (1580?–1660)

The deathbed confession of a servant opened Vincent's eyes to the crying spiritual needs of the peasantry of France. This seems to have been a crucial moment in the life of the man from a small farm in Gascony, France, who had become a priest with little more ambition than to have a comfortable life.

It was the Countess de Gondi (whose servant he had helped) who persuaded her husband to endow and support a group of able and zealous missionaries who would work among poor tenant farmers and country people in general. Vincent was too humble to accept leadership at first, but after working for some time in Paris among imprisoned galley slaves, he returned to lead what is now known as the Congregation of the Mission, or the Vincentians. These priests, with vows of poverty, chastity, obedience, and stability, were to devote themselves entirely to the people in smaller towns and villages.

Later Vincent established confraternities of charity for the spiritual and physical relief of the poor and sick of each parish. From these, with the help of St. Louise de Marillac, came the Daughters of Charity, "whose convent is the sickroom, whose chapel is the parish church, whose cloister is the streets of the city." He organized the rich women of Paris to collect funds for his missionary projects, founded several hospitals, collected relief funds for the victims of war, and ransomed over twelve hundred galley slaves from North Africa. He was zealous in conducting retreats for clergy at a time when there was great laxity, abuse, and ignorance among them. He was a pioneer in clerical training and was instrumental in establishing seminaries.

Most remarkably, Vincent was by temperament a very irascible person— even his friends admitted it. He said that except for the grace of God he would have been "hard and repulsive, rough and cross." But he became a tender and affectionate man, very sensitive to the needs of others.

Pope Leo XIII made him the patron of all charitable societies. Outstanding among these, of course, is the Society of St. Vincent de Paul, founded in 1833 by his admirer Blessed Frédéric Ozanam (September 7).

COMMENT: The Church is for all God's children, rich and poor, peasants and scholars, the sophisticated and the simple. But obviously the greatest concern of the Church must be for those who need the most help—those made helpless by sickness, poverty, ignorance, or cruelty. Vincent de Paul is a particularly appropriate patron for all Christians today, when hunger has become starvation, and the high living of the rich stands in more and more glaring contrast to the physical and moral degradation in which many of God's children are forced to live.

QUOTE: "Strive to live content in the midst of those things that cause your discontent. Free your mind from all that troubles you, God will take care of things. You will be unable to make haste in this [choice] without, so to speak, grieving the heart of God, because he sees that you do not honor him sufficiently with holy trust. Trust in him, I beg you, and you will have the fulfillment of what your heart desires" (St. Vincent de Paul, *Letters*).

* * *

SEPTEMBER 28 + OPTIONAL
Lorenzo Ruiz and Companions
MARTYRS (1600?–1637)

Lawrence (Lorenzo) was born in Manila of a Chinese father and a Filipino mother, both Christians. Thus he learned Chinese and Tagalog from them and Spanish from the Dominicans whom he served as altar boy and sacristan. He became a professional calligrapher, transcribing documents in beautiful penmanship. He was a full member of the Confraternity of the Holy Rosary under Dominican auspices. He married and had two sons and a daughter.

His life took an abrupt turn when he was accused of murder. Nothing further is known except the statement of two Dominicans that "he was sought by the authorities on account of a homicide to which he was present or which was attributed to him."

At that time three Dominican priests, Antonio Gonzalez, Guillermo Courtet, and Miguel de Aozaraza, were about to sail to Japan in spite of a violent persecution there. With them was a Japanese priest, Vicente Shiwozuka de la Cruz, and a layman named Lazaro, a leper. Lorenzo, having taken asylum with them, was allowed to accompany them. But only when they were at sea did he learn that they were going to Japan.

They landed at Okinawa. Lorenzo could have gone on to Taiwan, but "I decided to stay with the Fathers, because the Spaniards would hang me there." In Japan they were soon found out, arrested, and taken to Nagasaki. The site of wholesale bloodshed where the first atomic bomb was dropped had known tragedy before. The fifty thousand Catholics who once lived there were dispersed or killed by persecution.

They were subjected to an unspeakable kind of torture: After huge quantities of water were forced down their throats, they were made to lie down. Long boards were placed on their stomachs and guards then stepped on the ends of the boards, forcing the water to spurt violently from mouth, nose, and ears.

The superior, Antonio, died after some days. Both the Japanese priest and Lazaro broke under torture, which included the insertion of bamboo needles under their fingernails. But both were brought back to courage by their companions.

In Lorenzo's moment of crisis, he asked the interpreter, "I would like to know if, by apostatizing, they will spare my life." The interpreter was noncommittal, but Lorenzo, in the ensuing hours, felt his faith grow strong. He became bold, even audacious, with his interrogators.

The five were put to death by being hanged upside down in pits. Boards fitted with semicircular holes were fitted around their waists and stones put on top to increase the pressure. They were tightly bound, to slow circulation and prevent a speedy death. They were allowed to hang for three days. By that time Lorenzo and Lazaro were dead. The three Dominican priests, still alive, were beheaded.

In 1987, Blessed John Paul II canonized these six and ten others, Asians and Europeans, men and women, who spread the faith in the Philippines, Taiwan, and Japan. Lorenzo Ruiz is the first canonized Filipino martyr.

COMMENT: We ordinary Christians of today—how would we stand up in the circumstances these martyrs faced? We sympathize with the two who temporarily denied the faith. We understand Lorenzo's terrible moment of temptation. But we see also the courage—unexplainable in human terms— which surged from their store of faith. Martyrdom, like ordinary life, is a miracle of grace.

QUOTE: When government officials asked, "If we grant you life, will you renounce your faith?" Lorenzo responded: "That I will never do, because I am a Christian, and I shall die for God, and for him I will give many thousands of lives if I had them. And so, do with me as you please."

• • •

SEPTEMBER 28 + OPTIONAL
Wenceslaus
MARTYR (907?–929)

If saints have been falsely characterized as "otherworldly," the life of Wenceslaus stands as an example to the contrary: He stood for Christian values in the midst of the political intrigues which characterized tenth-century Bohemia.

He was born in 907 near Prague, son of the Duke of Bohemia. His saintly grandmother, Ludmilla, raised him and sought to promote him as ruler of Bohemia in place of his mother, who favored the anti-Christian factions. Ludmilla was eventually murdered, but rival Christian forces enabled Wenceslaus to assume leadership of the government.

His rule was marked by efforts toward unification within Bohemia, support of the Church and peacemaking negotiations with Germany, a policy that caused him trouble with the anti-Christian opposition. His brother Boleslav joined in the plotting, and in September of 929 invited Wenceslaus to Alt-Bunglou for the celebration of the feast of Sts. Cosmas and Damian (September 26). On the way to Mass, Boleslav attacked his brother, and in the struggle, Wenceslaus was killed by supporters of Boleslav.

Although his death resulted primarily from political upheaval, Wenceslaus was hailed as a martyr for the faith and his tomb became a pilgrimage shrine. He is hailed as the patron of the Bohemian people and the Czech Republic.

COMMENT: "Good King Wenceslaus" was able to incarnate his Christianity in a world filled with political unrest. While we are often victims of violence of a different sort, we can easily identify with his struggle to bring harmony to society. The call to become involved in social change and in political activity is addressed to Christians; the values of the Gospel are sorely needed today.

QUOTE: "While recognizing the autonomy of the reality of politics, Christians who are invited to take up political activity should try to make their choices consistent with the Gospel and, in the framework of a legitimate plurality, to give both personal and collective witness to the seriousness of their faith by effective and disinterested service of all people" (Pope Paul VI, *A Call to Action*, 46).

• • •

Michael, Gabriel, and Raphael

ARCHANGELS

Angels—messengers from God—appear frequently in Scripture, but only these three are named.

Michael appears in Daniel's vision as "the great prince" who defends Israel against its enemies (12:1). In the book of Revelation, Michael leads God's armies to final victory over the forces of evil (12:7). Devotion to Michael is the oldest angelic devotion, rising in the East in the fourth century. The Church in the West began to observe a feast honoring Michael and the angels in the fifth century.

Gabriel also makes an appearance in Daniel's visions, announcing Michael's role in God's plan (10:4–14). His best-known appearance is an encounter with a young Jewish girl named Mary, who consents to bear the Messiah (Luke 1:26–38).

Raphael's activity is confined to the Old Testament story of Tobit. There he guides Tobit's son, Tobiah, through a series of fantastic adventures that lead to a threefold happy ending: Tobiah's marriage to Sarah, the healing of Tobit's blindness and the restoration of the family fortune.

The memorials of Gabriel (March 24) and Raphael (October 24) were added to the Roman calendar in 1921. The 1970 revision of the calendar joined their feasts to Michael's.

COMMENT: Each of these archangels performs a different mission in Scripture: Michael protects; Gabriel announces; Raphael guides. Earlier belief that inexplicable events were due to the actions of spiritual beings has given way to a scientific worldview and a different sense of cause and effect. Yet believers still experience God's protection, communication and guidance in ways that defy description. We have every reason to believe in angels.

QUOTE: "For the honor we pay the angelic creatures in whom you delight redounds to your own surpassing glory, and by their great dignity and splendor you show how infinitely great you are, to be exalted above all things, through Christ our Lord" (*Roman Missal*, Preface for this feast).

* * *

SEPTEMBER 30 + MEMORIAL
Jerome
PRIEST AND DOCTOR (345–420)

Most of the saints are remembered for some outstanding virtue or devotion that they practiced, but Jerome is frequently remembered for his bad temper! It is true that he had a very bad temper and could use a vitriolic pen, but his love for God and his Son Jesus Christ was extraordinarily intense; anyone who taught error was an enemy of God and truth, and St. Jerome went after him or her with his mighty and sometimes sarcastic pen.

He was above all a Scripture scholar, translating most of the Old Testament from the Hebrew. He also wrote commentaries that are a great source of scriptural inspiration for us today. He was an avid student, a thorough scholar, a prodigious letter writer, and a consultant to monk, bishop, and pope. St. Augustine (August 28) said of him, "What Jerome is ignorant of, no mortal has ever known."

St. Jerome is particularly important for having made a translation of the Bible that came to be called the *Vulgate*. It is not the most critical edition of the Bible, but its acceptance by the Church was fortunate. As a modern scholar says, "No man before Jerome or among his contemporaries and very few men for many centuries afterwards were so well qualified to do the work." The Council of Trent called for a new and corrected edition of the *Vulgate* and declared it the authentic text to be used in the Church.

In order to be able to do such work, Jerome prepared himself well. He was a master of Latin, Greek, Hebrew, and Chaldaic. He began his studies at his birthplace, Stridon in Dalmatia (now Croatia). After his preliminary education he went to Rome, the center of learning at that time, and then to

Trier, Germany, where Jerome the scholar was very much in evidence. He spent several years in each place, always trying to find the very best teachers. He once served as private secretary for Pope Damasus (December 11).

After these preparatory studies, he traveled extensively in Palestine, marking each spot of Christ's life with an outpouring of devotion. Mystic that he was, he spent five years in the desert of Chalcis so that he might give himself up to prayer, penance, and study. Finally he settled in Bethlehem where he lived in the cave believed to have been the birthplace of Christ. On September 30, 420, Jerome died in Bethlehem. He is buried in the Basilica of St. Mary Major in Rome.

COMMENT: Jerome was a strong, outspoken man. He had the virtues and the unpleasant fruits of being a fearless critic and all the usual moral problems of a man. He was, as someone has said, no admirer of moderation whether in virtue or against evil. He was swift to anger, but also swift to feel remorse, even more severe on his own shortcomings than on those of others. A pope is said to have remarked, on seeing a picture of Jerome striking his breast with a stone, "You do well to carry that stone, for without it the Church would never have canonized you" (*Butler's Lives of the Saints*).

QUOTE: "In the remotest part of a wild and stony desert, burnt up with the heat of the scorching sun so that it frightens even the monks that inhabit it, I seemed to myself to be in the midst of the delights and crowds of Rome. In this exile and prison to which for the fear of hell I had voluntarily condemned myself, I many times imagined myself witnessing the dancing of the Roman maidens as if I had been in the midst of them: in my cold body and in my parched-up flesh, which seemed dead before its death, passion was able to live. Alone with this enemy, I threw myself in spirit at the feet of Jesus, watering them with my tears, and I tamed my flesh by fasting whole weeks. I am not ashamed to disclose my temptations, but I grieve that I am not now what I then was" (*Letter to* St. *Eustochium*).

• • •

Thérèse of the Child Jesus
VIRGIN AND DOCTOR (1873–1897)

"I prefer the monotony of obscure sacrifice to all ecstasies. To pick up a pin for love can convert a soul." These are the words of Thérèse of the Child Jesus, a Carmelite nun who lived a cloistered life of obscurity in the convent of Lisieux, France. And her preference for hidden sacrifice did indeed convert souls. Few saints of God are more popular than this young nun. Her autobiography, *The Story of a Soul,* is read and loved throughout the world. Thérèse Martin entered the convent at the age of fifteen and died in 1897 at the age of twenty-four.

Life in a Carmelite convent is indeed uneventful and consists mainly of prayer and hard domestic work. But Thérèse possessed that holy insight that redeems the time, however dull that time may be. She saw in quiet suffering redemptive suffering, suffering that was indeed her apostolate. Thérèse said she came to the Carmel convent "to save souls and pray for priests." And shortly before she died, she wrote: "I want to spend my heaven doing good on earth."

She was canonized in 1925, and two years later she and Francis Xavier (December 3) were declared copatrons of the missions.

On October 19, 1997, Blessed John Paul II proclaimed her a Doctor of the Church, the third woman to be so recognized in light of her holiness and the influence in the Church of her teaching on spirituality. Her parents, Louis and Zélie (October 1), were beatified in 2008.

COMMENT: Thérèse has much to teach our age of the image, the appearance, the "sell." We have become a dangerously self-conscious people, painfully aware of the need to be fulfilled, yet knowing we are not. Thérèse, like so many saints, sought to serve others, to do something outside herself, to forget herself in quiet acts of love. She is one of the great examples of the Gospel paradox that we gain our life by losing it, and that the seed that falls to the ground must die in order to live (John 12).

Preoccupation with self separates modern men and women from God, from their fellow human beings, and ultimately from themselves. We must relearn to forget ourselves, to contemplate a God who draws us out of ourselves, and to serve others as the ultimate expression of selfhood. These are the insights of St. Thérèse of Lisieux, and they are more valid today than ever.

COMMENT: All her life St. Thérèse suffered from illness. As a young girl she underwent a three-month malady characterized by violent crises, extended delirium, and prolonged fainting spells. Afterward, she was ever frail, and yet she worked hard in the laundry and refectory of the convent. Psychologically, she endured prolonged periods of darkness when the light of faith seemed all but extinguished. The last year of her life she slowly wasted away from tuberculosis. And yet shortly before her death on September 30 she murmured, "I would not suffer less."

Truly she was a valiant woman who did not whimper about her illnesses and anxieties. Here was a person who saw the power of love, that divine alchemy which can change everything, including weakness and illness, into service and redemptive power for others. Is it any wonder that she is patron of the missions? Who else but those who embrace suffering with their love really convert the world?

• • •

OCTOBER 1 + OPTIONAL
Blesseds Louis Martin and Zélie Guérin
HUSBAND (1823–1894), WIFE (1831–1877),
PARENTS

The Church's beatification of a couple is a rare event. The only other recent example is the 2001 beatification of Luigi and Maria Beltrame Quattrocchi.

Of the Martin's nine children, two daughters and two sons died in infancy. St. Thérèse of the Child Jesus (October 1) and three of her sisters entered the Carmelites in Lisieux, and the fourth sister, Leonie, joined the Monastery of the Visitation.

Born into a military family in Bordeaux, Louis learned to be a watchmaker. His desire to join the Canons Regular of St. Augustine at the St. Bernard Pass in the Swiss Alps vanished because he did not know Latin. After further studies in Paris, he moved to Alçenon, where he worked as a jeweler and watchmaker, enjoying the opportunity to fish nearby.

Zélie Guérin was also born into a military family. She sought without success to enter the Daughters of Charity of St. Vincent de Paul. Having mastered the craft of making Point d' Alçenon lace by hand, she opened her own shop and did very well.

When Zélie and Louis met in Alçenon, she felt that he was the man whom God intended her to marry. That happened on July 13, 1858. Their surviving daughters were Marie, Pauline, Leonie, Celine, and Marie-Francoise-Thérèse. Life in the devout Martin household is fondly described in Thérèse's book, *The Story of a Soul*.

Zélie continued her lacemaking business, which Louis helped to manage. After her death in 1877 from breast cancer, Louis and his daughters moved to Lisieux, where his brother-in-law worked as a pharmacist. His wife, Celine, helped Louis raise his daughters. The entrance of Thérèse into the Carmelites at the age of fifteen was a great sacrifice for him. His daughter Celine looked after Louis until he entered a mental sanitarium in Caen in 1894 and died a few months later.

Many married couples attended the beatification Mass celebrated in Lisieux by Cardinal Jose Saraiva Martins on October 19, 2008, World Mission Sunday. St. Thérèse of the Child Jesus was named copatron of the missions in 1927.

COMMENT: In life Louis and Zélie knew great joy and excruciating sorrow. They firmly believed that God was with them throughout every challenge that married life, parenting, and their occupations presented.

QUOTE: Thérèse once wrote, "God gave me a father and a mother more worthy of heaven than of earth."

• • •

Guardian Angels

Perhaps no aspect of Catholic piety is as comforting to parents as the belief that an angel protects their little ones from dangers real and imagined. Yet guardian angels are not only for children. Their role is to represent individuals before God, to watch over them always, to aid their prayer, and to present their souls to God at death.

The concept of an angel assigned to guide and nurture each human being is a development of Catholic doctrine and piety based on Scripture but not directly drawn from it. Jesus's words in Matthew 18:10 best support this belief: "See that you do not despise one of these little ones, for I say to you that their angels in heaven always look upon the face of my heavenly Father."

Devotion to the angels began to develop with the birth of the monastic tradition. St. Benedict (July 11) gave it impetus and St. Bernard of Clairvaux (August 20), a great twelfth-century reformer, was such an eloquent spokesman for the guardian angels that angelic devotion assumed its current form in his day.

A feast in honor of the guardian angels was first observed in the sixteenth century. In 1615 Pope Paul V added it to the Roman calendar.

COMMENT: Devotion to the angels is, at base, an expression of faith in God's enduring love and providential care extended to each person day-in and day-out until life's end.

QUOTE: "May the angels lead you into paradise; may the martyrs come to welcome you and take you to the holy city, the new and eternal Jerusalem" (*Rite for Christian Burial*).

• • •

Theodora Guérin

VIRGIN (1798–1856)

Trust in God's Providence enabled Mother Theodora to leave her homeland, sail halfway around the world, and found a new religious congregation.

Born in Etables, France, Anne-Thérèse's life was shattered by her father's murder when she was fifteen. For several years she cared for her mother and younger sister. She entered the Sisters of Providence in 1823, taking the name Sister Saint Theodore. An illness during novitiate left her with lifelong fragile health. This did not keep her from becoming an accomplished teacher.

At the invitation of the bishop of Vincennes, she and five sisters were sent in 1840 to Saint Mary-of-the-Woods, Indiana, to teach and to care for the sick poor. She was to establish a motherhouse and novitiate. Only later did she learn that her French superiors had already decided the sisters in the United States should form a new religious congregation under her leadership.

She and her community persevered despite fires, crop failures, prejudice against Catholic women religious, misunderstandings, and separation from their original religious congregation.

She once told her sisters, "Have confidence in the Providence that so far has never failed us. The way is not yet clear. Grope along slowly. Do not press matters; be patient, be trustful." Another time, she asked, "With Jesus, what shall we have to fear?"

She is buried in the Church of the Immaculate Conception in Saint Mary-of-the-Woods, Indiana, and was beatified in 1998. Eight years later she was canonized.

COMMENT: God's work gets done by people ready to take risks and to work hard—always remembering what St. Paul told the Corinthians, "I planted, Apollos watered, but God caused the growth" (1 Corinthians 3:6). Every holy person has a strong sense of God's providence.

QUOTE: During his homily at the canonization Mass, Pope Benedict XVI said that Mother Theodora "is a beautiful spiritual figure and a model of the Christian life. She was always open for the missions the Church entrusted to her, and she found the strength and the boldness to put them [the missions] into practice in the Eucharist, in prayer and in an infinite trust in Divine Providence. Her inner strength moved her to address particular attention to the poor, and above all to children."

• • •

Francis of Assisi

RELIGIOUS (1181?–1226)

Francis of Assisi was a poor little man who astounded and inspired the Church by taking the Gospel literally—not in a narrow fundamentalist sense, but by actually following all that Jesus said and did, joyfully, without limit and without a sense of self-importance.

Serious illness brought the young Francis to see the emptiness of his frolicking life as leader of Assisi's youth. Prayer—lengthy and difficult—led him to a self-emptying like that of Christ, climaxed by embracing a leper he met on the road. It symbolized his complete obedience to what he had heard in prayer: "Francis! Everything you have loved and desired in the flesh it is your duty to despise and hate, if you wish to know my will. And when you have begun this, all that now seems sweet and lovely to you will become intolerable and bitter, but all that you used to avoid will turn itself to great sweetness and exceeding joy."

From the cross in the neglected field-chapel of San Damiano, Christ told him, "Francis, go out and build up my house, for it is nearly falling down." Francis became the totally poor and humble workman.

He must have suspected a deeper meaning to "build up my house." But he would have been content to be for the rest of his life, the poor "nothing" man, actually putting brick on brick in abandoned chapels. He gave up all his possessions, piling even his clothes before his earthly father (who was demanding restitution for Francis's "gifts" to the poor) so that he would be totally free to say, "Our Father in heaven." He was, for a time, considered to be a religious fanatic, begging from door to door when he could not get money for his work, evoking sadness or disgust from his former friends, ridicule from the unthinking.

But genuineness will tell. A few people began to realize that this man was actually trying to be Christian. He really believed what Jesus said: "Announce the kingdom! Possess no gold or silver or copper in your purses, no traveling bag, no sandals, no staff" (Luke 9:1–3).

Francis's first Rule for his followers was a collection of texts from the Gospels. He initially had no idea of founding a religious order, but once it began he protected it and accepted all the legal structures needed to support it. His devotion and loyalty to the Church were absolute and highly exemplary at a time when various movements promoting reform tended to break the Church's unity.

He was torn between a life devoted entirely to prayer and a life of active preaching of the Good News. He decided in favor of the latter, but always returned to solitude when he could. He wanted to be a missionary in Syria or in Africa, but was prevented by shipwreck and illness in both cases. He tried to convert the sultan of Egypt during the Fifth Crusade.

During the last years of his relatively short life (he died at forty-four), he was half blind and seriously ill. Two years before his death, he received the stigmata, the real and painful wounds of Christ, in his hands, feet, and side.

On his deathbed, he said over and over again the last addition to his Canticle of the Creatures, "Be praised, O Lord, for our Sister Death." He sang Psalm 141, and at the end asked his superior to have his clothes removed when the last hour came and for permission to expire lying naked on the earth, in imitation of his Lord.

COMMENT: Francis of Assisi was poor only that he might be Christ-like. He recognized creation as another manifestation of the beauty of God. In 1979 he was named patron of ecology. Francis did great penance (apologizing to "Brother Body" later in life) that he might be totally disciplined for the will of

God. His poverty had a sister, humility, by which he meant total dependence on the good God. But all this was, as it were, preliminary to the heart of his spirituality: living the Gospel life, summed up in the charity of Jesus and perfectly expressed in the Eucharist.

QUOTE: "We adore you and we bless you, Lord Jesus Christ, here and in all the churches which are in the whole world, because by your holy cross you have redeemed the world" (St. Francis).

• • •

OCTOBER 5 + OPTIONAL
Maria Faustina Kowalska
VIRGIN (1905–1938)

St. Maria Faustina's name is forever linked to the annual feast of the Divine Mercy (celebrated on the Second Sunday of Easter), the divine mercy chaplet and the divine mercy prayer recited each day by many people at 3:00 P.M.

Born in what is now west-central Poland (part of Germany before World War I), Helena was the third of ten children. She worked as a housekeeper in three cities before joining the Congregation of the Sisters of Our Lady of Mercy in 1925. She worked as a cook, gardener, and porter in three of their houses.

In addition to carrying out her work faithfully, generously serving the needs of the sisters and the local people, she also had a deep interior life. This included receiving revelations from the Lord Jesus, messages that she recorded in her diary at the request of Christ and of her confessors.

At a time when some Catholics had an image of God as such a strict judge that they might be tempted to despair about the possibility of being forgiven, Jesus chose to emphasize his mercy and forgiveness for sins acknowledged and confessed. "I do not want to punish aching mankind," he once told St. Maria Faustina, "but I desire to heal it, pressing it to my merciful heart" (*Diary*, 1588). The two rays emanating from Christ's heart, she said, represent the blood and water poured out after Jesus's death (John 19:34).

Because Sister Maria Faustina knew that the revelations she had already received did not constitute holiness itself, she wrote in her diary: "Neither graces, nor revelations, nor raptures, nor gifts granted to a soul make it perfect, but rather the intimate union of the soul with God. These gifts are merely ornaments of the soul, but constitute neither its essence nor its perfection. My sanctity and perfection consist in the close union of my will with the will of God" (*Diary*, 1107).

Sister Maria Faustina died of tuberculosis in Kraków on October 5, 1938. Pope John Paul II beatified her in 1993 and canonized her seven years later.

COMMENT: Devotion to God's Divine Mercy bears some resemblance to devotion to the Sacred Heart of Jesus. In both cases, sinners are encouraged not to despair, not to doubt God's willingness to forgive them if they repent. As Psalm 136 says in each of its twenty-six verses, "God's love [mercy] endures forever."

QUOTE: Four years after Faustina's beatification, Pope John Paul II visited the Sanctuary of Divine Mercy at Lagiewniki (near Kraków) and addressed members of her congregation. He said: "The message of divine mercy has always been very close and precious to me. It is as though history has written it in the tragic experience of World War II. In those difficult years, this message was a particular support and an inexhaustible source of hope, not only for those living in Krakow, but for the entire nation. This was also my personal experience, which I carried with me to the See of Peter and which, in a certain sense, forms the image of this pontificate. I thank divine providence because I was able to contribute personally to carrying out Christ's will, by instituting the feast of Divine Mercy. Here, close to the remains of Blessed Faustina, I thank God for the gift of her beatification. I pray unceasingly that God may have 'mercy on us and on the whole world' (Quote from the Chaplet of Divine Mercy)."

• • •

Blessed Francis Xavier Seelos
PRIEST (1819–1867)

Zeal as a preacher and a confessor led Fr. Seelos to works of compassion as well.

Born in southern Bavaria, he studied philosophy and theology in Munich. On hearing about the work of the Redemptorists among German-speaking Catholics in the United States, he came to this country in 1843. Ordained at the end of 1844, he was assigned for six years to St. Philomena Parish in Pittsburgh as an assistant to St. John Neumann (January 5). The next three years Fr. Seelos was superior in the same community and began his service as novice master.

Several years in parish ministry in Maryland followed, along with responsibility for training Redemptorist students. During the Civil War, he went to Washington, D.C., and successfully appealed to President Lincoln that those students not be drafted for military service.

For several years he preached in English and in German throughout the Midwest and in the Middle Atlantic states. Assigned to St. Mary of the Assumption Church community in New Orleans, he served his Redemptorist confreres and parishioners with great zeal. In 1867 he died of yellow fever, having contracted that disease while visiting the sick. He was beatified in 2000.

COMMENT: Fr. Seelos worked in many different places but always with the same zeal: to help people know God's saving love and compassion. He preached about the works of mercy and then engaged in them, even risking his own health.

QUOTE: "To the abandoned and the lost he preached the message of Jesus Christ, 'the source of eternal salvation' (Hebrews 5:9), and in the hours spent in the confessional he convinced many to return to God. Today, Blessed Francis Xavier Seelos invites the members of the Church to deepen their union with Christ in the sacraments of penance and the Eucharist" (Pope John Paul II, beatification homily).

• • •

Bruno
PRIEST (1030?–1101)

This saint has the honor of having founded a religious order, which, as the saying goes, has never had to be reformed because it was never deformed. No doubt both the founder and the members would reject such high praise, but it is an indication of the saint's intense love of a penitential life in solitude.

He was born in Cologne, became a famous teacher at Rheims and was appointed chancellor of that archdiocese at the age of forty-five. He supported Pope Gregory VII (May 25) in his fight against the decadence of the clergy and took part in the removal of his own scandalous archbishop, Manasses. Bruno suffered the plundering of his house for his pains.

He had a dream of living in solitude and prayer and persuaded a few friends to join him in a hermitage. After a while he felt the place unsuitable and, through a friend, was given some land that was to become famous for his foundation "in the Chartreuse" (from which comes the word *Carthusians*). The climate, mountainous terrain, and inaccessibility guaranteed silence, poverty, and small numbers.

Bruno and his friends built an oratory with small individual cells at a distance from each other. They met for Matins and Vespers each day, and spent the rest of the time in solitude, eating together only on great feasts. Their chief work was copying manuscripts.

The pope, hearing of Bruno's holiness, called for his assistance in Rome. When the pope had to flee Rome, Bruno pulled up stakes again and spent his last years (after refusing a bishopric) in the wilderness of Calabria (southern Italy).

He was never formally canonized because the Carthusians were averse to all occasions of publicity. Pope Clement X extended his feast to the whole Church in 1674.

COMMENT: If there is always a certain uneasy questioning of the contemplative life, there is an even greater puzzlement about the extremely penitential combination of community and hermit life lived by the Carthusians.

QUOTE: "Members of those communities which are totally dedicated to contemplation give themselves to God alone in solitude and silence and through constant prayer and ready penance. No matter how urgent may be the needs of the active apostolate, such communities will always have a distinguished part to play in Christ's Mystical Body" (Decree on the Renewal of Religious Life, 7).

•   •   •

OCTOBER 6 + MEMORIAL (CANADA)
Blessed Marie-Rose Durocher
VIRGIN (1811–1849)

Canada was one diocese from coast to coast during the first eight years of Marie-Rose Durocher's life. Its half-million Catholics had received civil and religious liberty from the English only forty-four years before. When Marie-Rose was twenty-nine, Bishop Ignace Bourget became bishop of Montreal. He would be a decisive influence in her life.

He faced a shortage of priests and sisters and a rural population that had been largely deprived of education. Like his counterparts in the United States, he scoured Europe for help and founded four communities, one of which was the Sisters of the Holy Names of Jesus and Mary. Its first sister and reluctant foundress was Marie-Rose.

She was born in a little village near Montreal in 1811, the tenth of eleven children. She had a good education, was something of a tomboy, rode a horse named Caesar, and could have married well. At sixteen she felt the desire to become a religious but was forced to abandon the idea because of her weak constitution. At eighteen, when her mother died, her priest brother invited her and her father to come to his parish in Beloeil, not far from Montreal. For thirteen years she served as housekeeper, hostess, and parish worker. She became well known for her graciousness, courtesy, leadership, and tact; she was, in fact, called "the saint of Beloeil." Perhaps she was too tactful during two years when her brother treated her coldly.

As a young woman she had hoped there would someday be a community of teaching sisters in every parish, never thinking she would found one. But her spiritual director, Fr. Pierre Telmon, O.M.I., after thoroughly (and severely) leading her in the spiritual life, urged her to found a community herself. Bishop Bourget concurred, but Marie shrank from the prospect. She was in poor health, and her father and her brother needed her.

She finally agreed and, with two friends, Melodie Dufresne and Henriette Cere, entered a little home in Longueuil, across the St. Lawrence River from Montreal. With them were thirteen young girls already assembled for boarding school. Longueuil became successively her Bethlehem, Nazareth, and Gethsemane. She was thirty-two and would live only six more years— years filled with poverty, trials, sickness, and slander. The qualities she had nurtured in her "hidden" life came forward—a strong will, intelligence and common sense, great inner courage, and yet a great deference to directors. Thus was born an international congregation of women religious dedicated to education in the faith.

She was severe with herself and by today's standards quite strict with her sisters. Beneath it all, of course, was an unshakable love of her crucified Savior.

On her deathbed the prayers most frequently on her lips were "Jesus, Mary, Joseph! Sweet Jesus, I love you. Jesus, be to me Jesus!" Before she died, she smiled and said to the sister with her, "Your prayers are keeping me here—let me go."

She was beatified in 1982.

COMMENT: The Christian triad has always been and will always be prayer, penance, and charity. In our day we have seen a great burst of charity, a genuine interest in the poor. Countless Christians have experienced a deep form of prayer. But penance? We squirm when we read of terrible physical penance done by people like Marie-Rose. That is not for most people, of course. But the pull of a materialistic consumer culture oriented to pleasure and entertainment is impossible to resist without some form of deliberate and Christ-conscious abstinence. That is part of the way to answer Jesus's call to repent and turn completely to God.

QUOTE: To a novice leaving religious life, Marie-Rose said: "Do not imitate those persons who, after having spent a few months as postulant or novice in a community, dress differently, even ludicrously. You are returning to the secular state. My advice is, follow the styles of the day, but from afar, as it were."

* * *

OCTOBER 7 + MEMORIAL

Our Lady of the Rosary

St. Pius V (April 30) established this feast in 1573 to thank God for the victory of Christians over the Turks at Lepanto—a victory attributed to the praying of the rosary. Clement XI extended the feast to the universal Church in 1716.

The development of the rosary has a long history. First, a practice developed of praying 150 Our Fathers in imitation of the 150 Psalms. Then there was a parallel practice of praying 150 Hail Marys. Soon a mystery of Jesus's life was attached to each Hail Mary. Though Mary's giving the rosary to St. Dominic is recognized as a legend, the development of this prayer form owes much to the followers of St. Dominic. One of them, Alan de la Roche, was known as "the apostle of the rosary." He founded the first Confraternity of the Rosary in the fifteenth century. In the sixteenth century, the rosary was developed to include fifteen mysteries (joyful, sorrowful, and glorious). In 2002, Pope John Paul II added five luminous mysteries to this devotion.

COMMENT: The purpose of the rosary is to help us meditate on the great mysteries of our salvation. Pius XII called it a compendium of the gospel. The main focus is on Jesus—his birth, life, death, and resurrection. The Our Fathers remind us that Jesus's Father is the initiator of salvation. The Hail Marys remind us to join with Mary in contemplating these mysteries. They also make us aware that Mary was and is intimately joined with her Son in all the mysteries of his earthly and heavenly existence. The Glorys remind us that the purpose of all life is the glory of the Trinity.

The rosary appeals to many. It is simple. The constant repetition of words helps create an atmosphere in which to contemplate the mysteries of God. We sense that Jesus and Mary are with us in the joys and sorrows of life. We grow in hope that God will bring us to share in the glory of Jesus and Mary forever.

QUOTE: "The rosary, though clearly Marian in character, is at heart a Christ-centered prayer. It has all the depth of the gospel message in its entirety. It is an echo of the prayer of Mary, her perennial Magnificat for the work of the redemptive Incarnation which began in her virginal womb.... It can be said that the rosary is, in some sense, a prayer-commentary on the final chapter of the Vatican II Constitution *Lumen Gentium*, a chapter that discusses the wondrous presence of the Mother of God in the mystery of Christ and the Church" (Pope John Paul II, *The Rosary of the Virgin Mary*).

* * *

OCTOBER 9 + OPTIONAL
Denis and Companions
BISHOP AND MARTYR; MARTYRS (D. 258?)

This martyr and patron of France is regarded as the first bishop of Paris. His popularity is due to a series of legends, especially those connecting him with the great abbey church of St. Denis in Paris. He was for a time confused with the writer now called Pseudo-Dionysius.

The best hypothesis contends that Denis was sent to Gaul from Rome in the third century and was beheaded in the persecution under Emperor Valerius in 258.

According to one of the legends, after he was martyred on Montmartre (literally, "mountain of martyrs") in Paris, he carried his head to a village northeast of the city. St. Genevieve built a basilica over his tomb at the beginning of the sixth century.

COMMENT: Again we have the case of a saint about whom almost nothing is known, yet one whose cult has been a vigorous part of the Church's history for centuries. We can only conclude that the deep impression the saint made on the people of his day reflected a life of unusual holiness. In all such cases, there are two fundamental facts: A great man gave his life for Christ, and the Church has never forgotten him—a human symbol of God's eternal mindfulness.

QUOTE: "Martyrdom is part of the Church's nature since it manifests Christian death in its pure form, as the death of unrestrained faith, which is otherwise hidden in the ambivalence of all human events. Through martyrdom the Church's holiness, instead of remaining purely subjective, achieves by God's grace the visible expression it needs. As early as the second century one who accepted death for the sake of Christian faith or Christian morals was looked on and revered as a *martus* (witness). The term is scriptural in that Jesus Christ is the 'faithful witness' absolutely (Revelation 1:5; 3:14)" (Karl Rahner, *Theological Dictionary*).

• • •

OCTOBER 9 + OPTIONAL
John Leonardi
PRIEST (1541?–1609)

"I am only one person! Why should I do anything? What good would it do?" Today, as in any age, people seem plagued with the dilemma of getting involved. In his own way John Leonardi answered these questions. He chose to become a priest.

After his ordination, he became very active in the works of the ministry, especially in hospitals and prisons. The example and dedication of his work attracted several young laymen who began to assist him. They later became priests themselves.

John lived after the Protestant Reformation and the Council of Trent (1545–1563). He and his followers projected a new congregation of diocesan priests. For some reason the plan, which was ultimately approved, provoked great political opposition. John was exiled from his hometown of Lucca, Italy, for almost the entire remainder of his life. He received encouragement and help from St. Philip Neri (May 26) who gave him his lodgings—along with the care of his cat!

In 1579, John formed the Confraternity of Christian Doctrine and published a compendium of Christian doctrine that remained in use until the nineteenth century.

Fr. Leonardi and his priests became a great power for good in Italy, and their congregation was confirmed by Pope Clement VIII in 1595. He died at the age of sixty-eight from a disease caught when tending those stricken by the plague.

By the deliberate policy of the founder, the Clerks Regular of the Mother of God have never had more than fifteen churches and today form only a very small congregation.

COMMENT: What can one person do? If you have ever glanced through a *Christopher Notes* pamphlet you know—plenty! In the life of each saint one thing stands clear: God and one person are a majority! What one individual, following God's will and plan for his or her life, can do is more than our mind could ever hope for or imagine. Each of us, like John Leonardi, has a mission to fulfill in God's plan for the world. Each one of us is unique and has been given talent to use for the service of our brothers and sisters for the building up of God's Kingdom.

QUOTE: "Do not be afraid any longer, little flock, for your Father is pleased to give you the kingdom. Sell your belongings and give alms. Provide money bags for yourselves that do not wear out, an inexhaustible treasure in heaven that no thief can reach nor moth destroy" (Luke 12:32–33).

• • •

OCTOBER 9 + OPTIONAL
Blessed John Henry Newman
PRIEST (1801–1890)

John Henry Newman, the nineteenth-century's most important English-speaking Roman Catholic theologian, spent the first half of his life as an Anglican and the second half as a Roman Catholic. He was a priest, popular preacher, writer, and eminent theologian in both Churches.

Born in London, England, he studied at Oxford's Trinity College, was a tutor at Oriel College, and for seventeen years was vicar of the university church, St. Mary the Virgin. He eventually published eight volumes of *Parochial and Plain Sermons* as wells as two novels. His poem, "Dream of Gerontius," was set to music by Sir Edward Elgar.

After 1833, Newman was a prominent member of the Oxford Movement, which emphasized the Church's debt to the Church Fathers and challenged any tendency to consider truth as completely subjective.

Historical research made Newman suspect that the Roman Catholic Church was in closest continuity with the Church that Jesus established. In 1845, he was received into full communion as a Catholic. Two years later he was ordained a Catholic priest in Rome and joined the Congregation of the Oratory, founded three centuries earlier by St. Philip Neri (April 26). Returning to England, Newman founded Oratory houses in Birmingham and London, and for seven years served as rector of the Catholic University of Ireland.

Before Newman, many Catholic theologians tended to ignore history, preferring instead to draw deductions from first principles—much as plane geometry does. After Newman, the lived experience of believers was recognized as a key part of theological reflection.

Newman eventually wrote forty books and twenty-one thousand letters that survive. Most famous are *Essay on the Development of Christian Doctrine, On Consulting the Faith in Matters of Doctrine, Apologia Pro Vita Sua* (his spiritual autobiography up to 1864), and *Essay on the Grammar of Assent*. He accepted Vatican I's teaching on papal infallibility while noting its limits, which many people who favored that definition were reluctant to do.

When Newman was named a cardinal in 1879, he took as his motto *Cor ad cor loquitur* (Heart speaks to heart). He was buried at Rednal (near Birmingham) eleven years later. After his grave was exhumed in 2008, a new tomb was prepared at the oratory church in Birmingham.

Three years after Newman died, a Newman Club for Catholic students began at the University of Pittsburgh. In time, his name was linked to ministry centers at many public and private colleges and universities in the United States.

Pope Benedict XVI beatified Newman on September 19, 2010, at Crofton Park (near Birmingham). The pope noted Newman's emphasis on the vital place of revealed religion in civilized society, but also praised his pastoral zeal for the sick, the poor, the bereaved, and those in prison.

COMMENT: John Henry Newman has been called "the absent Father of Vatican II" because his writings on conscience, religious liberty, Scripture, the vocation of laypeople, the relation of Church and state, and other topics were extremely influential in the shaping of the Council's documents. Although Newman was not always understood or appreciated, he steadfastly preached the Good News by word and example.

QUOTE: Newman composed this prayer: "God has created me to do Him some definite service. He has committed some work to me which he has not committed to another. I have a mission; I may never know it in this life, but I shall be told it in the next. I am a link in a chain, a bond of connection between persons; He has not created me for naught. I shall do good—I shall do His work. I shall be an angel of peace while not intending it, if I do but keep His commandments. Therefore, I will trust him."

• • •

OCTOBER 11 (JUNE 3) + OPTIONAL
Blessed John XXIII
POPE (1881–1963)

Although few people had as great an impact on the twentieth century as Pope John XXIII, he avoided the limelight as much as possible. Indeed, one writer has noted that his ordinariness seems one of his most remarkable qualities.

The firstborn son of a farming family in Sotto il Monte, near Bergamo in northern Italy, Angelo Giuseppe Roncalli was always proud of his down-to-earth roots. In Bergamo's diocesan seminary, he joined the Secular Franciscan Order.

After his ordination in 1904, Angelo returned to Rome for canon law studies. He soon worked as his bishop's secretary, Church history teacher in the seminary, and as publisher of the diocesan paper.

His service as a stretcher-bearer for the Italian army during World War I gave him a firsthand knowledge of war. In 1921 he was made national director of the Society for the Propagation of the Faith. He still found time to teach patristics at a seminary in the Eternal City.

In 1925 he became a papal diplomat, serving first in Bulgaria, then in Turkey, and finally in France (1944–1953). During World War II, he became well acquainted with Orthodox Church leaders, and with the help of Germany's ambassador to Turkey, Archbishop Roncalli helped save an estimated twenty-four thousand Jewish people.

Named a cardinal and appointed patriarch of Venice in 1953, he finally shepherded a local church. A month short of entering his seventy-eighth year, he was elected pope, taking the name John, after his father and the two patrons of Rome's cathedral, St. John Lateran. He took his work very seriously, but not himself. His wit soon became proverbial, and he began meeting with political and religious leaders from around the world. In 1962 he was deeply involved in efforts to resolve the Cuban missile crisis.

His most famous encyclicals were *Mother and Teacher* (1961) and *Peace on Earth* (1963). Pope John XXIII enlarged the membership in the College of Cardinals and made it more international. At his address at the opening of the Second Vatican Council, he criticized the "prophets of doom" who "in these modern times see nothing but prevarication and ruin." Pope John XXIII set a tone for the council when he said, "The Church has always opposed…errors. Nowadays, however, the Spouse of Christ prefers to make use of the medicine of mercy rather than that of severity."

On his deathbed he said: "It is not that the Gospel has changed; it is that we have begun to understand it better. Those who have lived as long as I have…were enabled to compare different cultures and traditions, and know that the moment has come to discern the signs of the times, to seize the opportunity and to look far ahead."

He died on June 3, 1963. Blessed John Paul II beatified him in 2000.

COMMENT: Throughout his life, Angelo Roncalli cooperated with God's grace, believing that the job at hand was worthy of his best efforts. His sense of God's providence made him the ideal person to promote a new dialogue with Protestant and Orthodox Christians, as well as with Jews and Muslims. In the sometimes-noisy St. Peter's Basilica, many people immediately became silent on seeing the tomb of Pope John XXIII, grateful for the gift of his life and holiness. After his beatification, his tomb was moved into the basilica itself.

QUOTE: In 1903, young Angelo wrote in his spiritual journal: "From the saints I must take the substance, not the accidents of their virtues. I am not St. Aloysius, nor must I seek holiness in his particular way, but according to the requirements of my own nature, my own character and the different conditions of my life. I must not be the dry, bloodless reproduction of a model, however perfect. God desires us to follow the examples of the saints by absorbing the vital sap of their virtues and turning it into our own life-blood, adapting it to our own individual capacities and particular circumstances. If St. Aloysius had been as I am, he would have become holy in a different way" (*Journal of a Soul*).

• • •

OCTOBER 14 + OPTIONAL
Callistus I
POPE AND MARTYR (D. 223?)

The most reliable information about this saint comes from his enemy, St. Hippolytus (August 13), the first antipope, later a martyr for the Church. A negative principle is used: If some worse things had happened, Hippolytus would surely have mentioned them.

Callistus was a slave in the imperial Roman household. Put in charge of the bank by his master, he lost the money deposited, fled, and was caught. After serving time for a while, he was released to make some attempt to recover the money. Apparently he carried his zeal too far, being arrested for brawling in a Jewish synagogue. This time he was condemned to work in the mines of Sardinia. He was released through the influence of the emperor's mistress and lived at Anzio (site of a famous World War II beachhead).

After winning his freedom, Callistus was made superintendent of the public Christian burial ground in Rome (still called the catacombs of St. Callistus), probably the first land owned by the Church. The pope ordained him a deacon and made him his friend and adviser.

He was elected pope by a majority vote of the clergy and laity of Rome and thereafter was bitterly attacked by the losing candidate, St. Hippolytus, who let himself be set up as the first antipope in the history of the Church. The schism lasted about eighteen years.

Hippolytus is venerated as a saint. He was banished during the persecution of 235 and was reconciled to the Church. He died from his sufferings in Sardinia. He attacked Callistus on two fronts—doctrine and discipline. Hippolytus seems to have exaggerated the distinction between Father and Son (almost making two gods), possibly because theological language had not yet been refined. He also accused Callistus of being too lenient, for reasons we may find surprising: (1) Callistus admitted to Holy Communion those who had already done public penance for murder, adultery, fornication; (2)

he held marriages between free women and slaves to be valid—contrary to Roman law; (3) he authorized the ordination of men who had been married two or three times; (4) he held that mortal sin was not a sufficient reason to depose a bishop; (5) he held to a policy of leniency toward those who had denied their faith during persecution.

Callistus was martyred during a local disturbance in Trastevere (Rome) and is the first pope (except for Peter) to be commemorated as a martyr in the earliest martyrology of the Church.

COMMENT: The life of this man is another reminder that the course of Church history, like that of true love, never did run smooth. The Church had to (and still must) go through the agonizing struggle to state the mysteries of the faith in language that, at the very least, sets up definite barriers to error. On the disciplinary side, the Church had to preserve the mercy of Christ against rigorism while still upholding the Gospel ideal of radical conversion and self-discipline. Every pope—indeed every Christian—must walk the difficult path between reasonable indulgence and reasonable rigorism.

QUOTE: His contemporaries, Jesus said, were "like children who sit in marketplaces and call to one another, 'We played the flute for you, but you did not dance, we sang a dirge but you did not mourn.' For John [the Baptist] came neither eating nor drinking, and they said, 'He is possessed by a demon.' The Son of Man came eating and drinking and they said, 'Look, he is a glutton and a drunkard, a friend of tax collectors and sinners'" (Matthew 11:16b–19a).

● ● ●

OCTOBER 15 + MEMORIAL
Teresa of Jesus
VIRGIN AND DOCTOR (1515–1582)

Teresa lived in an age of exploration as well as political, social, and religious upheaval. It was the sixteenth century, an age of turmoil and reform. She was born before the Protestant Reformation and died almost twenty years after the closing of the Council of Trent.

The gift of God to Teresa in and through which she became holy and left her mark on the Church and the world is threefold: She was a woman, she was a contemplative, she was an active reformer.

As a woman, Teresa stood on her own two feet, even in the man's world of her time. She was "her own woman," entering the Carmelites despite strong opposition from her father. She is a person wrapped not so much in silence as in mystery. Beautiful, talented, outgoing, adaptable, affectionate, courageous, enthusiastic, she was totally human. Like Jesus, she was a mystery of paradoxes: wise, yet practical; intelligent, yet much in tune with her experience; mystic, yet an energetic reformer. A holy woman, a womanly woman.

Teresa was a woman "for God," a woman of prayer, discipline, and compassion. Her heart belonged to God. Her ongoing conversion was an arduous, lifelong struggle, involving ongoing purification and suffering. She was misunderstood, misjudged, opposed in her efforts at reform. Yet she struggled on, courageous and faithful; she struggled with her own mediocrity, her illness, her opposition. And in the midst of all this she clung to God in life and in prayer. Her writings on prayer and contemplation are drawn from her experience: powerful, practical, and graceful. A woman of prayer; a woman for God.

Teresa was a woman for others. Though a contemplative, she spent much of her time and energy seeking to reform herself and the Carmelites, to lead them back to the full observance of the primitive Rule. She founded over a half-dozen new monasteries. She traveled, wrote, fought—always to renew, to reform. In her self, in her prayer, in her life, in her efforts to reform, in all the people she touched, she was a woman for others, a woman who inspired and gave life.

Her writings, especially *The Way of Perfection* and *The Interior Castle,* have helped generations of believers.

In 1970 the Church gave her the title she had long held in the popular mind: Doctor of the Church. She and St. Catherine of Siena (April 29) were the first women so honored.

COMMENT: Ours is a time of turmoil, a time of reform, and a time of liberation. Modern women have in Teresa a challenging example. Promoters of renewal, promoters of prayer, all have in Teresa a woman to reckon with, one whom they can admire and imitate.

QUOTE: Teresa knew well the continued presence and value of suffering (physical illness, opposition to reform, difficulties in prayer), but she grew to be able to embrace suffering, even desire it: "Lord, either to suffer or to die." Toward the end of her life she exclaimed: "Oh, my Lord! How true it is that whoever works for you is paid in troubles! And what a precious price to those who love you if we understand its value."

• • •

OCTOBER 16 + OPTIONAL
Hedwig
RELIGIOUS (1174?–1243)

Rarely do humans realize the possibilities of the wise use of earthly power and worldly wealth. Hedwig was one of the few. Born to nobility toward the close of the twelfth century, she was married at an early age to Henry, duke of Silesia (now Poland). Through her persuasion and personal efforts, several monastic institutions of both men and women were established in Silesia. Several hospitals, one for lepers, were likewise founded. She was personally a great force in establishing peace in the surrounding areas during power struggles. To her great sorrow, she was unable to prevent a pitched battle between the forces of two of her sons, one of whom was dissatisfied over the partition of estates that Henry had made between them.

After she and her husband had made a mutual vow of celibacy, she lived mostly at the monastery at Trebnitz where, although not a formal member of the religious institute, she participated in the religious exercises of the community. She died in 1243 and was buried at Trebintz.

COMMENT: Whatever possessions we may be blessed with are not for our own needs or personal comfort alone, but are also to be used in the assistance of others. Use of these goods should always promote, never impede, progress in God's love. It is true that earthly things of themselves in no way contradict God's love, but rather are evidence of it; still, we can become so interested in and enticed by what we sense that we become forgetful of the God from whom these blessings come.

STORY: Hedwig sacrificed her wish to become a religious in later life in order to use her earthly goods to help the poor. She chose poverty, distrusting the comforts her means might have afforded her and denying herself even such basic necessities as shoes in winter. She wore the religious habit, lived the life of a religious, but would not give up the administration of her possessions because she used these goods to help the poor. She lived her life and used her possessions so that she and those she was able to help might better appreciate the supernatural life of God's grace.

• • •

OCTOBER 16 + OPTIONAL
Margaret Mary Alacoque
VIRGIN (1647–1690)

Margaret Mary was chosen by Christ to arouse the Church to a realization of the love of God symbolized by the heart of Jesus.

Her early years were marked by sickness and a painful home situation. "The heaviest of my crosses was that I could do nothing to lighten the cross my mother was suffering." After considering marriage for some time, Margaret entered the Order of Visitation nuns at the age of twenty-four.

A Visitation nun was "not to be extraordinary except by being ordinary," but the young nun was not to enjoy this anonymity. A fellow novice (shrewdest of critics) termed Margaret humble, simple, and frank, but above all kind and patient under sharp criticism and correction. She could not meditate in the formal way expected, though she tried her best to give up her "prayer of simplicity." Slow, quiet, and clumsy, she was assigned to help an infirmarian who was a bundle of energy.

On December 27, 1674, three years a nun, she received the first of her revelations. She felt "invested" with the presence of God, though always afraid of deceiving herself in such matters. The request of Christ was that his love for humanity be made evident through her. During the next thirteen months, he appeared to her at intervals. His human heart was to be the symbol of his divine-human love. By her own love she was to make up for the coldness and ingratitude of the world—by frequent and loving Holy Communion, especially on the first Friday of each month, and by an hour's vigil of prayer every Thursday night in memory of his agony and isolation in Gethsemane. He also asked that a feast of reparation be instituted.

Like all saints, Margaret had to pay for her gift of holiness. Some of her own sisters were hostile. Theologians who were called in declared her visions delusions and suggested that she eat more heartily. Later, parents of children she taught called her an impostor, an unorthodox innovator. A new confessor, St. Claude de la Colombière, a Jesuit, recognized her genuineness and supported her. Against her great resistance, Christ called her to be a sacrificial victim for the shortcomings of her own sisters and to make this known.

After serving as novice mistress and assistant superior, she died at the age of forty-three while being anointed. "I need nothing but God, and to lose myself in the heart of Jesus."

COMMENT: Our scientific, materialistic age cannot "prove" private revelations. Theologians, if pressed, admit that we do not *have* to believe in them. But it is impossible to deny the message Margaret Mary heralded: God loves us with a passionate love. Her insistence on reparation and prayer and the reminder of final judgment should be sufficient to ward off superstition and superficiality in devotion to the Sacred Heart while preserving its deep Christian meaning.

QUOTE: Christ said to St. Margaret Mary: "Behold this Heart which has so loved men that it has spared nothing, even to exhausting and consuming itself, in order to testify its love. In return, I receive from the greater part only ingratitude, by their irreverence and sacrileges, and by the coldness and contempt they have for me in this Sacrament of love.... I come into the heart I have given you in order that through your fervor you may atone for the offenses which I have received from lukewarm and slothful hearts that dishonor me in the Blessed Sacrament" (third apparition).

• • •

OCTOBER 16 + MEMORIAL (CANADA)

Marguerite d'Youville

RELIGIOUS (1701–1771)

We learn compassion from allowing our lives to be influenced by compassionate people, by seeing life from their perspective and reconsidering our own values.

Born in Varennes, Canada, Marie Marguerite Dufrost de Lajemmerais had to interrupt her schooling at the age of twelve to help her widowed mother. Eight years later she married Francois d'Youville; they had six children, four of whom died young. Despite the fact that her husband gambled, sold liquor illegally to Native Americans, and treated her indifferently, she cared for him compassionately before his death in 1730.

Even though she was caring for two small children and running a store to help pay off her husband's debts, Marguerite still helped the poor. Once her children were grown, she and several companions rescued a Quebec hospital that was in danger of failing. She called her community the Institute of the Sisters of Charity of Montreal; the people called them the "Grey Nuns" because of the color of their habit. In time, a proverb arose among the poor people of Montreal, "Go to the Grey Nuns; they never refuse to serve." In time, five other religious communities traced their roots to the Grey Nuns.

The General Hospital in Montreal became known as the Hotel Dieu (House of God) and set a standard for medical care and Christian compassion. When the hospital was destroyed by fire in 1766, she knelt in the ashes, led the *Te Deum* (a hymn to God's providence in all circumstances) and began the rebuilding process. She fought the attempts of government officials to restrain her charity and established the first foundling home in North America.

Blessed John XXIII, who beatified her in 1959, called her the "Mother of Universal Charity." She was canonized in 1990.

COMMENT: Saints deal with plenty of discouragement, plenty of reasons to say, "Life isn't fair!" and wonder where God is in the rubble of their lives. We honor saints like Marguerite because they show us that, with God's grace and their cooperation, suffering can lead to compassion rather than to bitterness.

QUOTE: "More than once the work which Marguerite undertook was hindered by nature or people. In order to work to bring that new world of justice and love closer, she had to fight some hard and difficult battles" (Blessed John Paul II, canonization homily).

. . .

OCTOBER 17 + MEMORIAL
Ignatius of Antioch
BISHOP AND MARTYR (D. 107?)

Born in Syria, Ignatius converted to Christianity and eventually became bishop of Antioch. In the year 107, Emperor Trajan visited Antioch and forced the Christians there to choose between death and apostasy. Ignatius would not deny Christ and thus was condemned to be put to death in Rome.

Ignatius is well known for the seven letters he wrote on the long journey from Antioch to Rome. Five of these letters are to churches in Asia Minor; they urge the Christians there to remain faithful to God and to obey their superiors. He warns them against heretical doctrines, providing them with the solid truths of the Christian faith.

The sixth letter was to Polycarp, bishop of Smyrna, who was later martyred for the faith (February 23). The final letter begs the Christians in Rome not to try to stop his martyrdom. "The only thing I ask of you is to allow me to offer the libation of my blood to God. I am the wheat of the Lord; may I be ground by the teeth of the beasts to become the immaculate bread of Christ."

Ignatius bravely met the lions in the Circus Maximus.

COMMENT: Ignatius's great concern was for the unity and order of the Church. Even greater was his willingness to suffer martyrdom rather than deny his Lord Jesus Christ. Ignatius did not draw attention to his own suffering, but to the love of God which strengthened him. He knew the price of commitment and would not deny Christ, even to save his own life.

QUOTE: "I greet you from Smyrna together with the Churches of God present here with me. They comfort me in every way, both in body and in soul. My chains, which I carry about on me for Jesus Christ, begging that I may happily make my way to God, exhort you: persevere in your concord and in your community prayers" (Ignatius of Antioch, *Letter to the Church at Tralles*).

* * *

OCTOBER 18 + FEAST
Luke
EVANGELIST

Luke wrote one of the major portions of the New Testament, a two-volume work comprising the third Gospel and the Acts of the Apostles. In the two books he shows the parallel between the life of Christ and that of the Church. He is the only Gentile Christian among the Gospel writers. Tradition holds him to be a native of Antioch, and Paul calls him "the beloved physician" (Colossians 4:14). His Gospel was probably written between A.D. 70 and 85.

Luke appears in Acts during Paul's second journey, remains at Philippi for several years until Paul returns from his third journey, accompanies Paul to Jerusalem and remains near him when he is imprisoned in Caesarea. During these two years, Luke had time to seek information and interview persons who had known Jesus. He accompanied Paul on the dangerous journey to Rome where he was a faithful companion. "Luke is the only one with me," Paul writes (2 Timothy 4:11).

COMMENT: Luke wrote as a Gentile for Gentile Christians. This Gospel reveals Luke's expertise in classic Greek style as well as his knowledge of Jewish sources.

The character of Luke may best be seen by the emphases of his Gospel, which has been given a number of subtitles: (1) The Gospel of Mercy: Luke emphasizes Jesus's compassion and patience with the sinners and the suffering. He has a broadminded openness to all, showing concern for Samaritans, lepers, publicans, soldiers, public sinners, unlettered shepherds, and the poor. Luke alone records the stories of the sinful woman, the lost sheep and coin, the prodigal son, the good thief. (2) The Gospel of Universal Salvation: Jesus died for all. He is the son of Adam, not just of David, and Gentiles are his friends too. (3) The Gospel of the Poor: "Little people" are prominent—Zechariah and Elizabeth, Mary and Joseph, shepherds, Simeon and the elderly widow, Anna. He is also concerned with what we now call "evangelical poverty." (4) The Gospel of Absolute Renunciation: He stresses the need for total dedication to Christ. (5) The Gospel of Prayer and the Holy Spirit: He shows Jesus at prayer before every important step of his ministry. The Spirit is bringing the Church to its final perfection. (6) The Gospel of Joy: Luke succeeds in portraying the joy of salvation that permeated the primitive Church.

QUOTE: Luke's Gospel ends: "Then [Jesus] led them [out] as far as Bethany, raised his hands, and blessed them. As he blessed them he parted from them and was taken up to heaven. They did him homage and then returned to Jerusalem with great joy, and they were continually in the temple praising God" (Luke 24:50–53).

• • •

OCTOBER 19 + MEMORIAL (U.S.A.)

Isaac Jogues, Jean de Brébeuf, and Companions

PRIESTS AND MARTYRS; MARTYRS

Isaac Jogues (1607–1646). Isaac Jogues and his companions were the first officially recognized martyrs of the North American continent. As a young Jesuit, Isaac Jogues, a man of learning and culture, taught literature in France. He gave up that career to work among the Huron Native Americans in the

New World, and in 1636 he and his companions, under the leadership of John de Brébeuf, arrived in Quebec. The Hurons were constantly warred upon by the Iroquois, and in a few years Fr. Jogues was captured by the Iroquois and imprisoned for thirteen months. His letters and journals tell how he and his companions were led from village to village, how they were beaten, tortured, and forced to watch as their Huron converts were mangled and killed.

An unexpected chance for escape came to Isaac Jogues through the Dutch, and he returned to France, bearing the marks of his sufferings. Several fingers had been cut, chewed, or burnt off. Pope Urban VIII gave him permission to offer Mass with his mutilated hands: "It would be shameful that a martyr of Christ be not allowed to drink the Blood of Christ." Welcomed home as a hero, Fr. Jogues might have sat back, thanked God for his safe return and died peacefully in his homeland. But his zeal led him back to fulfill his dreams. In a few months, he sailed for his missions among the Hurons.

In 1646 he and Jean de Lalande, who had offered his services to the missioners, set out for Iroquois country in the belief that a recently signed peace treaty would be observed. They were captured by a Mohawk war party, and on October 18, Fr. Jogues was tomahawked and beheaded. Jean de Lalande was killed the next day at Ossernenon, a village near Albany, New York.

The first of the Jesuit missionaries to be martyred was René Goupil who, with Lalande, had offered his services as an oblate. He was tortured along with Isaac Jogues in 1642, and was tomahawked for having made the Sign of the Cross on the brow of some children.

Jean de Brébeuf (1593–1649). Jean de Brébeuf was a French Jesuit who came to Canada at the age of thirty-two and labored there for twenty-four years. He went back to France when the English captured Quebec (1629) and expelled the Jesuits, but returned to his missions four years later. Although medicine men blamed the Jesuits for a smallpox epidemic among the Hurons, Jean remained with them.

He composed catechisms and a dictionary in Huron and saw seven thousand converted before his death. He was captured by the Iroquois and died after four hours of extreme torture at Sainte Marie, near Georgian Bay, Canada.

Fr. Anthony Daniel, working among Hurons who were gradually becoming Christian, was killed by the Iroquois on July 4, 1648. His body was thrown into his chapel, which was set on fire.

Gabriel Lalemant had taken a fourth vow—to sacrifice his life for the Native Americans. He was horribly tortured to death along with Fr. Brébeuf.

Fr. Charles Garnier was shot to death as he baptized children and catechumens during an Iroquois attack.

Fr. Noel Chabanel was killed before he could answer his recall to France. He had found it exceedingly hard to adapt to mission life. He could not learn the language, the food and life of the Native Americans revolted him, plus he suffered spiritual dryness during his whole stay in Canada. Yet he made a vow to remain until death in his mission.

These eight Jesuit martyrs of North America were canonized in 1930. Shrines in Auriesville, New York, and Midland, Ontario, honor them.

COMMENT: Faith and heroism planted belief in Christ's cross deep in our land. The Church in North America sprang from the blood of martyrs. Are we as eager to keep that cross standing in our midst? Do we bear witness to deep-seated faith in us, the Good News of the cross (redemption) into our home, our work, our social world?

QUOTE: "My confidence is placed in God who does not need our help for accomplishing his designs. Our single endeavor should be to give ourselves to the work and to be faithful to him, and not to spoil his work by our shortcomings" (from a letter of Isaac Jogues to a Jesuit friend in France, September 12, 1646, a month before he died).

* * *

OCTOBER 20 + MEMORIAL (U.S.A.)

Paul of the Cross

PRIEST (1694-1775)

Born in northern Italy, Paul became a soldier and fought the Turks for a year but then devoted himself to solitary prayer. In 1720 he founded the Congregation of the Passion, which received its first papal approval in 1741 and final approval in 1769. Members combined devotion to Christ's passion with preaching to the poor and rigorous penances. Known as Passionists, they take a fourth vow to spread the memory of Christ's passion among the faithful. Paul later founded a group of contemplative nuns dedicated to promoting devotion to Christ's passion.

Elected superior general in 1747, he was known throughout Italy as a zealous preacher and spiritual director. Paul's times of prayer and solitude strengthened his preaching, which emphasized Christ's passion as a demonstration of God's love for all people. We enter into the life of the Trinity through appreciating Christ's humanity as well as his divinity. Paul spent much of his life in Rome, near the Basilica of Sts. John and Paul on the Caelian Hill. Over two thousand of his letters and several short writings have survived.

He was canonized in 1867.

COMMENT: Paul lived at a time when significant numbers of Christians regarded Jesus as a great moral teacher but no more, when his miracles as recorded in the Gospels began to be doubted, when God was generally becoming more distant from people's lives. His devotion to Christ's passion must have seemed eccentric if not bizarre to many people. Yet it was that devotion that nurtured Paul's compassion and supported a preaching ministry that touched the hearts of many listeners. He was one of the most popular preachers of his day, known for both his words and his generous acts of mercy.

QUOTE: Paul wrote that God's love "penetrates the inner core of one's being, changes the lover into his beloved. And on a higher level where love is merged with sorrow and sorrow mingled with love, there results a certain blend of love and sorrow that is so complex that the love can no longer be distinguished from the sorrow nor the sorrow from the love."

●　●　●

OCTOBER 22 + OPTIONAL (U.S.A.)

Blessed John Paul II

POPE (1920–2005)

"Open wide the doors to Christ," urged John Paul II during the homily at the Mass when he was installed as pope in 1978.

Born in Wadowice, Poland, Karol Jozef Wojtyla had lost his mother, father, and older brother before his twenty-first birthday. Karol's promising academic career at Krakow's Jagiellonian University was cut short by the outbreak of World War II. While working in a quarry and a chemical factory, he enrolled in an underground seminary in Krakow. Ordained in 1946, he was immediately sent to Rome, where he earned a doctorate in theology.

Back in Poland, a short assignment as assistant pastor in a rural parish preceded his very fruitful chaplaincy to university students. Soon he earned a doctorate in philosophy and began teaching that subject at Poland's University of Lublin.

Communist officials allowed him to be appointed auxiliary bishop of Krakow in 1958, considering him a relatively harmless intellectual. They could not have been more wrong!

He attended all four sessions of Vatican II and contributed especially to its Pastoral Constitution on the Church in the Modern World. Appointed as archbishop of Krakow in 1964, he was named a cardinal three years later.

Elected pope in October 1978, he took the name of his short-lived, immediate predecessor. Pope John Paul II was the first non-Italian pope in 455 years. In time, he made pastoral visits to 124 countries, including several with small Christian populations.

He promoted ecumenical and interfaith initiatives, especially the 1986 Day of Prayer for World Peace in Assisi. He visited Rome's Main Synagogue and the Western Wall in Jerusalem; he also established diplomatic relations between the Holy See and Israel. He improved Catholic-Muslim relations and in 2001 visited a mosque in Damascus, Syria.

The Great Jubilee of the Year 2000, a key event in John Paul's ministry, was marked by special celebrations in Rome and elsewhere for Catholics and other Christians. Relations with the Orthodox Churches improved considerably during his ministry as pope.

"Christ is the center of the universe and of human history" was the opening line of his 1979 encyclical *Redeemer of the Human Race.* In 1995, he described himself to the United Nation General Assembly as "a witness to hope."

His 1979 visit to Poland encouraged the growth of the Solidarity movement there and the collapse of communism in Central and Eastern Europe ten years later. He began World Youth Day and traveled to several countries for those celebrations. He very much wanted to visit China and the Soviet Union but the governments in those countries prevented that.

One of the most well-remembered photos of his pontificate was his one-on-one conversation in 1983 with Mehmet Ali Agca, who had attempted to assassinate him two years earlier.

In his twenty-seven years of papal ministry, John Paul II wrote fourteen encyclicals and five books, canonized 482 saints, and beatified 1,338 people.

In the last years of his life, he suffered from Parkinson's disease and was forced to cut back on some of his activities.

Pope Benedict XVI beatified John Paul II on May 1, 2011, Divine Mercy Sunday. On July 5, 2013, Pope Francis signed a decree accepting the second miracle attributed to Blessed Pope John Paul II.

COMMENT: Before John Paul's funeral Mass in St. Peter's Square, hundreds of thousands of people had waited patiently for a brief moment to pray before his body, which lay in state inside St. Peter's for several days. The media coverage of his funeral was unprecedented.

Cardinal Joseph Ratzinger, then dean of the College of Cardinals and later Pope Benedict XVI, presided at the funeral Mass and concluded his homily by saying; "None of us can ever forget how, in that last Easter Sunday of his life, the Holy Father, marked by suffering, came once more to the window of the Apostolic Palace and one last time gave his blessing *urbi et orbi* ('to the city and to the world').

"We can be sure that our beloved pope is standing today at the window of the Father's house, that he sees us and blesses us. Yes, bless us, Holy Father. We entrust your dear soul to the Mother of God, your Mother, who guided you each day and who will guide you now to the glory of her Son, our Lord Jesus Christ. Amen."

QUOTE: In his 1999 *Letter to the Elderly*, Pope John Paul wrote: "Grant, O Lord of life...when the moment of our definitive 'passage' comes, that we may face it with serenity, without regret for what we shall leave behind. For in meeting you, after having sought you for so long, we shall find once more every authentic good which we have known here on earth, in the company of all those who have gone before us marked with the sign of faith and hope...Amen."

■ ■ ■

OCTOBER 23 + OPTIONAL
John of Capistrano
PRIEST (1386–1456)

It has been said the Christian saints are the world's greatest optimists. Not blind to the existence and consequences of evil, they base their confidence on the power of Christ's redemption. The power of conversion through Christ extends not only to sinful people but also to calamitous events.

Imagine being born in the fourteenth century. One-third of the population and nearly 40 percent of the clergy were wiped out by the bubonic plague. The Western Schism split the Church with two or three claimants to the Holy See at one time. England and France were at war. The city-states of Italy were constantly in conflict. No wonder that gloom dominated the spirit of the culture and the times.

John Capistrano was born in 1386. His education was thorough. His talents and success were great. When he was twenty-six he was made governor of Perugia. Imprisoned after a battle against the Malatestas, he resolved to change his way of life completely. At the age of thirty he entered the Franciscan novitiate and was ordained a priest four years later.

His preaching attracted great throngs at a time of religious apathy and confusion. He and twelve Franciscan brethren were received in the countries of central Europe as angels of God. They were instrumental in reviving a dying faith and devotion.

The Franciscan Order itself was in turmoil over the interpretation and observance of the Rule of St. Francis. Through John's tireless efforts and his expertise in law, the heretical Fraticelli were suppressed and the "Spirituals" were freed from interference in their stricter observance.

He helped bring about a reunion with the Greek and Armenian Churches, unfortunately only a brief arrangement.

When the Turks captured Constantinople in 1453, he was commissioned to preach a crusade for the defense of Europe. Gaining little response in Bavaria and Austria, he decided to concentrate his efforts in Hungary. He led the army to Belgrade. Under the great General Janos Hunyadi, they gained an overwhelming victory, and the siege of Belgrade was lifted. Worn out by his superhuman efforts, Capistrano was an easy prey to an infection after the battle. He died October 23, 1456.

COMMENT: John Hofer, a biographer of John Capistrano, recalls a Brussels organization named after the saint. Seeking to solve problems in a fully Christian spirit, its motto was: "Initiative, Organization, Activity." These three words characterized John's life. He was not one to sit around, ever. His deep Christian optimism drove him to battle problems at all levels with the confidence engendered by a deep faith in Christ.

QUOTE: On the saint's tomb in the Croatian town of Ilok, the governor had this message inscribed: "This tomb holds John, by birth of Capistrano, a man worthy of all praise, defender and promoter of the faith, guardian of the Church, zealous protector of his order, an ornament to all the world, lover of truth and religious justice, mirror of life, surest guide in doctrine; praised by countless tongues, he reigns blessed in heaven." That is a fitting epitaph for a real and successful optimist.

• • •

Anthony Claret
BISHOP (1807–1870)

The "spiritual father of Cuba" was a missionary, religious founder, social reformer, queen's chaplain, writer and publisher, archbishop, and refugee. He was a Spaniard whose work took him to the Canary Islands, Cuba, Madrid, Paris, and the First Vatican Council.

In his spare time as weaver and designer in the textile mills of Barcelona, he learned Latin and printing: the future priest and publisher was preparing. Ordained at twenty-eight, he was prevented by ill health from entering religious life as a Carthusian or as a Jesuit, but went on to become one of Spain's most popular preachers.

He spent ten years giving popular missions and retreats, always placing great emphasis on the Eucharist and devotion to the Immaculate Heart of Mary. Her rosary, it was said, was never out of his hand. At forty-two, beginning with five young priests, he founded a religious institute of missionaries, known today as the Claretians.

He was appointed to head the much-neglected archdiocese of Santiago in Cuba. He began its reform by almost ceaseless preaching and hearing of confessions, and suffered bitter opposition mainly for opposing concubinage and giving instruction to black slaves. A hired assassin (whose release from prison Anthony had obtained) slashed open his face and wrist. Anthony succeeded in getting the would-be assassin's death sentence commuted to a prison term. His solution for the misery of Cubans was family-owned farms producing a variety of foods for the family's own needs and for the market. This invited the enmity of the vested interests who wanted everyone to work on a single cash crop—sugar. Besides all his religious writings are two books he wrote in Cuba: *Reflections on Agriculture* and *Country Delights*.

He was recalled to Spain for a job he did not relish—being chaplain for the queen. He went on three conditions: He would reside away from the palace, he would come only to hear the queen's confession and instruct the children, and he would be exempt from court functions. In the revolution of 1868, he fled with the queen's party to Paris, where he preached to the Spanish colony.

All his life Anthony was interested in the Catholic press. He founded the Religious Publishing House, a major Catholic publishing venture in Spain, and wrote or published two hundred books and pamphlets.

At Vatican I, where he was a staunch defender of the doctrine of infallibility, he won the admiration of his fellow bishops. Cardinal Gibbons of Baltimore remarked of him, "There goes a true saint." At the age of sixty-three, he died in exile near the border of Spain.

COMMENT: Jesus foretold that those who are truly his representatives would suffer the same persecution as he did. Besides fourteen attempts on his life, Anthony had to undergo such a barrage of the ugliest slander that the very name *Claret* became a byword for humiliation and misfortune. The powers of evil do not easily give up their prey.

No one needs to go looking for persecution. All we need to do is be sure we suffer because of our genuine faith in Christ, not for our own whims and imprudences.

STORY: Queen Isabella II once said to Anthony, "No one tells me things as clearly and frankly as you do." Later she told her chaplain, "Everybody is always asking me for favors, but you never do. Isn't there something you would like for yourself?" He replied, "That you let me resign." The queen made no more offers.

● ● ●

OCTOBER 28 + FEAST

Simon and Jude

APOSTLES

Jude is so named by John, Luke, and Acts. Matthew and Mark call him Thaddeus. He is not mentioned elsewhere in the Gospels, except, of course, where all the apostles are mentioned. Scholars hold that he is not the author of the Letter of Jude. Actually, Jude had the same name as Judas Iscariot.

Evidently because of the disgrace of that name, it was shortened to Jude in English.

Simon is mentioned on all four lists of the apostles. On two of them he is called "the Zealot." The Zealots were a Jewish sect that represented an extreme of Jewish nationalism. For them, the messianic promise of the Old Testament meant that the Jews were to be a free and independent nation. God alone was their king, and any payment of taxes to the Romans—the very domination of the Romans—was a blasphemy against God. No doubt some of the Zealots were the spiritual heirs of the Maccabees, carrying on their ideals of religion and independence. But many were the counterparts of modern terrorists. They raided and killed, attacking both foreigners and "collaborating" Jews. They were chiefly responsible for the rebellion against Rome which ended in the destruction of Jerusalem in A.D. 70.

COMMENT: As in the case of all the apostles except for Peter, James, and John, we are faced with men who are really unknown, and we are struck by the fact that their holiness is simply taken to be a gift of Christ. He chose some unlikely people: a former Zealot, a former (crooked) tax collector, an impetuous fisherman, two "sons of thunder," and a man named Judas Iscariot.

It is a reminder that we cannot receive too often. Holiness does not depend on human merit, culture, personality, effort, or achievement. It is entirely God's creation and gift.

God needs no Zealots to bring about the kingdom by force. Jude, like all the saints, is the saint of the impossible: Only God can create his divine life in human beings. And God wills to do so, for all of us.

QUOTE: "Just as Christ was sent by the Father, so also he sent the apostles, filled with the Holy Spirit. This he did so that, by preaching the gospel to every creature (cf. Mark 16:15), they might proclaim that the Son of God, by his death and resurrection, had freed us from the power of Satan (cf. Acts 26:18) and from death, and brought us into the kingdom of his Father" (Constitution on the Sacred Liturgy, 6).

• • •

All Saints

The earliest certain observance of a feast in honor of all the saints is an early fourth-century commemoration of "all the martyrs." In the early seventh century, after successive waves of invaders plundered the catacombs, Pope Boniface IV gathered up some twenty-eight wagonloads of bones and reinterred them beneath the Pantheon, a Roman temple dedicated to all the gods. The pope rededicated the shrine as a Christian Church. According to Bede, the pope intended "that the memory of all the saints might in the future be honored in the place which had formerly been dedicated to the worship not of gods but of demons" (*On the Calculation of Time*).

But the rededication of the Pantheon, like the earlier commemoration of all the martyrs, occurred in May. Many Eastern Churches still honor all the saints in the spring, either during the Easter season or immediately after Pentecost.

How the Western Church came to celebrate this feast in November is a puzzle to historians. The Anglo-Saxon theologian Alcuin observed the feast on November 1 in 800, as did his friend Arno, bishop of Salzburg. Rome finally adopted that date in the ninth century.

COMMENT: This feast first honored martyrs. Later, when Christians were free to worship according to their consciences, the Church acknowledged other paths to sanctity. In the early centuries the only criterion was popular acclaim, even when the bishop's approval became the final step in placing a commemoration on the calendar. The first papal canonization occurred in 993; the lengthy process now required to prove extraordinary sanctity took form in the last five hundred years. Today's feast honors the obscure as well as the famous—the saints each of us has known.

QUOTE: "After this I had a vision of a great multitude, which no one could count, from every nation, race, people, and tongue. They stood before the throne and before the Lamb, wearing white robes and holding palm branches in their hands.... [One of the elders] said to me, 'These are the ones who have survived the time of great distress; they have washed their robes and made them white in the blood of the Lamb' " (Revelation 7:9, 14).

* * *

NOVEMBER 2
All Souls

The Church has encouraged prayer for the dead from the earliest times as an act of Christian charity. "If we had no care for the dead," Augustine noted, "we would not be in the habit of praying for them." Yet pre-Christian rites for the deceased retained such a strong hold on the superstitious imagination that a liturgical commemoration was not observed until the early Middle Ages, when monastic communities began to mark an annual day of prayer for their departed members.

In the middle of the eleventh century, St. Odilo, abbot of Cluny (France), decreed that all Cluniac monasteries offer special prayers and sing the Office for the Dead on November 2, the day after the feast of All Saints. The custom spread from Cluny and was finally adopted throughout the Roman Church.

The theological underpinning of the feast is the acknowledgment of human frailty. Since few people achieve perfection in this life but, rather, go to the grave still scarred with traces of sinfulness, some period of purification may be necessary before a soul comes face-to-face with God. The Council of Trent affirmed this purgatory state and insisted that the prayers of the living can speed the process of purification.

Superstition easily clung to the observance. Medieval popular belief held that the souls in purgatory could appear on this day in the form of witches, toads or will-o'-the-wisps. Graveside food offerings supposedly eased the rest of the dead.

Observances of a more religious nature have survived. These include public processions or private visits to cemeteries and decorating graves with flowers and lights. This feast is observed with great fervor in Mexico.

COMMENT: Whether or not one should pray for the dead is one of the great arguments that divide Christians. Appalled by the abuse of indulgences in the Church of his day, Martin Luther rejected the concept of purgatory. Yet prayer for a loved one is, for the believer, a way of erasing any distance, even death. In prayer we stand in God's presence in the company of someone we love, even if that person has gone before us into death.

QUOTE: "We must not make purgatory into a flaming concentration camp on the brink of hell—or even a 'hell for a short time.' It is blasphemous to think of it as a place where a petty God exacts final punishment.... St. Catherine of Genoa, a mystic of the fifteenth century, wrote that the 'fire' of purgatory is God's love 'burning' the soul so that, at last, the soul is wholly aflame. It is the pain of wanting to be made totally worthy of One who is seen as infinitely lovable, the pain of desire for union that is now absolutely assured, but not yet fully tasted" (Leonard Foley, O.F.M., *Believing in Jesus*).

• • •

NOVEMBER 3 + OPTIONAL
Martin de Porres
RELIGIOUS (1579–1639)

"Father unknown" is the cold legal phrase once used on baptismal records. "Half-breed" and "war souvenir" were cruel names inflicted by those of "pure" blood. Like many others, Martin might have grown to be a bitter man, but he did not. It was said that even as a child he gave his heart and his goods to the poor and despised.

He was the son of a freed woman of Panama, probably black but also possibly of Native American stock, and a Spanish grandee of Lima, Peru. His parents never married each other. Martin inherited the features and dark complexion of his mother. That irked his father, who didn't acknowledge his son for eight years. After the birth of a sister, the father abandoned the family. Martin was reared in poverty, locked into a low level of Lima's society.

When he was twelve, his mother apprenticed him to a barber-surgeon. He learned how to cut hair and also how to draw blood (a standard medical treatment then), care for wounds, and prepare and administer medicines.

After a few years in this medical apostolate, Martin applied to the Dominicans to be a "lay helper," not feeling himself worthy to be a religious brother. After nine years, the example of his prayer and penance, charity and humility led the community to request him to make full religious profession. Many of his nights were spent in prayer and penitential practices; his days were filled with nursing the sick and caring for the poor. It was particularly impressive that he treated all people regardless of their color, race, or status. He was instrumental in founding an orphanage, took care of slaves brought from Africa, and managed the daily alms of his priory with practicality as well as generosity. He became the procurator for both priory and city, whether it was a matter of "blankets, shirts, candles, candy, miracles, or prayers!" When his priory was in debt, he said, "I am only a poor mulatto. Sell me. I am the property of the order. Sell me."

Side by side with his daily work in the kitchen, laundry, and infirmary, Martin's life reflected God's extraordinary gifts: ecstasies that lifted him into the air, light filling the room where he prayed, bilocation, miraculous knowledge, instantaneous cures, and a remarkable rapport with animals. His charity extended to beasts of the field and even to the vermin of the kitchen. He would excuse the raids of mice and rats on the grounds that they were underfed; he kept stray cats and dogs at his sister's house.

He became a formidable fundraiser, obtaining thousands of dollars for dowries for poor girls so that they could marry or enter a convent.

Many of his fellow religious took him as their spiritual director, but he continued to call himself a "poor slave." He was a good friend of another Dominican saint of Peru, Rose of Lima (August 23).

COMMENT: Racism is a sin almost nobody confesses. Like pollution, it is a "sin of the world" that is everybody's responsibility but apparently nobody's fault. One could hardly imagine a more fitting patron of Christian forgiveness (on the part of those discriminated against) and Christian justice (on the part of reformed racists) than Martin de Porres.

QUOTE: In 1962, Blessed John XXIII remarked at the canonization of Martin: "He excused the faults of others. He forgave the bitterest injuries, convinced that he deserved much severer punishments on account of his own sins. He tried with all his might to redeem the guilty; lovingly he comforted the sick; he provided food, clothing and medicine for the poor; he helped, as best he could, farm laborers and Negroes, as well as mulattoes, who were looked upon at that time as akin to slaves; thus he deserved to be called by the name the people gave him: 'Martin of Charity.' "

• • •

NOVEMBER 4 + MEMORIAL
Charles Borromeo
BISHOP (1538–1584)

The name of St. Charles Borromeo is associated with reform. He lived during the time of the Protestant Reformation and had a hand in the reform of the whole Church during the final years of the Council of Trent (1545–1563).

Although he belonged to Milanese nobility and was related to the powerful Medici family, he desired to devote himself to the Church. When his uncle, Cardinal de Medici, was elected pope in 1559 as Pius IV, he made Charles cardinal-deacon and administrator of the archdiocese of Milan while he was still a layman and a young student. Because of his intellectual qualities, he was entrusted with several important offices connected with the Holy See and later appointed secretary of state with responsibility for the papal states. The untimely death of his elder brother brought Charles to a definite decision to be ordained a priest, despite relatives' insistence that he marry. Soon after he was ordained a priest at the age of twenty-five, he was consecrated archbishop of Milan.

Because of his work at the Council of Trent, he was not allowed to take up residence in Milan until the Council was over. Charles had encouraged the pope to renew the council in 1562 after it had been suspended for ten years. Working behind the scenes, St. Charles deserves the credit for keeping the Council in session when at several points it was on the verge of breaking up. He took upon himself the task of the entire correspondence during the final phase.

Eventually Charles was allowed to devote his time to the archdiocese of Milan, where the religious and moral picture was far from bright. The reform needed in every phase of Catholic life among both clergy and laity was initiated at a council of all the bishops under him. Specific regulations were drawn up for bishops and other clergy: If the people were to be converted to a better life, the bishops had to be the first to give a good example and renew their apostolic spirit.

Charles took the initiative in giving good example. He allotted most of his income to charity, forbade himself all luxury, and imposed severe penances upon himself. He sacrificed wealth, high honors, esteem, and influence to become poor. During the plague and famine of 1576, he tried to feed sixty to seventy thousand people daily. To do this he borrowed large sums of money that required years to repay. Whereas the civil authorities fled at the height of the plague, he stayed in the city, where he ministered to the sick and the dying, helping those in want.

Work and the heavy burdens of his high office began to affect his health. He died at the age of forty-six.

COMMENT: St. Charles made his own the words of Christ: "I was hungry and you gave me food, I was thirsty and you gave me drink, a stranger and you welcomed me, naked and you clothed me, ill and you cared for me, in prison and you visited me" (Matthew 25:35–36). Charles saw Christ in his neighbor and knew that charity done for the least of his flock was charity done for Christ.

QUOTE: "Christ summons the Church, as she goes her pilgrim way, to that continual reformation of which she always has need, insofar as she is a human institution here on earth. Consequently, if, in various times and circumstances, there have been deficiencies in moral conduct or in Church discipline, or even in the way that Church teaching has been formulated— to be carefully distinguished from the deposit of faith itself—these should be set right at the opportune moment and in the proper way" (Decree on Ecumenism, 6).

• • •

NOVEMBER 9 + FEAST

Dedication of St. John Lateran

Most Catholics think of St. Peter's as the pope's main church, but this is not so. St. John Lateran is the cathedral of the diocese of Rome, the home church of its bishop.

The first basilica on the site was built in the fourth century when Constantine donated land he had received from the wealthy Lateran family. That structure and its successors suffered fire, earthquake, and the ravages of war, but the Lateran remained the church where popes were consecrated until Pope Gregory XI returned from Avignon in the fourteenth century to find the church and the adjoining papal palace in ruins.

Pope Innocent X commissioned the present structure in 1646. One of Rome's most imposing churches, the Lateran has a towering facade crowned with fifteen colossal statues of Christ, John the Baptist, John the Evangelist, and twelve Doctors of the Church. Beneath its high altar rests the remains of the small wooden table on which, according to tradition, St. Peter celebrated Mass.

COMMENT: Unlike the commemorations of other Roman churches (St. Mary Major, August 5; Sts. Peter and Paul, November 18), this anniversary is a feast. The dedication of a church is a feast for all its parishioners. In a sense, St. John Lateran is the parish church of all Catholics, because it is the pope's cathedral. This church is the spiritual home of the people who are the Church.

QUOTE: "What was done here, as these walls were rising, is reproduced when we bring together those who believe in Christ. For, by believing they are hewn out, as it were, from mountains and forests, like stones and timber; but by catechizing, baptism and instruction they are, as it were, shaped, squared, and planed by the hands of the workers and artisans. Nevertheless, they do not make a house for the Lord until they are fitted together through love" (St. Augustine, *Sermon 36*).

• • •

Leo the Great
POPE AND DOCTOR (D. 461)

With apparently strong conviction about the importance of the bishop of Rome in the Church and of the Church as the ongoing sign of Christ's presence in the world, Leo the Great displayed endless dedication as pope. Elected in 440, he worked tirelessly as "Peter's successor," guiding his fellow bishops as "equals in the episcopacy and infirmities."

Leo is known as one of the best administrative popes of the ancient Church. His work branched into four main areas, indicative of his notion of the pope's total responsibility for the flock of Christ. He worked at length to control the heresies of Pelagianism (overemphasizing human freedom), Manichaeism (seeing everything material as evil) and others, placing demands on their followers so as to secure true Christian beliefs. A second major area of his concern was doctrinal controversy within the Church in the East, to which he responded with a classic letter setting down the Church's teaching on the two natures of Christ. With strong faith, he also led the defense of Rome against a barbarian attack, taking the role of peacemaker.

In these three areas, Leo's work has been highly regarded. His growth to sainthood has its basis in the spiritual depth with which he approached the pastoral care of his people, which was the fourth focus of his work. He is known for his spiritually profound sermons. An instrument of the call to holiness, well-versed in Scripture and ecclesiastical awareness, Leo had the ability to reach the everyday needs and interests of his people. One of his sermons is used in the Office of Readings on Christmas.

COMMENT: At a time when there is widespread criticism of Church structures, we also hear criticism that bishops and priests—indeed, all of us—are too preoccupied with administration of temporal matters. Pope Leo is an example of a great administrator who used his talents in areas where spirit and structure are inseparably combined: doctrine, peace, and pastoral care. He avoided an "angelism" that tries to live without the body, as well as the "practicality" that deals only in externals.

STORY: It is said of Leo that his true significance rests in his doctrinal insistence on the mysteries of Christ and the Church and in the supernatural charisms of the spiritual life given to humanity in Christ and in his body, the Church. Thus Leo held firmly that everything he did and said as pope for the administration of the Church represented Christ, the head of the Mystical Body, and St. Peter, in whose place Leo acted.

• • •

Martin of Tours
BISHOP (316?–397)

A conscientious objector who wanted to be a monk; a monk who was maneuvered into being a bishop; a bishop who fought paganism but pleaded for mercy for heretics—such was Martin of Tours, one of the most popular saints and one of the first not to be a martyr.

Born of pagan parents in what is now Hungary and raised in Italy, this son of a veteran was forced at the age of fifteen to serve in the army. He became a Christian catechumen and was baptized at eighteen. It was said that he lived more like a monk than a soldier. At twenty-three he refused a war bonus and told his commander: "I have served you as a soldier; now let me serve Christ. Give the bounty to those who are going to fight. But I am a soldier of Christ and it is not lawful for me to fight." After great difficulties, he was discharged and went to be a disciple of Hilary of Poitiers (January 13).

He was ordained an exorcist and worked with great zeal against the Arians. He became a monk, living first at Milan and later on a small island. When Hilary was restored to his see after exile, Martin returned to France and established what may have been the first French monastery near Poitiers. He lived there for ten years, forming his disciples and preaching throughout the countryside.

The people of Tours demanded that he become their bishop. He was drawn to that city by a ruse—the need of a sick person—and was brought to the church, where he reluctantly allowed himself to be consecrated bishop.

Some of the consecrating bishops thought his rumpled appearance and unkempt hair indicated that he was not dignified enough for the office.

Along with St. Ambrose (December 7), Martin rejected Bishop Ithacius's principle of putting heretics to death—as well as the intrusion of the emperor into such matters. Martin prevailed upon the emperor to spare the life of the heretic Priscillian. For his efforts, Martin was accused of the same heresy, and Priscillian was executed after all. Martin then pleaded for a cessation of the persecution of Priscillian's followers in Spain. He still felt he could cooperate with Ithacius in other areas, but afterward his conscience troubled him about this decision.

As death approached, his followers begged him not to leave them. He prayed, "Lord, if your people still need me, I do not refuse the work. Your will be done."

COMMENT: Martin's worry about cooperation with evil reminds us that almost nothing is either all black or all white. The saints are not creatures of another world: they face the same perplexing decisions that we do. Any decision of conscience always involves some risk. If we choose to go north, we may never know what would have happened had we gone east, west, or south. A hypercautious withdrawal from all perplexing situations is not the virtue of prudence; it is, in fact, a bad decision, for, as it is said, not to decide is to decide.

STORY: On a bitterly cold day, a famous legend goes, Martin met a poor man, almost naked, trembling in the cold and begging from passersby at the city gate. Martin had nothing but his weapons and his clothes. He drew his sword, cut his cloak into two pieces, gave one to the beggar and wrapped himself in the other half. Some of the bystanders laughed at his now odd appearance; others were ashamed at not having relieved the man's misery. That night in his sleep Martin saw Christ dressed in the half of the garment he had given away, and heard him say, "Martin, still a catechumen, has covered me with this garment."

• • •

NOVEMBER 12 + MEMORIAL

Josaphat

BISHOP AND MARTYR (1580?–1623)

In 1964, newspaper photos of Pope Paul VI embracing Athenagoras I, the Orthodox patriarch of Constantinople, marked a significant step toward the healing of a division in Christendom that has spanned for more than nine centuries.

In 1595, when today's saint was a boy, the Orthodox bishop of Brest-Litovsk (famous in World War I) in present-day Belarus and five other bishops representing millions of Ruthenians, sought reunion with Rome. John Kunsevich (Josaphat became his name in religious life) was to dedicate his life and die for the same cause. Born in what is now Ukraine, he went to work in Wilno and was influenced by clergy adhering to the Union of Brest (1596). He became a Basilian monk, then a priest, and soon was well known as a preacher and as an ascetic.

He became bishop of Vitebsk (now in Belarus) at a relatively young age and faced a difficult situation. Most monks, fearing interference in liturgy and customs, did not want union with Rome. By synods, catechetical instruction, reform of the clergy and personal example, however, Josaphat was successful in winning the greater part of the Orthodox in that area to the union.

But the next year a dissident hierarchy was set up, and his opposite number spread the accusation that Josaphat had "gone Latin" and that all his people would have to do the same. He was not enthusiastically supported by the Latin bishops of Poland.

Despite warnings, he went to Vitebsk, still a hotbed of trouble. Attempts were made to foment trouble and drive him from the diocese: A priest was sent to shout insults to him from his own courtyard. When Josaphat had him removed and shut up in his house, the opposition rang the town hall bell, and a mob assembled. The priest was released, but members of the mob broke into the bishop's home. He was struck with a halberd, then shot, and his body thrown into the river. It was later recovered and is now buried in St. Peter's Basilica in Rome. He was the first saint of the Eastern Church to be formally canonized by Rome.

His death brought a movement toward Catholicism and unity, but the controversy continued, and the dissidents, too, had their martyr. When Poland was partitioned, the Russians forced most Ruthenians to join the Russian Orthodox Church.

COMMENT: The seeds of separation were sown in the fourth century when the Roman Empire was divided into East and West. The actual split came over relatively unimportant customs (unleavened bread, Saturday fasting, celibacy). No doubt the political involvement of religious leaders on both sides was a large factor, and doctrinal disagreement was present. But no reason was enough to justify the present tragic division in Christendom, which is 64 percent Roman Catholic, 13 percent Eastern (mostly Orthodox) and 23 percent Protestant, and this when the 71 percent of the world that is not Christian should be experiencing unity and Christ-like charity from Christians!

STORY: Surrounded by an angry mob shortly before his death, Josaphat said, "You people of Vitebsk want to put me to death. You make ambushes for me everywhere, in the streets, on the bridges, on the highways and in the marketplace. I am here among you as your shepherd and you ought to know that I should be happy to give my life for you. I am ready to die for the holy union, for the supremacy of St. Peter and of his successor the Supreme Pontiff."

* * *

NOVEMBER 13 + MEMORIAL (U.S.A.)
Frances Xavier Cabrini
VIRGIN (1850–1917)

Frances Xavier Cabrini was the first United States citizen to be canonized. Her deep trust in the loving care of her God gave her the strength to be a valiant woman doing the work of Christ.

Refused admission to the religious congregation that had educated her to be a teacher, she began charitable work at the House of Providence Orphanage in Cadogno, Italy. In September 1877, she made her vows there and took the religious habit.

When the bishop closed the orphanage in 1880, he named Frances prioress of the Missionary Sisters of the Sacred Heart. Seven young women from the orphanage joined with her.

Since her early childhood in Italy, Frances had wanted to be a missionary in China but, at the urging of Pope Leo XIII, Frances went west instead of east. She traveled with six sisters to New York City to work with the thousands of Italian immigrants living there.

She found disappointment and difficulties with every step. When she arrived in New York City, the house intended to be her first orphanage in the United States was not available. The archbishop advised her to return to Italy. But Frances, truly a valiant woman, left the archbishop's residence all the more determined to establish that orphanage. And she did.

In thirty-five years Frances Xavier Cabrini founded sixty-seven institutions dedicated to caring for the poor, the abandoned, the uneducated, and the sick. Seeing great need among Italian immigrants who were losing their faith, she organized schools and adult education classes.

As a child, she was always frightened of water, unable to overcome her fear of drowning. Yet, despite this fear, she traveled across the Atlantic Ocean more than thirty times. She died of malaria in her own Columbus Hospital in Chicago.

COMMENT: The compassion and dedication of Mother Cabrini is still seen in hundreds of thousands of her fellow citizens, not yet canonized, who care for the sick in hospitals, nursing homes, and state institutions. We complain of increased medical costs in an affluent society, but the daily news shows us millions who have little or no medical care and who are calling for new Mother Cabrinis to become citizen-servants of their land.

QUOTE: At her canonization on July 7, 1946, Venerable Pius XII said, "Although her constitution was very frail, her spirit was endowed with such singular strength that, knowing the will of God in her regard, she permitted nothing to impede her from accomplishing what seemed beyond the strength of a woman."

* * *

NOVEMBER 15 + OPTIONAL

Albert the Great

BISHOP AND DOCTOR (1206–1280)

Albert the Great was a thirteenth-century German Dominican who influenced decisively the Church's stance toward Aristotelian philosophy brought to Europe by the spread of Islam.

Students of philosophy know him as the teacher of Thomas Aquinas. Albert's attempt to understand Aristotle's writings established the climate in which Thomas Aquinas developed his synthesis of Greek wisdom and Christian theology. But Albert deserves recognition on his own merits as a curious, honest, and diligent scholar.

He was the eldest son of a powerful and wealthy German lord of military rank. He was educated in the liberal arts. Despite fierce family opposition, he entered the Dominican novitiate.

His boundless interests prompted him to write a compendium of all knowledge: natural science, logic, rhetoric, mathematics, astronomy, ethics, economics, politics, and metaphysics. His explanation of learning took twenty years to complete. "Our intention," he said, "is to make all the aforesaid parts of knowledge intelligible to the Latins."

He achieved his goal while serving as an educator at Paris and Cologne, as Dominican provincial, and even as bishop of Regensburg for a short time. He defended the mendicant orders and preached a crusade in Germany and Bohemia.

Albert, a Doctor of the Church, is the patron of scientists and philosophers.

COMMENT: An information glut faces Christians today in all branches of learning. One needs only to read current Catholic periodicals to experience the varied reactions to the findings of the social sciences, for example, in regard to Christian institutions, Christian lifestyles, and Christian theology.

Ultimately, in canonizing Albert, the Church seems to point to his openness to truth, wherever it may be found, as his claim to holiness. His characteristic curiosity prompted Albert to mine deeply for wisdom within a philosophy his Church warmed up to with great difficulty.

QUOTE: "There are some who desire knowledge merely for its own sake; and that is shameful curiosity. And there are others who desire to know, in order that they may themselves be known; and that is vanity, disgraceful too. Others again, desire knowledge in order to acquire money or preferment by it; that too is a discreditable quest. But there are also some who desire knowledge, that they may build up the souls of others with it and that is charity. Others, again, desire it that they may themselves be built up thereby; and that is prudence. Of all these types, only the last two put knowledge to the right use" (St. Bernard, *Sermon on the Canticle of Canticles*).

• • •

NOVEMBER 16 + OPTIONAL
Margaret of Scotland
WIFE AND MOTHER (1050?–1093)

Margaret of Scotland was a truly liberated woman in the sense that she was free to be herself. For her, that meant freedom to love God and serve others.

Not Scottish by birth, Margaret was the daughter of Princess Agatha of Hungary and the Anglo-Saxon Prince Edward Atheling. She spent much of her youth in the court of her great-uncle, the English king, Edward the Confessor. Her family fled from William the Conqueror and was shipwrecked off the coast of Scotland. King Malcolm befriended them and was captivated by the beautiful, gracious Margaret. They were married at the castle of Dunfermline in 1070.

Malcolm was good-hearted but rough and uncultured, as was his country. Because of Malcolm's love for Margaret, she was able to soften his temper, polish his manners, and help him become a virtuous king. He left all domestic affairs to her and often consulted her in state matters.

Margaret tried to improve her adopted country by promoting the arts and education. For religious reform, she instigated synods and was present for the discussions that tried to correct religious abuses among priests and laypeople, such as simony, usury, and incestuous marriages. With her husband, she founded several churches.

Margaret was not only a queen, but a mother. She and Malcolm had six sons and two daughters. Margaret personally supervised their religious instruction and other studies.

Although she was very much caught up in the affairs of the household and country, she remained detached from the world. Her private life was austere. She had certain times for prayer and reading Scripture. She ate sparingly and slept little in order to have time for devotions. She and Malcolm kept two Lents, one before Easter and one before Christmas. During these times she always rose at midnight for Mass. On the way home, she would wash the feet of six poor persons and give them alms. She was always surrounded by beggars in public and never refused them. It is recorded that she never sat down to eat without first feeding nine orphans and twenty-four adults.

In 1093, King William Rufus made a surprise attack on Alnwick castle. King Malcolm and his oldest son, Edward, were killed. Margaret, already on her deathbed, died four days after her husband.

COMMENT: There are two ways to be charitable: the clean way and the messy way. The clean way is to give money or clothing to organizations that serve the poor. The messy way is dirtying your own hands in personal service to the poor. Margaret's outstanding virtue was her love of the poor. Although very generous with material gifts, Margaret also visited the sick and nursed them with her own hands. She and her husband served orphans and the poor on their knees during Advent and Lent. Like Christ, she was charitable the messy way.

QUOTE: "When [Margaret] spoke, her conversation was seasoned with the salt of wisdom. When she was silent, her silence was filled with good thoughts. So thoroughly did her outward bearing correspond with the staidness of her character that it seemed as if she has been born the pattern of a virtuous life" (Turgot, St. Margaret's confessor).

• • •

NOVEMBER 16 + OPTIONAL
Gertrude
VIRGIN (1256?–1302)

Gertrude, a Benedictine nun in Helfta (Saxony), was one of the great mystics of the thirteenth century. Together with her friend and teacher St. Mechtild, she practiced a spirituality called "nuptial mysticism," that is, she came to see herself as the bride of Christ. Her spiritual life was a deeply personal union with Jesus and his Sacred Heart, leading her into the very life of the Trinity.

But this was no individualistic piety. Gertrude lived the rhythm of the liturgy, where she found Christ. In the liturgy and Scripture, she found the themes and images to enrich and express her piety. There was no clash between her personal prayer life and the liturgy.

COMMENT: Gertrude's life is another reminder that the heart of the Christian life is prayer: private and liturgical, ordinary or mystical, always personal.

QUOTE: "Lord, you have granted me your secret friendship by opening the sacred ark of your divinity, your deified heart, to me in so many ways as to be the source of all my happiness; sometimes imparting it freely, sometimes as a special mark of our mutual friendship. You have so often melted my soul with your loving caresses that, if I did not know the abyss of your overflowing condescensions, I should be amazed were I told that even your Blessed Mother had been chosen to receive such extraordinary marks of tenderness and affection" (adapted from *The Life and Revelations of St. Gertrude*).

• • •

NOVEMBER 17 + MEMORIAL
Elizabeth of Hungary
RELIGIOUS (1207–1231)

In her short life Elizabeth manifested such great love for the poor and suffering that she has become the patron of Catholic charities and of the

Secular Franciscan Order. The daughter of the king of Hungary, Elizabeth chose a life of penance and asceticism when a life of leisure and luxury could easily have been hers. This choice endeared her in the hearts of the common people throughout Europe.

At the age of fourteen, Elizabeth was married to Louis of Thuringia (a German principality), whom she deeply loved. She bore three children. Under the spiritual direction of a Franciscan friar, she led a life of prayer, sacrifice, and service to the poor and sick. Seeking to become one with the poor, she wore simple clothing. Daily she would take bread to hundreds of the poorest in the land, who came to her gate.

After six years of marriage, her husband died in the crusades, and she was grief-stricken. Her husband's family looked upon her as squandering the royal purse and mistreated her, finally throwing her out of the palace. The return of her husband's allies from the crusades resulted in her being reinstated, since her son was legal heir to the throne.

In 1228 Elizabeth joined the Secular Franciscan Order, spending the remaining few years of her life caring for the poor in a hospital that she founded in honor of St. Francis. Elizabeth's health declined, and she died before her twenty-fourth birthday in 1231. Her great popularity resulted in her canonization four years later.

COMMENT: Elizabeth understood well the lesson Jesus taught when he washed his disciples' feet at the Last Supper: The Christian must be one who serves the humblest needs of others, even if one serves from an exalted position. Of royal blood, Elizabeth could have lorded it over her subjects. Yet she served them with such a loving heart that her brief life won for her a special place in the hearts of many. Elizabeth is also an example to us in her following the guidance of a spiritual director. Growth in the spiritual life is a difficult process. We can play games very easily if we don't have someone to challenge us or to share experiences so as to help us avoid pitfalls.

QUOTE: "Today, there is an inescapable duty to make ourselves the neighbor of every individual, without exception, and to take positive steps to help a neighbor whom we encounter, whether that neighbor be an elderly person, abandoned by everyone, a foreign worker who suffers the injustice of being despised, a refugee, an illegitimate child wrongly suffering for a sin of which the child is innocent, or a starving human being who awakens our conscience by calling to mind the words of Christ: 'As long as you did it for one of the least of these my brothers and sisters, you did it for me' (Matthew 25:40)" (Pastoral Constitution on the Church in the Modern World, 27).

• • •

NOVEMBER 18 + OPTIONAL
Rose Philippine Duchesne
VIRGIN (1769–1852)

Born in Grenoble, France, of a family that was among the new rich, Philippine learned political skills from her father and a love of the poor from her mother. The dominant feature of her temperament was a strong and dauntless will, which became the material—and the battlefield—of her holiness. Without telling her parents, she entered the convent at nineteen and remained despite their opposition. As the French Revolution broke, the convent was closed, and she began taking care of the poor and sick, opened a school for homeless children, and risked her life helping priests in the underground.

When the situation cooled, she personally rented her old convent, now a shambles, and tried to revive its religious life. The spirit was gone, and soon there were only four nuns left. They joined the infant Society of the Sacred Heart, whose young superior, St. Madeleine Sophie Barat, would be her lifelong friend. In a short time Philippine was a superior and supervisor of the novitiate and a school. But her ambition since hearing tales of missionary work in Louisiana as a little girl was to go to America and work among the Indians. At forty-nine, she thought this would be her work. With four nuns, she spent eleven weeks at sea en route to New Orleans and seven weeks more on the Mississippi to St. Louis. She then met one of the many disappointments of her life. The bishop had no place for them to live and work among Native Americans. Instead, he sent her to what she sadly called "the remotest village in the U.S.," St. Charles, Missouri. With characteristic drive and courage, she founded the first free school for girls west of the Mississippi.

It was a mistake. Though she was as hardy as any of the pioneer women in the wagons rolling west, cold and hunger drove them out—to Florissant, Missouri, where she founded the first Catholic Native American school, adding others in the territory. "In her first decade in America, Mother Duchesne suffered practically every hardship the frontier had to offer, except the threat of Indian massacre—poor lodging, shortages of food, drinking water, fuel and money, forest fires and blazing chimneys, the vagaries of the Missouri climate, cramped living quarters and the privation of all privacy, and the crude manners of children reared in rough surroundings and with only the slightest training in courtesy" (Louise Callan, R.S.C.J., *Philippine Duchesne*).

Finally, at seventy-two, in poor health and retired, she got her lifelong wish. A mission was founded at Sugar Creek, Kansas, among the Potawatomi. She was taken along. Though she could not learn their language, they soon named her "Woman-Who-Prays-Always." While others taught, she prayed. Legend has it that Native American children sneaked behind her as she knelt and sprinkled bits of paper on her habit, and came back hours later to find them undisturbed. She died in 1852 at the age of eighty-three and was canonized in 1988.

COMMENT: Divine grace channeled her iron will and determination into humility and selflessness, and a desire not to be made superior. Still, even saints can get involved in silly situations. In an argument with a priest over a minor change in the sanctuary, he threatened to remove her tabernacle. She patiently let herself be criticized by younger nuns for not being progressive enough. For thirty-one years, she hewed to the line of a dauntless love and an unshakable observance of her religious vows.

QUOTE: She once said: "We cultivate a very small field for Christ, but we love it, knowing that God does not require great achievements but a heart that holds back nothing for self.... The truest crosses are those we do not choose ourselves.... He who has Jesus has everything."

• • •

NOVEMBER 18 + OPTIONAL
Dedication of the Churches of Peter and Paul

St. Peter's is probably the most famous church in Christendom. Massive in scale and a veritable museum of art and architecture, it began on a much humbler scale. Vatican Hill was a simple cemetery where believers gathered at St. Peter's tomb to pray. In 319 Constantine built on the site a basilica that stood for more than a thousand years until, despite numerous restorations, it threatened to collapse. In 1506 Pope Julius II ordered it razed and reconstructed, but the new basilica was not completed and dedicated for more than two centuries.

St. Paul's Outside the Walls stands near the Abbazia delle Tre Fontane, where St. Paul is believed to have been beheaded. The largest church in Rome until St. Peter's was rebuilt, the basilica also rises over the traditional site of its namesake's grave. The most recent edifice was constructed after a fire in 1823. The first basilica was also Constantine's doing.

Constantine's building projects enticed the first of a centuries-long parade of pilgrims to Rome. From the time the basilicas were first built until the empire crumbled under "barbarian" invasions, the two churches, although miles apart, were linked by a roofed colonnade of marble columns.

COMMENT: Peter, the rough fisherman whom Jesus named the rock on which the Church is built, and the educated Paul, reformed persecutor of Christians, Roman citizen, and missionary to the Gentiles, are the original odd couple. The major similarity in their faith-journeys is the journey's end: Both, according to tradition, died a martyr's death in Rome, Peter on a cross and Paul beneath the sword. Their combined gifts shaped the early Church, and believers have prayed at their tombs from the earliest days.

QUOTE: "It is extraordinarily interesting that Roman pilgrimage began at an... early time. Pilgrims did not wait for the Peace of the Church [Constantine's edict of toleration] before they visited the tombs of the Apostles. They went to Rome a century before there were any public churches and when the Church was confined to the *tituli* [private homes] and the catacombs. The two great pilgrimage sites were exactly as today—the tombs, or memorials, of St. Peter upon the Vatican Hill and the tomb of St. Paul off the Ostian Way" (H.V. Morton, *This Is Rome*).

• • •

NOVEMBER 21 + MEMORIAL
Presentation of Mary

Mary's presentation was celebrated in Jerusalem in the sixth century. A church was built there in honor of this mystery. The Eastern Church was more interested in the feast, but it does appear in the West in the eleventh century. Although the feast at times disappeared from the calendar, in the sixteenth century it became a feast of the universal Church.

As with Mary's birth, we read of Mary's presentation in the temple only in apocryphal literature. In what is recognized as an unhistorical account, the *Protoevangelium of James* tells us that Anna and Joachim offered Mary to God in the temple when she was three years old. This was to carry out a promise made to God when Anna was still childless.

Though it cannot be proven historically, Mary's presentation has an important theological purpose. It continues the impact of the feasts of the Immaculate Conception (December 8) and of the birth of Mary (September 8). It emphasizes that the holiness conferred on Mary from the beginning of her life on earth continued through her early childhood and beyond.

COMMENT: It is sometimes difficult for modern Westerners to appreciate a feast like this. The Eastern Church, however, was quite open to this feast and even somewhat insistent about celebrating it. Even though the event has no basis in history, it stresses an important truth about Mary: From the beginning of her life, she was dedicated to God. She herself became a greater temple than any made by hands. God came to dwell in her in a marvelous manner and sanctified her for her unique role in God's saving work. At the same time, the magnificence of Mary enriches her children. They, too, are temples of God and sanctified in order that they might enjoy and share in God's saving work.

QUOTE: "Hail, holy throne of God, divine sanctuary, house of glory, jewel most fair, chosen treasure house, and mercy seat for the whole world, heaven showing forth the glory of God. Purest Virgin, worthy of all praise, sanctuary dedicated to God and raised above all human condition, virgin soil, unplowed field, flourishing vine, fountain pouring out waters, virgin bearing a child, mother without knowing man, hidden treasure of innocence, ornament of sanctity, by your most acceptable prayers, strong with the authority of motherhood, to our Lord and God, Creator of all, your Son who was born of you without a father, steer the ship of the Church, and bring it to a quiet harbor" (adapted from a homily by St. Germanus on the Presentation of the Mother of God).

●　●　●

NOVEMBER 22 + MEMORIAL

Cecilia

VIRGIN AND MARTYR

Although Cecilia is one of the most famous of the Roman martyrs, the familiar stories about her are apparently not founded on authentic material. There is no trace of honor being paid her in early times. A fragmentary inscription of the late fourth century refers to a church named after her, and her feast was celebrated at least in 545.

According to legend, Cecilia was a young Christian of high rank betrothed to a Roman named Valerian. Through her influence Valerian was converted, and was martyred along with his brother. The legend about Cecilia's death says that after being struck three times on the neck with a sword, she lived for three days and asked the pope to convert her home into a Church.

Since the time of the Renaissance, she has usually been portrayed with a viola or a small organ.

COMMENT: Like any good Christian, Cecilia sang in her heart and sometimes with her voice. She has become a symbol of the Church's conviction that good music is an integral part of the liturgy, of greater value to the church than any other art. It may be useful to recall Vatican II's teaching about Church music (see below).

QUOTE: "Liturgical action is given a more noble form when sacred rites are solemnized in song, with the assistance of sacred ministers and the active participation of the people…. Choirs must be diligently promoted, but bishops and other pastors must ensure that, whenever the sacred action is to be celebrated with song, the whole body of the faithful may be able to contribute that active participation which is rightfully theirs…. Gregorian chant, other things being equal, should be given pride of place in liturgical services. But other kinds of sacred music, especially polyphony, are by no means excluded…. Religious singing by the people is to be skillfully fostered, so that in devotions and sacred exercises, as also during liturgical services, the voices of the faithful may ring out" (Constitution on the Sacred Liturgy, 112–118).

* * *

NOVEMBER 23 + OPTIONAL

Clement I

POPE AND MARTYR (D. 101)

Clement of Rome was the third successor of St. Peter and reigned as pope during the last decade of the first century. The accounts of his martyrdom were composed about the fourth or fifth century. The Basilica of St. Clement in Rome, one of the earliest parish churches of that city, is probably built on the site of Clement's home. Clement's *First Epistle to the Corinthians* was preserved and widely read in the early Church. This letter from the church of Rome, authored by Clement (not to be confused with the writer now called Pseudo-Clement), to the church in Corinth, concerns a split that alienated a large number of the laity from the clergy. Clement deplores the unauthorized and unjustifiable division in the Corinthian church and urges unity. He cites the cause of the quarrel as "envy and jealousy."

COMMENT: Clement urged charity to heal the division in the church of Corinth, for "without charity, nothing is pleasing to God." Today many people in the Church have experienced polarization regarding worship, how we speak of God and other issues. May we modern Christians take to heart the exhortation of Clement, implementing these words of St. Paul: "And over all these put on love, that is, the bond of perfection" (Colossians 3:14).

QUOTE: "Charity unites us to God…. There is nothing mean in charity, nothing arrogant. Charity knows no schism, does not rebel, does all things in concord. In charity all the elect of God have been made perfect" (St. Clement, *First Epistle to the Corinthians*).

• • •

NOVEMBER 23 + OPTIONAL

Columban

ABBOT (543?–615)

Columban was the greatest of the Irish missionaries who worked on the European continent. As a young man who was greatly tormented by temptations of the flesh, Columban sought the advice of a religious woman who had lived a hermit's life for years. He saw in her answer a call to leave the world. He went first to a monk on an island in Lough Erne, then to the great monastic seat of learning at Bangor.

After many years of seclusion and prayer, he traveled to Gaul (modern-day France) with twelve companion missionaries. They won wide respect for the rigor of their discipline, their preaching, and their commitment to charity and religious life in a time characterized by clerical laxity and civil strife. Columban established several monasteries in Europe that became centers of religion and culture.

Like all saints, he met opposition. Ultimately he had to appeal to the pope against complaints of Frankish bishops, for vindication of his orthodoxy and approval of Irish customs. He reproved the king for his licentious life, insisting that he marry. Since this threatened the power of the queen mother, Columban was deported to Ireland. His ship ran aground in a storm, and he continued his work in Europe, ultimately arriving in Italy, where he found favor with the king of the Lombards. In his last years he established the famous monastery of Bobbio, where he died. His writings include a treatise on penance and against Arianism, sermons, poetry, and his monastic rule.

COMMENT: Now that public sexual license is approaching the extreme, we need the Church's jolting memory of a young man as concerned about chastity as Columban. And now that the comfort-captured Western world stands in tragic contrast to starving millions, we need the challenge to austerity and discipline of a group of Irish monks. They were too strict, we say; they went too far. How far shall we go?

QUOTE: Writing to the pope about a doctrinal controversy in Lombardy, Columban said: "We Irish, living in the farthest parts of the earth, are followers of St. Peter and St. Paul and of the disciples who wrote down the sacred canon under the Holy Spirit. We accept nothing outside this evangelical and apostolic teaching.... I confess I am grieved by the bad repute of the chair of St. Peter in this country.... Though Rome is great and known afar, she is great and honored with us only because of this chair.... Look after the peace of the Church, stand between your sheep and the wolves."

• • •

NOVEMBER 23 + OPTIONAL (MEXICO)
Blessed Miguel Agustín Pro
MARTYR (1891–1927)

¡Viva Cristo Rey! (Long live Christ the King) were the last words Fr. Pro uttered before he was executed for being a Catholic priest and serving his flock.

Born into a prosperous, devout family in Guadalupe de Zacatecas, he entered the Jesuits in 1911 but three years later fled to Granada, Spain, because of religious persecution in Mexico. He was ordained in Belgium in 1925.

He immediately returned to Mexico, where he served a church forced to go underground. He celebrated the Eucharist clandestinely and ministered the other sacraments to small groups of Catholics.

He and his brother Roberto were arrested on trumped-up charges of attempting to assassinate Mexico's president. Roberto was spared, but Miguel was sentenced to face a firing squad on November 23, 1927. His funeral became a public demonstration of faith. He was beatified in 1988.

COMMENT: In 1927 when Fr. Miguel Pro was assassinated, no one could have predicted that fifty-two years later the bishop of Rome would visit Mexico, be welcomed by its president, and celebrate open-air Masses before thousands of people. Blessed John Paul II made additional trips to Mexico in 1990, 1993, 1999, and 2002. Those who outlawed the Catholic Church in Mexico did not count on the deeply rooted faith of its people and the willingness of many of them, like Miguel Pro, to die as martyrs.

QUOTE: During his homily at the beatification Mass, Pope John Paul II said that Fr. Pro "is a new glory for the beloved Mexican nation, as well as for the Society of Jesus. His life of sacrificing and intrepid apostolate was always inspired by a tireless evangelizing effort. Neither suffering nor serious illness, neither the exhausting ministerial activity, frequently carried out in difficult and dangerous circumstances, could stifle the radiating and contagious joy which he brought to his life for Christ and which nothing could take away (see John 16:22). Indeed, the deepest root of self-sacrificing surrender for the lowly was his passionate love for Jesus Christ and his ardent desire to be conformed to him, even unto death."

• • •

NOVEMBER 24 + MEMORIAL
Andrew Dung-Lac and Companions
PRIEST AND MARTYR; MARTYRS

Andrew was one of 117 people martyred in Vietnam between 1820 and 1862. Members of this group were beatified on four different occasions between 1900 and 1951. All of them were canonized by Blessed John Paul II in 1988.

Christianity came to Vietnam (then three separate kingdoms) through the Portuguese. Jesuits opened the first permanent mission at Da Nang in 1615. They ministered to Japanese Catholics who had been driven from Japan.

The king of one of the kingdoms banned all foreign missionaries and tried to make all Vietnamese deny their faith by trampling on a crucifix. Like the priest-holes in Ireland during English persecution, many hiding places were offered in homes of the faithful.

Severe persecutions were again launched three times in the nineteenth century. During the six decades after 1820, between 100,000 and 300,000 Catholics were killed or subjected to great hardship. Foreign missionaries martyred in the first wave included priests of the Paris Mission Society and Spanish Dominican priests and tertiaries.

Persecution broke out again in 1847 when the emperor suspected foreign missionaries and Vietnamese Christians of sympathizing with a rebellion led by one of his sons.

The last of the martyrs were seventeen laypersons, one of them a nine-year-old, executed in 1862. That year a treaty with France guaranteed religious freedom to Catholics, but it did not stop all persecution.

By 1954 there were over a million and a half Catholics—about 7 percent of the population—in the north. Buddhists represented about 60 percent. Persistent persecution forced some 670,000 Catholics to abandon lands, homes, and possessions and flee to the south. In 1964, there were still 833,000 Catholics in the north, but many were in prison. In the south, Catholics were enjoying the first decade of religious freedom in centuries, their numbers swelled by refugees.

During the Vietnam Conflict, Catholics again suffered in the north and again moved to the south in great numbers. Now the whole country remains under communist rule.

COMMENT: It may help a people who associate Vietnam only with U.S. involvement in that war to realize that the cross has long been a part of the lives of the people of that country. Even as we ask again the unanswered questions about United States involvement and disengagement, the faith rooted in Vietnam's soil proves hardier than the forces that would destroy it.

QUOTE: "The Church in Vietnam is alive and vigorous, blessed with strong and faithful bishops, dedicated religious, and courageous and committed laypeople....The Church in Vietnam is living out the gospel in a difficult and complex situation with remarkable persistence and strength" (statement of three U.S. archbishops returning from Vietnam in January, 1989).

• • •

NOVEMBER 25 + OPTIONAL
Catherine of Alexandria
VIRGIN AND MARTYR (DIED C. 310)

According to the *Legend of St. Catherine*, this young woman converted to Christianity after receiving a vision. At the age of eighteen, she debated fifty pagan philosophers. Amazed at her wisdom and debating skills, they became Christians—as did about two hundred soldiers and members of the emperor's family. All of them were martyred.

Sentenced to be executed on a spiked wheel, Catherine touched the wheel and it shattered. She was beheaded. Centuries later, angels are said to have carried the body of St. Catherine to a monastery at the foot of Mt. Sinai.

Devotion to St. Catherine spread as a result of the Crusades. She was invoked as the patron of students, teachers, librarians, and lawyers. Catherine is one of the Fourteen Holy Helpers, venerated especially in Germany and Hungary.

COMMENT: The pursuit of God's wisdom may not lead to riches or earthly honors. In Catherine's case, this pursuit contributed to her martyrdom. She was not, however, foolish in preferring to die for Jesus rather than live only by denying him. All the rewards that her tormenters offered her would rust, lose their beauty, or in some other way become a poor exchange for Catherine's honesty and integrity in following Jesus Christ.

QUOTE: "Therefore I [King Solomon] prayed, and prudence was given me; / I pleaded, and the spirit of Wisdom came to me. / I preferred her to scepter and throne, / And deemed riches nothing in comparison with her, / nor did I liken any priceless gem to her; / Because all gold, in view of her, is a little sand, / and before her, silver is to be accounted mire. / Beyond health and comeliness I loved her, / And I chose to have her rather than the light, / because the splendor of her never yields to sleep. / Yet all good things together came to me in her company, / and countless riches at her hands; / And I rejoiced in them all, because Wisdom is their leader, / though I had not known that she is the mother of these" (Wisdom 7:7–12).

• • •

NOVEMBER 30 + FEAST

Andrew

APOSTLE

Andrew was St. Peter's brother and was called with him. "As [Jesus] was walking by the Sea of Galilee, he saw two brothers, Simon who is now called Peter, and his brother Andrew, casting a net into the sea; they were fishermen. He said to them, 'Come after me, and I will make you fishers of men.' At once they left their nets and followed him" (Matthew 4:18–20).

John the Evangelist presents Andrew as a disciple of John the Baptist. When Jesus walked by one day, John said, "Behold, the Lamb of God." Andrew and another disciple followed Jesus. "Jesus turned and saw them following him and said to them, 'What are you looking for?' They said to him, 'Rabbi' (which translated means Teacher), 'where are you staying?' He said to them, 'Come, and you will see.' So they went and saw where he was staying, and they stayed with him that day" (John 1:38–39a).

Little else is said about Andrew in the Gospels. Before the multiplication of the loaves, it was Andrew who spoke up about the boy who had the barley loaves and fishes (see John 6:8–9). When the Gentiles went to see Jesus, they came to Philip, but Philip then had recourse to Andrew (see John 12:20–22).

Legend has it that Andrew preached the Good News in what is now modern Greece and Turkey and was crucified at Patras.

COMMENT: As in the case of all the apostles except Peter and John, the Gospels give us little about the holiness of Andrew. He was an apostle. That is enough. He was called personally by Jesus to proclaim the Good News, to heal with Jesus's power and to share his life and death. Holiness today is no different. It is a gift that includes a call to be concerned about the Kingdom, an outgoing attitude that wants nothing more than to share the riches of Christ with all people.

STORY: "The Twelve called together the community of the disciples and said, 'It is not right for us to neglect the word of God to serve at table. Brothers, select from among you seven reputable men, filled with the Spirit and wisdom, whom we shall appoint to this task, whereas we shall devote ourselves to prayer and to the ministry of the word'" (Acts 6:2–4).

• • •

Blessed Charles de Foucauld

PRIEST AND HERMIT (1858–1916)

Born into an aristocratic family in Strasbourg, France, Charles was orphaned at the age of six, raised by his devout grandfather, rejected the Catholic faith as a teenager, and joined the French army. Inheriting a great deal of money from his grandfather, Charles went to Algeria with his regiment, but not without his mistress, Mimi.

When he refused to give her up, he was dismissed from the army. Later he reenlisted in Algeria after he had left Mimi. He resigned from the army when he was refused permission to make a scientific exploration of nearby Morocco. With the help of a Jewish rabbi, Charles disguised himself as a Jew and in 1883 began a one-year exploration that he recorded in a book that was well received.

Inspired by the Jews and Muslims whom he met, when he returned to France he resumed the practice of his Catholic faith in 1886. He joined a Trappist monastery in Ardeche, France, and later transferred to one in Akbes, Syria. He left it and in 1897 began to work as gardener and sacristan for the Poor Clare nuns in Nazareth and later in Jerusalem. He returned to France and was ordained a priest in 1901.

Later that year he returned to Beni-Abbes, Morocco, intending to found a monastic religious community in North Africa, offering hospitality to Christians, Muslims, Jews, or people with no religion. He lived a peaceful, hidden life but attracted no companions.

A former army comrade invited him to live among the Tuareg people in Algeria. Charles learned their language enough to write a Tuareg-French and French-Tuareg dictionary and to translate the Gospels into Tuareg. In 1905 he came to Tamanrasset, where he lived the rest of his life. His two-volume collection of Tuareg poetry was published after his death.

In early 1909 he visited France and established an association of laypeople who pledged to live by the Gospels. His return to Tamanrasset was welcomed by the Tuareg. In 1915 he wrote to Louis Massignon: "The love of God, the love for one's neighbor.... All religion is found there.... How to get to that point? Not in a day since it is perfection itself: it is the goal we must always aim for, which we must unceasingly try to reach and that we will only attain in heaven."

The outbreak of World War I led to attacks on the French in Algeria. Seized in a raid by another tribe, Charles and two French soldiers coming to visit him were shot to death on December 1, 1916.

Five religious congregations, associations, and spiritual institutes (Little Brothers of Jesus, Little Sisters of the Sacred Heart, Little Sisters of Jesus, Little Brothers of the Gospel, and Little Sisters of the Gospel) draw inspiration from the peaceful, largely hidden yet hospitable life that characterized Charles. He was beatified on November 13, 2005.

COMMENT: The life of Charles de Foucauld was eventually centered on God and was animated by prayer and humble service, which he hoped would draw Muslims to Christ. Those who are inspired by his example, no matter where they live, seek to live their faith humbly yet with deep religious conviction.

QUOTE: In his homily at the beatification Mass, Cardinal José Saraiva Martins noted that Charles chose as his motto, "Iesus Caritas, Jesus Love." In 1916, Charles wrote: "There is, I believe, a word from the Gospel that has a more profound impression on me nor has transformed my life more than this: 'Whatever you do for the least of my brothers, you do for me.' If we reflect that these words are those from the uncreated Truth, those from the mouth of He who said, 'This is my body...this is my blood,' what forces drives us to seek and to love Jesus in these 'least ones, these sinners, these poor ones.'"

• ⊛ •

Francis Xavier

PRIEST (1506–1552)

Jesus asked, "What profit would there be for one to gain the whole world and forfeit his life?" (Matthew 16:26a). These words were repeated to a young teacher of philosophy who had a highly promising career in academics, with success and a life of prestige and honor before him.

Francis Xavier, twenty-four at the time, and living and teaching in Paris, did not heed these words at once. They came from a good friend, Ignatius of Loyola (July 31), whose tireless persuasion finally won the young man to Christ. Francis then made the spiritual exercises under the direction of Ignatius, and in 1534 joined his little community (the infant Society of Jesus). Together at Montmartre they vowed poverty, chastity, and apostolic service according to the directions of the pope.

From Venice, where he was ordained priest in 1537, Francis Xavier went on to Lisbon and from there sailed to the East Indies, landing at Goa, on the west coast of India. For the next ten years he labored to bring the faith to such widely scattered peoples as the Hindus, the Malayans, and the Japanese.

Wherever he went, he lived with the poorest people, sharing their food and rough accommodations. He spent countless hours ministering to the sick and the poor, particularly to lepers. Very often he had no time to sleep or even to say his breviary but, as we know from his letters, he was filled always with joy.

Francis went through the islands of Malaysia, then up to Japan. He learned enough Japanese to preach to simple folk, to instruct and to baptize, and to establish missions for those who were to follow him. From Japan he had dreams of going to China, but this plan was never realized. Before reaching the mainland, he died. He and Thérèse of Lisieux were declared copatrons of missions in 1927.

COMMENT: All of us are called to "go and preach to all nations" (see Matthew 28:19). Our preaching is not necessarily on distant shores but to our families, our children, our spouse, our coworkers. And we are called to preach not with words, but by our everyday lives. Only by sacrifice, the giving up of all selfish gain, could Francis Xavier be free to bear the Good News to the world. Sacrifice is leaving yourself behind at times for a greater good, the good of prayer, the good of helping someone in need, the good of just listening to another. The greatest gift we have is our time. Francis gave his to others.

STORY: Francis died on the island of Sancian, a hundred miles southwest of Hong Kong. In his final sickness he had to be removed from the ship because the Portuguese sailors feared that kindness to him would offend their master. They were forced to leave him on the sands of the shore, exposed to a bitter wind, but a Portuguese merchant led him into a ramshackle hut. He prayed continually, between spasms of delirium and the doubtful therapy of bleeding. He grew weaker and weaker. "I [Anthony, his friend] could see that he was dying, and put a lighted candle in his hand. Then, with the name of Jesus on his lips, he gave his spirit to his Creator and Lord with great peace and repose."

* * *

DECEMBER 4 + OPTIONAL
John Damascene
PRIEST AND DOCTOR (676?–749)

John spent most of his life in the monastery of St. Sabas, near Jerusalem, and all of his life under Muslim rule, indeed, protected by it. He was born in Damascus, received a classical and theological education, and followed his father in a government position under the Arabs. After a few years he resigned and went to the monastery of St. Sabas.

He is famous in three areas. First, he is known for his writings against the iconoclasts, who opposed the veneration of images. Paradoxically, it was the Eastern Christian Emperor Leo who forbade the practice, and it was because John lived in Muslim territory that his enemies could not silence him. Second, he is famous for his treatise *Exposition of the Orthodox Faith*, a summary of the Greek fathers (of which he became the last). It is said that this book is for Eastern schools what the *Summa* of Aquinas became for the West. Thirdly, he is known as a poet, one of the two greatest of the Eastern Church, the other being Romanus the Melodist. His devotion to the Blessed Mother and his sermons on her feasts are well known.

COMMENT: John defended the Church's understanding of the veneration of images and explained the faith of the Church in several other controversies. For over thirty years he combined a life of prayer with these defenses and his other writings. His holiness expressed itself in putting his literary and preaching talents at the service of the Lord.

QUOTE: "The saints must be honored as friends of Christ and children and heirs of God, as John the theologian and evangelist says: 'But as many as received him, he gave them the power to be made the sons of God....' Let us carefully observe the manner of life of all the apostles, martyrs, ascetics and just men who announced the coming of the Lord. And let us emulate their faith, charity, hope, zeal, life, patience under suffering, and perseverance unto death, so that we may also share their crowns of glory" (*Exposition of the Orthodox Faith*).

* * *

DECEMBER 4 + OPTIONAL
Blessed Adolph Kolping
PRIEST (1813–1865)

The rise of the factory system in nineteenth-century Germany brought many single men into cities where they faced new challenges to their faith. Fr. Adolph Kolping began a ministry to them, hoping that they would not be lost to the Catholic faith as was happening to workers elsewhere in industrialized Europe.

Born in the village of Kerpen, Adolph became a shoemaker at an early age because of his family's economic situation. Ordained in 1845, he ministered to young workers in Cologne, establishing a choir, which by 1849 had grown into the Young Workmen's Society. A branch of this began in St. Louis, Missouri, in 1856. Nine years later there were over four hundred *Gesellenvereine* (workman's societies) around the world. Today this group has over 450,000 members in over sixty countries across the globe.

More commonly called the Kolping Society, this group emphasizes the sanctification of family life and the dignity of labor. Fr. Kolping worked to improve conditions for workers and greatly assisted those in need. He and St. John Bosco (January 31) in Turin had similar interests in working with young men in big cities. He told his followers, "The needs of the times will teach you what to do."

Fr. Kolping once said, "The first thing that a person finds in life and the last to which he holds out his hand, and the most precious that he possess, even if he does not realize it, is family life."

He and Blessed John Duns Scotus are buried in Cologne's Minoritenkirche, originally served by the Conventual Franciscans. The Kolping Society's international headquarters is across from this church.

Kolping members journeyed to Rome from Europe, America, Africa, Asia, and Oceania for Fr. Kolping's beatification in 1991, the one hundredth anniversary of Pope Leo XIII's revolutionary encyclical *Rerum Novarum* (On the Social Order). Fr. Kolping's personal witness and apostolate helped prepare for that encyclical.

COMMENT: Some people thought that Fr. Kolping was wasting his time and talents on young working men in industrialized cities. In some countries, the Catholic Church was seen by many workers as the ally of owners and the enemy of workers. Men like Adolph Kolping showed that was not true.

QUOTE: "Adolph Kolping gathered skilled workers and factory laborers together. Thus he overcame their isolation and defeatism. A faith society gave them the strength to go out into their everyday lives as Christ's witnesses before God and the world. To come together, to become strengthened in the assembly, and thus to scatter again is and still remains our duty today. We are not Christians for ourselves alone, but always for others too" (Blessed John Paul II, beatification homily).

• • •

DECEMBER 6 + OPTIONAL
Nicholas
BISHOP (D. 350?)

The absence of the hard facts of history is not necessarily an obstacle to the popularity of saints, as the devotion to St. Nicholas shows. Both the Eastern and Western Churches honor him, and it is claimed that, after the Blessed Virgin, he is the saint most pictured by Christian artists. And yet, historically, we can pinpoint only the fact that Nicholas was the fourth-century bishop of Myra, a city in Lycia, a province of Asia Minor.

As with many of the saints, however, we are able to capture the relationship that Nicholas had with God through the admiration that Christians have had for him—an admiration expressed in the colorful stories that have been told and retold through the centuries.

Perhaps the best-known story about Nicholas concerns his charity toward a poor man who was unable to provide dowries for his three daughters of marriageable age. Rather than see them forced into prostitution, Nicholas secretly tossed a bag of gold through the poor man's window on three separate occasions, thus enabling the daughters to be married. Over the centuries, this particular legend evolved into the custom of gift-giving on the saint's feast. In the English-speaking countries, St. Nicholas became, by a twist of the tongue, Santa Claus—further expanding the example of generosity portrayed by this holy bishop.

COMMENT: The critical eye of modern history makes us take a deeper look at the legends surrounding St. Nicholas. But perhaps we can utilize the lesson taught by his legendary charity, look deeper at our approach to material goods in the Christmas season, and seek ways to extend our sharing to those in real need.

QUOTE: "In order to be able to consult more suitably the welfare of the faithful according to the condition of each one, a bishop should strive to become duly acquainted with their needs in the social circumstances in which they live.... He should manifest his concern for all, no matter what their age, condition, or nationality, be they natives, strangers, or foreigners" (Decree on the Pastoral Office of Bishops, 16).

• • •

DECEMBER 7 + MEMORIAL

Ambrose

BISHOP AND DOCTOR (340?–397)

One of Ambrose's biographers observed that at the last judgment people would still be divided between those who admired Ambrose and those who heartily disliked him. He emerges as the man of action who cut a furrow through the lives of his contemporaries. Even royal personages were numbered among those who were to suffer crushing divine punishments for standing in Ambrose's way.

When the Empress Justina attempted to wrest two basilicas from Ambrose's Catholics and give them to the Arians, he dared the eunuchs of the court to execute him. His own people rallied behind him in the face of imperial troops. In the midst of riots, he both spurred and calmed his people with bewitching new hymns set to exciting Eastern melodies.

In his disputes with the Emperor Auxentius, he coined the principle: "The emperor is in the Church, not above the Church." He publicly admonished Emperor Theodosius for the massacre of seven thousand innocent people. The emperor did public penance for his crime. This was Ambrose, the fighter, sent to Milan as Roman governor and chosen while yet a catechumen to be the people's bishop.

There is yet another side of Ambrose—one which influenced Augustine (August 28), whom Ambrose converted. Ambrose was a passionate little man with a high forehead, a long melancholy face, and great eyes. We can picture him as a frail figure clasping the codex of sacred Scripture. This was the Ambrose of aristocratic heritage and learning.

Augustine found the oratory of Ambrose less soothing and entertaining but far more learned than that of other contemporaries. Ambrose's sermons were often modeled on Cicero, and his ideas betrayed the influence of contemporary thinkers and philosophers. He had no scruples in borrowing at length from pagan authors. He gloried in the pulpit in his ability to parade his spoils—"gold of the Egyptians"—taken over from the pagan philosophers.

His sermons, his writings, and his personal life reveal him as an otherworldly man involved in the great issues of his day. Humanity, for Ambrose, was, above all, spirit. In order to think rightly of God and the human soul, the closest thing to God, no material reality at all was to be dwelt upon. He was an enthusiastic champion of consecrated virginity.

The influence of Ambrose on Augustine will always be open for discussion. The *Confessions* reveal some manly, brusque encounters between Ambrose and Augustine, but there can be no doubt of Augustine's profound esteem for the learned bishop.

Neither is there any doubt that Monica (August 27) loved Ambrose as an angel of God who uprooted her son from his former ways and led him to his convictions about Christ. It was Ambrose, after all, who placed his hands on the shoulders of the naked Augustine as he descended into the baptismal fountain to put on Christ.

COMMENT: Ambrose exemplifies for us the truly catholic character of Christianity. He is a man steeped in the learning, law, and culture of the ancients and of his contemporaries. Yet, in the midst of active involvement in this world, this thought runs through Ambrose's life and preaching: The hidden meaning of the Scriptures calls our spirit to rise to another world.

QUOTE: "Women and men are not mistaken when they regard themselves as superior to mere bodily creatures and as more than mere particles of nature or nameless units in modern society. For by their power to know themselves in the depths of their being they rise above the entire universe of mere objects.... Endowed with wisdom, women and men are led through visible realities to those which are invisible" (Pastoral Constitution on the Church in the Modern World, 14–15).

• • •

Immaculate Conception

A feast called the Conception of Mary arose in the Eastern Church in the seventh century. It came to the West in the eighth century. In the eleventh century it received its present name, the Immaculate Conception. In the eighteenth century, it became a feast of the universal Church.

In 1854 Pius IX solemnly proclaimed: "The most Blessed Virgin Mary, in the first instant of her conception, by a singular grace and privilege granted by almighty God, in view of the merits of Jesus Christ, the savior of the human race, was preserved free from all stain of original sin."

It took a long time for this doctrine to develop. While many Fathers and Doctors of the Church considered Mary the greatest and holiest of the saints, they often had difficulty in seeing Mary as sinless—either at her conception or throughout her life. This is one of the Church teachings that arose more from the piety of the faithful than from the insights of brilliant theologians. Even such champions of Mary as Bernard (August 20) and Thomas Aquinas (January 28) could not see theological justification for this teaching.

Two Franciscans, William of Ware and Blessed John Duns Scotus, helped develop the theology. They point out that Mary's Immaculate Conception enhances Jesus's redemptive work. Other members of the human race are cleansed from original sin after birth. In Mary, Jesus's work was so powerful as to prevent original sin at the outset.

COMMENT: In Luke 1:28 the angel Gabriel, speaking on God's behalf, addresses Mary as "full of grace" (or "highly favored"). In that context this phrase means that Mary is receiving all the special divine help necessary for the task ahead. However, the Church grows in understanding with the help of the Holy Spirit. The Spirit led the Church, especially non-theologians, to the insight that Mary had to be the most perfect work of God next to the incarnation. Or rather, Mary's intimate association with the Incarnation called for the special involvement of God in Mary's whole life. The logic of piety helped God's people to believe that Mary was full of grace and free of sin from the first moment of her existence. Moreover, this great privilege of Mary is the highlight of all that God has done in Jesus. Rightly understood, the incomparable holiness of Mary shows forth the incomparable goodness of God.

QUOTE: "[Mary] gave to the world the Life that renews all things, and she was enriched by God with gifts appropriate to such a role.

"It is no wonder, then, that the usage prevailed among the holy Fathers whereby they called the mother of God entirely holy and free from all stain of sin, fashioned by the Holy Spirit into a kind of new substance and new creature. Adorned from the first instant of her conception with the splendors of an entirely unique holiness, the Virgin of Nazareth is, on God's command, greeted by an angel messenger as 'full of grace' (cf. Luke 1:28). To the heavenly messenger she replies: 'Behold the handmaid of the Lord, be it done to me according to thy word' (Luke 1:38)" (Dogmatic Constitution on the Church, 56).

● ● ●

DECEMBER 9 + MEMORIAL (MEXICO)
Juan Diego
CATECHIST (1474–1548)

First called *Cuauhtlatohuac* ("The eagle who speaks"), Juan Diego's name is forever linked with Our Lady of Guadalupe because it was to him that she first appeared at Tepeyac Hill on December 9, 1531. The most famous part of his story is told in connection with the feast or Our Lady of Guadalupe (December 12). After the roses gathered in his tilma were transformed into the miraculous image of Our Lady of Guadalupe, however, little more is said about Juan Diego.

In time he lived near the shrine constructed at Tepeyac, revered as a holy, unselfish and compassionate catechist who taught by word and especially by example.

During his 1990 pastoral visit to Mexico, Blessed John Paul II confirmed the long-standing liturgical cult in honor of Juan Diego, beatifying him. Juan Diego was canonized in 2002.

COMMENT: God counted on Juan Diego to play a humble yet huge role in bringing the Good News to the peoples of Mexico. Overcoming his own fear and the doubts of Bishop Juan de Zumarraga, Juan Diego cooperated with God's grace in showing his people that the Good News of Jesus is for everyone. Pope John Paul II used the occasion of this beatification to urge Mexican laypeople to assume their responsibilities for passing on the Good News and witnessing to it.

QUOTE: "In accepting the Christian message without forgoing his indigenous identity, Juan Diego discovered the profound truth of the new humanity, in which all are called to be children of God. Thus he facilitated the fruitful meeting of two worlds and became the catalyst for the new Mexican identity, closely united to Our Lady of Guadalupe, whose mestizo face expresses her spiritual motherhood, which embraces all Mexicans. That is why the witness of his life must continue to be the inspiration for the building up of the Mexican nation, encouraging brotherhood among all its children and ever helping to reconcile Mexico with its origins, values, and traditions." (Blessed John Paul II, canonization homily).

● ● ●

DECEMBER 11 + OPTIONAL

Damasus I

POPE (305?–384)

To his secretary St. Jerome (September 30), Damasus was "an incomparable person, learned in the Scriptures, a virgin doctor of the virgin Church, who loved chastity and heard its praises with pleasure."

Damasus seldom heard such unrestrained praise. Internal political struggles, doctrinal heresies, uneasy relations with his fellow bishops and those of the Eastern Church marred the peace of his pontificate.

The son of a Roman priest, possibly of Spanish extraction, Damasus started as a deacon in his father's church and served as a priest in what later became the basilica of San Lorenzo in Rome. He served Pope Liberius (352–366) and followed him into exile.

When Liberius died, Damasus was elected bishop of Rome, but a minority elected and consecrated another deacon, Ursinus, as pope. The controversy between Damasus and the antipope resulted in violent battles in two basilicas, scandalizing the bishops of Italy. At the synod Damasus called on the occasion of his birthday, he asked them to approve his actions. The bishops' reply was curt: "We assembled for a birthday, not to condemn a man unheard." Supporters of the antipope even managed to get Damasus accused of a grave crime—probably sexual—as late as A.D. 378. He had to clear himself before both a civil court and a Church synod.

As pope his lifestyle was simple in contrast to other ecclesiastics of Rome, and he was fierce in his denunciation of Arianism and other heresies. A misunderstanding of the Trinitarian terminology used by Rome threatened amicable relations with the Eastern Church, and Damasus was only moderately successful in dealing with that challenge.

During his pontificate Christianity was declared the official religion of the Roman state (380), and Latin became the principal liturgical language as part of the pope's reforms. His encouragement of St. Jerome's biblical studies led to the Vulgate, the Latin translation of Scripture that the Council of Trent (twelve centuries later) declared to be "authentic in public readings, disputations, preachings."

COMMENT: The history of the papacy and the Church is inextricably mixed with the personal biography of Damasus. In a troubled and pivotal period of Church history, he stands forth as a zealous defender of the faith who knew when to be progressive and when to entrench.

Damasus makes us aware of two qualities of good leadership: alertness to the promptings of the Spirit and service. His struggles are a reminder that Jesus never promised his rock protection from hurricane winds nor his followers immunity from difficulties. His only guarantee is final victory.

QUOTE: "He who walking on the sea could calm the bitter waves, who gives life to the dying seeds of the earth; he who was able to loose the mortal chains of death, and after three days' darkness could bring again to the upper world the brother for his sister Martha: He, I believe, will make Damasus rise again from the dust" (epitaph Damasus wrote for himself).

• • •

DECEMBER 12 + FEAST (U.S.A.)

Our Lady of Guadalupe

The feast in honor of Our Lady of Guadalupe goes back to the sixteenth century. Chronicles of that period tell us the story.

A poor Indian named Cuauhtlatohuac was baptized and given the name Juan Diego (December 9). He was a fifty-seven-year-old widower and lived in a small village near Mexico City. On Saturday morning, December 9, 1531, he was on his way to a nearby barrio to attend Mass in honor of Our Lady.

He was walking by a hill called Tepeyac when he heard beautiful music like the warbling of birds. A radiant cloud appeared and within it a young Native American maiden dressed like an Aztec princess. The lady spoke to him in his own language and sent him to the bishop of Mexico City, a Franciscan named Juan de Zumarraga. The bishop was to build a chapel in the place where the lady appeared.

Eventually the bishop told Juan Diego to have the lady give him a sign. About this same time Juan Diego's uncle became seriously ill. This led poor Diego to try to avoid the lady. The lady found Diego, nevertheless, assured him that his uncle would recover and provided roses for Juan to carry to the bishop in his cape or tilma.

When Juan Diego opened his tilma in the bishop's presence, the roses fell to the ground and the bishop sank to his knees. On Juan Diego's tilma appeared an image of Mary, exactly as she had appeared at the hill of Tepeyac. It was December 12, 1531.

COMMENT: Mary's appearance to Juan Diego as one of his people is a powerful reminder that Mary and the God who sent her accept all peoples.

In the context of the sometimes rude and cruel treatment of the Indians by the Spaniards, the apparition was a rebuke to the Spaniards and an event of vast significance for Native Americans. While a number of them had converted before this incident, they now came in droves. According to a contemporary chronicler, nine million Indians became Catholic in a very short time. In these days when we hear so much about God's preferential option for the poor, Our Lady of Guadalupe cries out to us that God's love for and identification with the poor is an age-old truth that stems from the gospel itself.

QUOTE: Mary to Juan Diego: "My dearest son, I am the eternal Virgin Mary, Mother of the true God, Author of Life, Creator of all and Lord of the Heavens and of the Earth…and it is my desire that a church be built here in this place for me, where, as your most merciful Mother and that of all your people, I may show my loving clemency and the compassion that I bear to the Indians, and to those who love and seek me" (from an ancient chronicle).

●　●　●

DECEMBER 13 + MEMORIAL

Lucy

VIRGIN AND MARTYR (D. 304)

Every little girl named Lucy must bite her tongue in disappointment when she first tries to find out what there is to know about her patron saint. The older books will have a lengthy paragraph detailing a small number of traditions. Newer books will have a lengthy paragraph showing that there is little basis in history for these traditions. The single fact survives that a disappointed suitor accused Lucy of being a Christian and she was executed in Syracuse (Sicily) in the year 304. But it is also true that her name is mentioned in Eucharistic Prayer I, geographical places are named after her, a popular song has her name as its title, and down through the centuries many thousands of little girls have been proud of the name Lucy.

One can easily imagine what a young Christian woman had to contend with in pagan Sicily in the year 300. If you have trouble imagining, just glance at today's pleasure-at-all-costs world and the barriers it presents against leading a good Christian life.

Her friends must have wondered aloud about this hero of Lucy's, an obscure itinerant preacher in a far-off captive nation that had been destroyed more than two hundred years before. Once a carpenter, he had been crucified by the Roman soldiers after his own people turned him over to the Roman authorities. Lucy believed with her whole soul that this man had risen from the dead. Heaven had put a stamp on all he said and did. To give witness to her faith, she made a vow of virginity.

What a hubbub this caused among her pagan friends! The kindlier ones just thought her a little strange. To be pure before marriage was an ancient Roman ideal, rarely found but not to be condemned. To exclude marriage altogether, however, was too much. She must have something sinister to hide, the tongues wagged.

Lucy knew of the heroism of earlier virgin martyrs. She remained faithful to their example and to the example of the carpenter, whom she knew to be the Son of God.

COMMENT: If you are a little girl named Lucy, you need not be disappointed. Your patron is a genuine, authentic heroine, first-class, an abiding inspiration for you and for all Christians. The moral courage of the young Sicilian martyr shines forth as a guiding light, just as bright for today's youth as it was in A.D. 304.

QUOTE: "The Gospel tells us of all that Jesus suffered, of the insults that fell upon him. But, from Bethlehem to Calvary, the brilliance that radiates from his divine purity spread more and more and won over the crowds. So great was the austerity and the enchantment of his conduct.

"So may it be with you, beloved daughters. Blessed be the discretion, the mortifications and the renouncements with which you seek to render this virtue more brilliant.... May your conduct prove to all that chastity is not only a possible virtue but a social virtue, which must be strongly defended through prayer, vigilance and the mortification of the senses" (Blessed John XXIII, *Letter to Women Religious*).

* * *

John of the Cross
PRIEST AND DOCTOR (1541–1591)

John is a saint because his life was a heroic effort to live up to his name: "of the Cross." The folly of the cross came to full realization in time. "Whoever wishes to come after me must deny himself, take up his cross, and follow me" (Mark 8:34b) is the story of John's life. The paschal mystery—through death to life—strongly marks John as reformer, mystic-poet and theologian-priest.

Ordained a Carmelite priest at twenty-five (1567), John met Teresa of Jesus (October 15) and, like her, vowed himself to the primitive Rule of the Carmelites. As partner with Teresa and in his own right, John engaged in the work of reform and came to experience the price of reform: increasing opposition, misunderstanding, persecution, and imprisonment. He came to know the cross acutely—to experience the dying of Jesus—as he sat month after month in his dark, damp, narrow cell with only his God!

Yet, the paradox! In this dying of imprisonment John came to life, uttering poetry. In the darkness of the dungeon, John's spirit came into the Light. There are many mystics, many poets; John is unique as mystic-poet, expressing in his prison-cross the ecstasy of mystical union with God in the *Spiritual Canticle*.

But as agony leads to ecstasy, so John had his *Ascent to Mt. Carmel*, as he named it in his prose masterpiece. As man-Christian-Carmelite, he experienced in himself this purifying ascent; as spiritual director, he sensed it in others; as psychologist-theologian, he described and analyzed it in his prose writings. His prose works are outstanding in underscoring the cost of discipleship, the path of union with God: rigorous discipline, abandonment, purification. Uniquely and strongly John underlines the Gospel paradox: The cross leads to resurrection, agony to ecstasy, darkness to light, abandonment to possession, denial to self to union with God. If you want to save your life, you must lose it. John is truly "of the Cross." He died at forty-nine—a life short, but full.

COMMENT: John in his life and writings has a crucial word for us today. We tend to be rich, soft, and comfortable. We shrink even from words like *self-denial, mortification, purification, asceticism, discipline*. We run from the cross. John's message—like the Gospel—is loud and clear: *Don't*—if you really want to live!

QUOTE: Thomas Merton said of John: "Just as we can never separate asceticism from mysticism, so in St. John of the Cross we find darkness and light, suffering and joy, sacrifice and love united together so closely that they seem at times to be identified."

In John's words: "Never was fount so clear, undimmed and bright; From it alone, I know proceeds all light, although 'tis night."

• • •

Hildegard of Bingen

VIRGIN AND DOCTOR (1098–1179)

Abbess, artist, author, composer, mystic, pharmacist, poet, preacher, theologian—where to begin describing this remarkable woman who was added to the calendar of saints in May 2012 and formally proclaimed a Doctor of the Church five months later?

Born into a noble family, she was instructed for ten years by Blessed Jutta, a very holy woman. When Hildegard was eighteen, she then became a Benedictine nun at the Monastery of St. Disibodenberg, becoming its prioress in 1136. Ordered by her confessor to write down the visions that she had received since the age of three, Hildegard took ten years to write *Scivias* (*Know the Ways*). Pope Eugene III read it and in 1147 encouraged her to continue writing. Her *Book of the Merits of Life* and *Book of Divine Works* followed. She wrote over three hundred letters to people who sought her advice; she also composed short works on medicine and physiology. Hildegard sought advice form St. Bernard of Clairvaux (August 20).

Hildegard's visions caused her to see human beings as "living sparks" of God's love, coming from God as daylight comes from the sun. Sin destroyed the original harmony of creation; Christ's redeeming death and resurrection opened up new possibilities. Virtuous living reduces the estrangement from God and others that sin causes.

Like all mystics, she saw the harmony of God's creation and the place of women and men in that. This unity was not apparent to many of her contemporaries.

Hildegard was no stranger to controversy. The monks near her original foundation protested vigorously when she moved her monastery to Bingen, overlooking the Rhine River. She confronted Emperor Frederick Barbarossa for supporting at least three antipopes. Hildegard challenged the Cathars, who rejected the Catholic Church and claimed to follow a more pure Christianity.

Between 1152 and 1162, she often preached in the Rhineland. Her monastery was placed under interdict because she had permitted the burial of a young man who had been excommunicated. She insisted that he had been reconciled with the Church and had received its sacraments before dying. She protested bitterly when the local bishop forbade the celebration of or reception of the Eucharist at that monastery, a sanction that was lifted only a few months before she died.

COMMENT: During his general audiences on September 1 and 8, 2010, Pope Benedict XVI spoke about Hildegard. He praised the humility with which she received God's gifts and the obedience she gave Church authorities. He praised the "rich theological content" of her mystical visions that sum up the history of salvation from creation to the end of time.

The pope closed his second talk by saying: "Let us always invoke the Holy Spirit, so that he may inspire in the Church holy and courageous women, like St. Hildegard of Bingen, who, developing the gifts they have received from God, make their own special and valuable contribution to the spiritual development of our communities and of the Church in our time."

QUOTE: Hildegard once wrote: "In the year 1141…a fiery light, flashing intensely, came from the open vault of heaven and poured through my whole brain. Like a flame that is hot without burning, it kindled all my heart and all my breast, just as the sun warms anything on which its rays fall. And suddenly I could understand what such books as the Psalter, the Gospels and the other Catholic volumes both of the Old and New Testament actually set forth."

• • •

Peter Canisius
PRIEST AND DOCTOR (1521–1597)

The energetic life of Peter Canisius should demolish any stereotypes we may have of the life of a saint as dull or routine. Peter lived his seventy-six years at a pace which must be considered heroic, even in our time of rapid change. A man blessed with many talents, Peter is an excellent example of the scriptural man who develops his talents for the sake of the Lord's work

He was one of the most important figures in the Catholic Reformation in Germany. His was such a key role that he has often been called the "second apostle of Germany" in that his life parallels the earlier work of Boniface (June 5).

Although Peter once accused himself of idleness in his youth, he could not have been idle too long, for at the age of nineteen he received a master's degree from the university at Cologne. Soon afterward he met Peter Faber, the first disciple of Ignatius Loyola (July 31), who influenced Peter so much that he joined the recently formed Society of Jesus.

At this early age Peter had already taken up a practice he continued throughout his life—a process of study, reflection, prayer, and writing. After his ordination in 1546, he became widely known for his editions of the writings of St. Cyril of Alexandria (June 27) and St. Leo the Great (November 10). Besides this reflective literary bent, Peter had a zeal for the apostolate. He could often be found visiting the sick or prisoners, even when his assigned duties in other areas were more than enough to keep most people fully occupied.

In 1547 Peter attended several sessions of the Council of Trent, whose decrees he was later assigned to implement. After a brief teaching assignment at the Jesuit college at Messina, Peter was entrusted with the mission to Germany—from that point on his life's work. He taught in several universities and was instrumental in establishing many colleges and seminaries. He wrote a catechism that explained the Catholic faith in a way that common people could understand—a great need of that age.

Renowned as a popular preacher, Peter packed churches with those eager to hear his eloquent proclamation of the Gospel. He had great diplomatic ability, often serving as a reconciler between disputing factions. In his letters (filling eight volumes), one finds words of wisdom and counsel to people in all walks of life. At times he wrote unprecedented letters of criticism to leaders of the Church—yet always in the context of a loving, sympathetic concern.

At seventy Peter suffered a paralytic seizure, but he continued to preach and write with the aid of secretary until his death in his hometown (Nijmegten, the Netherlands) on December 21, 1597.

COMMENT: Peter's untiring efforts are an apt example for those involved in the renewal of the Church or the growth of moral consciousness in business or government. He is regarded as one of the creators of the Catholic press and can easily be a model for the Christian author or journalist. Teachers can see in his life a passion for the transmission of truth. Whether we have much to give, as Peter Canisius did, or whether we have only a little to give, as did the poor widow in the Gospel (see Luke 21:1–4), the important thing is to give our all. It is in this way that Peter is so exemplary for Christians in an age of rapid change. We are called to understand our world but not automatically accept its values.

QUOTE: When asked if he felt overworked, Peter replied, "If you have too much to do, with God's help you will find time to do it all."

• • •

DECEMBER 23 + OPTIONAL
John of Kanty
PRIEST (1390?–1473)

John was a country lad who made good in the big city and the big university of Kraków, Poland. After brilliant studies he was ordained a priest and became a professor of theology. The inevitable opposition which saints encounter led to his being ousted by rivals and sent to be a parish priest at Olkusz. An extremely humble man, he did his best, but his best was not to the liking of his parishioners. Besides, he was afraid of the responsibilities of his position. But in the end he won his people's hearts. After some time he returned to Kraków and taught Scripture for the remainder of his life.

He was a serious man, and humble, but known to all the poor of Kraków for his kindness. His goods and his money were always at their disposal, and time and again they took advantage of him. He kept only the money and clothes absolutely needed to support himself. He slept little, and then on the floor, ate sparingly, and took no meat. He made a pilgrimage to Jerusalem, hoping to be martyred by the Turks. He made four pilgrimages to Rome, carrying his luggage on his back. When he was warned to look after his health, he was quick to point out that, for all their austerity, the fathers of the desert lived remarkably long lives.

COMMENT: John of Kanty is a typical saint: He was kind, humble, and generous, he suffered opposition, and led an austere, penitential life. Most Christians in an affluent society can understand all the ingredients except the last: Anything more than mild self-discipline seems reserved for athletes and ballet dancers. Christmas, at least, is a good time to reject self-indulgence.

STORY: The old breviary included this story: John of Kanty was once accosted by robbers, who took his money. They asked if he had any more, and he replied in the negative. When they had gone, he discovered some coins sewn in his cloak, ran after the robbers, shouted for them to stop and gave them the coins. They were so amazed that they gave back what they had taken.

* * *

DECEMBER 25 + SOLEMNITY
Birth of Our Lord Jesus Christ

On this day the Church focuses especially on the newborn child, God become human, who embodies for us all the hope and peace we seek. We need no other special saint today to lead us to Christ in the manger, although his mother, Mary, and Joseph, caring for his foster son, help round out the scene.

But if we were to select a patron for today, perhaps it might be appropriate for us to inspire an anonymous shepherd, summoned to the birthplace by a wondrous and even disturbing vision in the night, a summons from an angelic choir, promising peace and goodwill. A shepherd willing to seek out something that might just be too unbelievable to chase after, and yet compelling enough to leave behind the flocks in the field and search for a mystery.

On the day of the Lord's birth, let an unnamed, non-celebrity at the edge of the crowd model for us the way to discover Christ in our own hearts—somewhere between skepticism and wonder, between mystery and faith. And, like Mary and the shepherd, let us treasure that discovery in our hearts.

COMMENT: The precise dating in the Scripture readings for today sounds like a textbook on creationism. If we focus on the time frame, however, we miss the point. It lays out the story of a love affair: creation, the deliverance of the Hebrews from slavery in Egypt, the rise of Israel under David. It climaxes with the birth of Jesus. From the beginning, some scholars insist, God intended to enter the world as one of us, the beloved people. Praise God!

QUOTE: "For God so loved the world that he gave his only Son, so that everyone who believes in him may not perish but may have eternal life" (John 3:16).

• • •

DECEMBER 26 + FEAST
Stephen
MARTYR (D. 36?)

All we know of Stephen is found in Acts of the Apostles, 6—7. It is enough to tell us what kind of man he was.

At that time, as the number of disciples continued to grow, the Hellenists [Greek-speaking Christians] complained against the Hebrews [Hebrew-speaking Christians] because their widows were being neglected in the daily distribution. So the twelve called together the community of the disciples and said, "It is not right for us to neglect the word of God to serve at table. Brothers, select from among you seven reputable men, filled with the Spirit and wisdom, whom we shall appoint to this task, whereas we shall devote ourselves to prayer and to the ministry of the word.' The proposal was acceptable to the whole community, so they chose Stephen, a man filled with faith and the holy Spirit" (Acts 6:1–5).

Acts says that Stephen was a man filled with grace and power, who worked great wonders among the people. Certain Jews, members of the Synagogue of Roman Freedmen, debated with Stephen but proved no match for the wisdom and spirit with which he spoke. They persuaded others to make the charge of blasphemy against him. He was seized and carried before the Sanhedrin.

In his speech, Stephen recalled God's guidance through Israel's history, as well as Israel's idolatry and disobedience. He then claimed that his persecutors were showing this same spirit. "You always oppose the holy Spirit; you are just like your ancestors" (Acts 7:51b).

His speech brought anger from the crowd. "But [Stephen], filled with the holy Spirit, looked up intently to heaven and saw the glory of God and Jesus standing at the right hand of God, and he said, 'Behold, I see the heavens opened and the Son of Man standing at the right hand of God....' They threw him out of the city, and began to stone him.... As they were stoning

Stephen, he called out, 'Lord Jesus, receive my spirit.... Lord, do not hold this sin against them' " (Acts 7:55–56, 58a, 59, 60b).

COMMENT: Stephen died as Jesus did: falsely accused, brought to unjust condemnation because he spoke the truth fearlessly. He died with his eyes trustfully fixed on God, and with a prayer of forgiveness on his lips. A "happy" death is one that finds us in the same spirit, whether our dying is as quiet as Joseph's or as violent as Stephen's: dying with courage, total trust and forgiving love.

STORY: "The witnesses laid down their cloaks at the feet of a young man named Saul....

"Now Saul was consenting to his execution. On that day there broke out a severe persecution of the church in Jerusalem.... Saul, meanwhile, was trying to destroy the church; entering house after house and dragging out men and women, he handed them over for imprisonment....

"Still breathing murderous threats against the disciples of the Lord...as he was nearing Damascus, a light from the sky suddenly flashed around [Saul]. He fell to the ground and heard a voice saying to him, 'Saul, Saul, why are you persecuting me?' He said, 'Who are you, sir?' The reply came, 'I am Jesus, whom you are persecuting' " (Acts 7:58b; 8:1, 3; 9:1a, 3–5).

• • •

DECEMBER 27 + FEAST

John

APOSTLE AND EVANGELIST

It is God who calls; human beings answer. The vocation of John and his brother James is stated very simply in the Gospels, along with that of Peter and his brother Andrew: Jesus called them; they followed. The absoluteness of their response is indicated by the account. James and John "were in a boat, with their father Zebedee, mending their nets. He called them, and immediately they left their boat and their father and followed him" (Matthew 4:21b–22).

For the three former fishermen—Peter, James, and John—that faith was to be rewarded by a special friendship with Jesus. They alone were privileged to be present at the Transfiguration, the raising of the daughter of Jairus and the agony in Gethsemane. But John's friendship was even more special. Tradition assigns to him the fourth Gospel, although most modern Scripture scholars think it unlikely that the apostle and the evangelist are the same person.

John's own Gospel refers to him as "the disciple whom Jesus loved" (see John 13:23; 19:26; 20:2), the one who reclined next to Jesus at the Last Supper, and the one to whom he gave the exquisite honor, as he stood beneath the cross, of caring for his mother. "Woman, behold your son.... Behold, your mother" (John 19:26b, 27b).

Because of the depth of his Gospel, John is usually thought of as the eagle of theology, soaring in high regions that other writers did not enter. But the ever-frank Gospels reveal some very human traits. Jesus gave James and John the nickname, "sons of thunder." While it is difficult to know exactly what this meant, a clue is given in two incidents.

In the first, as Matthew tells it, they (Mark says their mother) asked that they might sit in the places of honor in Jesus's kingdom—one on his right hand, one on his left. When Jesus asked them if they could drink the cup he would drink and be baptized with his baptism of pain, they blithely answered, "We can!" Jesus said that they would indeed share his cup, but that sitting at his right hand was not his to give. It was for those to whom it had been reserved by the Father. The other apostles were indignant at the mistaken ambition of the brothers, and Jesus took the occasion to teach them the true nature of authority: "Whoever wishes to be first among you shall be your slave. Just so, the Son of Man did not come to be served but to serve and to give his life as a ransom for many" (Matthew 20:27–28).

On another occasion the "sons of thunder" asked Jesus if they should not call down fire from heaven upon the inhospitable Samaritans, who would not welcome Jesus because he was on his way to Jerusalem. But Jesus "turned and rebuked them" (see Luke 9:51–55).

On the first Easter, Mary Magdalene "ran and went to Simon Peter and to the other disciple whom Jesus loved, and told them, 'They have taken the Lord from the tomb, and we don't know where they put him'" (John 20:2). John recalls, perhaps with a smile, that he and Peter ran side by side, but then "the other disciple ran faster than Peter and arrived at the tomb first" (John 20:4b). He did not enter, but waited for Peter and let him go in first. "Then the other disciple also went in, the one who had arrived at the tomb first, and he saw and believed" (John 20:8).

John was with Peter when the first great miracle after the resurrection took place—the cure of the man crippled from birth—which led to their spending the night in jail together. The mysterious experience of the resurrection is perhaps best contained in the words of Acts: "Observing the boldness of Peter and John and perceiving them to be uneducated, ordinary men, they [the questioners] were amazed, and they recognized them as the companions of Jesus" (Acts 4:13).

The apostle John is traditionally considered the author of the Fourth Gospel, three New Testament letters and the book of Revelation. His Gospel is a very personal account. He sees the glorious and divine Jesus already in the incidents of his mortal life. At the Last Supper, John's Jesus speaks as if he were already in heaven. It is the Gospel of Jesus's glory.

COMMENT: It is a long way from being eager to sit on a throne of power or to call down fire from heaven to becoming the man who could write: "The way we came to know love was that he laid down his life for us; so we ought to lay down our lives for our brothers" (1 John 3:16).

QUOTE: A persistent story has it that John's "parishioners" grew tired of his one sermon, which relentlessly emphasized: "Love one another." Whether the story is true or not, it is based in John's writing. He wrote what may be called a summary of the Bible: "We have come to know and to believe in the love God has for us. God is love, and whoever remains in love remains in God and God in him" (1 John 4:16).

• • •

DECEMBER 28 + FEAST

Holy Innocents

MARTYRS

Herod "the Great," king of Judea, was unpopular with his people because of his connections with the Romans and his religious indifference. Hence he was insecure and fearful of any threat to his throne. He was a master politician and a tyrant capable of extreme brutality. He killed his wife, his brother, and his sister's two husbands, to name only a few.

Matthew 2:1–18 tells this story: Herod was "greatly troubled" when astrologers from the East came asking the whereabouts of "the newborn king of the Jews," whose star they had seen. They were told that the Jewish Scriptures named Bethlehem as the place where the Messiah would be born. Herod cunningly told them to report back to him so that he could also "do him homage." They found Jesus, offered him their gifts and, warned by an angel, avoided Herod on their way home. Jesus escaped to Egypt.

Herod became furious and "ordered the massacre of all the boys in Bethlehem and its vicinity two years old and under." The horror of the massacre and the devastation of the mothers and fathers led Matthew to quote Jeremiah: "A voice was heard in Ramah, / sobbing and loud lamentation; / Rachel weeping for her children" (Matthew 2:18). Rachel was the wife of Jacob/Israel. She is pictured as weeping at the place where the Israelites were herded together by the conquering Assyrians for their march into captivity.

COMMENT: The Holy Innocents are few in comparison to the victims of genocide and abortion of our day. But even if there had been only one, we recognize the greatest treasure God put on the earth—a human person, destined for eternity and graced by Jesus's death and resurrection.

QUOTE: "Purify us as we faithfully serve these, your mysteries, by which you grant justification even to those who lack understanding" (Prayer over the Gifts, feast of the Holy Innocents).

• • •

DECEMBER 29 + OPTIONAL

Thomas Becket

BISHOP AND MARTYR (1118–1170)

A strong man who eventually learned that a person cannot compromise with evil and who later became a strong churchman, a martyr and a saint—that was Thomas Becket, archbishop of Canterbury, murdered in his cathedral on December 29, 1170.

His career had been a stormy one. While archdeacon of Canterbury, he was made chancellor of England at the age of thirty-six by his friend King Henry II. When Henry felt it advantageous to make his chancellor the archbishop of Canterbury, Thomas gave him fair warning: He might not accept all of Henry's intrusions into Church affairs. Nevertheless, he was made archbishop (1162), resigned his chancellorship and reformed his whole way of life!

Troubles began. Henry insisted upon usurping Church rights. At one time, supposing some conciliatory action possible, Thomas came close to compromise. He momentarily approved the Constitutions of Clarendon, which would have denied the clergy the right of trial by a Church court and prevented them from making direct appeal to Rome. But Thomas rejected the Constitutions, fled to France for safety, and remained in exile for seven years. When he returned to England, he suspected it would mean certain death. Because Thomas refused to remit censures he had placed upon bishops favored by the king, Henry cried out in a rage, "Will no one rid me of this troublesome priest?" Four knights, taking his words as his wish, slew Thomas in the Canterbury cathedral.

Within three years Thomas was a saint of the Church and his tomb a shrine of pilgrimage. Henry II himself did penance at Thomas's tomb, but a later Henry (VIII) despoiled that tomb and scattered the saint's relics. Thomas Becket, however, remains a hero-saint down to our own times.

COMMENT: No one becomes a saint without struggle, especially with himself. Thomas knew he must stand firm in defense of truth and right, even at the cost of his life. We also must take a stand in the face of pressures—against dishonesty, deceit, destruction of life—at the cost of popularity, convenience, promotion, and even greater goods.

QUOTE: In T.S. Eliot's powerful drama *Murder in the Cathedral*, Becket faces a final temptation to seek martyrdom for earthly glory and revenge. With real insight into his situation, Thomas responds: "The last temptation is the greatest treason: To do the right deed for the wrong reason."

• • •

DECEMBER 31 + OPTIONAL
Sylvester I
POPE (D. 335)

When you think of this pope, you think of the Edict of Milan, the emergence of the Church from the catacombs, the building of the great basilicas—St. John Lateran, St. Peter's, and others—the Council of Nicea and other critical events. But for the most part, these events were planned or brought about by Emperor Constantine.

A great store of legends has grown up around the man who was pope at this most important time, but very little can be established historically. We know for sure that his papacy lasted from 314 until his death in 335. Reading between the lines of history, we are assured that only a very strong and wise man could have preserved the essential independence of the Church in the face of the overpowering figure of the Emperor Constantine. The bishops in general remained loyal to the Holy See and at times expressed apologies to Sylvester for undertaking important ecclesiastical projects at the urging of Constantine.

COMMENT: It takes deep humility and courage in the face of criticism for a leader to stand aside and let events take their course when asserting one's authority would only lead to useless tension and strife. Sylvester teaches a valuable lesson for Church leaders, politicians, parents and others in authority.

QUOTE: To emphasize the continuity of holy orders, the recent Roman breviary in its biographies of popes ends with important statistics. On the feast of St. Sylvester it recounts: "He presided at seven December ordinations at which he created forty-two priests, twenty-five deacons and sixty-five bishops for various sees." The Holy Father is indeed the heart of the Church's sacramental system, an essential element of its unity.

APPENDIX

Selected Bibliography of Saint Resources from Franciscan Media

Audio

Anderson, Carl and Fr. Jose Granados. *Called to Love: Approaching John Paul II's Theology of the Body*, read by Brian Patrick.

Bodo, Murray. *Francis: The Journey and the Dream*; foreword by John Michael Talbot; read by the author

Caster, Fr. Gary. *The Little Way of Lent: Meditations in the Spirit of St. Thérèse of Lisieux*, read by the author.

Houselander, Caryll. *The Reed of God*, read by Sherry Kennedy Brownrigg.

Kolodiejchuk, Brian, M.C., ed. *Jesus Is My All in All: Praying with the "Saint of Calcutta,"* read by Brian Patrick and Julie O'Neil.

Loehr, Gina. *The Four Teresas*, read by the author.

Martin, James S.J. *My Life With the Saints*, read by the author.

McBride, Alfred O.PRAEM. *Holding Jesus: Reflections on Mary, the Mother of God*, read by the author.

Padgett, Chris. *The Rosary Project: A Celebration of Prayer and Song*, read and performed by the author.

St. Thérèse of Lisieux. *Story of a Soul: The Autobiography of St. Thérèse of Lisieux*, translated by John Beevers; read by Sherry Kennedy Brownrigg.

Books

Allegri, Renzo. *Padre Pio: Man of Hope.*

Aquilina, Mike. *Good Pope, Bad Pope: Their Lives, Our Lessons.*

Beckett, Sister Wendy. *Sister Wendy on the Art of Saints.*

Beckwith, Barbara. *Joan of Arc: God's Warrior, a Seven-day Retreat.*

Bodo, Murray. *Francis: The Journey and the Dream.*

___. *Mystics: 10 Who Show Us the Ways of God.*

___. *Francis and Jesus.*

Gasnick, Roy, O.F.M., and Julien Grycan. *Serra: American Founding Father.*

Cameron, Fr. Peter John, O.P. *Mysteries of the Virgin Mary: Living our Lady's Graces.*

Carroll, Kathleen M. *St. Francis: A Short Biography.*

___. *A Mary Christmas.*

Caster, Fr. Gary. *Joseph, the Man Who Raised Jesus.*

___. *Mary, In Her Own Words: The Mother of God in Scripture.*

___. *The Little Way of Lent: Meditations in the Spirit of St. Thérèse of Lisieux.*

Catholic Update Guide to Mary.

Cavins, Emily. *Lily of the Mohawks: The Story of St. Kateri.*

Padgett, Chris. *Wholly Mary: Mother of God.*

Delio, Ilia, O.S.F. *Clare of Assisi: A Heart Full of Love.*

Edmisten, Karen. *Through the Year With Mary: 365 Reflections.*

___. *The Rosary: Keeping Company With Jesus and Mary.*

Engelbert, Omer. *St. Francis of Assisi.*

Franciscan Sisters of Perpetual Adoration. *Eucharistic Adoration: Reflections in the Franciscan Tradition.*

Friedman, Greg, O.F.M. *Lent with the Saints: Daily Reflections.*

Hill, Brennan R. *8 Spiritual Heroes: Their Search for God.*

Houdek, Diane M. *Advent with St. Francis: Daily Reflections.*

___ *Lent with St. Francis: Daily Reflections.*

Hutchinson, Gloria. *Praying the Rosary.*

Lochran, John. *The Miracle of Lourdes: A Message of Healing and Hope.*

Loehr, Gina. *The Four Teresas.*

Martin, Ralph, and Peter Williamson, eds. *John Paul II and the New Evangelization: How You Can Bring the Good News to Others.*

McBride, Alfred, O.PRAEM. *Holding Jesus: Reflections on Mary, the Mother of God.*

Michalenko, Sr. Sophia, C.M.S.T. *The Life of Faustina Kowalska: The Authorized Biography.*

Mills, David. *Discovering Mary: Answers to Questions About the Mother of God.*

Mother Teresa. *Loving Jesus.*

___. *One Heart Full of Love.*

___. *The Blessings of Love.*

___. *The Gift of Joy: Daily Reflections.*

___. *Total Surrender.*

Mueller, Joan, O.S.F. *St. Clare: A Short Biography.*

Niemier, Roch, O.F.M. *In the Footsteps of Francis and Clare.*

Novena in Honor of St. Anthony.

O'Neel, Brian. *39 Saints You Should Know.*

___. *Saint Who?: 39 Holy Unknowns.*

Pasquale, Gianluigi, ed. *Padre Pio's Spiritual Direction for Every Day.*

Perotta, Louise. *Help Me Pray: Learning From the Saints.*

Pope John Paul II. *Reasons for Hope: Daily Readings.*

Rigney, Melanie. *Sisterhood of Saints: Daily Guidance and Inspiration.*

Rodriguez, Janel. *Meet John Paul II: The People's Pope.*

Schorn, Joel. *God's Doorkeepers: Padre Pio, Solanus Casey and Andre Bessette.*

___. *Holy Simplicity: The Little Way of Mother Teresa, Dorothy Day & Thérèse of Lisieux.*

Treece, Patricia. *Meet John XXIII: Joyful Pope and Father to All.*

___. *Meet Padre Pio: Beloved Mystic, Miracle Worker and Spiritual Guide.*

___. *Quiet Moments With Padre Pio: 120 Readings.*

___. *Through the Year With Padre Pio: Daily Readings.*

Wintz, Jack, O.F.M. *A Retreat With Pope John Paul II: Be Not Afraid.*

___. *Saint Anthony of Padua: His Life, Legends and Devotions.*

Video

Assisi Pilgrimage: Walking in Faith with Francis and Clare, written and directed by Greg Friedman, O.F.M. (2-hours, with extensive commentary by Franciscan experts)

The Heroes and Heroines Series (People of Hope, People of Courage, People of Prayer)

In the Footprints of Francis and the Sultan: A Model for Peacemaking, Kathleen Warren, O.S.F., and Jayasri (Joyce) Hart

Women Who Inspire (St. Katharine Drexel and Blessed Teresa of Kolkata)

These resources can be ordered from Franciscan Media (1-800-488-0488, 8–5 EST) or www.FranciscanMedia.org.

• • •

INDEX

Lorenzo Ruiz and Companions,
  September 28
Louis, August 25
Louis Martin, Blessed, October 1
Louis Mary de Montfort, April 28
Lucy, December 13
Luke, October 18
Marcellinus, June 2
Margaret Mary Alacoque, October
  16
Margaret of Scotland, November 16
Marguerite Bourgeoys, January 12
Marguerite d'Youville, October 16
Maria Faustina Kowalska, October 5
Maria Goretti, July 6
Marianne Cope, January 23
Marie-Rose Durocher, Blessed,
  October 6
Mark, April 25
Martha, July 29
Martin I, April 13
Martin de Porres, November 3
Martin of Tours, November 11
Martyrdom of John the Baptist,
  August 29
Mary (birth), September 8
Mary Magdalene, July 22
Mary Magdalene de' Pazzi, May 25
Mary, Mother of God, January 1
Mary of the Cross MacKillop,
  August 8
Matthew, September 21
Matthias, May 14

Maximilian Mary Kolbe, August 14
Methodius, February 14
Michael, September 29
Miguel Agustín Pro, Blessed,
  November 23
Monica, August 27
Most Holy Name of Jesus, January 3
Most Holy Name of the Blessed
  Virgin Mary, September 12
Nereus, May 12
Nicholas, December 6
Norbert, June 6
Our Lady of Fatima, May 13
Our Lady of Guadalupe, December
  12
Our Lady of Lourdes, February 11
Our Lady of Mount Carmel, July 16
Our Lady of Sorrows, September 15
Our Lady of the Rosary, October 7
Pancras, May 12
Patrick, March 17
Paul, June 29
Paul (conversion), January 25
Paul Chong Hasang, September 20
Paul Miki and Companions,
  February 6
Paul of the Cross, October 20
Paulinus of Nola, June 22
Pedro de San José Betancur, April
  25
Perpetua, March 7
Peter, June 2
Peter, June 29